Pro JSF and HTML5

Building Rich Internet Components
Second Edition

Hazem Saleh

Allan Lykke Christensen

Zubin Wadia

Apress·

Pro JSF and HTML5

ISBN-13 (pbk): 978-1-4302-5010-4

ISBN-13 (electronic): 978-1-4302-5011-1

President and Publisher: Paul Manning
Lead Editor: Steve Anglin
Developmental Editor: Douglas Pundick
Technical Reviewer: Chad Darby
Editorial Board: Steve Anglin, Mark Beckner, Ewan Buckingham, Gary Cornell, Louise Corrigan, Jonathan Gennick, Jonathan Hassell, Robert Hutchinson, Michelle Lowman, James Markham, Matthew Moodie, Jeff Olson, Jeffrey Pepper, Douglas Pundick, Ben Renow-Clarke, Dominic Shakeshaft, Gwenan Spearing, Matt Wade, Tom Welsh
Coordinating Editor: Jill Balzano
Copy Editor: Brendan Frost
Compositor: SPi Global
Indexer: SPi Global
Artist: SPi Global
Cover Designer: Anna Ishchenko

Distributed to the book trade worldwide by Springer Science+Business Media New York, 233 Spring Street, 6th Floor, New York, NY 10013. Phone 1-800-SPRINGER, fax (201) 348-4505, e-mail orders-ny@springer-sbm.com, or visit www.springeronline.com. Apress Media, LLC is a California LLC and the sole member (owner) is Springer Science + Business Media Finance Inc (SSBM Finance Inc). SSBM Finance Inc is a Delaware corporation.

For information on translations, please e-mail rights@apress.com, or visit www.apress.com.

Apress and friends of ED books may be purchased in bulk for academic, corporate, or promotional use. eBook versions and licenses are also available for most titles. For more information, reference our Special Bulk Sales–eBook Licensing web page at www.apress.com/bulk-sales.

Any source code or other supplementary materials referenced by the author in this text is available to readers at www.apress.com. For detailed information about how to locate your book's source code, go to www.apress.com/source-code/.

I dedicate this book to my son (Ali), my daughter (Nada), my beautiful wife (Naglaa), and the wonderful JSF and Java EE community.

—Hazem Saleh

For my beautiful wife (Sau Kibuka), my son (Nikholai Mukalazi), and my daughter (Mackenzie Ndiga).

—Allan Lykke Christensen

For my daughter, Eva.

—Zubin Wadia

Contents at a Glance

About the Authors...xiii

About the Technical Reviewer xv

Introduction xvii

■Chapter 1: JSF Introduction 1

■Chapter 2: JSF Under the Hood—Part 1 29

■Chapter 3: JSF Under the Hood—Part 2 63

■Chapter 4: JSF Under the Hood—Part 3 93

■Chapter 5: JSF 2.2: What's New? 123

■Chapter 6: Going Deep: JSF Custom Components 145

■Chapter 7: Basic JSF2 HTML5 Components 167

■Chapter 8: Advanced JSF2 HTML5 Components 191

■Chapter 9: JSF Component Libraries 215

■Chapter 10: Creating a Basic JSF 2.2 Application 241

■Chapter 11: JSF2 Advanced Topics 267

■Chapter 12: JSF2 Security and Performance 289

■Chapter 13: Applying It All: The Mega App 307

Index 385

Contents

About the Authors..xiii

About the Technical Reviewer xv

Introduction xvii

■Chapter 1: JSF Introduction 1

What Is JSF? 1

JSF Evolution: 1.0–2.2... 3

JSF Architecture.. 5

Developing Your First JSF Application 6

Required Software.. 6

Developing the firstApplication.. 7

Building and deploying the firstApplication.. 19

JSF Life Cycle.. 20

Restore View... 21

Apply Request Values 23

Process Validations... 24

Update Model Values 24

Invoke Application 25

Render Response... 26

The Immediate Attribute 26

Summary.. 28

■ Chapter 2: JSF Under the Hood—Part 1 29

Managed Beans 29

Declaring Managed Beans 29

Initializing Managed Beans 31

Managing Managed Beans Dependency 34

Accessing Managed Beans from Java Code 36

@Named and @inject Annotations 36

Expression Language 37

Unified Expression Language 38

Value Expression 40

Method Expression 42

The Flash Scope 46

Navigation 51

Implicit Navigation 51

Rule-Based Navigation 52

Advanced Navigation 55

Exception Handling 58

Summary 61

■ Chapter 3: JSF Under the Hood—Part 2 63

Conversion and Validation in the JSF LifeCycle 63

Conversion 64

Converter Interface 64

Standard JSF Converters 66

Building Custom JSF Converter 70

Validation 74

Validator Interface 75

Standard JSF Validators 76

Building Custom JSF Validator 77

JSR 303 Bean Validation with JSF 80

Overriding Standard Messages 88

Summary 92

■**Chapter 4: JSF Under the Hood—Part 3** **93**

JSF Events 93

Faces Events 96

Phase Events 107

System Events 110

View Parameters 117

Summary 122

■**Chapter 5: JSF 2.2: What's New?** **123**

Big Ticket Features 123

HTML5-Friendly Markup 124

Resource Library Contracts 127

Faces Flows 132

Stateless Views 136

Other Significant Changes 137

UIData supports the Collection Interface rather than List 137

WAI-ARIA support 137

<f:viewAction /> 138

File Upload 140

Ajax request delay 142

New XML namespaces 142

Backwards Compatibility 143

Summary 143

■**Chapter 6: Going Deep: JSF Custom Components** **145**

Understanding the JSF Component Architecture 145

The RandomText Custom Component 146

Step 1—Create the Component Model and Logic 147

Step 2—Creating the Custom Component 150

Step 3—Create a Custom Renderer Class 156

Step 4—Create a Tag Library Descriptor...158

Example of using the RandomText component 161

Packaging Components...166

Summary 166

■Chapter 7: Basic JSF2 HTML5 Components...167

Input Color Custom Component..168

Creating the Composite Component..169

Using the Composite Component 169

Supporting Lists..171

Ajax-enabling the Component 172

Fallback for Unsupported Browsers 174

Input Date Picker Custom Component...176

Creating the Composite Component..177

Creating a Backing Bean for the Composite Component..178

Using the Composite Component 180

Fallback for Unsupported Browsers 182

Slider Custom Component...184

Creating the Composite Component..185

Using the Composite Component 186

Spinner Custom Component..187

Creating the Composite Component..188

Using the Composite Component 189

Summary 190

■Chapter 8: Advanced JSF2 HTML5 Components...191

Media Component 191

Media Elements Introduced in HTML5...191

Creating the JSF Media Component 195

Progress Bar Component 208

Summary 214

■Chapter 9: JSF Component Libraries 215

PrimeFaces 215

Component Overview 216

Integrating and Customizing PrimeFaces 221

RichFaces 226

Component Overview 229

Integrating and Customizing RichFaces 233

Summary 240

■Chapter 10: Creating a Basic JSF 2.2 Application 241

Structuring Weather Application...241

Constructing JSF Pages 245

Leveraging Faces Flow...254

Composing Managed Beans (JPA Entity Beans)...260

Application Back End (EJB 3.2 + JPA 2.1)...263

Summary 266

■Chapter 11: JSF2 Advanced Topics 267

Design Considerations for JSF Applications...267

Minimizing Use of Session-Scope 267

Container-Managed Security 268

State Saving 270

Contexts and Dependency Injection (CDI)...271

Ajaxifying JSF Applications 272

Using the <f:ajax> tag..272

Using the JavaScript API...273

Testing JSF Applications 278

What Is Arquillian?...279

Setting Up Arquillian and Drone..279

Writing Tests Using Arquillian and Drone 282

Summary..287

■Chapter 12: JSF2 Security and Performance...289

JSF Application Security...289

Authentication...290

Authorization...291

Data Protection...293

Applying Managed Security in the Weather Application...293

JSF Application Performance...300

Refresh Period...300

Skip Comments...300

Project Stage...301

State Saving Method...301

Response Buffer...301

Number of Views in a Session...302

Apache MyFaces Specific Tuning...303

Stateless JSF...304

Best Practices...305

Summary...305

■Chapter 13: Applying It All: The Mega App...307

Mega App Specification...307

Mega App Wireframes...309

Mega App Architecture...315

Constructing Data Model...317

Constructing Service Layer (EJBs)...320

Composing Page Templates...347

Composing JSF Pages and Backing Beans...351

Applying Security...377

Error Handling...380

Composing JSF Components...380

Packaging and Deploying the Mega App...382

Summary...384

Index...385

About the Authors

Hazem Saleh has ten years of experience in Java EE, Portal, and open-source technologies. He worked as a technical consultant for many clients in Europe (Sweden), North America (USA, Canada), South America (Peru), Africa (Egypt, Morocco), and Asia (Qatar, Kuwait, KSA). He is an Apache MyFaces committer and the founder of many open-source projects. Besides being the author of *JavaScript Unit Testing* (Packt Publishing) and a coauthor of *The Definitive Guide to Apache MyFaces and Facelets* (Apress), Hazem is also an author of many technical articles, a developerWorks contributing author, and a technical speaker in both local and international conferences such as the IBM Regional Technical Exchange (Johannesburg), CON-FESS (Vienna), and JavaOne (San Francisco, Moscow, and Shanghai). Hazem is now working for IBM Egypt as an advisory software engineer. He is a WebSphere Portal and Web 2.0 SME, and an IBM Certified Expert IT Specialist (L2).

Allan Lykke Christensen is a Senior Technology Manager at the LEGO Group in Denmark, where he manages experienced software developers and drives agile practices and software excellence. In the past Allan has run his own software company and been the vice-president of Danish ICT Management, an international consulting firm with focus on ICT in developing economies. At Danish ICT Management he was responsible for daily management of software teams in Uganda, Kenya, Bangladesh, and Denmark. In his daily work he was also responsible for project planning and execution. He has been developing and implementing IT projects for more than 14 years. His expertise covers a wide range—he has developed workflow systems, information systems, e-learning tools, knowledge management systems, and websites. He has worked as team leader on several major European Commission–financed ICT projects in various developing economies. He is the coauthor of *The Definitive Guide to Apache MyFaces and Facelets* (Apress, 2008) and has made countless presentations and training sessions on software development–related topics around the world. Allan is also the lead developer of the Converge project aiming at implementing an open source editorial content management system for media houses. More information can be found on http://www.getconverge.com.

Zubin Wadia has twelve years of experience implementing Java, .NET, open-source, and mobile solutions across a variety of consumer and enterprise use-cases. He has been a practitioner of Java since 1999 and designed one of the earliest JSF applications for large-scale enterprise use in 2005. He is the co-author of *The Definitive Guide to Apache MyFaces and Facelets* (Apress), a foundational book focused on practical JSF development. Zubin is the CTO of ImageWork Technologies, a leading Systems Integration firm focused on delivering innovative content management solutions to government and Fortune 500 clients. He is a graduate of Singularity University, a highly competitive future-focused program for technology leaders sponsored by NASA and Google. In 2010, he co-founded CiviGuard, a real-time public safety platform named to the "100 Brilliant Companies" list by *Entrepreneur* magazine in 2011. In 2013, he co-founded Quipio, a critically acclaimed app for effortless self-expression that's been featured multiple times on the App Store.

About the Technical Reviewer

Chád Darby is an author, instructor, and speaker in the Java development world. As a recognized authority on Java applications and architectures, he has presented technical sessions at software development conferences worldwide (USA, UK, India, Russia, and Australia). In his fifteen years as a professional software architect, he's had the opportunity to work for Blue Cross/Blue Shield, Merck, Boeing, Red Hat, and a handful of startup companies.

Chád is a contributing author to several Java books, including *Professional Java E-Commerce* (Wrox Press), *Beginning Java Networking* (Wrox Press), and *XML and Web Services Unleashed* (Sams Publishing). Chád has Java certifications from Sun Microsystems and IBM. He holds a B.S. in Computer Science from Carnegie Mellon University.

You can read Chád's blog at www.luv2code.com and follow him on Twitter @darbyluvs2code.

Introduction

This book is an ideal resource for Java developers intending to build sophisticated, enterprise-grade web experiences with HTML5-enabled JSF. Java web developers today have an unprecedented variety of libraries, frameworks, and components available for creating rich and meaningful applications. The result is an ecosystem that delivers incredible productivity at an individual level.

That being said, most software is built in team environments with shared code bases, multiple service endpoints, complex views, and diverse functional areas. A multitude of choices can end up being counterproductive in team environments, resulting in the accrual of technical debt and multiple implementation patterns for similar use-cases. Component-based frameworks like JavaServer Faces (JSF) are designed to curb such behavior in team environments, while still giving developers latitude to customize when a use-case requires it.

In *Pro JSF* and *HTML5* we show you how to leverage the full potential of JSF, a server-side component-oriented Java web framework that sets the standard for developer team productivity. It offers developers a rich array of standard and third-party interface components that can be used to compose complex views in an intuitive, reusable, and repeatable way. The latest standard, JSF 2.2, allows HTML5-enabled components to be used in the composition of views. We demonstrate how a developer can couple the power and expressivity of HTML5 with the discipline and repeatability of JSF components to deliver rich user experiences.

This book provides solid coverage for foundational and advanced topics of JavaServer Faces (especially JSF 2.2). The first four chapters cover the JSF life cycle, architecture, managed beans and integration with CDI (Context and Dependency Injection), expression language, exception handling, conversion and validation, JSF events (Faces events, Phase events, and System events), and view parameters. Chapter 5 covers the new features of JSF 2.2, such as faces flow, resource library contracts, HTML5 friendly markup, and Ajax file uploading.

Chapters 6, 7, and 8 detail the process of creating HTML5-enabled components in the JSF 2.2 world with a number of interactive examples. Chapter 9 covers the basics of two popular JSF component libraries (PrimeFaces and RichFaces) with two interactive examples.

In Chapter 10, a basic JSF 2.2 application is developed that utilizes Java EE 7 technologies (CDI, JPA 2.1, and EJB 3.2) in order to facilitate bean management, transaction management, and persistence in the JSF application. Chapter 11 covers JSF advanced topics such as application design considerations, unit testing, and Ajax queuing.

Chapter 12 covers important topics relating to JSF application security including authentication, authorization, and data protection. The chapter shows how to apply container-managed security in an example application. Chapter 12 also covers JSF performance considerations to help ensure that your applications run smoothly and responsively.

Finally, Chapter 13 gathers most of the topics covered in the book and puts them into practice in the form of an advanced application that implements real-world use-cases.

We want this book to serve as a progressive guide to the component-oriented framework beginner, and as a reference for the seasoned JSF developer who is looking to maximize JSF 2.2's significantly upgraded capabilities. We wish you happy reading and productive coding!

CHAPTER 1

JSF Introduction

This chapter will explain what the JavaServer Faces (JSF) framework is, how the framework evolved over time, key aspects of its architecture, and details about its signature request processing life cycle. Beyond explanations, we'll go hands-on and guide you through your first JSF application from scratch using JSF 2.1 and Maven 3; you will learn how to deploy your JSF 2.1 application on two different web containers (GlassFish and Tomcat). If you are already familiar with JSF at a basic component level, a deeper understanding of the request life cycle will serve you well when tasked with more complex applications.

What Is JSF?

JSF is a server-side component-oriented Java web framework that simplifies the process of developing rich Java enterprise web applications. JSF excels at delivering a highly customizable yet standardized approach to building application user interfaces. The user interface tier is usually the most challenging and variable part of any application. It is also the difference between a successful application that is widely adopted and evolved consistently versus one that is reluctantly adopted and frequently changed to meet user desires.

JSF provides a powerful platform for solving the common problems that frequently appear during Java enterprise web application development, such as validation, conversion, navigation, templating, and page flows. Providing a standard way for resolving the common problems of web application development makes JSF an excellent framework that reduces the development and maintenance time of web applications.

This is especially true when your development team is large and distributed, a common scenario encountered in the enterprise. Building user experiences around a set of standardized JSF components allows for a fair degree of customization and expression, but also establishes a "shared DNA" for how an application should look, behave, and respond across different implementations.

JSF offers APIs and tag libraries for

- Providing UI components for rapid development of applications.

- Wiring component events into Java server-side code.

- Binding UI components with POJOs (Plain Old Java Objects).

- Providing a set of useful built-in validators and converters, and offering a mechanism for creating custom ones in order to fulfill specific requirements.

- Handling exceptions.

- Handling navigation between application pages.

- Creating page templates and application templates.

- Defining page flows in a manner that reflects application requirements.

- Handling the localization and internationalization of user interface.

- Creating "real-time" pages that auto-update with data from back ends and APIs.

- Creating custom components by extending framework classes and providing an implementation for custom component views, events, and state.

JSF is a large framework that allows developers to work with it at a variety of levels. One can break each level into a distinct role that can be performed by one or more developers depending on the complexity and scale of the application. Figure 1-1 shows different JSF roles according to the JSF specification. The JSF roles include the following:

- Page author.

- Component writer.

- Application developer.

- Tools provider.

- JSF implementor.

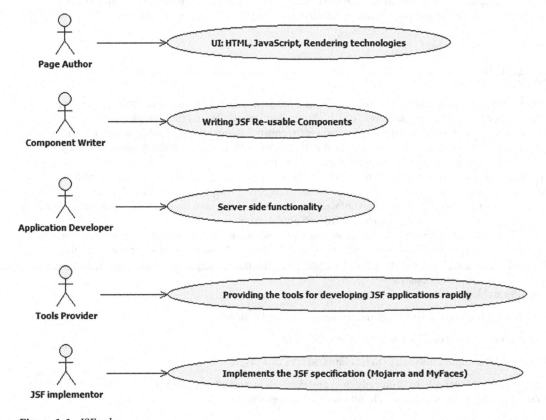

Figure 1-1. *JSF roles*

As shown in Figure 1-1, the page author is responsible for creating the user interface of the page(s). Page author should have knowledge of markup, styling, and scripting languages such as HTML5, CSS3, and JavaScript. Page author should also have knowledge of rendering technologies such as JavaServer Pages (JSP).

Unlike the application developer, the page author is focused on developing a pleasing and effective user experience for the application. JSF's component architecture abstracts away a significant amount of complexity, allowing the page author to be productive even if they have little familiarity with programming languages such as Java and C#.

The component writer is responsible for developing reusable JSF components that can be used by the page author. Reusable JSF components can be collected into "component libraries." Think of this as a palette of components that are easy to discover, customize, and integrate into your applications. Component libraries are a big contributing factor to force-multiplying productivity across large developer teams. Two popular and comprehensive JSF component libraries are PrimeFaces and RichFaces.

Reusable JSF components should support the following capabilities:

- *Encoding:* converting the internal component's properties and attributes into suitable markup in the pages that use the component (such as HTML).

- *Decoding:* converting incoming requests with related headers and parameters into related properties and attributes of the component.

- Adding to this, the component should support request-time events, validation, conversion, and statefulness. Conversion is the process of converting an incoming request to a suitable form for the component. Statefulness means that the component must retain its original state for the new requests. This can be done by saving and restoring the component state across the different requests.

The application developer is responsible for developing the server-side functionality of the JSF application. The application developer is focused on developing Java, EJB, or any other language capable of running on the JVM (Java Virtual Machine). Adding to this, the application developer can define the persistence storage mechanism of the JSF application (inclusive of the data and the content model) and expose data and business logic objects to be used from the JSF page.

The tools provider is responsible for developing the tools that help JSF developers to build JSF applications. These tools include IDE (Integrated Development Environments) plug-ins and extensions and page generators. The JSF implementor is responsible for providing a standards-compliant runtime or implementation of the JSF specification for all of the previous roles. Examples of the available implementations of the JSF specification are Oracle Mojarra (`http://javaserverfaces.java.net/`) and Apache MyFaces (`http://myfaces.apache.org/`).

JSF Evolution: 1.0–2.2

JSF 1.0 was released in March 2004; it represented a significant evolution in the way the web tier was implemented. But with these advantages also came limitations that needed to be circumvented in order for JSF to gain widespread adoption in the community. Some of these limitations were related to component performance and others were related to open defects.

The Expert Group worked hard on the specification and, in May 2004, released version 1.1, which eliminated some of JSF 1.0's greatest performance issues and had many defect fixes which made the JSF framework usable within the next-generation web applications. With JSF 1.1, the Expert Group had achieved most of the early goals they set out to achieve in Java Specification Request (JSR) 127. These goals were related to creation of a standard GUI component framework that can be supported by development tools that allowed JSF developers to create custom components by extending base framework components, defining APIs for input validation and conversion, and specifying a model for GUI localization and internationalization.

■ **Note** You can read the JSR 127 at `http://jcp.org/en/jsr/detail?id=127`.

In May 2006, JSF 1.2 was released with Java Enterprise Edition 5.0. JSF 1.2 had significant enhancements to address some of the user community's real-world issues with JSF 1.1. JSF 1.2 had many features, some of which were

- Unified expression language between the JSF and the JSP.
- Solving the integration issues of the JSF with both the JSP and the JSTL.
- Allowing the single component to override the conversion and the validation messages.
- Enhancing the security of the client side state saving.

■ **Note**   JSR 252 is the JSF 1.2 specification; you can read it at http://jcp.org/en/jsr/detail?id=252.

In July 2009, JSF 2.0 was released with Java Enterprise Edition 6.0. JSF 2.0 introduced a big set of features and enhancements. Some of the features and enhancements were

- Composite components.
- Full templating support.
- Complete Ajax support.
- Enhancing the JSF navigation.
- Supporting the view parameters.
- Supporting more scopes in the application.
- Providing exception handling mechanism.
- Improving the validation by the JSR 303 integration.
- Standardizing the resource-loading mechanism.
- Minimizing XML usage by supporting annotations for most of the configurations.

In July 2010, JSF 2.1 was mainly a maintenance release for JSF 2.0. It included bug fixes and enhancements. Some of them were

- Allowing the JSP document syntax (.jspx files) to be treated as Facelets files.
- Pluggable Facelet cache mechanism.

■ **Note**   JSR 314 specification gathers the JSF 2.0 in its final release and the JSF 2.1 in its maintenance releases; you can read the specification at http://jcp.org/en/jsr/detail?id=314.

As of the writing time of this chapter, JSF 2.2 specification and implementation are still in progress and are not released yet. JSF 2.2 is expected to be released with the Java Enterprise Edition 7.0 release. The main features of JSF 2.2 are

- Standardizing the flow APIs by introducing the FacesFlow.
- Multi-templating.
- Adding new JSF elements and attributes that are **HTML5 specific**.

■ **Note**   JSR 344 is the JSF 2.2 specification; you can read its early draft review at
http://jcp.org/en/jsr/detail?id=344.

Throughout the book's chapters, we will discuss these features in more details using practical, easy-to-follow examples.

JSF Architecture

JSF architecture is based on the MVC (Model View Controller) 2 pattern. Unlike the MVC1 pattern, the MVC2 pattern decouples the view from the controller from the model. Figure 1-2 shows the JSF MVC2 architecture.

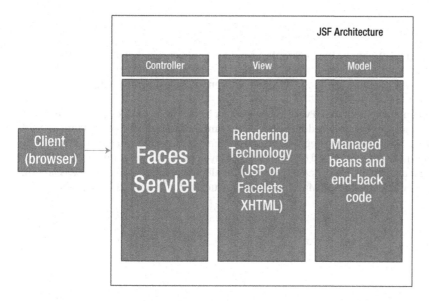

Figure 1-2. *The JSF MVC2 architecture*

In JSF, the MVC2 pattern is fulfilled as follows:

- Controller, which is represented by the JSF Faces Servlet. The Faces Servlet is responsible for handling the request dispatching and the pages navigation. The Faces Servlet orchestrates the JSF life cycle by invoking the JSF Lifecycle object that is responsible for handling the JSF request processing life cycle.

- Model, which is represented by the JSF managed beans and the back-end code. The JSF managed bean is simply a POJO that conforms to the JavaBeans naming conventions and can be accessed from the JSF application (pages and other managed beans). A JSF managed bean must have a scope that controls its life span; it can be in the request, view, flow, session, application, or none scope. Every JSF managed bean should to be registered in the faces-config.xml (the JSF configuration file) or registered using annotations (managed beans will be covered in detail in Chapter 2).

- View, which is the rendering technology of JSF. The rendering technology defines the page layout and content. The default rendering technology for JSF since its 2.0 version is the Facelets XHTML (however, you still have the option to use JSP as the JSF rendering technology, although it is not recommended).

You may wonder how the JSF runtime works in order to simplify the application development for the JSF developers, and how the controller orchestrates the work with both the model and the view in JSF. Such questions will be answered in the "JSF Life Cycle" section.

Developing Your First JSF Application

Now, it is the time to stop the theory for a while and start working with the JSF framework. Let's see how to develop and run your first JSF 2.1 application.

Required Software

Before going into the details of your first JSF 2.1 application example, I would like to mention that all of the examples of this book are based on the Apache Maven 3 software, version 3.0.4, to perform the compilation and the assembly of the compiled sources into a deployable Java EE WAR file. Maven 3 can be downloaded from http://maven.apache.org/download.html.

Apache Maven is a powerful build management tool. Every Maven project has a "project object model" file that is called (pom.xml). The (pom.xml) file includes the project dependencies to compile and build the project into a target artifact. In order to build a project, Maven gets the dependencies from the (pom.xml) file and then downloads these dependencies on the local disk if they were not found on it; after this, Maven performs the compilation and the assembly for the compiled sources into a target artifact. The target artifact for all of the examples in the book is Java EE web application WAR file. One of the powerful features of Maven is its strict structure for its applications, as shown in Figure 1-3.

Figure 1-3. *The Maven project structure*

As shown, the project root contains two main subfolders (src and target) and the (pom.xml) file. The src directory contains the source code of the application and the target directory contains the generated artifacts. The src directory has a number of subdirectories; each one of these directories has a specific purpose:

- **src/main/java:** It contains the Java source code of the application.

- **src/main/resources:** It contains the resources that the application needs such as the resource bundles.

- **src/main/filters:** It includes the resource filters.

- **src/main/config:** It includes the configuration files.

- **src/main/webapp:** It includes the files of the JEE web application project.

- **src/test:** It includes the unit tests of the application.

- **src/site:** It includes the files used to generate the website of the Maven project.

Adding to the Apache Maven 3 software, all of the examples of this book use Oracle jdk1.6.0_27 (which can be downloaded from www.oracle.com/technetwork/java/javase/downloads/index.html), and the examples can run on any JSF 2.1 (and JSF 2.2 for the JSF 2.2 examples) capable runtime environment.

■ **Note**　Oracle GlassFish v3.1 (or later) and Apache Tomcat 7 are capable to run JSF 2.1 applications. I will show you how to run the firstApplication, which is based on JSF 2.1 on both Java web containers.

Developing the firstApplication

The firstApplication contains two pages. In the first page, you can enter your name and password as shown in Figure 1-4.

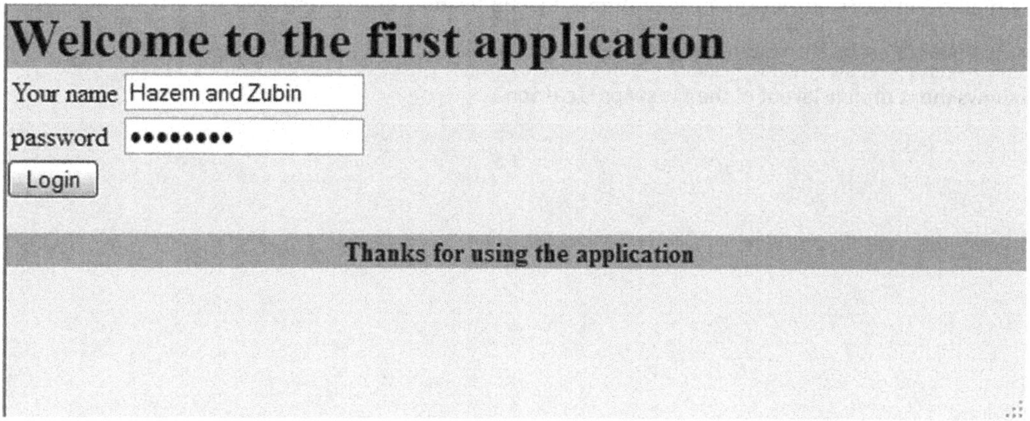

Figure 1-4. *The login page*

After clicking the "Login" button, you will be redirected to the welcome page, as shown in Figure 1-5.

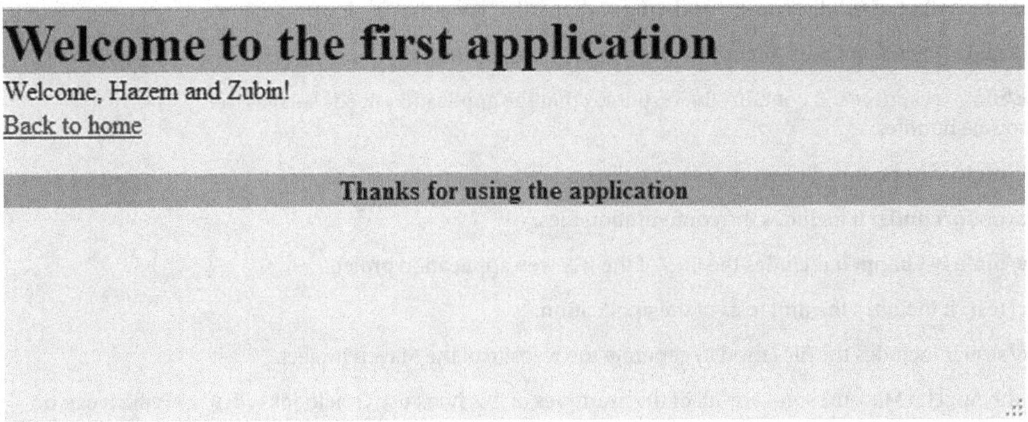

Welcome to the first application

Welcome, Hazem and Zubin!
Back to home

Thanks for using the application

Figure 1-5. *The welcome page*

The firstApplication has the following Maven structure:

- firstApplication/src/main/webapp/WEB-INF/faces-config.xml

- firstApplication/src/main/webapp/WEB-INF/web.xml

- firstApplication/src/main/webapp/WEB-INF/templates/simple.xhtml

- firstApplication/src/main/webapp/css/simple.css

- firstApplication/src/main/webapp/index.xhtml

- firstApplication/src/main/webapp/welcome.xhtml

- firstApplication/src/main/java/com/jsfprohtml5/firstapplication/model/User.java

- firstApplication/src/main/resources/com/jsfprohtml5/firstapplication/messages.properties

Figure 1-6 shows the complete layout of the firstApplication.

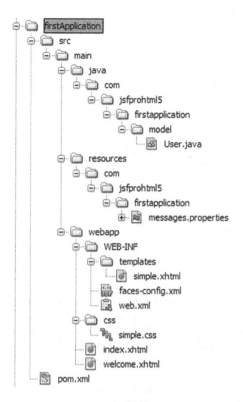

Figure 1-6. *The firstApplication Maven structure*

Configuration Files

There are two configuration files for the firstApplication, which are the web.xml and faces-config.xml. The web.xml file is the standard web module deployment descriptor in which the Faces Servlet is defined. The main purpose of the Faces Servlet is to intercept the requests to the JSF pages in order to prepare the JSF context before accessing the requested JSF page. Listing 1-1 shows the web.xml file of the firstApplication.

Listing 1-1. The web.xml of the firstApplication

```
<?xml version="1.0" encoding="UTF-8"?>

<web-app xmlns="http://java.sun.com/xml/ns/javaee"
              xmlns:xsi="http://www.w3.org/2001/XMLSchema-instance"
              xsi:schemaLocation="http://java.sun.com/xml/ns/javaee
http://java.sun.com/xml/ns/javaee/web-app_3_0.xsd"
              version="3.0">
    <context-param>
        <param-name>javax.faces.PROJECT_STAGE</param-name>
        <param-value>Development</param-value>
    </context-param>
```

```
<servlet>
    <servlet-name>Faces Servlet</servlet-name>
    <servlet-class>javax.faces.webapp.FacesServlet</servlet-class>
    <load-on-startup>1</load-on-startup>
</servlet>
<servlet-mapping>
    <servlet-name>Faces Servlet</servlet-name>
    <url-pattern>/faces/*</url-pattern>
</servlet-mapping>
<session-config>
    <session-timeout>
        30
    </session-timeout>
</session-config>
<welcome-file-list>
    <welcome-file>faces/index.xhtml</welcome-file>
</welcome-file-list>
</web-app>
```

In Listing 1-1, there are two main things you need to know: the first one is the definition of the Faces Servlet and its mapping to the (/faces/*) URL using the <url-pattern> element. The second one is the javax.faces.PROJECT_STAGE context parameter, which is set to Development (other possible values are Production, SystemTest, and UnitTest). Setting the project stage in the development mode makes the JSF framework generate additional messages in the page when finding a common development mistake. This feature can help the JSF developers to become more productive during the development time.

Finally, the <welcome-file> element specifies the welcome page of the application, which is the index.xhtml file; this will make any request to http://localhost:8080/firstApplication/ redirected to http://localhost:8080/firstApplication/faces/index.xhtml, which will trigger the Faces Servlet to prepare the JSF context before going to the index.xhtml page.

■ **Note** In any Servlet 3.0 container such as GlassFish v3, the web.xml file is optional. If the web.xml is omitted, the Faces Servlet will be automatically mapped to *.jsf, *.faces, and /faces/* URL patterns.

Now, let's move to the faces-config file, which includes the related JSF configuration. Actually, since JSF 2.0, the faces-config file becomes optional because most of the JSF configuration can be defined using the Java annotations. Listing 1-2 shows the firstApplication Faces configuration file.

Listing 1-2. The firstApplication Faces Configuration File

```
<faces-config version="2.1"
    xmlns="http://java.sun.com/xml/ns/javaee"
    xmlns:xsi="http://www.w3.org/2001/XMLSchema-instance"
    xsi:schemaLocation="http://java.sun.com/xml/ns/javaee
http://java.sun.com/xml/ns/javaee/web-facesconfig_2_1.xsd">
```

```
        <application>
                <resource-bundle>
                        <base-name>com.jsfprohtml5.firstapplication.messages</base-name>
                        <var>bundle</var>
                </resource-bundle>
        </application>
</faces-config>
```

Listing 1-2 defines the application resource bundle globally in order to be used from the JSF expression language (#{...}) using the bundle variable (the JSF expression language will be illustrated in detail in Chapter 3).

Facelets Pages

The firstApplication contains two main pages: the first page (index.xhtml) represents the home page, and the other page is the (welcome.xhtml) page, which represents the welcome page. Both pages refer to a template (simple.xhtml) page that is defined under the (firstApplication/src/main/webapp/WEB-INF/templates/), as shown in Listing 1-3.

Listing 1-3. The simple.xhtml Template File

```
<?xml version='1.0' encoding='UTF-8' ?>
<!DOCTYPE html>
<html xmlns="http://www.w3.org/1999/xhtml"
      xmlns:ui="http://java.sun.com/jsf/facelets"
      xmlns:f="http://java.sun.com/jsf/core"
      xmlns:h="http://java.sun.com/jsf/html">

<h:head>
  <title><ui:insert name="title">#{bundle['application.defaultpage.title']}</ui:insert></title>
  <link href="#{request.contextPath}/css/simple.css" rel="stylesheet" type="text/css"/>
</h:head>

<h:body>
    <div id="container">
        <div id="header">
            <ui:insert name="header">
                <h1>#{bundle['application.defaultpage.header.content']}</h1>
            </ui:insert>
        </div>

        <div id="content">
            <ui:insert name="content">
                #{bundle['application.defaultpage.body.content']}
            </ui:insert>
        </div>

        <div id="footer">
            <ui:insert name="footer">
                #{bundle['application.defaultpage.footer.content']}
            </ui:insert>
        </div>
    </div>
</h:body>
</html>
```

The <!DOCTYPE html> declares the template doctype: in the firstApplication pages, all the pages use this doctype, which represents the HTML5 doctype. In order to include the JSF HTML, core, and Facelets UI tags, the following declaration is used:

```
<html xmlns="http://www.w3.org/1999/xhtml"
      xmlns:ui="http://java.sun.com/jsf/facelets"
      xmlns:f="http://java.sun.com/jsf/core"
      xmlns:h="http://java.sun.com/jsf/html">
```

The first line is a standard XHTML practice, the second line declares the Facelets UI tags, the third line declares the JSF core tags, and finally the last line declares the JSF HTML tags to be used in the template page.

The <h:head> and <h:body> elements are replacements for the HTML <head> and <body> elements. The template consists of a container element whose ID is "container". The "container" element contains three sub-elements:

- **The header element:** The header of the page is defined inside the "header" div element.

- **The content element:** The content of the page is defined inside the "content" div element.

- **The footer element:** The footer of the page is defined inside the "footer" div element.

Inside the header, content, and the footer elements, there is a Facelets <ui:insert> tag. The Facelets <ui:insert> tag is used for declaring an initial default content that can be overridden by the pages that use the template. The content inside the <ui:insert> tag represents the initial value of the content. The #{...} represents the JSF expression language. The JSF expression language can be used for binding the JSF model with the JSF page; in the template page, it binds the resource bundle content with the page through the #{bundle['key name']}. The bundle variable is defined in the faces-config.xml, as shown in the "Configuration Files" section. Listing 1-4 shows the messages.properties resource bundle file.

Listing 1-4. The message.properties File

```
user.name = Your name
user.password = password
user.name.validation = You need to enter a username
user.password.validation = You need to enter a password

application.login = Login
application.loginpage.title = Login page

application.welcome = Welcome
application.welcomepage.title = Welcome page
application.welcomepage.return = Back to home

application.defaultpage.title = Default Title
application.defaultpage.header.content = Welcome to the first application
application.defaultpage.body.content = Your content here ...
application.defaultpage.footer.content = Thanks for using the application
```

The resource bundle is a set of key and value pairs. Using the JSF expression language, the values of the bundle keys are resolved in the runtime. For example, the #{bundle['application.defaultpage.header.content']} expression is evaluated to "Welcome to the first application" in the runtime.

The template file also includes a CSS (Cascading Style Sheets) file, which is the simple.css file. The simple.css is responsible for the template page layout. Listing 1-5 shows the simple.css file.

Listing 1-5. The simple.css File

```css
h1, p, body, html {
    margin:0;
    padding:0;
}

body {
    background-color:#EEEEEE;
}

#container {
    width:100%;
}

#header {
    background-color:#FFA500;
}

#header h1 {
    margin-bottom: 0px;
}

#content {
    float:left;
    width:100%;
}

#footer {
    clear:both;                 /*No floating elements are allowed on left or right*/
    background-color:#FFA500;
    text-align:center;
    font-weight: bold;
}

.errorMessage {
    color: red;
}
```

In order to change the page layout anytime without changing the HTML code of the web application, it is recommended to use CSS.

■ **Note** Since JSF 2.0, page templates are supported. Before JSF 2.0, the JSF developers had to download and configure a templating library (such as the Facelets library) in the JSF applications for defining the layout of the pages.

Listing 1-6 shows the index.xhtml page code, which represents the introductory page of the application.

Listing 1-6. The index.xhtml Page

```xml
<?xml version='1.0' encoding='UTF-8' ?>
<!DOCTYPE html>
<html xmlns="http://www.w3.org/1999/xhtml"
      xmlns:ui="http://java.sun.com/jsf/facelets"
      xmlns:h="http://java.sun.com/jsf/html">


<ui:composition template="/WEB-INF/templates/simple.xhtml">
    <ui:define name="title">
        #{bundle['application.loginpage.title']}
    </ui:define>
    <ui:define name="content">
        <h:form>
            <h:panelGrid columns="3">
                <h:outputText value="#{bundle['user.name']}"></h:outputText>
                <h:inputText id="userName"
                             value="#{user.name}"
                             required="true"
                             requiredMessage="#{bundle['user.name.validation']}">
                </h:inputText>
                <h:message for="userName" styleClass="errorMessage"/>

                <h:outputText value="#{bundle['user.password']}"></h:outputText>
                <h:inputSecret id="password"
                               value="#{user.password}"
                               required="true"
                               requiredMessage="#{bundle['user.password.validation']}">
                </h:inputSecret>
                <h:message for="password" styleClass="errorMessage"/>
            </h:panelGrid>

            <h:commandButton value="#{bundle['application.login']}" action="welcome">
            </h:commandButton> <br/><br/>
        </h:form>
    </ui:define>
</ui:composition>

</html>
```

In order to include the simple.xhtml template page in the index.xhtml page (or any other XHTML page), the <ui:composition> tag is used, specifying its template attribute with the relative path of the template page. The <ui:composition> tag includes <ui:define> tags. The <ui:define> tag is used for overriding the template content that is defined by the <ui:insert> tag if the tags are matched using the name attribute.

In the index.xhtml page, the "title" and the "content" of the template are overridden with the page title and the page content. The page content includes an <h:form> tag that is required for all the JSF input components which participate in the form submission.

In order to make the internal layout of the form, the <h:panelGrid> tag is used. The <h:panelGrid> tag is a layout container that renders the JSF components in a grid of rows and columns. The <h:panelGrid> tag has a columns attribute that specifies the number of the columns of the grid (which is "3" in the example). In the index.xhtml page, every row in the <h:panelGrid> represents an input field with its label and message. The first row is as follows:

```
<h:outputText value="#{bundle['user.name']}"></h:outputText>
<h:inputText id="userName"
                value="#{user.name}"
                required="true"
                requiredMessage="#{bundle['user.name.validation']}">
</h:inputText>
<h:message for="userName" styleClass="errorMessage"/>
```

The <h:outputText> defines the user name label, the <h:inputText> defines the "userName" input text, and finally the <h:message> defines the message of the "userName" input text in order to display the validation error messages. The <h:message> is linked with the input text using the for attribute specifying the ID of the input text (which is the "userName" in this case).

Setting the required attribute of the <h:inputText> tag to true creates a validation on the input text in order to avoid empty values. If an empty value is entered in the input text, then the message in the requiredMessage attribute will be displayed in the <h:message>. The value attribute of the <h:inputText> tag contains the following JSF value expression, #{user.name}, which links the name property of the User managed bean with the input text value that is entered by the user. The code of the User managed bean is listed in the "Managed Beans" section.

The second row of the <h:panelGrid> represents the "password" secret field with its label and message. It is the same idea of the first row with the difference that it uses the <h:inputSecret> tag in order to define a password input field, and the value of the <h:inputSecret> tag is linked with the password property of the User managed bean through the #{user.password} value expression. The <h:commandButton> renders an HTML submit button. In the page, the login command button is defined as follows:

```
<h:commandButton value="#{bundle['application.login']}" action="welcome"></h:commandButton>
```

The action attribute of the <h:commandButton> can accept a JSF method-binding expression for a managed bean action method to invoke when the command button is clicked. The managed bean action method must be a public method and it must return a String value or null. The returned String represents the logical outcome of the action and is used by the JSF runtime to determine the next page to display by looking if there is a matching navigation rule defined in the configuration file. However since JSF 2.0, implicit navigation is supported. This allows the action attribute to accept a String value that directly points to a target page without the need to define a navigation rule in the configuration file (for example: if the target page name is "foo.xhtml" then the action String outcome must be "foo" and the JSF runtime will append the ".xhtml" extension with the action String value in order to navigate correctly to the target page). In the index.xhtml page, the action attribute is set to "welcome", which means that when the login command button is clicked, the application will navigate to the welcome.xhtml page.

■ **Note** The JSF navigation is a topic that has many details, and it will be illustrated in more detail in the next chapters of the book. JSF validation and conversion will be illustrated in depth in Chapter 3.

Listing 1-7 shows the welcome.xhtml page code, which represents the welcome page of the application.

Listing 1-7. The welcome.xhtml Page Code

```
<?xml version='1.0' encoding='UTF-8' ?>
<!DOCTYPE html>
<html xmlns="http://www.w3.org/1999/xhtml"
```

```
        xmlns:ui="http://java.sun.com/jsf/facelets"
        xmlns:h="http://java.sun.com/jsf/html"
        xmlns:f="http://java.sun.com/jsf/core">

<ui:composition template="/WEB-INF/templates/simple.xhtml">
    <ui:define name="title">
        #{bundle['application.welcomepage.title']}
    </ui:define>
    <ui:define name="content">
        #{bundle['application.welcome']}, #{user.name}! <br/>
        <h:link value="#{bundle['application.welcomepage.return']}"
                outcome="index"></h:link> <br/><br/>
    </ui:define>
</ui:composition>
</html>
```

The welcome.xhtml page includes the simple.xhtml template page using the <ui:composition> tag. Like the index.xhtml page, in the welcome.xhtml page, the "title" and the "content" of the template are overridden with the page title and the page content. The page content displays a welcome message that includes the name property of the User managed bean using the #{user.name} value expression. The page content includes a link to the introductory page using the <h:link> tag. The <h:link> tag is a new tag that is introduced since JSF 2.0; it renders an HTML anchor element. The value attribute of the <h:link> is rendered as the anchor text and its outcome attribute is used to determine the target navigation page. In the welcome page, the outcome attribute value is set to "index", which makes an implicit navigation the "index.xhtml" page of the application.

Managed Beans

As illustrated in the Facelets pages section, there is a User managed bean that is binded with the input and output components of the index and the welcome pages. Listing 1-8 shows the User managed bean.

Listing 1-8. The User Managed Bean

```
package com.jsfprohtml5.firstapplication.model;

import java.io.Serializable;
import javax.faces.bean.ManagedBean;
import javax.faces.bean.SessionScoped;

@ManagedBean
@SessionScoped
public class User implements Serializable {
    private String name;
    private String password;

    public String getName() {
        return name;
    }

    public void setName(String name) {
        this.name = name;
    }
```

```
public String getPassword() {
    return password;
}

public void setPassword(String password) {
    this.password = password;
}
}
```

The User managed bean is a simple Java bean with two setters and getters for the name and the password properties. The @ManagedBean annotation is used for registering the User class as a JSF managed bean.

■ **Note**   The @ManagedBean annotation has an optional name attribute that describes the name of the managed bean to be used from the JSF expressions. In the User managed bean, the name attribute is omitted; this means that the managed bean name will be the same as the class name with the first character in lowercase, i.e., it will be used from the JSF expressions like #{user}.

The @SessionScoped annotation is used for setting the managed bean in the session scope. Other possible values can be (@RequestScoped, @ViewScoped, @ApplicationScoped, @NoneScoped [or @FlowScoped, which is supported in JSF 2.2]).

Dependencies

Now, let's move to the (pom.xml) dependencies of the firstApplication. Listing 1-9 shows the required dependencies of the firstApplication on GlassFish 3.1.2.

Listing 1-9. The GlassFish 3.1.2 Configuration in the pom.xml File

```
<dependencies>
            <dependency>
                        <groupId>javax</groupId>
                        <artifactId>javaee-web-api</artifactId>
                        <version>6.0</version>
                        <scope>provided</scope>
            </dependency>

            <dependency>
                        <groupId>javax.faces</groupId>
                        <artifactId>javax.faces-api</artifactId>
                        <version>2.1</version>
                        <scope>provided</scope>
            </dependency>

            <dependency>
                        <groupId>javax.servlet</groupId>
                        <artifactId>servlet-api</artifactId>
                        <version>2.5</version>
                        <scope>provided</scope>
            </dependency>
```

```
        <dependency>
                        <groupId>javax.servlet</groupId>
                        <artifactId>jsp-api</artifactId>
                        <version>2.0</version>
                        <scope>provided</scope>
        </dependency>

</dependencies>
```

As shown in the listing, the following dependencies are needed for compilation ONLY and will not be included in the lib folder of the web application because these dependencies are already shipped with the GlassFish 3.1.2 application server:

- Servlet API version 2.5.

- JSP API version 2.0.

- JavaEE Web API version 6.

- JSF API version 2.1.

Listing 1-10 shows the required dependencies of the firstApplication on Tomcat 7.

Listing 1-10. Tomcat 7 Configuration

```
<dependencies>
        <dependency>
                        <groupId>javax</groupId>
                        <artifactId>javaee-web-api</artifactId>
                        <version>6.0</version>
                        <scope>provided</scope>
        </dependency>

        <dependency>
                        <groupId>org.glassfish</groupId>
                        <artifactId>javax.faces</artifactId>
                        <version>2.1.6</version>
        </dependency>

        <dependency>
                        <groupId>javax.servlet</groupId>
                        <artifactId>servlet-api</artifactId>
                        <version>2.5</version>
                        <scope>provided</scope>
        </dependency>

        <dependency>
                        <groupId>javax.servlet</groupId>
                        <artifactId>jsp-api</artifactId>
                        <version>2.0</version>
                        <scope>provided</scope>
        </dependency>

</dependencies>
```

As shown in the listing, it is almost the same set of dependencies with one difference, which is replacing the JSF API v2.1 dependency which is in the provided scope:

```
<dependency>
            <groupId>javax.faces</groupId>
            <artifactId>javax.faces-api</artifactId>
            <version>2.1</version>
            <scope>provided</scope>
</dependency>
```

With the following dependency in the compile scope:

```
<dependency>
            <groupId>org.glassfish</groupId>
            <artifactId>javax.faces</artifactId>
            <version>2.1.6</version>
</dependency>
```

This replacement tells Maven to use the JSF 2.1.6 jar for compiling the firstApplication and to include the jar in the web application lib folder. I choose the 2.1.6 version specifically because it works fine on Tomcat 7.

Building and deploying the firstApplication

The firstApplication Maven project is available for download from the book web site: www.apress.com/9781430250104. In order to build and deploy the firstApplication, you need to install Maven 3 in your system.

■ **Note** The detailed steps for configuring Maven 3 are described in the Maven website: http://maven.apache.org/ download.html#Installation. The instructions show you how to install Maven in your system whether it is Windows, Linux, Solaris, or Mac OS X.

After installing Maven 3 in your system, you can simply build the firstApplication by executing the following Maven command from the command line. This command should be executed from the application directory that contains the pom.xml file:

```
mvn clean install
```

After executing this command, you can find the generated firstApplication-1.0.war file in the target folder. Let's see how to deploy the generated war files on both the Apache Tomcat 7 and the Oracle GlassFish 3.1.2.

■ **Note** Do not forget to use the proper pom.xml dependencies mentioned in the "Dependencies" section for generating the two war files correctly (one for the Apache Tomcat 7 and the other for the Oracle GlassFish 3.1.2).

Deploying the Application on Tomcat 7

In order to deploy the `firstApplication-1.0.war` file on the Apache Tomcat 7, you need to do the following:

- Copy the `firstApplication-1.0.war` file to the `${Tomcat_Installation_Directory}\webapps` directory.

- Start the Tomcat 7 server by executing the following command from the `${Tomcat_Installation_Directory}\bin` directory:

- `startup.bat` (For Windows)

- `startup.sh` (For Linux)

- Access the `firstApplication` from the following URL: `http://localhost:8080/firstApplication-1.0/`

Deploying the Application on GlassFish 3.1.2

In order to deploy the `firstApplication-1.0.war` file on the Oracle GlassFish 3.1.2, you need to do the following:

- Copy the `firstApplication-1.0.war` file to the `${GlassFish_Installation_Directory}\` `domains\`**`domain1`**`\autodeploy` directory (The **domain1** can be changed to any domain name).

- Start the GlassFish 3.1.2 server by executing the following command from the `${GlassFish_Installation_Directory}\bin` directory: `asadmin start-domain domain1`

- Access the `firstApplication` from the following URL: `http://localhost:8080/firstApplication/`

Although the `firstApplication` is a simple JSF application, it covered many basics of the JSF. You now know the following:

- How to create a JSF application from scratch.

- The basics of the JSF expressions.

- What JSF managed is and how to create and use from the JSF application.

- How to create a JSF page template and use the template from the application pages.

- How to configure and use a resource bundle from the JSF application.

- How to use the basic JSF HTML component tags.

- How to use the JSF required field validator in order to validate input fields.

- How to use Maven in order to manage deploying the JSF application easily on the different JSF 2.1 web containers.

JSF Life Cycle

Now, it is the time to know how the JSF works behind the scenes. Although developing JSF applications does not require understanding the details of the JSF life cycle, it is recommended to read this section in order to realize how the code you develop is executed in the JSF runtime container and in order to prepare yourself for advanced JSF development. The JSF request processing life cycle has six phases, as shown by Figure 1-7.

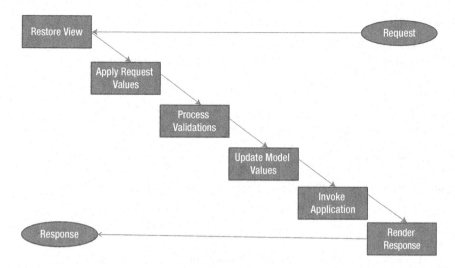

Figure 1-7. *The JSF request processing phases*

The six phases are as follows:

- Restore View.
- Apply Request Values.
- Process Validations.
- Update Model Values.
- Invoke Application.
- Render Response.

Restore View

Every JSF page is represented on the server as a tree of UI components that has one-to-one mapping with the user interface in the client (browser). In order to understand this correctly, let's see an example. Listing 1-11 shows a JSF XHTML page that allows the user enters his/her favorite food, beverage, and sport.

Listing 1-11. The favorites.xhtml Page

```
<html xmlns="http://www.w3.org/1999/xhtml"
      xmlns:h="http://java.sun.com/jsf/html">
<h:head>
  <title>Your Favorites</title>
</h:head>
<h:body>
    <h:form id="favForm">
        <h:panelGrid columns="3">
            <h:outputText value="Favorite Food"></h:outputText>
            <h:inputText id="favoriteFood" value="#{favorite.food}" required="true">
            </h:inputText>
```

```
            <h:message for="favoriteFood"/>

            <h:outputText value="Favorite Beverage"></h:outputText>
            <h:inputText id="favoriteBeverge" value="#{favorite.beverage}" required="true">
            </h:inputText>
            <h:message for="favoriteBeverge"/>

            <h:outputText value="Favorite Sport"></h:outputText>
            <h:inputText id="favoriteSport" value="#{favorite.sport}" required="true">
            </h:inputText>
            <h:message for="favoriteSport"/>
        </h:panelGrid>
        <h:commandButton value="Save my favorites" action="#{favorite.save}"/><br/><br/>
    </h:form>
</h:body>
</html>
```

The code in the favorites.xhtml page is represented as a tree of UI components, as shown in Figure 1-8.

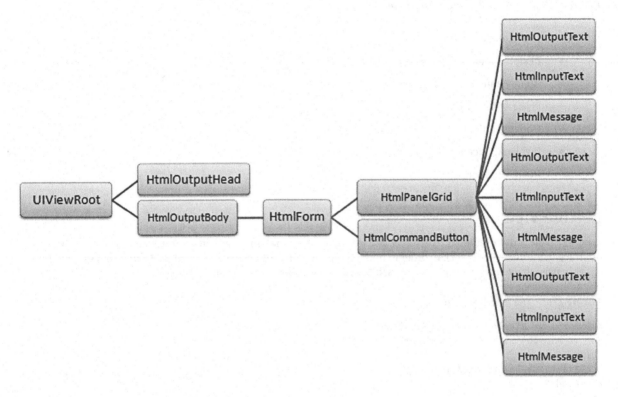

Figure 1-8. *The UI components tree of the favorites page*

In the "Restore View" phase, there are two cases:

- "Non Postback" requests: The "Non Postback" request refers to a new request to a page. If this case, the Restore View phase creates an empty UI components tree and stores it in the current FacesContext instance. For the "Non Postback" requests, the JSF life cycle directly proceeds to the last phase, which is the "Render Response" phase. In the "Render Response" phase, the empty UI components tree is populated with the JSF components in the page. Also, the UI components tree state is saved in the JSF view state for the next requests.

- "Postback" requests: The "Postback" request occurs when the content of the form is submitted to the same page using the HTTP POST method. In this case, the Restore View phase restores the UI components tree from the JSF view state that was generated from the previous page request.

Apply Request Values

The "Apply Request Values" phase is called after the UI components tree is restored. In this phase, every node in the UI components tree is assigned to the values submitted from the form. Figure 1-9 shows how the UI components tree is populated with the request values if the form is submitted with values, for example, "Fish" for the "favoriteFood", "Orange Juice" for the "favoriteBeverge", and "Football" for the "favoriteSport".

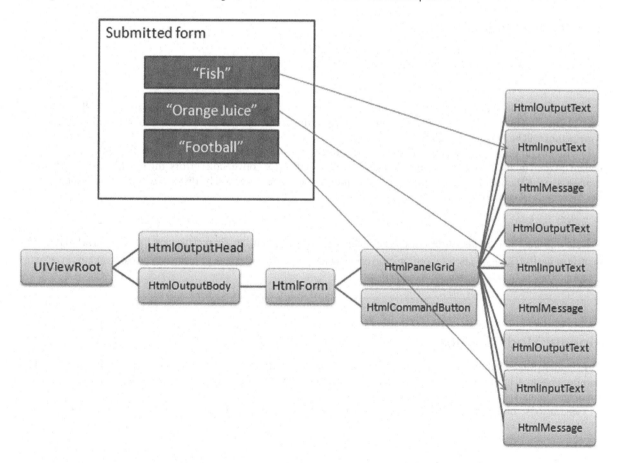

Figure 1-9. *UI components tree population with the request values*

■ **Note**   The "Apply Request Values" is applied to all the components which have a `value` attribute. In JSF, the components which have the `value` attribute must implement the `ValueHolder` interface. In order to apply the request values to all the value holder nodes in the UI components tree, the JSF runtime calls the `processDecodes()` method of the `UIViewRoot`, which causes the child components' `processDecodes()` method to be called as well in order to apply the request values for all of them.

Process Validations

The "Process Validations" phase is called after the "Apply Request Values" phase. In this phase, the conversion and the validation are performed in order. In the `favorites.xhtml`, a validation is performed on all the input fields in order to guarantee that they will always have non-empty values by setting the `"required"` attribute to `true`.

Conversion is about converting the HTTP request parameters to the corresponding Java types in order to eliminate the overhead required from the developer to implement this functionality for every web application. JSF has many built-in converters and it provides an interface in order to develop custom converters. Listing 1-12 shows an example of the JSF built-in date converter.

Listing 1-12.   An Example of the Built-in Date Converter

```
<h:inputText id="birthDate" value="#{user.birthDate}">
              <f:convertDateTime pattern="dd/MM/yyyy"/>
</h:inputText>
```

In this example, the `"birthDate"` input field is ensured to have a date with the following format `"dd/MM/yyyy"` and is converted to the `birthDate` (`Date` object) property in the `User` managed bean (more details of validations and conversions will be illustrated in Chapter 3).

When a component has a failing validation (or conversion), the component error message (`FacesMessage`) will be queued in the `FacesContext` instance. In case of validation (or conversion) errors, the JSF lifecycle directly proceeds to the "Render Response" phase, and the queued Faces messages will be displayed in the `<h:message>` or `<h:messages>` UI components.

■ **Note**   In order to apply the process validations in the UI components tree, the JSF runtime calls the `processValidators()` method of the `UIViewRoot`, which causes the child components' `processValidators()` method to be called as well in order to apply the conversion and the validation to all of them.

Update Model Values

The "Update Model Values" phase is called after completing the conversion and the validation of the values in the UI components tree. In this phase, the binding is done between the values in the UI components tree and the JSF model (managed beans).

Figure 1-10 shows how the JSF managed bean properties are updated with the values of the UI components tree.

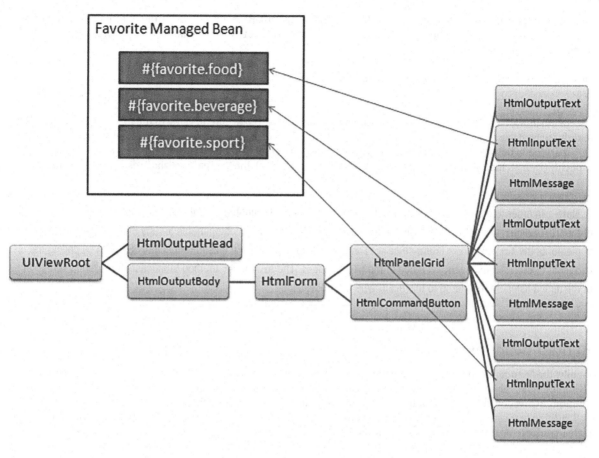

Figure 1-10. *The JSF managed bean properties update with the values of the UI components tree*

Note In order to perform the model values update, the JSF runtime calls the processUpdates() method of the UIViewRoot, which causes the child components' processUpdates() method to be called as well in order to apply the model updates to all of them. However, the UIInput components override the processUpdates() method in order to call the updateModel() for binding the user input with the managed bean property.

Invoke Application

The "Invoke Application" phase is called after completing the model values update. In this phase, the action code is executed. The action code in JSF can be in action methods and action listeners.

Note In the favorites.xhtml, the action code is represented in the #{favorite.save} action method.

In this phase, the navigation is performed by the JSF NavigationHandler after executing the custom action code. The action attribute can be set to a literal value. In the firstApplication, you already see a case where the action attribute is set to a literal value:

```
<h:commandButton value="#{bundle['application.login']}" action="welcome">
</h:commandButton>
```

In the literal value case, the JSF runtime directly passes the "welcome" literal value to the JSF NavigationHandler in order to navigate to the new page. The navigation handling results are displayed in the "Render Response" phase.

If an action outcome is not matching a navigation case implicitly (the outcome matching an existing page name) or explicitly (by matching a navigation rule defined in the faces-config), the NavigationHandler stays on the same page.

▪ **Note** In order to perform the "Invoke Application" phase, the JSF runtime calls the processApplication() method of the UIViewRoot, which broadcasts the queued events to the UICommand components (or any other UIComponent that implements the ActionSource interface or ActionSource2 interface [which was introduced in JSF 1.2]) by calling the broadcast(FacesEvent event) method of the UIComponent. The broadcast method broadcasts the action event to all of the action listeners registered to this event type for processing.

Render Response

Finally, the "Render Response" phase is called by the JSF runtime in order to render the final results to the user. The UI components tree is rendered to the client by calling the encodeXXX() methods on every component (the encode methods are responsible for generating the suitable markup for every component).

Adding to the rendering, the "Render Response" phase also stores the state of the UI components tree in the view state in order to be restored in the next requests.

The Immediate Attribute

Sometimes, you can have situations in your JSF application in which you want to skip the conversion and the validation in order to navigate to another page. For example, let's assume that in the favorites.xhtml page, you want to have a "Go Home" button that navigates to an index page "index.xhtml" as follows:

```
<h:form id="favForm">
        ...
        <h:inputText id="favoriteFood"
                            value="#{favorite.food}"
                            required="true">
        </h:inputText>
        ... <!-- other required fields -->
        <h:commandButton value="Save my favorites" action="#{favorite.save}"/>
        <h:commandButton value="Go home" action="index"/>
</h:form>
```

If you click the "Go home" button and you leave the required input fields empty, you will face the validation error messages as shown in Figure 1-11:

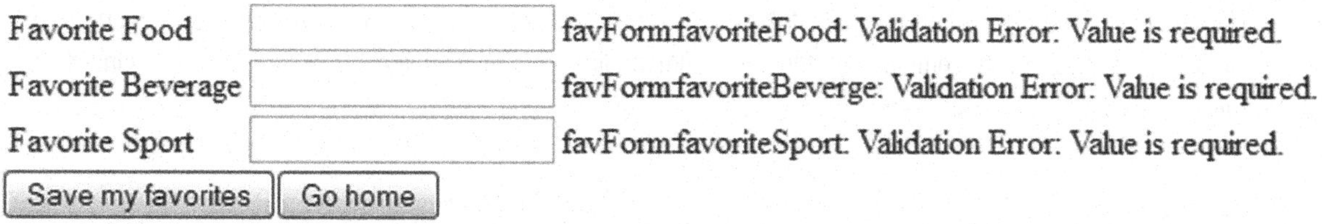

Favorite Food		favFormfavoriteFood: Validation Error: Value is required.
Favorite Beverage		favFormfavoriteBeverge: Validation Error: Value is required.
Favorite Sport		favFormfavoriteSport: Validation Error: Value is required.

Save my favorites Go home

Figure 1-11. *Validation errors due to the absence of "immediate" to true*

This is because the "Go home" command button makes a POST submit that triggers the JSF life cycle, and due to the validations on the input fields, the "Go home" operation could not be completed.

The JSF framework provides the "immediate" attribute, which allows skipping the conversion and the validation of the JSF life cycle. What the "immediate" attribute actually does is to allow the action event to be executed in the "Apply Request Values" phase. Setting the immediate attribute to true as follows resolves this issue:

```
<h:form id="favForm">
        ...
        <h:inputText id="favoriteFood"
                        value="#{favorite.food}"
                        required="true">
        </h:inputText>
        ... <!-- other required fields -->
        <h:commandButton value="Save my favorites" action="#{favorite.save}"/>
        <h:commandButton value="Go home" action="index" immediate="true"/>
</h:form>
```

■ **Note** The <h:link> and <h:button> are new components that have been introduced since JSF 2.0; they can be used to implement the GET navigation to target pages using the outcome attribute (you already saw an example of the <h:link> in the firstApplication). As a result of this, these new components can be used directly instead of the command button and command link **with the immediate attribute set to true** for doing the navigation without executing conversion and validation.

Adding to the UICommand components, the immediate attribute can be applied to the EditableValueHolder components (such as the input text). If the immediate attribute is set to true for an EditableValueHolder component, the conversion and the validation of the EditableValueHolder components will be executed in the "Apply Request Values" phase (before the "Process Validations" phase).

■ **Note**   ValueHolder components are those which have the value attribute such as (label and output text), and they implement the ValueHolder interface. The EditableValueHolder components are a subtype of the ValueHolder components that can have their values edited by the users such as the (input text). ActionSource components are those which can make actions such as (command button and command link), and they implement the ActionSource interface (or ActionSource2 since JSF 1.2).

Summary

After reading this chapter, you know what JSF is and you see how the JSF framework has evolved over time. You know the JSF architecture and have learned how to develop a JSF application that covered many interesting topics in the JSF world (basic UI components, managed beans, expression language, templating, resource bundles, and validation). Finally, you know how the JSF request processing life cycle works behind the scene. In the next chapters, all of the mentioned JSF topics in the chapter and other advanced topics will be illustrated in more detail.

CHAPTER 2

■ ■ ■

JSF Under the Hood—Part 1

This chapter illustrates important topics in the JSF framework. In this chapter, you will learn in detail about the JSF managed beans and the expression language (EL). You will also learn a bit about JSF navigation. Finally, you will learn how to utilize the JSF exception handling mechanism in your JSF web applications for empowering the applications error handling.

Managed Beans

The JSF managed bean is simply a POJO (Plain Old Java Object) that conforms to the JavaBeans naming conventions and can be accessed from the JSF application (pages and other managed beans). It is called **managed** because it is managed by the JSF framework which instantiates the bean class for you in a lazy manner when the JSF application needs to use it. The next sections will cover in detail how to declare managed beans, how to initialize managed beans, how to manage the dependencies between different managed beans, how to access managed beans, and finally how to utilize the @Named and @inject annotations for working with the JSF POJO model.

Declaring Managed Beans

In the first chapter, we had an example of the managed beans usage in the firstApplication. Listing 2-1 shows the User managed bean.

Listing 2-1. The User Managed Bean

```
package com.jsfprohtml5.firstapplication.model;

import java.io.Serializable;
import javax.faces.bean.ManagedBean;
import javax.faces.bean.SessionScoped;

@ManagedBean
@SessionScoped
public class User implements Serializable {
    private String name;
    private String password;

    public String getName() {
        return name;
    }
```

```
public void setName(String name) {
    this.name = name;
}

public String getPassword() {
    return password;
}

public void setPassword(String password) {
    this.password = password;
}
}
```

The User managed bean is a Java bean class with two setters and getters for the name and the password properties. The @ManagedBean annotation is used for registering the User class as a JSF managed bean. The @ManagedBean annotation has an optional name attribute that describes the name of the managed bean to be used from the JSF expressions. In the User managed bean, the name attribute is omitted; this means that the managed bean name will be the same as the class name with the first character in lowercase i.e., it will be used from the JSF expressions like #{user}.

A JSF managed bean must have a scope associated with it that controls its life span. The scope can be in:

- Request Scope (@RequestScoped), which means that the bean will be instantiated and will be alive as long as the HTTP request is alive.

- View Scope (@ViewScoped), which means that the bean will be instantiated and will be alive as long as the user is staying in the same view.

- Session Scope (@SessionScoped), which means that the bean will be instantiated and will be alive as long as the user's HTTP session is alive.

- Application Scope (@ApplicationScoped), which means that the bean will be instantiated and will be alive throughout the lifetime of the application.

- None scope (@NoneScoped), which means that the bean will not be instantiated and will not be stored in any scope as a **standalone** entity. The none scoped managed bean can be used and instantiated by another managed bean; in this case, the none scoped bean will have the scope of its caller managed bean which instantiates it (i.e., the none scoped managed beans will be alive as long as their caller managed beans are alive). You will see an example of this case in the "Managing managed beans dependency" section.

▪ **Note**   In the JSF 2.2, there is a new scope called "Flow Scope" (@FlowScoped). This flow will be illustrated in detail in the next chapter.

Adding to Annotations, Every JSF managed bean can also be registered in the faces-config.xml (the JSF configuration file). Listing 2-2 shows how the User managed bean can be defined in the faces-config.xml file instead of using annotations.

Listing 2-2. The User Managed Bean Definition in the faces-config.xml File

```
<managed-bean>
 <managed-bean-name>user</managed-bean-name>
 <managed-bean-class>com.jsfprohtml5.firstapplication.model.User</managed-bean-class>
 <managed-bean-scope>session</managed-bean-scope>
</managed-bean>
```

Initializing Managed Beans

JSF managed beans can be initialized from both the faces configuration file or using annotation. Listing 2-3 shows how to initialize the name property of the User managed bean with value "anonymous" from the faces configuration file.

Listing 2-3. Initializing the Name Property in the faces-config.xml

```
<managed-bean>
 <managed-bean-name>user</managed-bean-name>
 <managed-bean-class>com.jsfprohtml5.firstapplication.model.User</managed-bean-class>
 <managed-bean-scope>session</managed-bean-scope>
 <managed-property>
         <property-name>name</property-name>
                 <value>anonymous</value>
 </managed-property>
</managed-bean>
```

The <managed-property> element can be used for initializing the managed bean property. It has mainly two sub-elements:

- <property-name> element, which includes the name of the managed bean property.

- <value> element, which includes the initial value of the managed bean property.

Another way to initialize the managed bean properties is to use annotations. Listing 2-4 shows how to initialize the name property of the User managed bean with value "anonymous" using the @ManagedProperty annotation.

Listing 2-4. Initializing the Name Property Using the @ManagedProperty Annotation

```
@ManagedBean
@SessionScoped
public class User implements Serializable {

    @ManagedProperty(value="anonymous")
    private String name;
    private String password;

    // The setters and the getters ...
}
```

Using annotations, the @ManagedProperty annotation is used for initializing the name property of the User managed bean with the value "anonymous" using the value attribute.

It is important to note that the JSF managed beans can work perfectly with the different Java EE annotations. There are two Java EE annotations that are related to the JSF managed beans life cycle and can be used for initializing and de-initializing the managed beans:

- @PostConstruct

- @PreDestroy

Listing 2-5 shows an example of the @PostConstruct and the @PostDestroy annotations in the User managed bean.

Listing 2-5. The @PostConstruct and the @ PostDestroy Annotations

```java
import java.io.Serializable;
import javax.annotation.PostConstruct;
import javax.annotation.PreDestroy;
import javax.faces.bean.ManagedBean;
import javax.faces.bean.ManagedProperty;
import javax.faces.bean.SessionScoped;

@ManagedBean
@SessionScoped
public class User implements Serializable {

    @ManagedProperty(value="anonymous")
    private String name;
    private String password;

    // The setters and the getters ...

    @PostConstruct
    private void initialize() {
        System.out.println("Bean is initialized with the following user name: " + name);
    }

    @PreDestroy
    private void cleanUp() {
        System.out.println("You can do the cleanup here");
    }
}
```

The @PostConstruct method is called when the User managed bean is instantiated and initialized. This means that the output console will show the following message when the `initialize` method is called:

```
"Bean is initialized with the following user name: anonymous"
```

■ **Note** As you notice, the @PostConstruct and the @PreDestroy methods return types are void and take no arguments. The methods can also be private, public, protected, or package.

The @PreDestroy method is called before the User managed bean is destroyed. In this method, you can put the required cleanup and de-initialization code of the managed bean.

There are also many other Java EE annotations that are related to the data access and can be used perfectly with the JSF managed beans, such as @Resource, @PersistenceUnit, @PersistenceContext, @EJB, and @WebServiceRef. We will cover most of these annotations in the next chapters.

Adding to the ability of initializing simple attributes, you can also initialize the managed bean complex types such as lists and maps. Listing 2-6 introduces two new properties to the User managed bean: the favoriteSports List and spokenLanguages Map.

Listing 2-6. The User Managed Bean with the Two New Properties

```
import java.util.List;
import java.util.Map;
//...
public class User implements Serializable {
    private String name;
    private String password;

    private List<String> favoriteSports;
    private Map<String, String> spokenLanguages;

        // setters and getters ...
}
```

In order to initialize the favoriteSports List with some initial values, you can use the <list-entries> element in the <managed-property> element, as shown by Listing 2-7.

Listing 2-7. Initialization of the List Property in the Faces Configuration File

```
<managed-property>
        <property-name>favoriteSports</property-name>
        <list-entries>
                <value>Handball</value>
                <value>Football</value>
                <value>Basketball</value>
        </list-entries>
</managed-property>
```

In the XHTML page, you can iterate on the favoriteSportlist as shown in Listing 2-8 using the <ui:repeat>.

Listing 2-8. Displaying the favoriteSports Items in the XHTML Page

```
<b>You have the following initial list of favorite sports:</b>
<ul>
        <ui:repeat value="#{user.favoriteSport}" var="sport">
                <li>#{sport}</li>
        </ui:repeat>
</ul>
```

If you want to display a specific item in the favoriteSport list, you can use the [ ] operator. For example, the following #{user.favoriteSport[0]} will display the first item in the favoriteSport array, which is "Handball". In order to initialize the spokenLanguages Map with some initial values, you can use the <map-entries> element in the <managed-property> element, as shown by Listing 2-9.

Listing 2-9. Initialization of the Map Property in the Faces Configuration File

```
<managed-property>
        <property-name>spokenLanguages</property-name>
        <map-entries>
                <map-entry>
                        <key>EN</key>
```

```
                        <value>English</value>
            </map-entry>
            <map-entry>
                        <key>FR</key>
                        <value>French</value>
            </map-entry>
        </map-entries>
</managed-property>
```

In the XHTML page, you can display the spokenLanguages using the #{user.spokenLanguages}. If you want to display a specific map entry value, you can get it from its key using the [ ] operator as well. For example, using the #{user.spokenLanguages['EN']} will display "English".

■ **Note**   There is no equivalent JSF annotations for the <list-entries> and <map-entries> elements, so the only way to initialize maps and lists is to use the faces configuration file.

Managing Managed Beans Dependency

JSF supports IoC (inversion of control) for the managed beans, which means that the managed beans can be coupled in the runtime without needing to handle this coupling from the application code. Let's see how we can utilize IoC in our JSF applications. Listing 2-10 introduces a new property to the User managed bean, the profession property.

Listing 2-10. The New Profession Attribute in the User Managed Bean

```
public class User implements Serializable {
    ...
    private Profession profession;
        ...
    public Profession getProfession() {
        return profession;
    }

    public void setProfession(Profession profession) {
        this.profession = profession;
    }
}
```

Listing 2-11 shows the attributes of the Profession managed bean class.

Listing 2-11. The Profession Managed Bean

```
public class Profession implements Serializable {
    private String title;
    private String industry;

    public String getTitle() {
        return title;
    }
```

```
public void setTitle(String title) {
    this.title = title;
}

public String getIndustry() {
    return industry;
}

public void setIndustry(String industry) {
    this.industry = industry;
}
}
```

Associating the Profession managed bean instance with the User managed bean instance can be done using either the JSF configuration file or the JSF annotations. Listing 2-12 shows the part of the JSF configuration file which configures the Profession managed bean to be injected in the User managed bean when it is instantiated.

Listing 2-12. Configuring the Profession Instance to Be Injected in the User Instance

```
<managed-bean>
        <managed-bean-name>user</managed-bean-name>
        <managed-bean-class>com.jsfprohtml5.firstapplication.model.User</managed-bean-class>
        <managed-bean-scope>session</managed-bean-scope>
        <managed-property>
                <property-name>profession</property-name>
                <value>#{profession}</value>
        </managed-property>
        ...
</managed-bean>
<managed-bean>
        <managed-bean-name>profession</managed-bean-name>
        <managed-bean-class>com.jsfprohtml5.firstapplication.model.Profession</managed-bean-class>
        <managed-bean-scope>none</managed-bean-scope>
        <managed-property>
                <property-name>title</property-name>
                <value>Software Engineer</value>
        </managed-property>
        <managed-property>
                <property-name>industry</property-name>
                <value>IT</value>
        </managed-property>
</managed-bean>
```

The Profession managed bean is declared in the none scope in order to have the scope of its caller managed bean which instantiates it (which is the User managed bean in this case). In the User managed bean, a property initialization is defined for the profession property, and the #{profession} expression is used as the value for the profession property using the <managed-property> element.

After doing this configuration, the Profession managed bean will be instantiated and set in the session scope when the User managed bean is instantiated by the JSF framework. This means that the #{user.profession.title} expression will return the initial value for the profession title, which is "Software Engineer".

Accessing Managed Beans from Java Code

It is important to know how to access managed beans from the Java code. This is useful if you want to get the information of a specific managed bean (for example bean1) from another managed bean (for example bean2) that is not referring to bean1 directly. In order to access managed beans from the Java code, you need to use the ValueExpression class. Listing 2-13 shows how to get the information of the User managed bean from the Java code.

Listing 2-13. Getting the User Managed Bean Information from the Java Code

```
FacesContext context = FacesContext.getCurrentInstance();
Application application = context.getApplication();
ELContext elContext = context.getELContext();

ExpressionFactory expressionFactory = application.getExpressionFactory();

ValueExpression valueExpression = expressionFactory.createValueExpression
                                  (elContext, "#{user}", User.class);

User user = (User) valueExpression.getValue(elContext);
```

In order to retrieve the User managed bean information, a ValueExpression object is created using the createValueExpression API of the ExpressionFactory class. The createValueExpression API takes the following arguments:

- ELContext, which refers to the EL context used to parse the expression.

- The expression String to parse.

- The type that the result of the expression will be coerced to after the expression evaluation.

Using the ValueExpression object, you can get the value of the expression using the getValue(ELContext) API, and you can also use the ValueExpression object for setting a value to the expression in the runtime using the setValue(ELContext, value) API.

@Named and @inject Annotations

In future JSF specifications, the @ManagedBean will be deprecated so it is recommended to use the @Named CDI (Context and Dependency Injection) annotation instead of the @ManagedBean. You should know that the @ManagedBean is managed by the JSF framework, while the @Named annotation is not managed by the JSF framework. The @Named annotation is managed by the JEE application server which supports CDI. One advantage of the CDI over the JSF dependency injection is that in order to inject an instance using the CDI @inject annotation, this instance does not require to be annotated with any specific annotation, while in JSF, the @ManagedProperty requires the bean to be injected to be annotated with the @ManagedBean annotation.

Let's see how we can use the @Named annotation for the User managed bean instead of the @ManagedBean. Listing 2-14 shows the modified version of the User managed bean that utilizes the @Named annotation.

Listing 2-14. The @Named User Managed Bean

```
import java.io.Serializable;
import javax.enterprise.context.SessionScoped;
import javax.inject.Inject;
import javax.inject.Named;
```

```
@Named
@SessionScoped
public class User implements Serializable {
    private String name;
    private String password;
    @Inject
    private Profession profession;

    // ...

    public Profession getProfession() {
        return profession;
    }

    public void setProfession(Profession profession) {
        this.profession = profession;
    }

    //...
}
```

We need to note some changes that should be made in order to use CDI with our User managed bean:

- The @Named annotation replaces the @ManagedBean annotation.

- We used the javax.enterprise.context.SessionScoped instead of the javax.faces.bean.SessionScoped (in CDI, you must not use the javax.faces.bean.xxx package for specifying the bean scope; instead, you have to use the javax.enterprise.context.xxx package).

- We used the @inject annotation for injecting the Profession managed bean instance in the User managed bean instance instead of using the @ManagedProperty annotation.

■ **Note**   When using CDI, you need to create an empty beans.xml under the WEB-INF folder of the web application.

Expression Language

There are two **different** sets of ELs:

- The JSP EL.

- The JSF EL.

There are many differences between the two ELs. The JSP EL expressions start with the dollar sign ($), then followed by the left curly bracket ({), then followed by the JSP expression, and finally closed with the right curly bracket (}). The JSP EL executes immediately when the page is rendered (in the page compilation time). On the other hand, the JSF EL expressions start with the hash (#), then followed by the left curly bracket ({), then followed by the JSF expression, and finally closed with the right curly bracket (}). The JSF EL expressions execution is deferred, which means that the expressions are evaluated based on the JSF lifecycle context.

To be more specific, the JSF deferred expressions are available during the page postback as well as the page initial rendering, which means that the JSF deferred expressions can be evaluated in the request processing and the response rendering phases of the JSF framework, while the JSP immediate expressions are available ONLY during the page rendering (NOT the page postback) because they are evaluated once the page is rendered for the first time. This means that the JSP EL is always read-only value expressions, while the JSF EL can work in both read and write modes.

Unified Expression Language

Thanks to JSP 2.1, which was part of the Java EE 5, this mismatch is resolved by having a unified EL which essentially represents a union of the JSP and JSF ELs. The unified EL has the following features:

- Deferred evaluations of expressions.

- The expressions can work in both read and write modes.

- The JSTL tags can work with deferred expressions.

Listing 2-15 shows an example that shows how the <c:forEach> JSTL tag can work with the JSF deferred expression #{..}.

Listing 2-15. The JSF Deferred Expressions with the <c:forEach> Tag

```
<b>You have the following initial list of favorite sports:</b>
<ul>
        <c:forEach items="#{user.favoriteSport}" var="sport">
                <li>#{sport}</li>
        </c:forEach>
</ul>
```

As shown in the listing, this code can be a replacement for the code in Listing 2-16, which is part of the welcome.xhtml page in the firstApplication.

Listing 2-16. The Original JSF Deferred Expression with the <ui:repeat> Tag

```
<b>You have the following initial list of favorite sports:</b>
<ul>
        <ui:repeat value="#{user.favoriteSport}" var="sport">
                <li>#{sport}</li>
        </ui:repeat>
</ul>
```

Adding to this, you have the option to combine other JSTL tags with the JSF deferred expressions, as shown in Listing 2-17.

Listing 2-17. The JSF Deferred Expressions with the Different JSTL Tags

```
<b>You have the following initial list of favorite sports:</b>
<ul>
        <c:forEach items="#{user.favoriteSport}" var="sport">
                <c:choose>
                    <c:when test="#{sport == 'Football'}">
                            <li><b><u>Popular in Africa:</u></b> #{sport}</li>
                    </c:when>
                    <c:otherwise>
                            <li>#{sport}</li>
                    </c:otherwise>
                </c:choose>
        </c:forEach>
</ul>
```

The following JSTL tags are used with the JSF deferred expressions in the example:

- `<c:forEach>` for performing the iteration.

- `<c:choose>` for defining a group of mutually exclusive choices. It is like the Java `switch` statement.

- `<c:when>`, which is like the Java `case` statement.

- `<c:other>`, which is like the Java `default` statement.

In this example, the `<c:forEach>` iterates over the `#{user.favoriteSport}` list, and the current sport item is represented by the `#{sport}` expression. The `<c:when>` tag checks if the current sport `#{sport}` value is `'Football'` and when it finds this value, the following sentence `"Popular in Africa:"` is highlighted and underlined and appended to beginning of the list item. If the current sport does not equal `'Football'` then the `#{sport}` is displayed normally using the `<c:otherwise>` JSTL element. Figure 2-1 shows how the list items will appear.

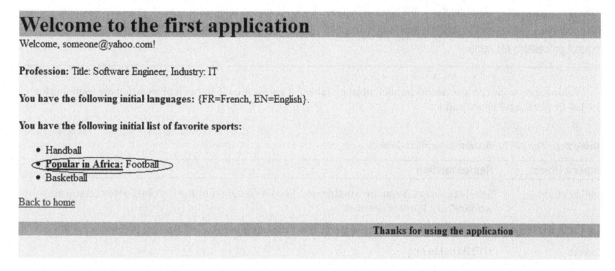

Figure 2-1. *The highlighted underlined list item*

Note that in order to work with JSTL, you need to include the JSTL URI in the declaration, as shown in the following bolded text:

```
<html xmlns="http://www.w3.org/1999/xhtml"
    xmlns:ui="http://java.sun.com/jsf/facelets"
    xmlns:h="http://java.sun.com/jsf/html"
    xmlns:f="http://java.sun.com/jsf/core"
    xmlns:c="http://java.sun.com/jsp/jstl/core">
```

In the JSF EL, there are two types of expressions:

- Value expression.

- Method expression.

In the next sections, we will dig into the details of both value and method expressions.

Value Expression

A value expression can be used for setting the value of a managed bean property or displaying the value of a managed bean property or any dynamically evaluated object. We have seen several examples so far for the value expressions. For example, the following #{user.name} expression in the welcome.xhtml page of the firstApplication represents a value expression that displays the name of the User managed bean:

Welcome, #{user.name}!

While the same #{user.name} expression in the login page (index.xhtml) of the firstApplication represents a value expression that sets the name of the User managed bean:

<h:inputText id="userName" value="#{user.name}" required="true"/>

■ **Note**　As we know from Chapter 1, the binding between the EditableValueHolder's (such as inputText and selectOneMenu) value and the JSF EL expression (model) is performed in the Update Model Values phase of the JSF request processing life cycle.

Value expressions can also access implicit objects. Table 2-1 shows the JSF implicit objects that are available for the JSF EL per the JSF specification.

Table 2-1. *The JSF EL Available Implicit Objects*

Implicit Object	Representation
Application	ServletContext if you are working on a Servlet container or the PortletContext if you are working on a Portlet container.
applicationScope	application scoped map (the application attributes map).
Cookie	HTTP cookie map.
facesContext	current FacesContext instance.
Component	UIComponent instance (will be detailed in "Creating Custom JSF Components" in chapters 6-8).
Cc	parent composite component (will be detailed in "Creating Custom JSF Components" in chapters 6-8).
Flash	flash scoped map (will be illustrated in detail in the flash scope section).
Header	request HTTP headers map.
headerValues	request HTTP headers map. However, every value of the map is a String[] that represents the header key values.
initParam	init parameters map of the application.
Param	request query parameters map.
paramValues	request query parameters map. However, every value of the map is a String[] that represents the parameter key values.
Request	ServletRequest if you are working on a Servlet container or the PortletRequest if you are working on a Portlet container.

(continued)

Table 2-1. (*continued*)

Implicit Object	Representation
requestScope	request scoped map (the request attributes map).
Resource	resource reference.
Session	HttpSession if you are working on a Servlet container or the PortletSession if you are working on a Portlet container.
sessionScope	session scoped map (the session attributes map).
View	UIViewRoot for the current view.
viewScope	view scoped map (the view attributes map).

The following example in Listing 2-18 shows how to show the request header information using the #{header} value expression.

Listing 2-18. Displaying the Request Header Information Using the Header Implicit Object

```
<table border="1">
        <th>Key</th>
        <th>Value</th>
        <c:forEach items="#{header}" var="header">
                <tr>
                        <td>#{header.key}</td>
                        <td>#{header.value}</td>
                </tr>
        </c:forEach>
</table>
```

The #{header} expression returns a map that represents the HTTP headers, and using the <c:forEach> JSTL tag, the header keys and values are displayed. Figure 2-2 shows the output of Listing 2-18.

Key	Value
host	localhost:8080
user-agent	Mozilla/5.0 (Windows NT 5.1; rv:17.0) Gecko/20100101 Firefox/17.0
accept	text/html,application/xhtml+xml,application/xml;q=0.9,*/*;q=0.8
accept-language	en,en-gb;q=0.5
accept-encoding	gzip, deflate
connection	keep-alive
referer	http://localhost:8080/Test2/
cookie	JSESSIONID=d7b1c5bc46ab0089781b4c60c92a
cache-control	max-age=0
content-type	application/x-www-form-urlencoded
content-length	174

Figure 2-2. *The HTTP headers information*

■ **Note** It is also possible to use the square brackets ([]) instead of the (.) inside the value expressions. Adding to accessing managed bean properties, square brackets can be used for accessing maps and arrays as we saw in the "Managed Beans" section examples.

Method Expression

A method expression can be used for executing public non-static methods of managed beans. Method expression can be invoked from

- action and actionListener attributes of the ActionSource (or ActionSource2) components such as (commandButton and commandLink).
- valueChangeListener attribute of the EditableValueHolder components such as (inputText and selectOneMenu).
- beforePhase and afterPhase attributes of the <f:view> tag.

In the firstApplication, we can modify the login commandButton's action attribute to have a method expression instead of the "welcome" String literal in the login page (index.xhtml) as shown in the bolded line in Listing 2-19.

Listing 2-19. The Modified Login Page

```
<?xml version='1.0' encoding='UTF-8' ?>
<!DOCTYPE html>
<html xmlns="http://www.w3.org/1999/xhtml"
      xmlns:ui="http://java.sun.com/jsf/facelets"
      xmlns:h="http://java.sun.com/jsf/html">

<ui:composition template="/WEB-INF/templates/simple.xhtml">
    <ui:define name="title">
        #{bundle['application.loginpage.title']}
    </ui:define>
    <ui:define name="content">
                    ...

        <h:commandButton value="#{bundle['application.login']}" action="#{user.login}"/>
            <br/><br/>
        </h:form>
    </ui:define>
</ui:composition>

</html>
```

The login() method in the User managed bean is simple, as shown in Listing 2-20.

Listing 2-20. The Login Action Method in the User Managed Bean

```java
public class User implements Serializable {

    ...

    public String login() {
        return "welcome";
    }

    ...

}
```

As shown in Listing 2-20, the method of the action attribute have the following signature:

- Returns a String (outcome) that is used for determining the navigation.

- Takes no argument.

Adding to this, if you are working with EditableValueHolders, you can invoke a method expression from the valueChangeListener attribute. Let's see an example to explain this. Listing 2-21 shows the beverages page, which contains a selectOneMenu component that holds a list of beverages and an outputText to show the price of the selected beverage.

Listing 2-21. The Beverages Page

```xml
<?xml version='1.0' encoding='UTF-8' ?>
<!DOCTYPE html>
<html xmlns="http://www.w3.org/1999/xhtml"
    xmlns:h="http://java.sun.com/jsf/html"
    xmlns:f="http://java.sun.com/jsf/core">

<h:head>
  <title>Beverages</title>
</h:head>

<h:body>
    <h:form>
        <h:outputText value="Select a beverage: " />
        <h:selectOneMenu value="#{beverage.name}"
                    valueChangeListener="#{beverage.beverageSelected}"
                    onchange="submit()">

            <f:selectItem itemLabel="---" itemValue="---"/>
            <f:selectItem itemLabel="Tea" itemValue="tea" />
            <f:selectItem itemLabel="Coffee" itemValue="coffee" />
            <f:selectItem itemLabel="Coca-Cola" itemValue="cocacola" />
        </h:selectOneMenu> <br/><br/>

        <h:outputText value="You will have to pay: #{beverage.price} USD"

                    rendered="#{beverage.price ne null}"/>
    </h:form>
</h:body>
</html>
```

The selectOneMenu component renders a combo-box with a list of beverage items (Tea, Coffee, Coca-Cola); when the user selects one of the available beverages, the form is submitted and the valueChangeListener method (the beverageSelected method of the Beverage managed bean) is executed to calculate the price of the selected beverage. You may notice that using the rendered attribute, the outputText will not be rendered if the beverage price is not available.

■ **Note**   ne stands for (not equal), it is also equivalent to != which is supported by EL. EL also supports the following relational operators:

1.   eq stands for (equal) and it is equivalent to ==.

2.   lt stands for (less than) and it is equivalent to <.

3.   le stands for (less than or equal) and it is equivalent to <=.

4.   gt stands for (greater than) and it is equivalent to >.

5.   ge stands for (greater than or equal) and it is equivalent to >=.

Listing 2-22 shows the Beverage managed bean.

Listing 2-22. The Beverage Managed Bean

```
import javax.faces.bean.ManagedBean;
import javax.faces.bean.RequestScoped;
import javax.faces.event.ValueChangeEvent;

@ManagedBean
@RequestScoped
public class Beverage {
    private String name;
    private Double price;

    public String getName() {
        return name;
    }

    public void setName(String name) {
        this.name = name;
    }

    public Double getPrice() {
        return price;
    }

    public void setPrice(Double price) {
        this.price = price;
    }
```

```
public void beverageSelected(ValueChangeEvent event) {
    String selectedBeverage = event.getNewValue().toString();
    if ("tea".equals(selectedBeverage)) {
        price = 2.0;
    } else if ("coffee".equals(selectedBeverage)) {
        price = 2.5;
    } else if ("cocacola".equals(selectedBeverage)) {
        price = 3.0;
    }
}
}
```

As shown in Listing 2-22, the method of the valueChangeListener attribute has the following signature:

- Returns void.

- Takes a single argument which is the ValueChangeEvent object.

The ValueChangeEvent object holds both the old value and the new selected value. The new selected value can be retrieved using getNewValue(). In the beverageSelected method, the new selected value is retrieved and a price is set according to the selected beverage item. Figure 2-3 shows the beverages example output.

Select a beverage: Coca-Cola ▾

You will have to pay: 3.0 USD

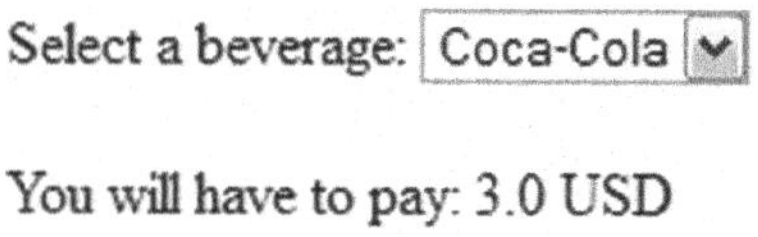

Figure 2-3. *The beverages example output*

So far, we have seen two examples of the JSF method expressions; in the following chapters, we will see many other examples.

■ **Note**   You do not have make a full page submission in order to execute the valueChangeListener method of the EditableValueHolder; otherwise, you can use the <f:ajax> tag in order to invoke the valueChangeListener method in an Ajaxified style (the <f:ajax> tag will be discussed in detail in Chapter 5).

It is important to note that if you are working on a Java EE 6 container (or later) which includes the Unified EL 2.1, you can invoke arbitrary methods with parameters. Let's see an example to explain this. Listing 2-23 shows the calculateAverage method of a custom Maths managed bean.

Listing 2-23. The calculateAverage Method of a Custom Maths Managed Bean

```
@ManagedBean
@RequestScoped
public class Maths {

    public Double calculateAverage (Double number1, Double number2) {
        return (number1 + number2) / 2;
    }
}
```

In the XHTML page, you can call the `calculateAverage` method by using `#{maths.calculateAverage(10.5,` `12.3)}`, which outputs `11.4`.

The Flash Scope

The flash scope is a new scope introduced since the JSF 2.0. The flash scope concept is inspired from RoR (Ruby on Rails). The flash scope means that "anything that is placed in the flash scope will be exposed to the next view encountered by the same user session and then cleared out." In other words, the objects in the flash scope will be available **ONLY** for the next request of the same browser **window**.

The flash scope is useful if you want to keep information for a short time for the next request only, whether the next request will result from an HTTP Redirect, a JSF form postback, or an HTTP GET for a new page. Let's see an example to understand the flash scope.

The survey application is a simple application that consists of three pages:

- `input.xhtml`, which asks the user for some information that is useful for the survey.

- `confirm.xhtml`, which displays the information entered by the user and asks the user to confirm or modify it.

- `final.xhtml`, which is a "Thank you" page.

Listing 2-24 shows the `input.xhtml` page.

Listing 2-24. The input.xhtml Page

```
<?xml version='1.0' encoding='UTF-8' ?>
<!DOCTYPE html>
<html xmlns="http://www.w3.org/1999/xhtml"
      xmlns:ui="http://java.sun.com/jsf/facelets"
      xmlns:h="http://java.sun.com/jsf/html"
      xmlns:f="http://java.sun.com/jsf/core">

<ui:composition template="/WEB-INF/templates/simple.xhtml">
    <ui:define name="title">
        #{bundle['survey.input.page']}
    </ui:define>
    <ui:define name="content">
        <h:form>
            <h:panelGrid columns="3">
                <h:outputText value="#{bundle['survey.user.name']} "></h:outputText>
                <h:inputText id="userName"
                             value="#{flash.userName}"
                             required="true">
                </h:inputText>
                <h:message for="userName" styleClass="errorMessage"/>
                <h:outputText value="#{bundle['survey.user.age']}"></h:outputText>
                <h:inputText id="age"
                             value="#{flash.age}"
                             required="true">
                    <f:convertNumber />
                </h:inputText>
                <h:message for="age" styleClass="errorMessage"/>
```

```
            <h:outputText value="#{bundle['survey.user.sex']}"></h:outputText>
            <h:selectOneMenu id="sex"
                            value="#{flash.sex}">
                <f:selectItem itemLabel="Male" itemValue="male"/>
                <f:selectItem itemLabel="Female" itemValue="female"/>
            </h:selectOneMenu>
            <h:message for="sex" styleClass="errorMessage"/>

            <h:outputText value="#{bundle['survey.user.monthyIncome']}"></h:outputText>
            <h:inputText id="monthlyIncome"
                        value="#{flash.monthlyIncome}"
                        required="true">
                <f:convertNumber />
            </h:inputText>
            <h:message for="monthlyIncome" styleClass="errorMessage"/>

            <h:outputText value="#{bundle['survey.user.yearlyTravelAbroad']}"></h:outputText>
            <h:inputText id="yearlyTravelsAbroad"
                        value="#{flash.travelsAbroad}"
                        required="true">
                <f:convertNumber />
            </h:inputText>
            <h:message for="yearlyTravelsAbroad" styleClass="errorMessage"/>

            <h:outputText value="#{bundle['survey.user.oftenTravelBy']}"></h:outputText>
            <h:selectOneMenu id="travelBy"
                            value="#{flash.travelBy}">
                <f:selectItem itemLabel="#{bundle['survey.travelby.plane']}" itemValue="plane"/>
                <f:selectItem itemLabel="#{bundle['survey.travelby.car']}" itemValue="car"/>
            </h:selectOneMenu>
            <h:message for="travelBy" styleClass="errorMessage"/>
        </h:panelGrid>

        <h:commandButton value="#{bundle['survey.actions.next']}"
                        action="confirm?faces-redirect=true"/>

        <br/><br/>
    </h:form>
  </ui:define>
</ui:composition>

</html>
```

In the input.xhtml page, the user is asked to enter name, age, sex, monthly income, yearly travels abroad, and how often the user travels by. The most important thing to notice in this page is the bolded lines, where the #{flash} EL is used for making the value binding between the EditableValueHolders and the flash scope. When the form data is valid and the user clicks the "Next" commandButton, the binding is done between the EditableValueHolder values and the flash attributes, and the page is redirected to the confirm.xhtml page. Listing 2-25 shows the initial code of the confirm.xhtml page.

Listing 2-25. The Initial Code of the confirm.xhtml Page

```
<?xml version='1.0' encoding='UTF-8' ?>
<!DOCTYPE html>
<html xmlns="http://www.w3.org/1999/xhtml"
      xmlns:ui="http://java.sun.com/jsf/facelets"
      xmlns:h="http://java.sun.com/jsf/html">

<ui:composition template="/WEB-INF/templates/simple.xhtml">
    <ui:define name="title">
        #{bundle['survey.confirm.page']}
    </ui:define>
    <ui:define name="content">
        <h:form>
            <h:outputText value="#{bundle['survey.information.confirm']}"/>
            <h:panelGrid columns="2">
                <h:outputText value="#{bundle['survey.user.name']}"/>
                <h:outputText value="#{flash.userName}"/>

                <h:outputText value="#{bundle['survey.user.age']}"/>
                <h:outputText value="#{flash.age}"/>

                <h:outputText value="#{bundle['survey.user.sex']}"/>
                <h:outputText value="#{flash.sex}"/>

                <h:outputText value="#{bundle['survey.user.monthyIncome']}"/>
                <h:outputText value="#{flash.monthlyIncome}"/>

                <h:outputText value="#{bundle['survey.user.yearlyTravelAbroad']}"/>
                <h:outputText value="#{flash.travelsAbroad}"/>

                <h:outputText value="#{bundle['survey.user.oftenTravelBy']}"></h:outputText>
                <h:outputText value="#{flash.travelBy}"/>
            </h:panelGrid>

            <h:commandButton value="#{bundle['survey.actions.save']}"
                             action="#{survey.save}"/>
            <h:commandButton value="#{bundle['survey.actions.modify']}"
                             action="input?faces-redirect=true"/>

            <br/><br/>
        </h:form>
    </ui:define>
</ui:composition>

</html>
```

The confirmation page displays all of the entered survey information using the #{flash.attributeName}. From this page, the user can either save the entered information and navigate to the final.xhtml page or modify the information in the input.xhtml page.

However, if you click the "Modify" commandButton in order to modify the entered information, you will find the input.xhtml fields are empty (in other words, the flash information is lost), which is logical because the flash scope life ends once the confirm.xhtml page is rendered. In order to resolve this issue, all you need to do to keep the flash information for the next request is to use the keep keyword as follows: #{flash.keep.attributeName}. Listing 2-26 shows the modified confirm.xhtml page.

Listing 2-26. The Modified confirm.xhtml Page

```
<?xml version='1.0' encoding='UTF-8' ?>
<!DOCTYPE html>
<html xmlns="http://www.w3.org/1999/xhtml"
      xmlns:ui="http://java.sun.com/jsf/facelets"
      xmlns:h="http://java.sun.com/jsf/html">

<ui:composition template="/WEB-INF/templates/simple.xhtml">
    <ui:define name="title">
        #{bundle['survey.confirm.page']}
    </ui:define>
    <ui:define name="content">
        <h:form>
            <h:outputText value="#{bundle['survey.information.confirm']}"/>
            <h:panelGrid columns="2">
                <h:outputText value="#{bundle['survey.user.name']}"/>
                <h:outputText value="#{flash.keep.userName}"/>

                <h:outputText value="#{bundle['survey.user.age']}"/>
                <h:outputText value="#{flash.keep.age}"/>

                <h:outputText value="#{bundle['survey.user.sex']}"/>
                <h:outputText value="#{flash.keep.sex}"/>

                <h:outputText value="#{bundle['survey.user.monthyIncome']}"/>
                <h:outputText value="#{flash.keep.monthlyIncome}"/>

                <h:outputText value="#{bundle['survey.user.yearlyTravelAbroad']}"/>
                <h:outputText value="#{flash.keep.travelsAbroad}"/>

                <h:outputText value="#{bundle['survey.user.oftenTravelBy']}"></h:outputText>
                <h:outputText value="#{flash.keep.travelBy}"/>
            </h:panelGrid>

            <h:commandButton value="#{bundle['survey.actions.save']}"
                             action="#{survey.save}"/>
            <h:commandButton value="#{bundle['survey.actions.modify']}"
                             action="input?faces-redirect=true"/>

            <br/><br/>
        </h:form>
    </ui:define>
</ui:composition>

</html>
```

Using the #{flash.keep.attributeName} will ensure keeping the flash attributes for the next request.

■ **Note** You cannot use the request scope in order to keep the information after the HTTP Redirect, because the HTTP Redirect creates a new request, which means that the current request information will be lost.

Listing 2-27 shows the code of the Survey managed bean, which includes a single method save() that retrieves the flash attributes and then prints them in the console.

Listing 2-27. The Survey Managed Bean

```
package com.jsfprohtml5.survey.model;

import java.io.Serializable;
import javax.faces.bean.ManagedBean;
import javax.faces.context.FacesContext;
import javax.faces.context.Flash;

@ManagedBean
public class Survey implements Serializable {
    public String save() {

        Flash flash = FacesContext.getCurrentInstance().getExternalContext().getFlash();

        // Read the information from the flash
        String userName = (String) flash.get("userName");
        Number age = (Number) flash.get("age");
        String sex = (String) flash.get("sex");
        Number monthlyIncome = (Number) flash.get("monthlyIncome");
        Number travelsAbroad = (Number) flash.get("travelsAbroad");
        String travelBy = (String) flash.get("travelBy");

        System.out.println("Flash information are: \n{\n" +
                "Name: " + userName + ", \n" +
                "Age: " + age + ", \n" +
                "Sex: " + sex + ", \n" +
                "monthlyIncome: " + monthlyIncome + ", \n" +
                "travelsAbroad: " + travelsAbroad + ", \n" +
                "travelBy: " + travelBy + "\n" +
                "}");

        // Save the information in the survey database ...
        // ...

        return "final?faces-redirect=true";
    }

}
```

You can get the Flash object using the getFlash() API of the ExternalContext. After this, you can retrieve the flash attributes using the get() method of the Flash object. Finally, you can do whatever you want with the retrieved flash attributes (such as persisting them in a structured database, or using them for starting a workflow ...).

░ **Note** The complete source code of the Survey application is available on the book web site at www.apress.com/9781430250104 (attached in the Chapter 2 source code zip file).

Navigation

In the JSF framework, there are two types of navigations:

- Implicit navigation.
- Rule-based navigation.

The next sections illustrate both navigation types with examples of when to use each of them.

Implicit Navigation

In the firstApplication, we already have two examples of page navigations. The first one was about the <h:commandButton>, which navigates from the index.xhtml page to the welcome.xhtml page:

```
<h:commandButton value="#{bundle['application.login']}" action="welcome"/>
```

The second example was about the <h:link>, which navigates from the welcome.xhtml page to the index.xhtml page:

```
<h:link value="#{bundle['application.welcomepage.return']}" outcome="index"/>
```

The mentioned two examples represent the first mentioned type of JSF navigations, which is called "*implicit navigation.*" Implicit navigation was introduced in the JSF framework in its 2.0 version. It is called implicit because using it, you do not have to define a navigation rule in the JSF configuration file (faces-config.xml); all that you need to do is to specify the relative path of the target page in the action or the outcome attributes (you do not need to mention the .xhtml extension of the target page because the JSF navigation system will append it for you and will navigate to the target page).

Using implicit navigation, you can also make an HTTP Redirect to the target page instead of forwarding the HTTP Request to the target page (which is the default behavior). This can be performed by using the faces-redirect parameter, as follows:

```
<h:commandButton value="#{bundle['application.login']}" action="welcome?faces-redirect=true"/>
```

Setting the faces-redirect parameter to true tells the JSF navigation system to make HTTP Redirect instead of the HTTP Request forwarding.

The most important advantage of the JSF implicit navigation is its simplicity; however, one of its drawbacks is the inflexibility that happens when you have a complex navigation in the JSF application and you need to rename one of the target navigation pages. In this case, you will have to revisit all the pages that include the target navigation page in order to change the old page name to the new page name. So it is recommended to use the JSF implicit navigation for small applications or for prototyping or for PoCs (Proof of Concepts).

Rule-Based Navigation

In rule-based navigation, the navigation rules are defined in the Faces configuration file (`faces-config.xml`). Rule-based navigation consists of a set of navigation rules. Every navigation rule can have one or more navigation case(s). Listing 2-28 shows a rule-based navigation example.

Listing 2-28. Rule-Based Navigation Example 1

```
<faces-config ...>

    <navigation-rule>
        <from-view-id>/index.xhtml</from-view-id>
        <navigation-case>
            <from-action>#{exampleBean.doAction}</from-action>
            <from-outcome>success</from-outcome>
            <to-view-id>/welcome.xhtml</to-view-id>
        </navigation-case>
        <navigation-case>
            <from-action>#{exampleBean.doAction}</from-action>
            <from-outcome>fail</from-outcome>
            <to-view-id>/invalid.xhtml</to-view-id>
        </navigation-case>
    </navigation-rule>

</faces-config>
```

As shown in the example, the navigation rule can contain the following elements:

- `<from-view-id>` (Optional), which represents the view from which the navigation starts.

- `<navigation-case>`, which can be from 1 to N inside the navigation rule.

The navigation case can contain the following elements:

- `<from-action>` (Optional), which holds an EL expression which refers to an action method that returns a String (outcome).

- `<from-outcome>`, which represents a String literal outcome. In the presence of the `<from-action>` element, the `<from-outcome>` value is compared with the `<from-action>` returned outcome, and if the two values are matched then the navigation proceeds to the `<to-view-id>`. If the `<from-action>` element is not present then the `<from-outcome>` is compared with the action attribute of the action source components, and if the two values are matched then the navigation proceeds to the `<to-view-id>` (will be illustrated in the next navigation example).

- `<to-view-id>`, which represents the target view.

Looking back in the example, starting from the `index.xhtml` page, the first navigation case fires when the #{exampleBean.doAction} action method is executed and returned the "success" outcome; in this case, the page will be forwarded to the `welcome.xhtml` page. The other navigation case fires when the #{exampleBean.doAction} action method is executed and returns the "fail" outcome; in this case, the page will be forwarded to the `invalid.xhtml` page. Listing 2-29 shows the important part of the ExampleBean managed bean.

Listing 2-29. The ExampleBean Managed Bean

```
@ManagedBean
@RequestScoped
public class ExampleBean implements Serializable {
    public String doAction() {
        if (validateInformation()) {
            return "success";
        } else {
            return "fail";
        }
    }

    private boolean validateInformation() {
        /* Some calls can be performed to the business services here ...  */
    }
}
```

As indicated in the preceding, the <from-action> element is an optional one, which means that the JSF navigation can work by specifying the <from-outcome> element only. Listing 2-30 shows two navigation cases without the <from-action> elements.

Listing 2-30. Rule-Based Navigation Example 2

```
<faces-config ...>

    <navigation-rule>
        <from-view-id>/index.xhtml</from-view-id>
        <navigation-case>
            <from-outcome>success</from-outcome>
            <to-view-id>/welcome.xhtml</to-view-id>
        </navigation-case>
        <navigation-case>
            <from-outcome>fail</from-outcome>
            <to-view-id>/invalid.xhtml</to-view-id>
        </navigation-case>
    </navigation-rule>

</faces-config>
```

When the <from-action> element is omitted, the <from-outcome> String literal is compared with the action attribute of the action source components (commandButton or commandLink). This means that if we have any commandButton or commandLink whose action's value (or evaluated expression value) is "success" then the first navigation case will fire, and when it is "fail" then the second navigation case will fire.

Adding to the action source components, the <from-outcome> String literal is also compared with the outcome attribute of the <h:link> and the <h:button> components.

■ **Note** The JSF (implicit and rule-based) navigation can be performed using

1. `<h:commandButton>` and `<h:commandLink>` via the `action` attribute.

2. `<h:button>` and `<h:link>` via the `outcome` attribute.

Both the `action` and the `outcome` attributes can accept a String literal or an EL expression, which refers to a method that returns a String (in the case of the `action` attribute) or an EL expression that evaluates to a String (in the case of the `outcome` attribute).

The `<from-view-id>` element can also be omitted, as shown in Listing 2-31.

Listing 2-31. Rule-Based Navigation Example 3

```
<navigation-rule>
        <navigation-case>
                <from-outcome>success</from-outcome>
                <to-view-id>/welcome.xhtml</to-view-id>
        </navigation-case>
        <navigation-case>
                <from-outcome>fail</from-outcome>
                <to-view-id>/invalid.xhtml</to-view-id>
        </navigation-case>
</navigation-rule>
```

When the `<from-view-id>` element is omitted, this means that the navigation cases will be available for all the pages of the application which means that for Listing 2-31, when the return result of the `action` or `outcome` attributes of the components in any page is matched with the `<from-outcome>` value, the corresponding navigation case will fire.

■ **Note** It is important to know that the navigation cases are executed in the order of their presence inside the `<navigation-rule>`.

One of the nice features of the JSF navigation is the support of the wildcards in the `<from-view-id>` element. This can be useful if you want to apply a navigation rule on a set of pages in the JSF application. Listing 2-32 shows an example.

Listing 2-32. Rule-Based Navigation Example 4

```
<navigation-rule>
                <from-view-id>/common/*</from-view-id>
                <navigation-case>
                        <from-outcome>success</from-outcome>
                        <to-view-id>/welcome.xhtml</to-view-id>
                </navigation-case>
```

```
        <navigation-case>
                <from-outcome>fail</from-outcome>
        <to-view-id>/invalid.xhtml</to-view-id>
        </navigation-case>
</navigation-rule>
```

The previous example means that the navigation cases will be applied only to all the pages under the common folder by using the /common/* pattern.

The default behavior of the rule-based navigation is forwarding the request to the target page; however, it is also possible to change this behavior by using an HTTP Redirect instead. Listing 2-33 shows how to make the navigations using the HTTP Redirect.

Listing 2-33. Rule-Based Navigation Example 5

```
<navigation-rule>
        <navigation-case>
                <from-outcome>success</from-outcome>
                <to-view-id>/welcome.xhtml</to-view-id>
                <redirect/>
        </navigation-case>
        <navigation-case>
                <from-outcome>fail</from-outcome>
                <to-view-id>/invalid.xhtml</to-view-id>
                <redirect/>
        </navigation-case>
</navigation-rule>
```

As shown in the previous listing, it is very simple to change a navigation case behavior from the HTTP Request forward to the HTTP Redirect. Using the <redirect/> element inside the <navigation-case>, the HTTP Redirect will be applied on this navigation case when it is matched.

Advanced Navigation

The last feature that we want to cover in the JSF navigation is the conditional navigation feature, which is useful in handling complex navigation cases. In order to understand this feature, let's see a detailed example. In this example, the user enters an average number of (his/her) sleeping hours daily in order to know if (his/her) sleeping hours are:

- Lower than the average (<7 hours).

- Normal (from 7 to 9 hours).

- Above the average (> 9 hours).

Figure 2-4 shows the example flow. The flow consists of four pages:

- input.xhtml represents the starting input page. In this page, the user inputs (his/her) number of sleeping hours and then clicks the "Check my sleeping hours" button to proceed to the next page.

- normal.xhtml represents the page that will be displayed if the user enters a number from 7 to 9.

- above.xhtml represents the page that will be displayed if the user enters a number more than 9.

- below.xhtml represents the page that will be displayed if the user enters a number less than 7.

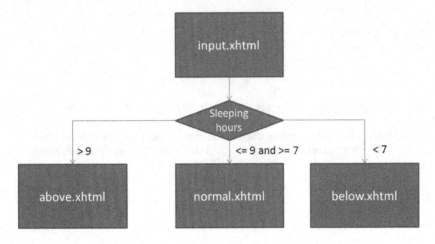

Figure 2-4. *The example flow*

Listing 2-34 shows the code of the starting input page (input.xhtml).

Listing 2-34. The input.xhtml Page

```
<?xml version='1.0' encoding='UTF-8' ?>
<!DOCTYPE html>
<html xmlns="http://www.w3.org/1999/xhtml"
      xmlns:h="http://java.sun.com/jsf/html"
      xmlns:f="http://java.sun.com/jsf/core">

<h:head>
  <title>Sleeping hours checker</title>
</h:head>

<h:body>
    <h:form>
        <h1>Sleeping hours checker</h1>
        <h:outputText value="Enter your sleeping hours: "/>
        <h:inputText id="sleepingHours"
                     value="#{sleeping.hours}"
                     required="true">
            <f:convertNumber integerOnly="true" maxIntegerDigits="2" />
        </h:inputText>
        <br/>
        <h:commandButton action="proceed" value="Check my sleeping hours"/>
    </h:form>
</h:body>
</html>
```

The form contains an input text, sleepingHours, which is required and accepts only integer numbers with two digits by using the <f:convertNumber integerOnly="true" maxIntegerDigits="2" /> converter.

■ **Note**   As known from Chapter 1, JSF conversion is about converting the HTTP request parameters to the corresponding Java types in order to eliminate the overhead required from the developer to implement this functionality for every web application. In this example, the `<f:convertNumber/>` converter registers a number converter to its parent input text component (`sleepingHours`), and by setting the `integerOnly` attribute to `true`, only the integer part of the input text value will be formatted and parsed. Setting the `maxIntegerDigits` to 2 means that the maximum number of the digits of the integer to be parsed and formatted will be 2 (the conversion and validation will be covered in detail in Chapter 3).

When the "`Check my sleeping hours`" commandButton is clicked, it produces the "proceed" outcome, and based on the user input, we want to display the proper result page. Thanks to the JSF conditional navigation, this can be done from the Faces configuration file, as shown in Listing 2-35.

Listing 2-35. The Conditional Navigation in the faces-config.xml File

```
<faces-config ...>

    <navigation-rule>
        <from-view-id>/input.xhtml</from-view-id>
        <navigation-case>
            <if>#{sleeping.hours le 9 and sleeping.hours ge 7}</if>
            <from-outcome>proceed</from-outcome>
            <to-view-id>/normal.xhtml</to-view-id>
        </navigation-case>
        <navigation-case>
            <if>#{sleeping.hours lt 7}</if>
            <from-outcome>proceed</from-outcome>
            <to-view-id>/below.xhtml</to-view-id>
        </navigation-case>
        <navigation-case>
            <if>#{sleeping.hours gt 9}</if>
            <from-outcome>proceed</from-outcome>
            <to-view-id>/above.xhtml</to-view-id>
        </navigation-case>
    </navigation-rule>

</faces-config>
```

The `<if>` element is a new one that has been introduced since JSF 2.0 (the conditional navigation feature was originally taken from the JBoss Seam and included as part of the JSF 2.0). In order to match a specific navigation case containing an `<if>` element, it is required that the content of the `<if>` element be evaluated to `true`. As you see in the previous listing, the `<if>` element content can be a complete JSF EL Expression; in the first navigation case, the `<if>` element checks that the #{`sleeping.hours`} value is less than 9 and greater than 7. If the first navigation case is matched, then the target navigation page will be the `normal.xhtml`. The second `<if>` element in the second navigation case checks that the #{`sleeping.hours`} value is less than 7. If the second navigation case is matched then the target navigation page will be the `below.xhtml`. Finally, the third `<if>` element in the third navigation case checks that the #{`sleeping.hours`} value is greater than 9. If the third navigation case is matched, then the navigation target page will be the `above.xhtml`.

■ **Tip**   It is important to know that the `<to-view-id>` can take a JSF EL expression that would be evaluated by the JSF navigation handler in order to obtain the view identifier.

Behind the scenes, the JSF navigation is handled by the NavigationHandler class. If a navigation case is matched by the NavigationHandler class, it will change the current view by making a call to the FacesContext. setViewRoot(UIViewRoot) API with the new view. It is useful to know how to work with the NavigationHandler class, because you may have to work with it directly from many places in your JSF application (such as phase listeners and exception handlers [there is an example for this one in the "Exception Handling" section]). Listing 2-36 shows an example of using the NavigationHandler.

Listing 2-36. An Example of Using the NavigationHandler Class

```
FacesContext context = FacesContext.getCurrentInstance();

NavigationHandler navigationHandler = context.getApplication().getNavigationHandler();
navigationHandler.handleNavigation(context, "#{myBean.handleFlow1}", "flow1");
```

The NavigationHandler class has a handleNavigation method with the following parameters:

1.   context: Represents the current JSF FacesContext.

2.   fromAction: A String that represents an action method expression ("#{myBean. handleFlow1}") that produced the specified outcome. It can be null.

3.   outcome: A String that represents the outcome ("flow1"). It can be null.

■ **Note**   When the outcome of a specific action is null, the NavigationHandler does nothing, which means that the current view will be redisplayed.

Exception Handling

Exception handling is one of the most important concerns that have to be taken care of in the Java EE web application. Exception handling has many benefits: it can display friendly messages for the application end users when an application error raises, which increases the trust of using the application from the end-user point of view; adding to this, exception handling allows application developers to easily troubleshoot and debug application defects. Since JSF 2.0, an exception handling mechanism is supported by the framework in order to have a centralized place for handling exceptions in the JSF applications.

Let's create a custom JSF exception handler to the firstApplication in order to understand how to handle exceptions in the JSF applications. In order to create a custom exception handler for the JSF application, we need to do three things:

- Creating a custom exception handler class which handles the application exceptions. This handler class should extend an exception handling wrapper class (such as the ExceptionHandlerWrapper class).

- Creating a custom exception handler factory class which is responsible for creating the instances of the exception handler class. The custom exception handler class should extend the JSF ExceptionHandlerFactory class.

Finally, registering the custom exception handler factory class in the faces-config.xml file, which is added to the firstApplication example. Listing 2-37 shows the custom exception handler class which extends the ExceptionHandlerWrapper class which is added to the firstApplication example.

Listing 2-37. The CustomExceptionHandler Class

```
package com.jsfprohtml5.firstapplication.exceptions;

import java.util.Iterator;
import javax.faces.FacesException;
import javax.faces.application.NavigationHandler;
import javax.faces.context.ExceptionHandler;
import javax.faces.context.ExceptionHandlerWrapper;
import javax.faces.context.FacesContext;
import javax.faces.event.ExceptionQueuedEvent;
import javax.faces.event.ExceptionQueuedEventContext;

public class CustomExceptionHandler extends ExceptionHandlerWrapper {
  private ExceptionHandler wrapped;

  public CustomExceptionHandler(ExceptionHandler wrapped) {
    this.wrapped = wrapped;
  }

  @Override
  public ExceptionHandler getWrapped() {
    return wrapped;
  }

  @Override
  public void handle() throws FacesException {
    Iterator i = getUnhandledExceptionQueuedEvents().iterator();

    while (i.hasNext()) {
      ExceptionQueuedEvent event = (ExceptionQueuedEvent) i.next();
      ExceptionQueuedEventContext context = (ExceptionQueuedEventContext) event.getSource();

      Throwable t = context.getException();

      FacesContext fc = FacesContext.getCurrentInstance();

      try {
      /* Here you can use the Throwable object in order to verify the exceptions you want to handle
      in the application */
        NavigationHandler navigationHandler = fc.getApplication().getNavigationHandler();

        navigationHandler.handleNavigation(fc, null, "error?faces-redirect=true");
```

```
        fc.renderResponse();
      } finally {
        i.remove();
      }
    }

    // Call the parent exception handler's handle() method
    getWrapped().handle();
  }

}
```

The core method of the CustomExceptionHandler class is the handle() method, which is responsible for handling the exceptions in the JSF application. It is important to note that the getUnhandledExceptionQueuedEvents() method can be used for getting all of the unhandled exceptions in the JSF application. Every item in the returned Iterable object represents an ExceptionQueuedEvent object. From the ExceptionQueuedEvent object, you can get the ExceptionQueuedEventContext object, from which you can retrieve the Throwable object. Using the Throwable object, you can verify the exceptions you want to handle in the applications. Finally, the NavigationHandler is used in order to navigate to the application error page (error.xhtml), and the ExceptionQueuedEvent is removed from the Iterable object. Listing 2-38 shows the error.xhtml page.

Listing 2-38. The Application Error Page

```
<?xml version='1.0' encoding='UTF-8' ?>
<!DOCTYPE html>
<html xmlns="http://www.w3.org/1999/xhtml"
      xmlns:h="http://java.sun.com/jsf/html">

<h:head>
  <title>Error</title>
  <link href="#{request.contextPath}/css/simple.css" rel="stylesheet" type="text/css"/>
</h:head>

<h:body>
    <h2 class="errorMessage">
        An error occurs. return to <a href="index.xhtml">login</a> page.
    </h2>
</h:body>
</html>
```

Secondly, we need to create the custom exception handler factory class that is responsible for creating the instances of the CustomExceptionHandler class. Listing 2-39 shows the CustomExceptionHandlerFactory class.

Listing 2-39. The CustomExceptionHandlerFactory Class

```
package com.jsfprohtml5.firstapplication.exceptions;

import javax.faces.context.ExceptionHandler;
import javax.faces.context.ExceptionHandlerFactory;

public class CustomExceptionHandlerFactory extends ExceptionHandlerFactory {

  private ExceptionHandlerFactory parent;
```

```
  public CustomExceptionHandlerFactory(ExceptionHandlerFactory parent) {
    this.parent = parent;
  }

  @Override
  public ExceptionHandler getExceptionHandler() {
    ExceptionHandler result = new CustomExceptionHandler(parent.getExceptionHandler());
    return result;
  }
}
```

Finally, we need to register the custom exception handler factory class in the faces-config.xml, as shown in Listing 2-40.

Listing 2-40. Registering the Custom Exception Handler Factory Class in the JSF Configuration File

```
<?xml version='1.0' encoding='UTF-8'?>

<faces-config version="2.1"
    xmlns="http://java.sun.com/xml/ns/javaee"
    xmlns:xsi="http://www.w3.org/2001/XMLSchema-instance"
    xsi:schemaLocation="http://java.sun.com/xml/ns/javaee http://java.sun.com/xml/ns/javaee/
web-facesconfig_2_1.xsd">

    <factory>
      <exception-handler-factory>
        com.jsfprohtml5.firstapplication.exceptions.MyExceptionHandlerFactory
      </exception-handler-factory>
    </factory>

        <!-- ... -->

</faces-config>
```

After setting up this exception handling mechanism in the firstApplication, if an exception is thrown from the firstApplication for whatever reason, the error.xhtml page will be displayed as Figure 2-5.

An error occurs. return to <u>login</u> page.

Figure 2-5. The error handling page (error.xhtml)

■ **Note**   The complete source code of the updated firstApplication example is available on the book web site at www.apress.com/9781430250104 (attached in the Chapter 2 source code zip file).

Summary

In this chapter, you learned in detail the different ways for declaring, initializing, and managing the dependencies of the JSF managed beans. You also learned in detail how to make use of the EL in your JSF applications. You now also know in detail how to efficiently use the JSF navigation system and finally how to utilize the JSF exception handling mechanism in order to empower your JSF application error handling.

CHAPTER 3

■ ■ ■

JSF Under the Hood—Part 2

JSF conversion and validation is one of the most important topics in the JSF framework which is covered in detail in this chapter. This chapter explains how conversion and validation works in the JSF request processing life cycle. You will learn how to use and customize the standard JSF converters and validators in your JSF application(s) and how to create your own custom converters and validators when the standard converters and validators do not fully fit the application's needs. Finally, you will understand how to utilize Java Bean Validation (JSR 303) APIs in order to empower and standardize your JSF application validation.

Conversion and Validation in the JSF LifeCycle

As we know from Chapter 1, conversion is about converting the HTTP request parameters to the corresponding Java types in order to eliminate the overhead required from the developer to implement this functionality for every web application, while validation is about validating the user input for certain condition(s). The conversion and the validation process in the JSF life cycle can occur in three phases, as shown in Figure 3-1.

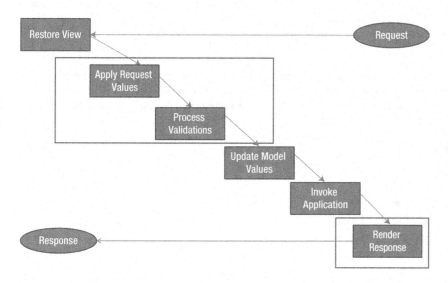

Figure 3-1. The possible JSF phases in which conversion and validation can happen

The figure illustrates how JSF conversions and validations can occur in

1. *Process Validations phase,* for all the components which do not have immediate attribute set to true.

2. *Apply Request Values phase,* for the components whose immediate="true".

3. *Render Response phase.*

In both the Process Validations phase and the Apply Request Values phase, the conversion from the HTTP Request String to the Java type occurs (using the getAsObject API in the JSF Converter interface), and then the JSF validation is performed. While in the Render Response phase, the conversion from the Java type to String occurs (using the getAsString API in the JSF Converter interface) in order to be ready for rendering.

■ **Note**　Notice that the immediate attribute can be applied to both the UICommand components (such as CommandButton and CommandLink) and to the EditableValueHolder components (such as inputText).

Conversion can be applied to all the ValueHolder components (this includes UIOutput and UIInput–which extends UIOutput–components), while the validation can be applied only on the EditableValueHolder components (this includes UIInput components). In the next sections, the JSF conversion and the validation will be illustrated in detail.

Conversion

In order to understand the JSF conversion, we need to know three main topics: the Converter interface APIs, the standard JSF converters, and finally how to build a custom converter in JSF. The next subsections illustrate these topics in detail.

Converter Interface

All of the JSF converters must implement the javax.faces.convert.Converter interface. The Converter interface describes a Java class that can perform Object-to-String and String-to-Object conversions between the model data objects and a String representation of these model objects that is suitable for rendering. Listing 3-1 shows the JSF Converter interface.

Listing 3-1. JSF Converter Interface

```
package javax.faces.convert;

import javax.faces.component.UIComponent;
import javax.faces.context.FacesContext;

public interface Converter {

    public Object getAsObject(FacesContext context, UIComponent component, String value);

    public String getAsString(FacesContext context, UIComponent component, Object value);
}
```

As shown in the `Converter` interface, it contains two APIs:

The first API is `getAsObject`, which performs the String-to-Object conversion; this API can be called in the Process Validations phase (or the Apply Request Values phase). It has three parameters:

1. `context`, which represents the JSF `FacesContext` instance of this request.

2. `component`, which represents the component whose value will be converted. This component instance can be used in order to retrieve the component attributes if the converter needs to use them.

3. `value`, which represents the `String` value to be converted to `Object`.

The second API is `getAsString`, which performs the Object-to-String conversion; this API is called in the Render Response phase. It takes three parameters:

1. `context`, which represents the JSF `FacesContext` instance of this request.

2. `component`, which represents the component whose value will be converted. This component instance can be used in order to retrieve the component attributes if the converter needs to use them.

3. `value`, which represents the `Object` value to be converted to `String`.

Every component can have one or more converter(s). If conversion could not be performed due to an error, the converter must throw `ConverterException`; in this case, the component that owns the converter will be marked as invalid, and `ConverterException` message will be received and added to `FacesContext` messages in order to be displayed by the `<h:message>` and `<h:messages>` components. Listing 3-2 shows an example illustrating how JSF conversion works for multiple `ValueHolder` components with attached converters.

Listing 3-2. Conversion Example for Multiple ValueHolder Components

```
<h:form>
            <h1>Test form</h1>
            <h:outputText value="Enter First Number: "/>
            <h:inputText id="firstNumber"
                            value="#{testBean.firstNumber}">
                    <f:convertNumber/>
            </h:inputText>
            <h:message for="firstNumber"/>
            <br/>
            <h:outputText value="Enter Second Number: "/>
            <h:inputText id="secondNumber"
                            value="#{testBean.secondNumber}">
                    <f:convertNumber/>
            </h:inputText>
            <h:message for="secondNumber"/>
            <br/>
            <h:commandButton value="submit"/>
</h:form>
```

In this example, we have a form that contains two `inputText` components. Every `inputText` component has an attached `<f:convertNumber>` converter. `<f:convertNumber/>` converter converts the user's entered value in the input text to a Java Number object, which is then binded with the attribute (`firstNumber` and `secondNumber`) of `TestBean` managed bean. If the user enters non-numeric values in both `inputText` components and then clicks the `"submit"` button, the user will see two conversion error messages in both the `<h:message/>` components which are attached to every input text. This is because JSF conversion (and also JSF validation) must be applied for every component that has converters (and/or validators), which means that the JSF validation process (which includes both conversion and validation) cannot be aborted midway because the framework has to collect all of the error messages in one shot.

Standard JSF Converters

Now, let's dive into the details of the JSF standard converters. Table 3-1 shows JSF standard converters.

Table 3-1. *JSF Standard Converters*

Converter ID	Description
javax.faces.Boolean	Implicit converter that can be applied to Boolean and boolean Java types.
javax.faces.Byte	Implicit converter that can be applied to Byte and byte Java types.
javax.faces.Character	Implicit converter that can be applied to Character and char Java types.
javax.faces.Short	Implicit converter that can be applied to Short and short Java types.
javax.faces.Integer	Implicit converter that can be applied to Integer and int Java types.
javax.faces.Long	Implicit converter that can be applied to Long and long Java types.
javax.faces.Float	Implicit converter that can be applied to Float and float Java types.
javax.faces.Double	Implicit converter that can be applied to Double and double Java types.
javax.faces.BigDecimal	Implicit converter that can be applied to BigDecimal Java type.
javax.faces.BigInteger	Implicit converter that can be applied to BigInteger Java type.
javax.faces.Number	Explicit converter that can be used to convert user input to Number Java type.
javax.faces.DateTime	Explicit converter that can be used to convert user input to java.util.Date Java type.

As shown in the table, the JSF converters have two types:

- Implicit converters.
- Explicit converters.

Implicit converters are applied automatically to the listed value types. For example, assume we have the following Calculator managed bean, as shown in Listing 3-3.

Listing 3-3. The Calculator Managed Bean

```
import java.io.Serializable;
import javax.faces.bean.ManagedBean;
import javax.faces.bean.RequestScoped;

@ManagedBean
@RequestScoped
public class Calculator implements Serializable {
    private Double firstNumber;
    private Double secondNumber;
    private Double result;
```

```
        public Double getFirstNumber() {
            return firstNumber;
        }

        public void setFirstNumber(Double firstNumber) {
            this.firstNumber = firstNumber;
        }

        public Double getSecondNumber() {
            return secondNumber;
        }

        public void setSecondNumber(Double secondNumber) {
            this.secondNumber = secondNumber;
        }

        public Double getResult() {
            return result;
        }

        public void setResult(Double result) {
            this.result = result;
        }

        public String calculateSum() {
            result = firstNumber + secondNumber;

            return null;
        }
    }
}
```

Listing 3-4 shows the XHTML file that uses the Calculator managed bean.

Listing 3-4. The Calculator XHTML Associated Page

```
<?xml version='1.0' encoding='UTF-8' ?>
<!DOCTYPE html>
<html xmlns="http://www.w3.org/1999/xhtml"
      xmlns:h="http://java.sun.com/jsf/html">

<h:head>
  <title>Calculator</title>
</h:head>

<h:body>
    <h:form>
        <h:panelGrid columns="2">
            <h:outputText value="First number:"/>
            <h:inputText id="fNumber"
                        value="#{calculator.firstNumber}"
                        required="true">
            </h:inputText>
```

```
        <h:outputText value="Second number:"/>
        <h:inputText id="sNumber"
                        value="#{calculator.secondNumber}"
                        required="true">
        </h:inputText>
    </h:panelGrid>

    <h:commandButton action="#{calculator.calculateSum}" value="Sum"/><br/>
    <h:outputText value="Result: #{calculator.result}"/>

    </h:form>
</h:body>
</html>
```

Both the #{calculator.firstNumber} and #{calculator.secondNumber} expressions are binded automatically with the firstNumber and the secondNumber attributes of the Calculator managed bean after being converted to Double using the implicit javax.faces.Double converter. Like the Double type, implicit converters are applied also on the Boolean, Byte, Character, Short, Integer, Long, Float, BigDecimal, and BigInteger Java types.

Explicit converters have to be attached to the components explicitly. Currently, the JSF core tag library provides the following tags that represent JSF explicit converters:

- <f:convertDateTime>

- <f:convertNumber>

- <f:converter>

<f:convertDateTime> converter converts the input String to java.util.Date object with any specified format. Listing 3-5 shows a sample managed bean that includes a java.util.Date attribute.

Listing 3-5. Sample Managed Bean that Includes Date Attribute

```
import java.io.Serializable;
import java.util.Date;
import javax.faces.bean.ManagedBean;
import javax.faces.bean.RequestScoped;

@ManagedBean
@RequestScoped
public class TestBean implements Serializable {
    // ...
    private Date birthDate;

    public Date getBirthDate() {
        return birthDate;
    }

    public void setBirthDate(Date birthDate) {
        this.birthDate = birthDate;
    }
    // ...
}
```

In order to convert the input String to `birthDate` attribute with the "dd-MM-yyyy" format, you can attach the `<f:convertDateTime>` to EditableValueHolder component as follows:

```
<h:outputText value="Date of birth:"/>
<h:inputText id="birthDate"
                value="#{testBean.birthDate}"
                required="true">
        <f:convertDateTime pattern="dd-MM-yyyy"/>
</h:inputText>
```

If the user enters a value in the `birthDate` field that cannot be converted to a Date object with the "dd-MM-yyyy" format, a conversion error message will be displayed. Listing 3-2 shows an example of `<f:convertNumber>` converter which converts the input String to a Java Number object. In addition, it has many formatting capabilities. Assume that we have the someNumber (of type Double) attribute of TestBean managed bean #{testBean.someNumber}, and we want to format it on the number format ###,###.###; this can be achieved using the pattern attribute of `<f:convertNumber>` as follows:

```
<h:outputText value="#{testBean.someNumber}">
        <f:convertNumber pattern="###,###.###"/>
</h:outputText>
```

Assuming that the #{testBean.someNumber} is evaluated to 123456.124 (for example), it will be displayed as 123,456.124.

■ **Note** You can read more about the Java `NumberFormat` at
http://docs.oracle.com/javase/7/docs/api/java/text/DecimalFormat.html

---

If we want to display only two fraction digits of the #{testBean.someNumber} number, we can use the maxFractionDigits attribute of the `<f:convertNumber>` tag as follows:

```
<h:outputText value="#{testBean.someNumber}">
        <f:convertNumber maxFractionDigits="2"/>
</h:outputText>
```

If the #{testBean.someNumber} is evaluated to 123456.124 for example, it will be displayed as 123,456.12.

Using both the currencyCode and the type (="currency") attributes of the `<f:convertNumber>`, we can format the number in currency format as follows:

```
<h:outputText value="#{testBean.someNumber}">
        <f:convertNumber currencyCode="EGP" type="currency"/>
</h:outputText>
```

If the #{testBean.someNumber} is evaluated to 2000 for example, it will be displayed as EGP2,000.00.

■ **Note** The currency codes are defined in ISO 4217. You can get the full list of currency codes from
http://en.wikipedia.org/wiki/ISO_4217

Using the `type="percent"` attribute of the `<f:convertNumber>`, you can format the number as a percentage.

```
<h:outputText value="#{testBean.someNumber}">
          <f:convertNumber type="percent"/>
</h:outputText>
```

If the `#{testBean.someNumber}` is evaluated to `0.3` for example, it will be displayed as 30%.

■ **Note**   Notice that you can override the different conversion messages by using the `converterMessage` attribute of `EditableValueHolders`. For example: <h:inputText id="someNumber" value="#{bean.someNumber}" converterMessage="Not a number!!!"/>

Will show a conversion error message "Not a number" if the number conversion fails.

Building Custom JSF Converter

In addition to all of the mentioned implicit and explicit converters provided by the JSF framework, JSF allows developers to create their own custom converters. Let's see an example to illustrate this idea. Assume we need to convert the user input `String` to a `Location` object. In order to achieve this requirement, we need to develop a custom converter (`LocationConverter` for example) which converts the input `String` to a `Location` object and then converts the `Location` object to a friendly String that can be displayed to the end user in the *Render Response phase*. Listing 3-6 shows the `Location` class that we need the user input to be converted to.

Listing 3-6. Location Class

```
package com.jsfprohtml5.example.model;

public class Location {
    private String address;
    private String city;
    private String country;

    public Location() {
    }

    public Location(String address, String city, String country) {
        this.address = address;
        this.city = city;
        this.country = country;
    }

    public String getAddress() {
        return address;
    }

    public void setAddress(String address) {
        this.address = address;
    }
```

```
    public String getCity() {
        return city;
    }

    public void setCity(String city) {
        this.city = city;
    }

    public String getCountry() {
        return country;
    }

    public void setCountry(String country) {
        this.country = country;
    }
}
```

Location class is a simple Java bean that contains three attributes (address, city, country). In order to implement our LocationConverter custom converter, we need to extend the JSF Converter interface and implement both the getAsObject and getAsString methods. Listing 3-7 shows the LocationConverter implementation.

Listing 3-7. LocationConverter Class

```
package com.jsfprohtml5.example.converters;

import com.jsfprohtml5.example.model.Location;
import javax.faces.application.FacesMessage;
import javax.faces.component.UIComponent;
import javax.faces.context.FacesContext;
import javax.faces.convert.Converter;
import javax.faces.convert.ConverterException;
import javax.faces.convert.FacesConverter;

@FacesConverter("com.jsfprohtml5.LocationConverter")
public class LocationConverter implements Converter {

    @Override
    public Object getAsObject(FacesContext context, UIComponent component, String value) {

        if (null == value || 0 == value.length()) {
            return null;
        }

        String locationParts[] = value.split(",");

        if (locationParts.length != 3
            || locationParts[0].length() == 0
              || locationParts[1].length() == 0
                || locationParts[2].length() == 0) {
```

```
        FacesMessage message = new FacesMessage("Invalid Location format (address, city, country).",
                                    "Use the following format {address, city, country)}.");

            message.setSeverity(FacesMessage.SEVERITY_ERROR);

        throw new ConverterException(message);
    }

    String address = locationParts[0];
    String city = locationParts[1];
    String country = locationParts[2];

    Location location = new Location(address, city, country);

    return location;
}

@Override
public String getAsString(FacesContext context, UIComponent component, Object value) {

    Location location = (Location) value;

    return location.getAddress() + ", " +
            location.getCity() + ", " +
            location.getCountry();
}

}
```

In the getAsObject() method which is called in the *Process Validations phase* (or in *Apply Request Values phase*), the conversion from the input String is converted to the Location object whose class is mentioned in Listing 3-6, and as shown in the bolded lines, if the input String does not meet the location format specification, a ConverterException with a faces error message is thrown. The location format is specified to be on the following form:

Address, City, Country

In getAsString() method which is called in the *Render Response phase*, the conversion from the Location object to the output rendering String is performed. It is important to notice the @FacesConverter annotation, which is used for registering the converter in the JSF application. The @FacesConverter annotation has two main attributes: value() attribute, which is taken to be the converter ID, and the forClass() attribute, which is taken to be the converter for class. For this example, we used only the value() attribute and declared our converter ID to be "com.jsfprohtml5.LocationConverter".

Instead of using @FacesConverter annotation, you can declare the converter in the JSF faces-config.xml file as follows:

```
<faces-config ...>
    <converter>
        <converter-id>com.jsfprohtml5.LocationConverter</converter-id>
        <converter-class>com.jsfprohtml5.example.converters.LocationConverter</converter-class>
    </converter>
</faces-config>
```

Now, let's see how to use LocationConverter in the JSF application. Listing 3-8 shows TestBean managed bean which includes a Location attribute (location).

Listing 3-8. TestBean Managed Bean Class

```
package com.jsfprohtml5.example.model;

import java.io.Serializable;
import java.util.Date;
import javax.faces.bean.ManagedBean;
import javax.faces.bean.RequestScoped;

@ManagedBean
@RequestScoped
public class TestBean implements Serializable {
    // ...
    private Location location;
    // ...
    public Location getLocation() {
        return location;
    }
    public void setLocation(Location location) {
        this.location = location;
    }
    // ...
    public String proceed() {
        return null;
    }
}
```

Listing 3-9 shows the LocationConverter converter XHTML test page.

Listing 3-9. LocationConverter XHTML Test Page

```
<?xml version='1.0' encoding='UTF-8' ?>
<!DOCTYPE html>
<html xmlns="http://www.w3.org/1999/xhtml"
      xmlns:h="http://java.sun.com/jsf/html"
      xmlns:f="http://java.sun.com/jsf/core">

<h:head>
  <title>Location Converter Test</title>
</h:head>

<h:body>
    <h:form>
        <h1>Converter Test</h1>
        <h:outputText value="Enter location: " />
        <h:inputText id="location"
                     value="#{testBean.location}"
                     required="true">
            <f:converter converterId="com.jsfprohtml5.LocationConverter" />
        </h:inputText>
```

```
        <br/>
        <h:commandButton action="#{testBean.proceed}" value="Proceed"/><br/>
        <h:outputText value="#{testBean.location}">
            <f:converter converterId="com.jsfprohtml5.LocationConverter" />
        </h:outputText>
<h:messages style="color: red"/>
    </h:form>
</h:body>
</html>
```

As shown in the bolded lines, in the converter test page, there is an input text and an output text which uses `LocationConverter` using `<f:converter>` tag. `<f:converter>` tag is a core tag that is mainly designed in order to avoid creating a TLD (Tag Library Descriptor) for every custom converter. Passing the ID of the custom converter, which is defined in the `@FacesConverter` annotation, to the `converterId` attribute of the `<f:converter>` tag will attach the custom converter to the parent `ValueHolder` component.

Figure 3-2 shows a conversion error that will be displayed when the user enters invalid location information that does not cope with the location (`Address, City, Country`) format.

Converter Test

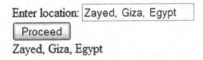

Enter location: Place

Proceed

- Invalid Location format (address, city, country).

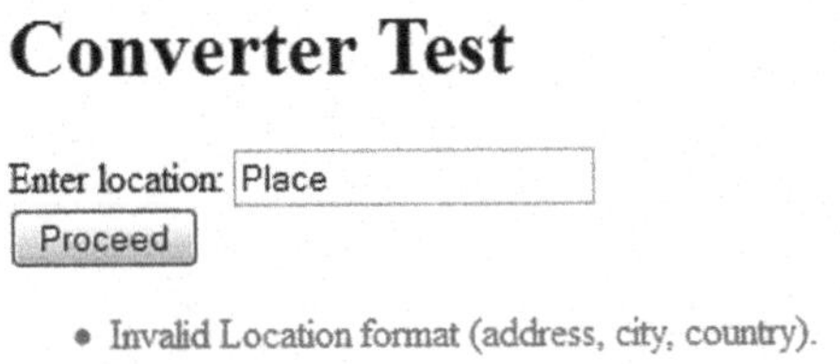

Figure 3-2. *LocationConverter error message*

Figure 3-3 shows the behavior of `LocationConverter` when the user inputs valid location information that copes with the location (`Address, City, Country`) format.

Converter Test

Enter location: Zayed, Giza, Egypt

Proceed

Zayed, Giza, Egypt

Figure 3-3. *LocationConverter behavior for input and output text*

Validation

In order to understand the JSF validation, we need to know four main topics: the `Validator` interface APIs, the standard JSF Validators, how to build a custom validator in JSF, and finally how to work with Java Bean Validation (JSR 303) APIs. The next subsections illustrate these topics in detail.

Validator Interface

The javax.faces.validator.Validator interface is the core interface for the JSF validators. The JSF Validator interface describes a Java class that can perform validation (checks on the correctness) on EditableValueHolder components. A single EditableValueHolder can have zero or more validators in the view. Listing 3-10 shows the JSF Validator interface.

Listing 3-10. JSF Validator Interface

```
package javax.faces.validator;

import java.util.EventListener;
import javax.faces.component.UIComponent;
import javax.faces.context.FacesContext;

public interface Validator extends EventListener {

    //...
    public void validate(FacesContext context, UIComponent component, Object value) throws
ValidatorException;
}
```

As shown in the Validator interface, it contains a single API. The validate API performs the required validation on the parent EditableValueHolder component's value; this API can be called in the *Process Validations phase* (or in *Apply Request Values phase* if immediate attribute of the EditableValueHolder is set to true). validate() API has three parameters:

1. context, which represents the JSF FacesContext instance of this request.

2. component, which represents the component whose value will be validated. This component instance can be used in order to retrieve the component attributes if the validator needs to use them.

3. value, which represents the String value to be validated.

For every component that has a validator (or more). If the validation fails, the validator must throw ValidatorException; in this case, the component that owns the validator will be marked as invalid, and a ValidatorException message will be received and added to the FacesContext messages in order to be displayed by the <h:message> component associated with the EditableValueHolder component and by the <h:messages> component.

Listing 3-11 shows an example to illustrate how validation works for multiple EditableValueHolder components with attached validators. Notice that in this example, number1 and number2 are attributes in TestBean managed bean and are of type Long.

Listing 3-11. Validation Example for Multiple EditableValueHolder Components

```
<h:form>
            <h:outputText value="Enter Number1: "/>
            <h:inputText id="number1"
                     value="#{testBean.number1}">
                            <f:validateRequired/>
                            <f:validateLongRange minimum="0" maximum="999"/>
            </h:inputText>
            <h:message for="number1"/>
```

```
                   <br/>
                   <h:outputText value="Enter Number2: "/>
                   <h:inputText id="number2"
                                required="true"
                                value="#{testBean.number2}">
                                          <f:validateLongRange minimum="0" maximum="999"/>
                   </h:inputText>
                   <h:message for="number2"/>
                   <br/>
                   <h:commandButton value="submit"/>
</h:form>
```

We have a form that contains two inputText components (number1 and number2). Every inputText component has two attached validators. Every input text has the following validators:

1. <f:validateRequired>, which is used to validate that the EditableValueHolder component will not contain empty input (using the required="true" attribute has the same effect).

2. <f:validateLongRange>, which is used to validate that the value of the long integer field is within a specified range (minimum and maximum).

<f:validateLongRange> is used in the example to verify that both input texts have a minimum value equal to 0 and a maximum value equal to 999. If the user enters empty values or out-of-range values in both inputText components and then clicks the "submit" command button, the user will see two validation error messages in both <h:message/> components that are associated with every inputText component. This explains what we said previously that the validation in JSF (like conversion) must be applied to every component that has one or more validator(s).

Standard JSF Validators

Now, let's dive into the details of the JSF standard validators. Table 3-2 shows the JSF standard validators.

Table 3-2. *JSF Standard Validators*

Validator Tag	Description
<f:validateRequired>	Used to validate that the EditableValueHolder (such as input text) value is required. Setting the required="true" attribute has the same effect.
<f:validateLongRange>	Used to validate that the EditableValueHolder value which is long integer is within a specified range.
<f:validateDoubleRange>	Used to validate that the EditableValueHolder value which is double is within a specified range.
<f:validateLength>	Used to validate that the EditableValueHolder value is within the specified length range.
<f:validateRegex>	Used to validate that the EditableValueHolder value is complaint with a specified Java regular expression.
<f:validateBean>	Used to assign the EditableValueHolder local value validation to the Java Bean Validation (JSR 303) APIs.

We already have seen examples of `<f:validateRequired>` and `<f:validateLongRange>` validators in Listing 3-11. `<f:validateDoubleRange>` is the same as the `<f:validateLongRange>`; however, it works with `Double` instead of `Long`. `<f:validateLength>` validator is used to validate that the `EditableValueHolder` value is within the specified length range. For example:

```
<h:inputText id="address"
                  required="true"
              value="#{person.address}">
                      <f:validateLength minimum="20" maximum="120"/>
</h:inputText>
```

As shown in this example, the `address` attribute of `person` managed bean is validated to have a length of minimum 20 and maximum 120 characters using the `<f:validateLength>` validator in the `"address"` input text.

`<f:validateRegex>` validator is used to validate that the `EditableValueHolder` value is complaint with a specified Java regular expression.

```
<h:inputText id="email"
        required="true"
        value="#{person.email}">
                    <f:validateRegex pattern="(.+@.+\.[a-zA-Z]+)?"/>
</h:inputText>
```

As shown in this example, the `email` attribute of `person` managed bean is validated to have a valid e-mail using the `"(.+@.+\.[a-zA-Z]+)?"` regular expression in the `pattern` field of the `<f:validateRegex>` validator for the `"email"` input text.

`<f:validateBean>` validator is used to assign the `EditableValueHolder` local value validation to the Java Bean Validation APIs (JSR 303). We will go into the details of this validator in the "JSR 303 Bean Validation with JSF" section.

You can override validation messages by using either the `requiredMessage` attribute of the `EditableValueHolders` for the required field validation error message or the `validatorMessage` attribute for general validation error messages on the `EditableValueHolder`. For example:

```
<h:inputText id="someNumber"
                  value="#{bean.someNumber}"
                  required="true"
              requiredMessage="You have to enter a number"
              validatorMessage="Number has to be minimum 10 and maximum 100">
            <f:validateLongRange minimum="10" maximum="100"/>
</h:inputText>
```

This will show a required field validation error message, "You have to enter a number," if the user does not enter a value in the input text, and will show a validation message, "Number has to be minimum 10 and maximum 100", if the user enters a number that is out of the range (less than 10 or greater than 100).

Building Custom JSF Validator

Adding to all of the mentioned built-in validators provided by the JSF framework, JSF allows the developers to create their own custom validators. Let's see an example to illustrate this. Assume we want to have an `EmailValidator` custom validator which validates that the user input is complaint with an e-mail format.

In order to implement our `EmailValidator` custom validator, we need to extend the `Validator` interface and implement `validate` method. Listing 3-12 shows the `EmailValidator` implementation.

Listing 3-12. EmailValidator Class

```java
package com.jsfprohtml5.example.validators;

import java.util.regex.Matcher;
import java.util.regex.Pattern;
import javax.faces.application.FacesMessage;
import javax.faces.component.UIComponent;
import javax.faces.context.FacesContext;
import javax.faces.validator.FacesValidator;
import javax.faces.validator.Validator;
import javax.faces.validator.ValidatorException;

@FacesValidator("com.jsfprohtml5.EmailValidator")
public class EmailValidator implements Validator {
    private static final String EMAIL_REGEX = "(.+@.+\\.[a-zA-Z]+)?";

    private Pattern pattern;
    private Matcher matcher;

    public EmailValidator() {
        pattern = Pattern.compile(EMAIL_REGEX);
    }

    @Override
    public void validate(FacesContext context,
                         UIComponent component,
                         Object value)
                         throws ValidatorException {

        matcher = pattern.matcher(value.toString());

        if (! matcher.matches()) {
            FacesMessage message = new FacesMessage("Invalid Email format",
                                         "Use for example: xyz@company.com");

                message.setSeverity(FacesMessage.SEVERITY_ERROR);

            throw new ValidatorException(message);
        }
    }
}
```

In the validate() method which is called in the *Process Validations phase* (or *Apply Request Values phase*), the validation occurs, and as shown in the bolded lines, if the input String does not meet the e-mail format, a ValidatorException with a Faces error message is thrown. It is important to notice the @FacesValidator annotation, which is used for registering the validator. The @FacesValidator annotation has one main attribute, the value() attribute, which is taken to be the ID of the validator. For this example, we use the value() attribute and declared our validator ID to be "com.jsfprohtml5.EmailValidator".

Instead of using the @FacesValidator annotation, you can declare the validator in the JSF faces-config.xml file as follows:

```
<faces-config ...>
    ...
    <validator>
        <validator-id>com.jsfprohtml5.EmailValidator</validator-id>
        <validator-class>com.jsfprohtml5.example.validators.EmailValidator</validator-class>
    </validator>
 ...
</faces-config>
```

Now, let's see how to use the EmailValidator in the JSF application. Listing 3-13 shows an updated version of TestBean managed bean (shown originally in Listing 3-8) which includes an email attribute of type (String).

Listing 3-13. Updated Version of TestBean Managed Bean

```
public class TestBean implements Serializable {
    // ...
    private String email;

    // ...
    public String getEmail() {
        return email;
    }
    public void setEmail(String email) {
        this.email = email;
    }
    // ...
}
```

Listing 3-14 shows the EmailValidator validator XHTML test page.

Listing 3-14. EmailValidator XHTML Test Page

```
<?xml version='1.0' encoding='UTF-8' ?>
<!DOCTYPE html>
<html xmlns="http://www.w3.org/1999/xhtml"
      xmlns:h="http://java.sun.com/jsf/html"
      xmlns:f="http://java.sun.com/jsf/core">
<h:head>
  <title>Email Validator Test</title>
</h:head>
<h:body>
    <h:form>
        <h1>Validator Test</h1>

            <h:outputText value="Enter Email: "/>
            <h:inputText id="email"
                    value="#{testBean.email}" required="true">
            <f:validator validatorId="com.jsfprohtml5.EmailValidator"/>
            </h:inputText>
        <br/>
```

```
        <h:commandButton action="#{testBean.proceed}" value="Proceed"/><br/>
        <h:messages style="color: red"/>
    </h:form>
</h:body>
</html>
```

As shown in the bolded lines, in the test page, there is an input text which uses the EmailValidator using the `<f:validator>` tag. The `<f:validator>` tag is a core tag that is mainly designed in order to avoid creating a TLD for every custom validator. Passing the ID of the custom validator which is defined in the @FacesValidator annotation to the validatorId attribute of the `<f:validator>` tag will attach the custom validator to the parent EditableValueHolder component.

Figure 3-4 shows a validation error that will be displayed when the user enters an invalid e-mail that does not cope with the e-mail format requirements.

Validator Test

Enter Email:  hazems@apache

Proceed

- Invalid Email format

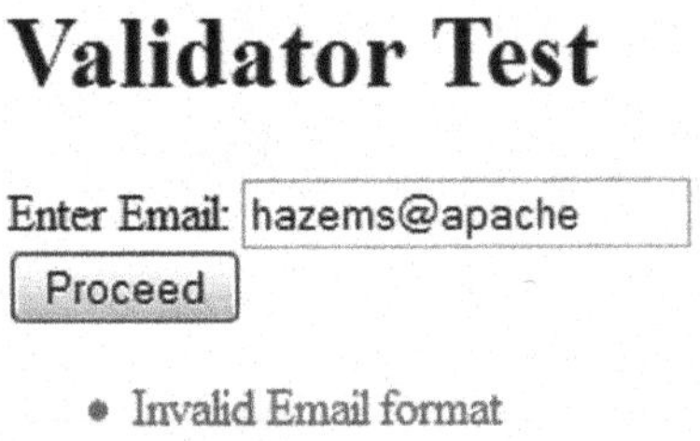

Figure 3-4. *EmailValidator error message*

Figure 3-5 shows the behavior of the EmailValidator when the user enters valid e-mail information that copes with the e-mail format requirements.

Validator Test

Enter Email: hazems@apache.org

Proceed

Figure 3-5. *EmailValidator valid form*

JSR 303 Bean Validation with JSF

JSR 303 Bean Validation was introduced in Java EE 6 in order to empower building validation in Java enterprise applications. JSR 303 comes with built-in validators (constraints) such as @NotNull, @Min, @Max, @Past, @Future, @Size, etc., and it also allows creating custom constraints on the application domain model (or generally on POJO). Adding to the JSF built-in and custom validators, and since JSF 2.0, there is default integration between JSF and JSR 303 Java Bean Validation APIs. In the next subsections, this sort of integration will be illustrated in a sample subscriber application.

In the subscriber application, the user can save (his/her) name, address, and e-mail for subscriptions, as shown in Figure 3-6.

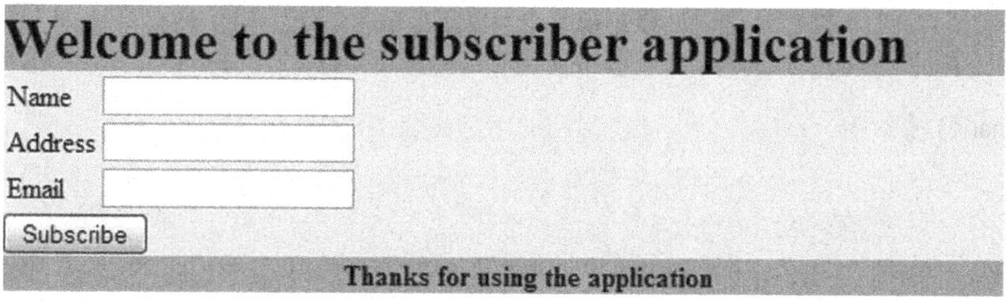

Welcome to the subscriber application

Name	
Address	
Email	

Subscribe

Thanks for using the application

Figure 3-6. *The subscriber application*

The user information is validated as follows:

1. All of the fields are required.

2. User name must be at least 4 characters and at most 30 characters.

3. Address must be at least 12 characters and at most 120 characters.

4. E-mail must be valid.

Technically speaking, we will implement the first validation requirement using the JSF required field validator. All of the other validations will be implemented using the JSR 303 APIs. In the validation requirement numbers 2 and 3, the JSR 303 @Size annotation will be used, while for requirement number 4, we will implement a custom JSR 303 constraint. Listing 3-15 shows a Person managed bean which is used in the application main XHTML page.

Listing 3-15. Person Managed Bean

```
package com.jsfprohtml5.subscriber.model;

import com.jsfprohtml5.subscriber.bean.validation.custom.EmailAddress;
import java.io.Serializable;
import javax.faces.bean.ManagedBean;
import javax.faces.bean.RequestScoped;
import javax.validation.constraints.Size;

@ManagedBean
@RequestScoped
public class Person implements Serializable {

    @Size(min = 4, max = 30)
    private String name;

    @Size(min = 12, max = 120)
    private String address;

    @EmailAddress
    private String email;

    public Person() {
    }

    public String subscribe() {
        return null;
    }
```

```
    public String getName() {
        return name;
    }
    public void setName(String name) {
        this.name = name;
    }

    public String getAddress() {
        return address;
    }
    public void setAddress(String address) {
        this.address = address;
    }

    public String getEmail() {
        return email;
    }
    public void setEmail(String email) {
        this.email = email;
    }
}
```

As shown in the bolded lines, we used the @size built-in Java Bean Validation annotation in order to control the sizes of name and address fields. The @size annotation has mainly two attributes, min and max, to validate the length of the annotated fields. @EmailAddress annotation is a custom constraint that we use to validate email attribute of Person managed bean. Listing 3-16 shows the code of the @EmailAddress annotation.

Listing 3-16. @EmailAddress Annotation

```
package com.jsfprohtml5.subscriber.bean.validation.custom;

import java.lang.annotation.Documented;
import java.lang.annotation.ElementType;
import java.lang.annotation.Retention;
import java.lang.annotation.RetentionPolicy;
import java.lang.annotation.Target;
import javax.validation.Constraint;
import javax.validation.Payload;

@Target({ElementType.FIELD, ElementType.METHOD})
@Constraint(validatedBy = EmailValidator.class)
@Retention(RetentionPolicy.RUNTIME)
@Documented
public @interface EmailAddress {
    String message() default "{email.invalid}";

    Class<?>[] groups() default {};

    Class<? extends Payload>[] payload() default {};
}
```

If you are familiar with Java annotations, using the @interface, you can create an annotation type. @Target annotation indicates the Java program elements to which the annotation type is applicable (in this example, these elements are Java fields and methods). Java Bean Validation specification (JSR 303) mandates that any constraint annotation defines the following attributes:

1. message attribute, which should be by default returning an error message. It can return either the actual error message text or the error message key by using the curly brackets as follows "{key}". In the previous code listing, it returns email.invalid key.

2. groups attribute, which allows specifying validation groups, to which this constraint belongs.

3. payload attribute, which can be used by clients of the Java Bean Validation API to assign custom payload objects to a constraint (outside of the scope of this book).

@Constraint annotation is a Java Bean Validation annotation which refers to the reference of the class that performs the validation logic using validatedBy attribute. Listing 3-17 shows the EmailValidator validation class implementation.

Listing 3-17. EmailValidator Validation Class

```
package com.jsfprohtml5.subscriber.bean.validation.custom;

import java.util.regex.Matcher;
import java.util.regex.Pattern;
import javax.validation.ConstraintValidator;
import javax.validation.ConstraintValidatorContext;

public class EmailValidator implements ConstraintValidator<EmailAddress, String> {
    private static final String EMAIL_REGEX = "(.+@.+\\.[a-zA-Z]+)?";

    private Pattern pattern;
    private Matcher matcher;

    @Override
    public void initialize(EmailAddress constraintAnnotation) {
        pattern = Pattern.compile(EMAIL_REGEX);
    }

    @Override
    public boolean isValid(String value, ConstraintValidatorContext context) {
        matcher = pattern.matcher(value);

        if (! matcher.matches()) {
            return false;
        }

        return true;
    }
}
```

As you will notice, EmailValidator constraint has the same logic of the JSF EmailValidator class that we developed in Listing 3-12. However, there is one main difference: in JSF validator, when the validation fails, the validator throws an exception, but in the Java Bean Validation, the validator returns false. The initialize() method is used for initializing the custom constraint; it is important to note that this method is guaranteed to be called before any of the other constraint implementation methods.

Now, after building our custom constraint, we are ready to use the built-in and custom constraints in our JSF XHTML page. Listing 3-18 shows the subscriber application main page (index.xhtml).

Listing 3-18. The Subscriber Application XHTML Page

```xml
<?xml version='1.0' encoding='UTF-8' ?>
<!DOCTYPE html>
<html xmlns="http://www.w3.org/1999/xhtml"
      xmlns:ui="http://java.sun.com/jsf/facelets"
      xmlns:h="http://java.sun.com/jsf/html"
      xmlns:f="http://java.sun.com/jsf/core">

<ui:composition template="/WEB-INF/templates/default.xhtml">
    <ui:define name="title">
        #{bundle['application.subscriber.title']}
    </ui:define>
    <ui:define name="content">
        <h:form>
            <h:panelGrid columns="3">
                <h:outputText value="#{bundle['user.name']}"></h:outputText>
                <h:inputText id="userName"
                             value="#{person.name}"
                             required="true"
                             requiredMessage="#{bundle['user.name.required']}">

                </h:inputText>
                <h:message for="userName" styleClass="errorMessage"/>

                <h:outputText value="#{bundle['user.address']}"></h:outputText>
                <h:inputText id="address"
                             value="#{person.address}"
                             required="true"
                             requiredMessage="#{bundle['user.address.required']}">

                </h:inputText>
                <h:message for="address" styleClass="errorMessage"/>

                <h:outputText value="#{bundle['user.email']}"></h:outputText>
                <h:inputText id="email"
                             value="#{person.email}"
                             required="true"
                             requiredMessage="#{bundle['user.email.required']}">

                </h:inputText>
                <h:message for="email" styleClass="errorMessage"/>
            </h:panelGrid>
```

```
            <h:commandButton value="#{bundle['application.subscribe']}"
                            action="#{person.subscribe}">
            </h:commandButton>

            <br/>

            <h:messages styleClass="errorMessage"/>
        </h:form>
    </ui:define>
</ui:composition>

</html>
```

As we notice in the code listing, we did nothing special; we used the JSF required field validator with all of the fields. It is important to note that all of the built-in or custom JSR 303 validators (@Size and @EmailValidator) will be applied automatically to the JSF components without doing any extra steps.As shown in Figure 3-7, Java Bean Validation errors are automatically attached to the JSF <h:message> and <h:messages> components.

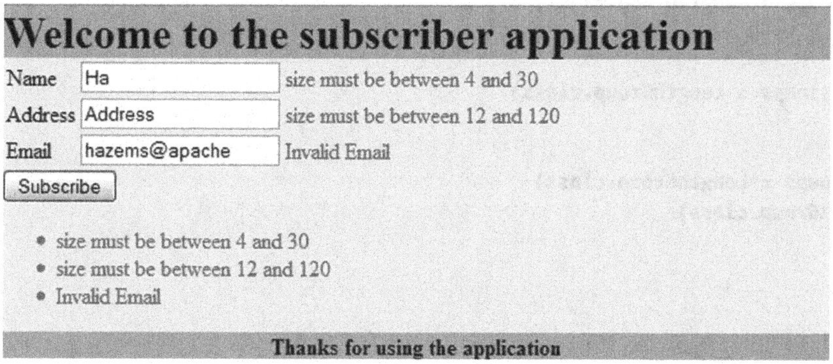

Figure 3-7. *Java Bean Validation errors in the JSF message components*

By default, all of the Java Bean Validation (JSR 303) validators will be enabled automatically in the JSF managed beans; in order to disable this behavior, you can set the javax.faces.validator.DISABLE_DEFAULT_BEAN_VALIDATOR context param in the web.xml to true as shown:

```
<context-param>
            <param-name>javax.faces.validator.DISABLE_DEFAULT_BEAN_VALIDATOR</param-name>
            <param-value>true</param-value>
</context-param>
```

One thing that is important to note is that Java Bean Validation is a standalone validation framework which is not part of the JavaServer Faces framework (although there is a decent integration between them, as we see in the subscriber application); this means that you need to provide a separate property file for the Java Bean Validation messages. As per JSR 303, this property file should be named ValidationMessages.properties with its locale variations for handling different locales, and the Java Bean Validation property files should be put under the default package (the root of the class path) of the JSF application.

■ **Note**   Covering the complete features of JSR 303 is outside of the scope of this book; you can read the complete JSR 303 specification at `http://jcp.org/en/jsr/detail?id=303`.

All of the validated fields in Listing 3-15 belong to the Default validation group of the Java Bean Validation framework; however, you have the option to specify many validation groups for the same constraint. A validation group is nothing more than a tag interface. Let's create two validation groups called (LengthGroup) and (EmailGroup). LengthGroup will group the length constraints in Person managed bean (@Size constraints), while EmailGroup will include the e-mail constraint in Person managed bean (@EmailAddress constraint). Then attach the validation groups to the constraints as shown in Listing 3-19.

Listing 3-19. Validation Groups in Person Managed Bean

```
@ManagedBean
@RequestScoped
public class Person implements Serializable {

    @Size(min = 4, max = 30, groups = LengthGroup.class)
    private String name;

    @Size(min = 12, max = 120, groups = LengthGroup.class)
    private String address;

    @Size(min = 5, max = 30, groups = LengthGroup.class)
    @EmailAddress(groups = EmailGroup.class)
    private String email;

    public Person() {
    }

    public String subscribe() {
        return null;
    }

    public String getName() {
        return name;
    }
    public void setName(String name) {
        this.name = name;
    }

    public String getAddress() {
        return address;
    }
    public void setAddress(String address) {
        this.address = address;
    }
```

```
        public String getEmail() {
            return email;
        }
        public void setEmail(String email) {
            this.email = email;
        }
}
```

JSF—by default—executes the constraints which are grouped under the Default validation group. In order to run specific validation groups on the EditableValueHolders, JSF provides a <f:validateBean> tag that can be used to select which validation groups are to be executed on the parent EditableValueHolder. This feature really gives a great control on the level of the input field validation. Listing 3-20 shows an updated index.xhtml of the subscriber application.

Listing 3-20. Updated index.xhtml Page

```
<?xml version='1.0' encoding='UTF-8' ?>
<!DOCTYPE html>
<html xmlns="http://www.w3.org/1999/xhtml"
      xmlns:ui="http://java.sun.com/jsf/facelets"
      xmlns:h="http://java.sun.com/jsf/html"
      xmlns:f="http://java.sun.com/jsf/core">

<ui:composition template="/WEB-INF/templates/default.xhtml">
    <ui:define name="title">
        #{bundle['application.subscriber.title']}
    </ui:define>
    <ui:define name="content">
        <h:form>
            <h:panelGrid columns="3">
                <h:outputText value="#{bundle['user.name']}"></h:outputText>
                <h:inputText id="userName"
                            value="#{person.name}"
                            required="true"
                            requiredMessage="#{bundle['user.name.required']}">

                <f:validateBean
validationGroups="com.jsfprohtml5.subscriber.bean.validation.groups.LengthGroup"/>
                </h:inputText>
                <h:message for="userName" styleClass="errorMessage"/>

                <h:outputText value="#{bundle['user.address']}"></h:outputText>
                <h:inputText id="address"
                            value="#{person.address}"
                            required="true"
                            requiredMessage="#{bundle['user.address.required']}">

                <f:validateBean
validationGroups="com.jsfprohtml5.subscriber.bean.validation.groups.LengthGroup"/>
                </h:inputText>
                <h:message for="address" styleClass="errorMessage"/>
```

```
                <h:outputText value="#{bundle['user.email']}"></h:outputText>
                <h:inputText id="email"
                             value="#{person.email}"
                             required="true"
                             requiredMessage="#{bundle['user.email.required']}">

            <f:validateBean
validationGroups="com.jsfprohtml5.subscriber.bean.validation.groups.LengthGroup,
com.jsfprohtml5.subscriber.bean.validation.groups.EmailGroup"/>

                </h:inputText>
                <h:message for="email" styleClass="errorMessage"/>
            </h:panelGrid>

            <h:commandButton value="#{bundle['application.subscribe']}"
                             action="#{person.subscribe}">
            </h:commandButton>

            <br/>

            <h:messages styleClass="errorMessage"/>
        </h:form>
    </ui:define>
</ui:composition>

</html>
```

As shown in the bolded lines, the `<f:validateBean>` tag can be attached to `EditableValueHolders`, and using the `validationGroups` attribute, you can specify the fully qualified name of the constraint classes (separated by commas) which you want to execute on the parent `EditableValueHolder`.

■ **Note** The complete Maven project of the subscriber application is included in the book web page at `apress.com` under *Chapter 3* resources.

Overriding Standard Messages

It is always useful to override the standard conversion and validation error messages in order to have a better user experience. Although you can customize the conversion and validation error messages by using the `validatorMessage`, `requiredMessage`, and `converterMessage` attributes of the `EditableValueHolder` components, it will require less effort and more accuracy to globally override the JSF standard conversion and validation messages on the application level than on every `EditableValueHolder` component.

In order to globally override the JSF standard conversion and validation messages, you will have to override the messages in your application message bundle by using the standard message keys. Table 3-3 shows the possible JSF standard message keys according to the JSF specification.

Table 3-3. *The JSF Standard Message Keys According to the JSF Specification*

Key	Default Message
javax.faces.component.UIInput.CONVERSION	{0}: Conversion error occurred.
javax.faces.component.UIInput.REQUIRED	{0}: Validation error: Value is required.
javax.faces.component.UIInput.UPDATE	{0}: An error occurred when processing your submitted information.
javax.faces.component.UISelectOne.INVALID	{0}: Validation error: Value is not valid
javax.faces.component.UISelectMany.INVALID	{0}: Validation error: Value is not valid
javax.faces.converter.BigDecimalConverter.DECIMAL	{2}: "{0}" must be a signed decimal number.
javax.faces.converter.BigDecimalConverter.DECIMAL_detail	{2}: "{0}" must be a signed decimal number consisting of zero or more digits, that may be followed by a decimal point and fraction. Example: {1}
javax.faces.converter.BigIntegerConverter.BIGINTEGER	{2}: "{0}" must be a number consisting of one or more digits. javax.faces.converter.BigIntegerConverter.BIGINTEGER_detail={2}: "{0}" must be a number consisting of one or more digits. Example: {1}
javax.faces.converter.BooleanConverter.BOOLEAN	{1}: "{0}" must be 'true' or 'false'.
javax.faces.converter.BooleanConverter.BOOLEAN_detail	{1}: "{0}" must be 'true' or 'false'. Any value other than 'true' will evaluate to 'false'.
javax.faces.converter.ByteConverter.BYTE	{2}: "{0}" must be a number between 0 and 255.
javax.faces.converter.ByteConverter.BYTE_detail	{2}: "{0}" must be a number between 0 and 255. Example: {1}
javax.faces.converter.CharacterConverter.CHARACTER	{1}: "{0}" must be a valid character.
javax.faces.converter.CharacterConverter.CHARACTER_detail	{1}: "{0}" must be a valid ASCII character.
javax.faces.converter.DateTimeConverter.DATE	{2}: "{0}" could not be understood as a date.
javax.faces.converter.DateTimeConverter.DATE_detail	{2}: "{0}" could not be understood as a date. Example: {1}
javax.faces.converter.DateTimeConverter.TIME	{2}: "{0}" could not be understood as a time.
javax.faces.converter.DateTimeConverter.TIME_detail	{2}: "{0}" could not be understood as a time. Example: {1}
javax.faces.converter.DateTimeConverter.DATETIME	{2}: "{0}" could not be understood as a date and time.
javax.faces.converter.DateTimeConverter.DATETIME_detail	{2}: "{0}" could not be understood as a date and time. Example: {1}
javax.faces.converter.DateTimeConverter.PATTERN_TYPE	{1}: A 'pattern' or 'type' attribute must be specified to convert the value "{0}".

(continued)

Table 3-3. (*continued*)

Key	Default Message
javax.faces.converter.DoubleConverter.DOUBLE	{2}: "{0}" must be a number consisting of one or more digits.
javax.faces.converter.DoubleConverter.DOUBLE_detail	{2}: "{0}" must be a number between 4.9E-324 and 1.7976931348623157E308. Example: {1}
javax.faces.converter.EnumConverter.ENUM	{2}: "{0}" must be convertible to an enum.
javax.faces.converter.EnumConverter.ENUM_detail	{2}: "{0}" must be convertible to an enum from the enum that contains the constant "{1}".
javax.faces.converter.EnumConverter.ENUM_NO_CLASS	{1}: "{0}" must be convertible to an enum from the enum, but no enum class provided.
javax.faces.converter.EnumConverter.ENUM_NO_CLASS_detail	{1}: "{0}" must be convertible to an enum from the enum, but no enum class provided.
javax.faces.converter.FloatConverter.FLOAT	{2}: "{0}" must be a number consisting of one or more digits.
javax.faces.converter.FloatConverter.FLOAT_detail	{2}: "{0}" must be a number between 1.4E-45 and 3.4028235E38. Example: {1}
javax.faces.converter.IntegerConverter.INTEGER	{2}: "{0}" must be a number consisting of one or more digits.
javax.faces.converter.IntegerConverter.INTEGER_detail	{2}: "{0}" must be a number between –2147483648 and 2147483647. Example: {1}
javax.faces.converter.LongConverter.LONG	{2}: "{0}" must be a number consisting of one or more digits.
javax.faces.converter.LongConverter.LONG_detail	{2}: "{0}" must be a number between –9223372036854775808 and 9223372036854775807. Example: {1}
javax.faces.converter.NumberConverter.CURRENCY	{2}: "{0}" could not be understood as a currency value.
javax.faces.converter.NumberConverter.CURRENCY_detail	{2}: "{0}" could not be understood as a currency value. Example: {1}
javax.faces.converter.NumberConverter.PERCENT	{2}: "{0}" could not be understood as a percentage.
javax.faces.converter.NumberConverter.PERCENT_detail	{2}: "{0}" could not be understood as a percentage. Example: {1}
javax.faces.converter.NumberConverter.NUMBER	{2}: "{0}" is not a number.
javax.faces.converter.NumberConverter.NUMBER_detail	{2}: "{0}" is not a number. Example: {1}
javax.faces.converter.NumberConverter.PATTERN	{2}: "{0}" is not a number pattern.
javax.faces.converter.NumberConverter.PATTERN_detail	{2}: "{0}" is not a number pattern. Example: {1}
javax.faces.converter.ShortConverter.SHORT	{2}: "{0}" must be a number consisting of one or more digits.

(*continued*)

Table 3-3. (*continued*)

Key	Default Message
javax.faces.converter.ShortConverter.SHORT_detail	{2}: "{0}" must be a number between –32768 and 32767 Example: {1}
javax.faces.converter.STRING	{1}: Could not convert "{0}" to a string.
javax.faces.validator.BeanValidator.MESSAGE	{0}
javax.faces.validator.DoubleRangeValidator.MAXIMUM	{1}: Validation error: Value is greater than allowable maximum of "{0}".
javax.faces.validator.DoubleRangeValidator.MINIMUM	{1}: Validation error: Value is less than allowable minimum of "{0}".
javax.faces.validator.DoubleRangeValidator.NOT_IN_RANGE	{2}: Validation error: Specified attribute is not between the expected values of {0} and {1}.
javax.faces.validator.DoubleRangeValidator.TYPE	{0}: Validation error: Value is not of the correct type.
javax.faces.validator.LengthValidator.MAXIMUM	{1}: Validation error: Length is greater than allowable maximum of "{0}".
javax.faces.validator.LengthValidator.MINIMUM	{1}: Validation error: Length is less than allowable minimum of "{0}".
javax.faces.validator.LongRangeValidator.MAXIMUM	{1}: Validation error: Value is greater than allowable maximum of "{0}".
javax.faces.validator.LongRangeValidator.MINIMUM	{1}: Validation error: Value is less than allowable minimum of "{0}".
javax.faces.validator.LongRangeValidator.NOT_IN_RANGE	{2}: Validation error: Specified attribute is not between the expected values of {0} and {1}.
javax.faces.validator.LongRangeValidator.TYPE	{0}: Validation error: Value is not of the correct type.

Let's see an example to see how this customization can be performed. The following code snippet shows an input text that is validated to be required and to have a value between 10 and 100.

```
<h:inputText id="someNumber"
             value="#{testBean.number}"
             required="true">

        <f:validateLongRange minimum="10" maximum="100"/>
</h:inputText>
<br/>
<h:commandButton action="#{testBean.proceed}" value="Proceed"/><br/>
```

When the user enters an out-of-range number and then clicks the "Proceed" command button, the following JSF default validation error message will appear to the user:

`xxx:someNumber: Validation Error: Specified attribute is not between the expected values of 10 and 100.`

In order to change the message, we need to do the following:

1. Override the `javax.faces.validator.LongRangeValidator.NOT_IN_RANGE` key in the application message bundle as follows:

   `javax.faces.validator.LongRangeValidator.NOT_IN_RANGE = {2}''s value must be minimum {0} and maximum {1}.`

2. Register the application message bundle in the `faces-config.xml` file as follows:

```
<faces-config ...>
        ...
    <application>
            <message-bundle>com.jsfprohtml5.application.Messages</message-bundle>
    </application>
        ...
</faces-config>
```

After doing these changes in the application's message bundle and in the `faces-config.xml` file, after inputting an out-of-range number in the input text and then clicking the "proceed" command button, the final error message will be

`xxx:someNumber's value must be minimum 10 and maximum 100.`

Summary

In this chapter, you learned in detail the JSF validation and conversion. You know the lifecycle of the JSF conversion, the JSF Converter interface, and the JSF standard converters, and you understand how to build custom JSF converters. You also learned the lifecycle of the JSF validation, the JSF Validator interface, and the JSF standard validators; how to build custom JSF validators; and finally how to work with Java Bean Validation (JSR 303) in JSF applications. At the end of the chapter, you learned how to empower your JSF application by customizing the JSF framework standard conversion and validation messages.

CHAPTER 4

■ ■ ■

JSF Under the Hood—Part 3

In this chapter, you will learn in detail how to empower your JSF applications by understanding the JSF event model. After you finish this chapter, you will understand the different JSF event types (JSF Faces events, Phase events, and System events). You will learn how to work with JSF events in your JSF applications. And in the last section, you will learn how to utilize the JSF view parameters in order to produce RESTful JSF pages that can be bookmarked by the end users and can be indexed by web search crawlers.

JSF Events

Before going into the details of JSF events, we need to understand first what an *event* is and what an *event listener* is. An event is usually an action performed by the user (such as clicking a button or changing a drop-down value). When an event occurs, a change (or set of changes) in the event source object occurs and is captured in an event object. The event object should tell what the source object of the event is and what changes to the event source (if any) occur. An event listener is usually a class that must be notified when a specific event (that the event listener class is interested in) occurs.

Generally, in the Java world, the two main components in the event model are represented as one interface and one class, as shown in Figure 4-1.

Figure 4-1. Java event model main interfaces

EventListener is a tagging interface with no methods that all of the event listener interfaces must extend, while EventObject class has mainly one method, getSource(), which returns the object on which the event initially occurred (the event source). Coping with the Java event model, JSF utilizes both EventObject and EventListener for building its event and listener model.

In order to define JSF listeners, all of the JSF listener interfaces extend EventListener interface. Figure 4-2 shows the main JSF event listeners (note that this diagram does not show the complete list of JSF listeners for simplicity).

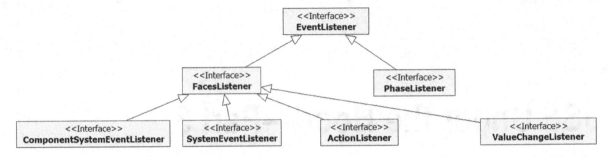

Figure 4-2. *JSF event listeners*

There are two types of JSF event listeners:

- **Faces Listener** is the base interface for action listener, value change listener, System event listener, and component System event listener.

- **Phase Listener** is the listener interface for the beginning and ending of each standard phase of the JSF request processing lifecycle.

Let's go into the details of the child listeners to understand who can create these listeners and when they can be executed. Figure 4-3 shows the two types of application-related event listeners:

- **ActionListener** interface, which is responsible for receiving action events.

- **ValueChangeListener** interface, which is responsible for receiving value change events.

Figure 4-3. *Application-related event listeners*

As shown in this figure, ActionSource component (or ActionSource2 component) may have more than one or more action listener(s). EditableValueHolder component (such as UIInput component) or ValueHolder component may have one or more value change listener(s).

System event listeners, by definition, listen for System events. System events, which were introduced in JSF 2.0, provide an elegant view on the JSF life cycle. Using System event listeners, the JSF developer can, for example, write custom code that will be executed in the application startup and teardown events or be executed when an exception is thrown in the application.

SystemEventListener is the main interface for System event listeners. SystemEventListener can listen for all SystemEvents types. System events can be triggered on the JSF application level (like application startup or application teardown or application exception) or on the JSF component level (like "before validating the component" or "after validating the component" or "before the view is rendered"). If System events occur on the component level, then in this case you may use the more specific event listener, which is ComponentSystemEventListener interface (shown in Figure 4-2) to handle. This is because ComponentSystemEventListener listens for ComponentSystemEvent (which extends SystemEvent).

Phase listeners allow handling the different Phase events. Phase events occur in the beginning and ending of each standard phase of the JSF request processing lifecycle. JSF request processing life cycle phases are

- Restore View.
- Apply Request Values.
- Process Validations.
- Update Model Values.
- Invoke Application.
- Render Response.

As shown in Figure 4-4, Lifecycle instance may have zero or more attached PhaseListeners, and UIViewRoot can have from zero to two instances of PhaseListeners. Phase listeners will be illustrated in detail in the "Phase Events" section.

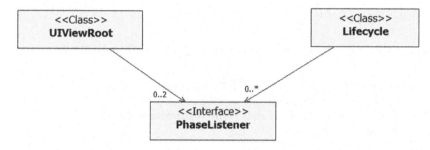

Figure 4-4. *PhaseListener interface*

■ **Note**   There is another listener which extends FacesListener (and is omitted from Figure 4-2 for simplicity): this listener is BehaviorListener. BehaviorListener listens for all of the BehaviorEvents of the JSF HTML components. These events will be illustrated in Chapter 5.

Now that we've covered the JSF event listener model, what about the JSF event model? Figure 4-5 shows the main classes in the JSF event hierarchy.

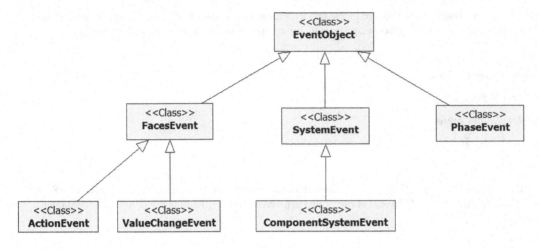

Figure 4-5. *The main classes in the JSF event object hierarchy*

In order to define JSF event objects, all of the JSF event objects extend EventObject class. There are three important things to notice:

- FacesEvent is the base class for events that can be triggered by UIComponents. It has two subclasses: ActionEvent class, which represents events that are triggered by ActionSource2 components, and ValueChangeEvent class, which represents events that are triggered by ValueHolder or EditableValueHolder components.

- SystemEvent is the base class for all the System events. ComponentSystemEvent class (extends SystemEvent) represents System events which are specific for UIComponents.

- PhaseEvent is a class that represents Phase events which occur in the beginning and ending of each standard phase of the JSF request processing lifecycle.

■ **Note**   It is important to know that all of the JSF event listener interfaces and event classes are located in (javax.faces.event) package. During the chapter and for simplicity, we will mention only the event listener interface name or the event class name without mentioning the fully qualified interface (or class) name.

Faces Events

Faces events are those events which can be triggered by UIComponents. Faces events include two types of events:

- Action Events.
- Value Change Events.

Action events are fired by ActionSource2 components such as (CommandButton or CommandLink components). An action event is fired when, for example, UICommand component is clicked. Value change events are fired by ValueHolder components such as (outputText component) or EditableValueHolder components such as (inputText or selectOneMenu components). A value change event is fired when the component's value is changed. Before going to the examples of both types of events, it is important to know when each of these events fire in the phases of the JSF life cycle. Figure 4-6 shows the execution time of both action and value change events.

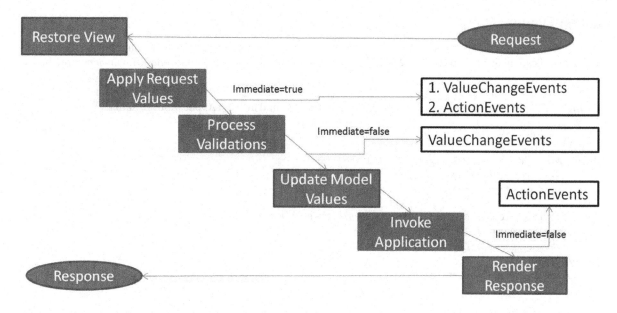

Figure 4-6. *The execution time of both action and value change events*

As shown in the figure, action events and value change events are executed at the end of the following three phases:

- Apply Request Values.
- Process Validations.
- Invoke Application.

These are four execution scenarios of both events:

- When the immediate attribute of the EditableValueHolder (or ValueHolder) component is set to true, then ValueChangeEvent is executed at the end of the "Apply Request Values" phase.

- When the immediate attribute of the ActionSource2 component is set to true, then ActionEvent is executed at the end of the "Apply Request Values" phase.

- When the immediate attribute of the EditableValueHolder (or ValueHolder) component is set to false, then ValueChangeEvent is executed at the end of the "Process Validations" phase.

- When the immediate attribute of the ActionSource2 component is set to false, then ActionEvent is executed at the end of the "Invoke Application" phase.

In the next two sections, we will see different examples on how to create listeners for both action and value change events.

■ **Note** From the explanation of the execution scenarios, it is important to note that by default (when immediate attribute is set to false) both action events and value change events are queued, which means that these events will not be fired once the user (for example) performs an action on a ActionSource2 component or makes a change in a value of an EditableValueHolder component. Both events will be queued until they are fired in the suitable time in the JSF request processing life cycle, as shown in the previous figure.

Action Events

In the previous chapters, we saw some examples of action events and action listeners with action methods. Let's recall the first application example in Chapter 2. Listing 4-1 shows an example of an action listener with an action method in the first application example.

Listing 4-1. An Example of an Action Listener with an Action Method in "First Application" Example

```
<?xml version='1.0' encoding='UTF-8' ?>
<!DOCTYPE html>
<html xmlns="http://www.w3.org/1999/xhtml"
      xmlns:ui="http://java.sun.com/jsf/facelets"
      xmlns:h="http://java.sun.com/jsf/html">

<ui:composition template="/WEB-INF/templates/simple.xhtml">
    <ui:define name="title">
        #{bundle['application.loginpage.title']}
    </ui:define>
    <ui:define name="content">

                             ...

        <h:commandButton value="#{bundle['application.login']}" action="#{user.login}"/>
            <br/><br/>
        </h:form>
    </ui:define>
</ui:composition>

</html>
```

As we see in Listing 4-1, we could create an action listener with an action method using the UICommand (CommandButton) action attribute. Listing 4-2 shows the #{user.login} action method code.

Listing 4-2. #{user.login} Action Method Code

```
public class User implements Serializable {

    ...

    public String login() {
        return "welcome";
    }

    ...
}
```

As you will notice, the action method is a method which takes no arguments and returns a String that represents the outcome.

■ **Note** Action methods are handled by the JSF built-in default action listener. The default action listener takes the returned outcome String from the action method and then delivers it to NavigationHandler to handle the navigation (if there is any).

If you do not need a navigation in your action method, then you can use action listener methods instead. Listing 4-3 shows a form that contains a CommandButton with an action listener method in order to calculate the factorial number of an input field.

Listing 4-3. An Example of an Action Listener Method

```
<h:form>

                <h:outputText value="Enter Number:"/>
                <h:inputText value="#{calc.number}">
                        <f:validateLongRange minimum="0" maximum="25"/>
                </h:inputText>

                <br/>
                <h:commandButton value="Calculate Factorial"
                                        actionListener="#{calc.findFactorial}">
                </h:commandButton>

                <br/>
                <h:outputText value="Result is: #{calc.result}" rendered="#{calc.result ne 0}"/>

                <h:messages/>

</h:form>
```

An action listener method can be attached to UICommand component using its actionListener attribute. As indicated in the preceding, an action listener method executes an action without returning any outcome for the JSF navigation, so the action listener method returns void and has ActionEvent as a parameter. Listing 4-4 shows Calc managed bean, which includes findFactorial action listener.

Listing 4-4. Calc Managed Bean

```
@ManagedBean
@RequestScoped
public class Calc implements Serializable {
    private int number;
    private long result;

    public int getNumber() {
        return number;
    }

    public void setNumber(int number) {
        this.number = number;
    }

    public long getResult() {
        return result;
    }

    public void setResult(long result) {
        this.result = result;
    }
```

```
    public void findFactorial(ActionEvent event) {
        result = 1;

        for (int i = 1; i <= number; i++) {
            result = result * i;
        }
    }
}
```

Adding to using the default action listener with either action method or action listener method, you can write your own custom action listener. This can be done by creating your action listener class, which implements ActionListener interface. Listing 4-5 shows CalcActionListener, which implements ActionListener. As shown, processAction() gets the current input number and then calculates the corresponding factorial of this number, and finally it sets the output in the result attribute of the Calc managed bean.

Listing 4-5. CalcActionListener Custom Action Listener

```
import javax.faces.context.FacesContext;
import javax.faces.event.AbortProcessingException;
import javax.faces.event.ActionEvent;
import javax.faces.event.ActionListener;

public class CalcActionListener implements ActionListener {

    @Override
    public void processAction(ActionEvent event) throws AbortProcessingException {
        FacesContext context = FacesContext.getCurrentInstance();

        Calc calc = context.getApplication().evaluateExpressionGet(context,
                                                        "#{calc}",
                                                        Calc.class);

        long result = 1;

        for (int i = 1; i <= calc.getNumber(); i++) {
            result = result * i;
        }

        calc.setResult(result);
    }

}
```

In order to attach the custom action listener to the UICommand component, you can use the <f:actionListener> tag inside the UICommand component. Listing 4-6 shows the updates on the form mentioned in Listing 4-3 with the custom action listener update.

Listing 4-6. An Example of Custom Action Listener in the XHTML Page

```
<h:form>

            <h:outputText value="Enter Number:"/>
            <h:inputText value="#{calc.number}">
                    <f:validateLongRange minimum="0" maximum="25"/>
            </h:inputText>

            <br/>
            <h:commandButton value="Calculate Factorial">
                    <f:actionListener type="com.jsfprohtml5.factorial.model.CalcActionListener"/>
            </h:commandButton>

            <br/>
            <h:outputText value="Result is: #{calc.result}" rendered="#{calc.number ne 0}"/>

            <h:messages/>

</h:form>
```

A best practice to follow is to use action methods for executing business actions, which may also include navigation to new pages, and to use action listener methods (or custom action listeners) to do some initialization work for actions (such as logging the actions, for example) before executing the actual business action. It is important to know that action listener methods (or custom action listeners) always execute before action methods in the same order that they are declared in the view and attached to the `ActionSource2` component. Listing 4-7 shows the factorial calculation form mentioned in Listing 4-3 with an update which combines both an action method and an action listener on the "`Calculate Factorial`" command button component.

Listing 4-7. Action Method and Action Listener Combination on the "Calculate Factorial" Command Component

```
<h:form>

            <h:outputText value="Enter Number:"/>
            <h:inputText value="#{calc.number}">
                    <f:validateLongRange minimum="0" maximum="25"/>
            </h:inputText>

            <br/>
            <h:commandButton value="Calculate Factorial"
                                        actionListener="#{calc.logFindFactorial}"
                                        action="#{calc.findFactorial}">
            </h:commandButton>

            <br/>
            <h:outputText value="Result is: #{calc.result}" rendered="#{calc.number ne 0}"/>

            <h:messages/>

</h:form>
```

The execution of #{calc.logFindFactorial} which logs findFactorial operation will be performed before the actual factorial calculation by #{calc.findFactorial}. Listing 4-8 shows the updates to Calc managed bean which is shown originally in Listing 4-4.

Listing 4-8. Updated Calc Managed Bean

```java
@ManagedBean
@RequestScoped
public class Calc implements Serializable {
    private long number;
    private long result;

    public long getNumber() {
        return number;
    }

    public void setNumber(long number) {
        this.number = number;
    }

    public long getResult() {
        return result;
    }

    public void setResult(long result) {
        this.result = result;
    }

    public void logFindFactorial(ActionEvent event) {
        System.out.println("Getting the factorial for: " + number);
    }

    public String findFactorial() {
        result = 1;

        for (int i = 1; i <= number; i++) {
            result = result * i;
        }

        System.out.println("Factorial(" + number + ") = " + result);

        return null;
    }
}
```

After entering a number in the number field and then clicking "Calculate Factorial" command button, the following lines will be printed in console as follows:

```
Getting the factorial for: 3
Factorial(3) = 6
```

Sometimes, you may need to set a value directly in your managed bean property before executing an action method; if you have this situation then you can use <f:setPropertyActionListener> tag inside your ActionSource2 component. Table 4-1 shows the main attributes of <f:setPropertyActionListener> tag.

Table 4-1. *Main Attributes of < f:setPropertyActionListener> Tag*

Attribute	Description
Value*	Represents ValueExpression to be stored as the value of the target attribute.
Target*	Represents ValueExpression that is the destination of the value attribute.

In order to understand how to use the <f:setPropertyActionListener> tag, let's see an example. Listing 4-9 shows an example of the <f:setPropertyActionListener> tag inside a CommandButton.

Listing 4-9. An Example of <f:setPropertyActionListener>

```
<h:commandButton value="Say Hi" action="page2">
          <f:setPropertyActionListener target="#{person.name}" value="Some user"/>
</h:commandButton>
```

As shown in the previous code listing, when the CommandButton is clicked, the name attribute of the Person managed bean will be set to "Some user" and then the current page will be forwarded to page2. Listing 4-10 shows Person managed bean.

Listing 4-10. Person Managed Bean

```
@ManagedBean
@SessionScoped
public class Person {
    private String name;

    public String getName() {
        return name;
    }
    public void setName(String name) {
        this.name = name;
    }
}
```

Person managed bean is a simple bean with only one attribute name with its setter and getter. After setting the name attribute of the Person managed bean to "Some user" using the <f:setPropertyActionListener> tag, then in page2, if we have the following expression in the page:

```
Hello, #{person.name}
```

This will produce

```
Hello, Some user
```

Value Change Events

A value change event is an event that is triggered when the value of a ValueHolder (or an EditableValueHolder) component is changed. Let's see an example of a value change listener. Assume that we want to display the capitals of set of countries that are shown in a JSF SelectOneMenu component when the user selects one of these countries and then clicks a CommandButton to get the capital of the selected country. Listing 4-11 shows the form which includes the country list.

Listing 4-11. An Example of Value Change Listener

```
<h:form>

            <h:outputLabel for="countries" value="Select a country: "/>
            <h:selectOneMenu id="countries" value="#{country.name}"
                                 valueChangeListener="#{country.findCapital}">

                    <f:selectItem itemLabel="---" itemValue="---"/>
                    <f:selectItem itemLabel="United States" itemValue="USA"/>
                    <f:selectItem itemLabel="Egypt" itemValue="Egypt"/>
                    <f:selectItem itemLabel="Denmark" itemValue="Denmark"/>
            </h:selectOneMenu>
            <h:commandButton value="Find Capital" /> <br/>

            <h:outputText value="Capital of #{country.name} is #{country.capital}"
                             rendered="#{country.capital ne null}"/>

</h:form>
```

As we see in the bolded lines, we have a selectOneMenu component that has four items that are added using <f:selectItem> tag. The first item represents no selection, while the rest of the items represent countries. selectOneMenu component has a valueChangeListener attribute which includes a value change listener method #{country.findCapital}. When the user selects one of the available countries and then clicks the CommandButton, then the form will be submitted and the value change listener method will be executed if the selectOneMenu value is changed. Listing 4-12 shows the Country managed bean.

Listing 4-12. Country Managed Bean

```
import javax.faces.bean.ManagedBean;
import javax.faces.bean.RequestScoped;
import javax.faces.event.ValueChangeEvent;

@ManagedBean
@RequestScoped
public class Country {
    private String name;
    private String capital;

    public String getName() {
        return name;
    }
    public void setName(String name) {
        this.name = name;
    }

    public String getCapital() {
        return capital;
    }
    public void setCapital(String capital) {
        this.capital = capital;
    }
```

```
public void findCapital(ValueChangeEvent event) {
    System.out.println("Old selected value is: " + event.getOldValue());
    System.out.println("New selected value is: " + event.getNewValue());

    String selectedCountryName = (String) event.getNewValue();

    if ("USA".equals(selectedCountryName)) {
        capital = "Washington";
    } else if ("Egypt".equals(selectedCountryName)) {
        capital = "Cairo";
    } else if ("Denmark".equals(selectedCountryName)) {
        capital = "Copenhagen";
    }
}
}
```

As you notice in the bolded lines, the value change listener method returns void and has ValueChangeEvent as a parameter. Using getOldValue() and getNewValue() methods of ValueChangeEvent, you can get the old and the new values of the ValueHolder (or EditableValueHolder) components. In our example, we get the new value which represents the new country selection, then get the suitable capital for the selected country, and finally set the result in the capital attribute in order to be displayed by the page, as shown in Listing 4-11.

Instead of firing the value change event by changing the value of the ValueHolder (or EditableValueHolder) component and click on a CommandButton or a CommandLink. You can fire the value change event when the value of the ValueHolder (or EditableValueHolder) component changes by submitting the form when the component's value changes. Listing 4-13 shows how to apply this behavior by removing the CommandButton and submitting the form on value change.

Listing 4-13. Executing the Value Change Listener by Submitting the Form on SelectOneMenu's Value Change

```
<h:form>

        <h:outputLabel for="countries" value="Select a country: "/>
        <h:selectOneMenu id="countries" value="#{country.name}"
valueChangeListener="#{country.findCapital}"
                                                    onchange="submit();">

            <f:selectItem itemLabel="---" itemValue="---"/>
            <f:selectItem itemLabel="United States" itemValue="USA"/>
            <f:selectItem itemLabel="Egypt" itemValue="Egypt"/>
            <f:selectItem itemLabel="Denmark" itemValue="Denmark"/>
        </h:selectOneMenu> <br/>

        <h:outputText value="Capital of #{country.name} is #{country.capital}"
                                    rendered="#{country.capital ne null}"/>

</h:form>
```

Adding to using the default value change listener, you can write your own custom value change listener. This can be done by creating a custom value change listener class that implements ValueChangeListener interface. Listing 4-14 shows CountryValueChangeListener, which utilizes ValueChangeListener and implements processValueChange(), which gets the new selected country and then finds its capital and finally sets the result in the capital attribute of the Country managed bean.

Listing 4-14. CountryValueChangeListener Custom Listener

```java
import javax.faces.context.FacesContext;
import javax.faces.event.AbortProcessingException;
import javax.faces.event.ValueChangeEvent;
import javax.faces.event.ValueChangeListener;

public class CountryValueChangeListener implements ValueChangeListener {

    @Override
    public void processValueChange(ValueChangeEvent event) throws AbortProcessingException {
        FacesContext context = FacesContext.getCurrentInstance();
        Country country = context.getApplication().evaluateExpressionGet(context,
                                                        "#{country}",
                                                        Country.class);

        String selectedCountryName = (String) event.getNewValue();

        if ("USA".equals(selectedCountryName)) {
            country.setCapital("Washington");
        } else if ("Egypt".equals(selectedCountryName)) {
            country.setCapital("Cairo");
        } else if ("Denmark".equals(selectedCountryName)) {
            country.setCapital("Copenhagen");
        }
    }
}
```

In order to attach the custom value change listener to the ValueHolder (or EditableValueHolder) component, you can use the <f:valueChangeListener> tag inside the component. Listing 4-15 shows the updates on the capital finder form mentioned in Listing 4-13 with the custom value change listener update.

Listing 4-15. An Example of Custom Value Change Listener in the XHTML Page

```html
<h:form>

            <h:outputLabel for="countries" value="Select a country: "/>
            <h:selectOneMenu id="countries" value="#{country.name}"
                                                        onchange="submit();">

                    <f:selectItem itemLabel="---" itemValue="---"/>
                    <f:selectItem itemLabel="United States" itemValue="USA"/>
                    <f:selectItem itemLabel="Egypt" itemValue="Egypt"/>
                    <f:selectItem itemLabel="Denmark" itemValue="Denmark"/>

                    <f:valueChangeListener type="com.jsfprohtml5.factorial.model
.CountryValueChangeListener"/>
            </h:selectOneMenu> <br/>

            <h:outputText value="Capital of #{country.name} is #{country.capital}"
                                        rendered="#{country.capital ne null}"/>

</h:form>
```

As shown in the previous bolded line, using `<f:valueChangeListener>` is very similar to `<f:actionListener>`; mainly, you need to specify the type attribute which refers to the fully qualified class name of the listener class.

Phase Events

Phase events occur in the beginning and ending of each standard phase of the JSF request processing lifecycle, as shown in Figure 4-7.

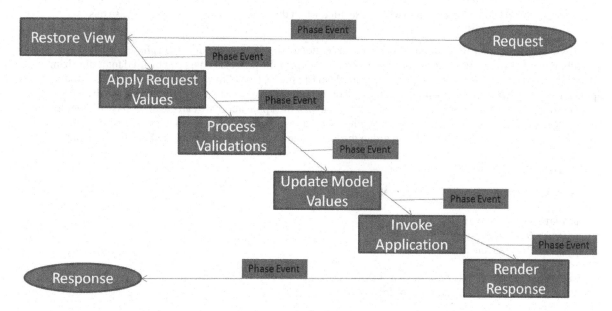

Figure 4-7. *Phase events execution time*

Phase events are handled by phase listeners. As shown in Figure 4-4, `Lifecycle` instance may have zero or more attached phase listeners, and `UIViewRoot` can have from zero to two instances of phase listeners. In order to create a phase listener, you need to implement the JSF `PhaseListener` interface. Listing 4-16 shows the code of the JSF `PhaseListener` interface.

Listing 4-16. PhaseListener Interface

```
package javax.faces.event;

import java.io.Serializable;
import java.util.EventListener;

public interface PhaseListener extends EventListener, Serializable {

    public void afterPhase(PhaseEvent event);

    public void beforePhase(PhaseEvent event);

    public PhaseId getPhaseId();
}
```

As shown in Listing 4-16, PhaseListener interface has the following methods:

- getPhaseId(): This method returns the identifier of the request processing phase, during which this listener is interested in processing PhaseEvent events. Legal values are the singleton instances defined by the PhaseId class, including PhaseId.ANY_PHASE to indicate an interest in being notified for all standard phases.

- beforePhase(): This method will be executed when the processing for a particular phase of the request processing lifecycle is about to begin.

- afterPhase(): This method will be executed when the processing for a particular phase has just been completed.

Phase listeners can be useful for debugging the execution of the different JSF life cycle phases. It can also be used for authorizing JSF application pages. Let's see an example to see how phase listeners can be used for authorizing JSF pages. Let's get back to the first application example in Chapter 2. One of the missing functionalities in that application is that the user can open directly the welcome application without having to pass through the login page. In order to secure the welcome page (or maybe other pages) in the application, we can create a phase listener for this. One thing that we need to modify in the application is to set a session flag to indicate that the user is authenticated by entering a non-empty username and password in the login page. Listing 4-17 shows the updated User managed bean.

Listing 4-17. Updated User Managed Bean

```
public class User implements Serializable {

    private String name;
    private String password;
    private Profession profession;

    private List<String> favoriteSports;
    private Map<String, String> spokenLanguages;

    ...

    public String login() {
        FacesContext context = FacesContext.getCurrentInstance();
        HttpSession session = (HttpSession) context.getExternalContext().getSession(true);

        // User passes through the login page and clicks the "login" button.
        session.setAttribute("isAuthenticated", true);

        return "welcome";
    }

    ...
}
```

As shown in the previous code listing, a session attribute "isAuthenticated" is added for marking the user as authenticated in the login() method (any entered non-empty username and password are accepted in the example). Listing 4-18 shows AuthorizationListener phase listener code.

Listing 4-18. AuthorizationListener Phase Listener

```
package com.jsfprohtml5.firstapplication.model;

import javax.faces.application.NavigationHandler;
import javax.faces.context.FacesContext;
import javax.faces.event.PhaseEvent;
import javax.faces.event.PhaseId;
import javax.faces.event.PhaseListener;
import javax.servlet.http.HttpSession;

public class AuthorizationListener implements PhaseListener {

    @Override
    public void afterPhase(PhaseEvent event) {
        FacesContext context = event.getFacesContext();
        String currentPage = context.getViewRoot().getViewId();

        boolean isLoginPage = currentPage.endsWith("index.xhtml");

        HttpSession session = (HttpSession) context.getExternalContext().getSession(true);
        Object isAuthenticated = session.getAttribute("isAuthenticated");

        if (!isLoginPage && isAuthenticated == null) {
            NavigationHandler navigationHandler = context.getApplication().getNavigationHandler();
            navigationHandler.handleNavigation(context, null, "index");
        }
    }

    @Override
    public void beforePhase(PhaseEvent event) {
        //Nothing ...
    }

    @Override
    public PhaseId getPhaseId() {
        return PhaseId.RESTORE_VIEW;
    }

}
```

In order to implement page authorization, we need to create a phase listener on the JSF life cycle after the RESTORE_VIEW phase is completed. In the afterPhase() API, the current page is retrieved using context.getViewRoot().getViewId(). When the page is not the login page (index.xhtml) and the user is not authenticated, then the user is forwarded to the login page using NavigationHandler. In order to install the phase listener on the JSF life cycle, you need to define it in the faces configuration file, as shown in Listing 4-19.

Listing 4-19. Defining the Phase Listener in the Faces Configuration File

```
<faces-config ...>

    ...

    <lifecycle>
        <phase-listener>
            com.jsfprohtml5.firstapplication.model.AuthorizationListener
        </phase-listener>
    </lifecycle>
</faces-config>
```

■ **Tip** If you want to apply a phase listener on a specific view instead of applying it on all the pages, you can do this by using the `<f:phaseListener>` tag as follows: `<f:phaseListener type="package.CustomPhaseListener">` (where `type` attribute represents the fully qualified phase listener Java class name to be created and registered). `<f:phaseListener>` tag registers a `PhaseListener` instance on the `UIViewRoot` in which this tag is nested.

System Events

System events are introduced in JSF 2.0 to allow the JSF developer to listen for and to react to advanced life cycle events. As illustrated earlier in the chapter, System events can occur on the JSF application level (like application startup or application teardown) or on the JSF component level. Unlike Faces events, System events are published immediately, which means that they are not queued to later life cycle processing phases. Table 4-2 shows the different types of System events that can occur on the application level (directly extends `SystemEvent`).

Table 4-2. *JSF System Events on the Application Level (Extends SystemEvent)*

System Event	Description
PostConstructApplicationEvent	Published immediately once the application startup completes.
PreDestroyApplicationEvent	Published immediately before the application shutdowns.
ExceptionQueuedEvent	Published when an unexpected exception in the JSF application is thrown. This can happen at any of the JSF life cycle processing phases.

   System events can also occur on the component level. Table 4-3 shows the most common types of System events that can occur on the component level. All of the following events extend from `ComponentSystemEvent`.

Table 4-3. *JSF System Events on the Component Level (Extends ComponentSystemEvent)*

System Event	Description
PreRenderComponentEvent	This event is published just before the rendering of the component.
PostAddToViewEvent	This event is published just after the component is added to the JSF view.
PreValidateEvent	This event is published just before the component is about to be validated.
PostValidateEvent	This event is published just after the component is validated.
PreDestroyViewMapEvent	This event is published just before the view scope map is about to be destroyed.
PostConstructViewMapEvent	This event is published just after the view scope map is created.
PreRenderViewEvent	This event is published just before the view (UIViewRoot) is about to be rendered.
PostRestoreStateEvent	This event is published just after the component state is restored.

In order to see how we can use System events in order to empower our JSF applications, let's get back to the subscriber application which we created in Chapter 3. Assume that we want to introduce a new drop-down item that will include list of professions, as shown in Figure 4-8. The list of professions is static in the application, so it will be loaded once when the application starts and will be unloaded before the application shuts down.

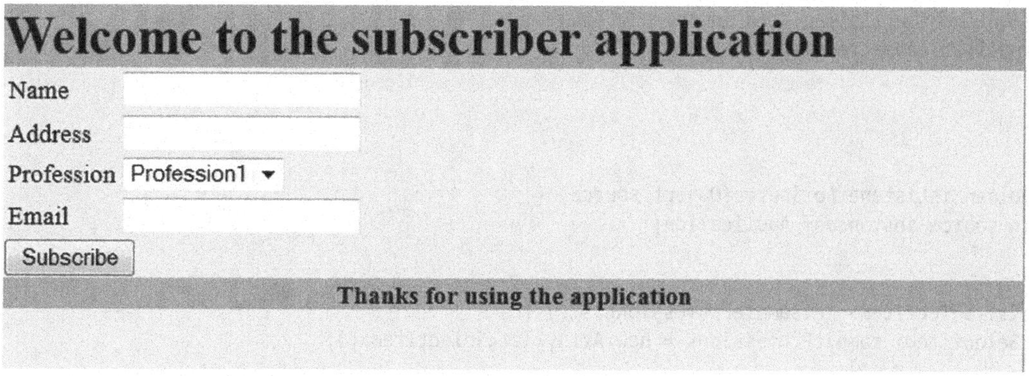

Figure 4-8. *The updated subscriber application screen*

In order to implement this functionality, we can use PostConstructApplicationEvent to load the static listing data just after the application starts and PreDestroyApplicationEvent to make any cleanup just before the application shutdowns.

Listing 4-20 shows our application's custom SystemEvent listener, which will be called just after the application starts and just before the application shuts down.

Listing 4-20. Subscriber Custom SystemEvent Listener

```
package com.jsfprohtml5.subscriber.model;

import java.util.ArrayList;
import java.util.List;
import java.util.Map;
import javax.faces.application.Application;
```

111

```java
import javax.faces.context.FacesContext;
import javax.faces.event.AbortProcessingException;
import javax.faces.event.PostConstructApplicationEvent;
import javax.faces.event.PreDestroyApplicationEvent;
import javax.faces.event.SystemEvent;
import javax.faces.event.SystemEventListener;
import javax.faces.model.SelectItem;

public class ListingLoader implements SystemEventListener {
    public static final String PROFESSIONS_KEY = "professions";

    @Override
    public void processEvent(SystemEvent event) throws AbortProcessingException {
        Map<String, Object> applicationMap = FacesContext.getCurrentInstance().
                                    getExternalContext().getApplicationMap();

        if (event instanceof PostConstructApplicationEvent) {

            //Load the listing data in the startup ...
            applicationMap.put(PROFESSIONS_KEY, getSampleProfessionList());
        } else if (event instanceof PreDestroyApplicationEvent) {

            //Unload the listing data in the shutdown ...
            applicationMap.remove(PROFESSIONS_KEY);
        }
    }

    @Override
    public boolean isListenerForSource(Object source) {
        return source instanceof Application;
    }

    private List<SelectItem> getSampleProfessionList() {
        List<SelectItem> sampleProfessions = new ArrayList<SelectItem>();

        sampleProfessions.add(new SelectItem("Profession1"));
        sampleProfessions.add(new SelectItem("Profession2"));
        sampleProfessions.add(new SelectItem("Profession3"));
        sampleProfessions.add(new SelectItem("Other"));

        return sampleProfessions;
    }
}
```

In order to implement SystemEventListener interface, we need to provide the implementation for two methods:

1. isListenerForSource(Object source): This method should return true if the event listener is interested in receiving events from the source object. For our listener, the event listener is interested only in receiving events from Application object.

processEvent(SystemEvent event): This method will be called once the SystemEvent is received and ready for processing. In our listener, event object is checked to be either PostConstructApplicationEvent or PreDestroyApplicationEvent. If it is a PostConstructApplicationEvent, the profession list is set in a map entry whose key is PROFESSIONS_KEY in the application map. In the PreDestroyApplicationEvent, any possible cleanup can be performed; in our listener, the profession list is just removed from the application map.

In order to allow our application's custom SystemEvent listener to execute in PostConstructApplicationEvent or PreDestroyApplicationEvent, we need to register our custom SystemEvent listener in the faces configuration file (faces-config.xml), as shown in Listing 4-21.

Listing 4-21. Registering Our Custom SystemEvent Listener in faces-config.xml

```
<faces-config ...>

    <application>

        <system-event-listener>
            <system-event-class>javax.faces.event.PostConstructApplicationEvent</system-event-class>
            <system-event-listener-class>com.jsfprohtml5.subscriber.model.ListingLoader
</system-event-listener-class>
        </system-event-listener>

        <system-event-listener>
            <system-event-class>javax.faces.event.PreDestroyApplicationEvent</system-event-class>
            <system-event-listener-class>com.jsfprohtml5.subscriber.model.ListingLoader
</system-event-listener-class>
        </system-event-listener>

        ...
    </application>
</faces-config>
```

Using the <system-event-listener> element inside the <application> element, we can register a System event listener on a specific System event. It has two main elements: the <system-event-class> element, which represents the fully qualified class name of the System event class, and the <system-event-listener-class> element, which represents the fully qualified class name of the System event listener class.

In our example, we declare two <system-event-listener> elements to allow our custom SystemEvent listener (ListingLoader) to receive events from both PostConstructApplicationEvent and PreDestroyApplicationEvent.

■ **Note** There is an optional element under the <system-event-listener>, which is <source-class> element. The <source-class> element can be used for specifying the fully qualified class name of the event source.

Now that we see an example of System events that can occur on the application level, let's see how to utilize the System events that can occur on the component level. Assume that we want to customize the error displaying way on the input fields of the subscriber application form so that when we have an error (or set of errors) in the validation, then input fields will be highlighted. This is actually a perfect use case for component System events. In order to implement this use case, we will need to utilize the postValidate event.

JSF introduces <f:event> tag that we can put directly as a child of any JSF HTML component in order to install ComponentSystemEventListener instances on it. Table 4-4 shows the attributes of <f:event> tag. Notice that the mentioned attributes of <f:event> tag are mandatory.

Table 4-4. *<f:event> Tag Attributes*

Attribute	Description
Type*	Value expression that evaluates to a String which represents the name of the event for which to install a listener. Valid values are preRenderComponent, preRenderView, postAddToView, preValidate, and postValidate. In addition to the mentioned valid values, the fully qualified class name of any java class that extends ComponentSystemEvent may be used as the value of the "type" attribute after annotating the extending class with @NamedEvent annotation.
Listener*	Method expression that must evaluate to a public method that takes a ComponentSystemEvent as a parameter, with a return type of void, or to a public method that takes no arguments with a return type of void.

In order to change the style of input component, we can put an <f:event> tag inside it. Listing 4-22 shows how to listen on the postValidate event in the user name input field.

Listing 4-22. Listening on the postValidate Event in the User Name Input Field

```
<h:inputText id="userName"
                            value="#{person.name}"
                            required="true"
                            requiredMessage="#{bundle['user.name.required']}">

        <f:event type="postValidate" listener="#{person.checkName}"/>
        <f:validateBean validationGroups="com.jsfprohtml5.subscriber.bean.validation.groups
.LengthGroup"/>
</h:inputText>
```

The JSF method expression #{person.checkName} checks if the user name input is valid. If user name is not valid, a specific style class is added to the input field. Listing 4-23 shows the code of checkName method.

Listing 4-23. checkName Method Code

```
@ManagedBean
@RequestScoped
public class Person implements Serializable {

    ...

    public void checkName(ComponentSystemEvent componentSystemEvent) {
        UIComponent component = componentSystemEvent.getComponent();

        if (component instanceof EditableValueHolder) {
            EditableValueHolder editableValueHolder = (EditableValueHolder) component;

            if (! editableValueHolder.isValid()) {
                component.getAttributes().put("styleClass", "invalidInput");
            } else {
                component.getAttributes().put("styleClass", "");
            }
        }
    }
}
```

As we see in the listing, the listener method has `ComponentSystemEvent` as a parameter. Using `getComponent()`, we can retrieve the component instance and then we check if the component is valid (passes validation phase) using `isValid()` method of `EditableValueHolder`. If the component is not valid, then `invalidInput` CSS style class is added to the `styleClass` attribute of the component. The `invalidInput` CSS style class is simple, as shown in Listing 4-24.

Listing 4-24. invalidInput Style Class

```
.invalidInput {
    background-color: red;
    color: white;
}
```

Figure 4-9 shows how the user name input field looks like when it does not pass the validation.

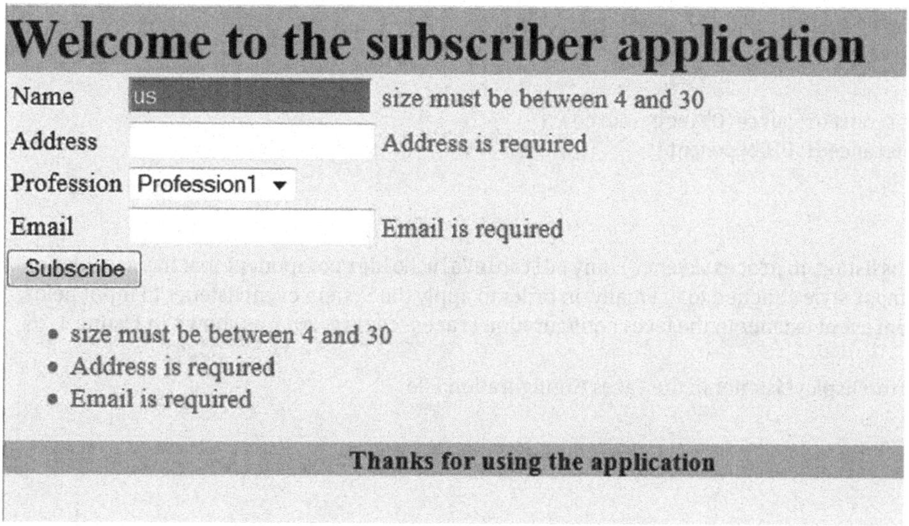

Figure 4-9. *Styling the user name input field when an error occurs*

Installing component System event listener on every input component using `<f:event>` for styling these input elements in case of having errors may not be efficient and will make us have a lot of duplication in all the application forms. So, we need a unified and simple way in our JSF application to control the error display in all of the input field.

In order to unify the control of the error display in all of the input fields, we can create a custom System event listener on `PostValidateEvent` and apply it to all input text elements in the application by setting input text class as the event source. Listing 4-25 shows `ErrorDisplayListener` class (our custom System event listener class).

Listing 4-25. ErrorDisplayListener Class

```
package com.jsfprohtml5.subscriber.model;

import javax.faces.component.EditableValueHolder;
import javax.faces.component.UIComponent;
import javax.faces.event.AbortProcessingException;
import javax.faces.event.SystemEvent;
import javax.faces.event.SystemEventListener;
```

```
public class ErrorDisplayListener implements SystemEventListener {

    @Override
    public void processEvent(SystemEvent event) throws AbortProcessingException {
        UIComponent component = (UIComponent) event.getSource();

        if (component instanceof EditableValueHolder) {
            EditableValueHolder editableValueHolder = (EditableValueHolder) component;

            if (! editableValueHolder.isValid()) {
                component.getAttributes().put("styleClass", "invalidInput");
            } else {
                component.getAttributes().put("styleClass", "");
            }
        }
    }

    @Override
    public boolean isListenerForSource(Object source) {
        return source instanceof UIComponent;
    }
}
```

As shown in the previous listing, in processEvent(), any EditableValueHolder component that has a validation error will have the invalidInput style attached to it. Finally, in order to apply the System event listener to input fields, we need to register the System event listener in the faces configuration (faces-config.xml), as shown in Listing 4-26.

Listing 4-26. Registering ErrorDisplayListener in the Faces Configuration File

```
<faces-config ...>

    <application>
        ...

        <system-event-listener>
            <source-class>javax.faces.component.html.HtmlInputText</source-class>
            <system-event-class>javax.faces.event.PostValidateEvent</system-event-class>
            <system-event-listener-class>com.jsfprohtml5.subscriber.model.ErrorDisplayListener
</system-event-listener-class>
        </system-event-listener>
    </application>

</faces-config>
```

Using the <source-class> element forces the source of postValidateEvent to be (javax.faces.component.html. HtmlInputText), which is the JSF input text element class. After writing and registering our custom System event listener, we will be able to automatically see the styled input elements when we have one or more validation error(s), as shown in Figure 4-10.

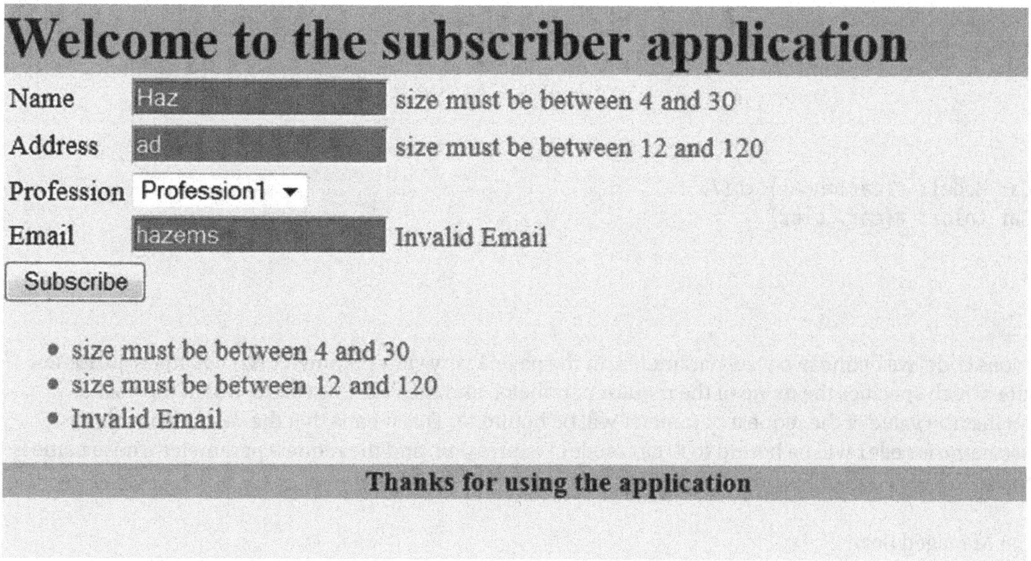

Welcome to the subscriber application

Name	Haz	size must be between 4 and 30
Address	ad	size must be between 12 and 120
Profession	Profession1 ▼	
Email	hazems	Invalid Email

[Subscribe]

- size must be between 4 and 30
- size must be between 12 and 120
- Invalid Email

Thanks for using the application

Figure 4-10. *Styled input elements when we have one or more validation errors*

■ **Note**   The updated applications (first application and subscriber application) are available for download from the book's web site at `http://www.apress.com/9781430250104`; you will be able to find the complete source inside the Chapter4 zip file.

View Parameters

In order to support bookmarkable pages, view parameters are introduced in JSF 2.0 to support having addressable pages. View parameters allow JSF pages to be RESTful, which means that they can be bookmarked by the end user(s) in the browser so that at any time they can get back to use these pages later. View parameters can be created in the JSF Facelets pages using `<f:viewParam>` tag. Listing 4-27 shows how to define `<f:viewParam>` tag inside a JSF page (car.xhtml).

Listing 4-27. Using <f:viewParam> Tag Inside a JSF Page (car.xhtml)

```
<html xmlns="http://www.w3.org/1999/xhtml"
      xmlns:ui="http://java.sun.com/jsf/facelets"
      xmlns:h="http://java.sun.com/jsf/html"
      xmlns:f="http://java.sun.com/jsf/core">

    <f:metadata>
        <f:viewParam name="model" value="#{car.model}"/>
        <f:viewParam name="color" value="#{car.color}"/>
    </f:metadata>
```

```
<h:head>
    <title>Car Information</title>
</h:head>

<h:body>
    <p>
        Car Model: #{car.model} <br/>
        Car Color: #{car.color}
    </p>
</h:body>
</html>
```

In the previous code, we define two view parameters in the page. Every view parameter has two main attributes, the name attribute, which specifies the name of the request parameter, and the value attribute, which represents a value expression that the value of the request parameter will be bound to. This means that the value of the request parameter whose name is model will be bound to #{car.model} expression, and the request parameter whose name is color will be bound to #{car.color} expression. Listing 4-28 shows Car managed bean.

Listing 4-28. Car Managed Bean

```
@ManagedBean
@RequestScoped
public class Car {
    private String model;
    private String color;

    public String getModel() {
        return model;
    }
    public void setModel(String model) {
        this.model = model;
    }

    public String getColor() {
        return color;
    }
    public void setColor(String color) {
        this.color = color;
    }
}
```

After calling car.xhtml page from the browser with the following parameters:

/car.xhtml?model=300D&color=black

This will produce the following content in car.xhtml page:

Car Model: 300D
Car Color: black

■ **Note** It is important to know that `<f:viewParam>` causes a `UIViewParameter` to be attached as metadata for the current view. `UIViewParameter` extends `UIInput`, which means that any actions that one would normally take on a UIInput instance are valid for instances of this class. So you can attach converters, validators, and value change listeners to the `<f:viewParam>` tag.

As shown in the previous tip, we can add both converter and validators to `<f:viewParam>` tag. Let's see how we can validate the view parameters in `car.xhtml` page. Let's modify the `Car` managed bean by adding a new attribute to describe the car number as shown in Listing 4-29.

Listing 4-29. Modifying Car Managed Bean

```
@ManagedBean
@RequestScoped
public class Car {
    //...
    private Long number;

    //...
    public Long getNumber() {
        return number;
    }
    public void setNumber(Long number) {
        this.number = number;
    }
}
```

In order to mandates that all of `Car` attributes are mandatory, then as we do with other `EditableValueHolder` components, we can set `required` attribute to `true`. In order to validate that Car number attribute is a valid number within a specific numeric range, we can use `<f:validateLongRange/>` inside `<f:viewParam>` tag. Listing 4-30 shows how we can validate the view parameters in `car.xhtml` page.

Listing 4-30. Modified car.xhtml Page to Utilize Validation

```
<html xmlns="http://www.w3.org/1999/xhtml"
     xmlns:ui="http://java.sun.com/jsf/facelets"
     xmlns:h="http://java.sun.com/jsf/html"
     xmlns:f="http://java.sun.com/jsf/core">

    <f:metadata>
        <f:viewParam name="model" value="#{car.model}"
                            required="true"
                                requiredMessage="You need to specify car model"/>

        <f:viewParam name="color" value="#{car.color}"
                            required="true"
                                requiredMessage="You need to specify car color"/>
```

```
        <f:viewParam name="number" value="#{car.number}"
                             required="true"
                             requiredMessage="You need to specify car number">

        <f:validateLongRange minimum="1" maximum="9999999999"/>
      </f:viewParam>
    </f:metadata>

    <h:head>
        <title>Car Information</title>
    </h:head>

    <h:body>
        <p>
            <h:outputText  value="Car Model: #{car.model}" rendered="#{car.model ne null}" /> <br/>
            <h:outputText  value="Car Color: #{car.color}" rendered="#{car.color ne null}"/> <br/>
            <h:outputText  value="Car Number: #{car.number}" rendered="#{car.number ne null}"/>
        </p>

        <h:messages  styleClass="errorMessage"/>
    </h:body>
</html>
```

Validation errors will be displayed in <h:messages/>; this can happen when for example the URL does not specify model and color and number parameters or when the number parameter represents an invalid number or out of range number (the assumed range is from 1 to 9999999999).

In order to support browser bookmarkability and search engine web crawlers, JSF 2.0 (and later) provides <h:link> component. If you set includeViewParams attribute of <h:link> component to true, this will generate the page view parameters as part of the generated URL of the <h:link> component. For example, if we added <h:link> component to the car.xhtml page in Listing 4-30 as follows:

<h:link includeViewParams="true" value="Can be bookmarked"/>

This will generate a URL on the following pattern:

<a href="/contextPath/car.xhtml?model=xxx&color=yyy&number=zzz">Can be bookmarked</a>

■ **Note**   Like <h:link> component, <h:button> component has includeViewParams attribute; however, <h:button> generates an HTML button that depends on JavaScript onclick action in order to view target page, which means that it cannot be reached by web search crawlers.

Adding to <h:link> and <h:button>, it is also possible to use includeViewParams parameter inside the JSF action attribute (as part of the JSF action outcome), Listing 4-31 shows a JSF input form in a new page (intro.xhtml) that allows the user to enter the car information, as displayed in Listing 4-30.

Listing 4-31. JSF Input Form for Entering Car Information (intro.xhtml)

```
<h:form>
            <h:panelGrid columns="3">
                <h:outputText value="Model:"></h:outputText>
                <h:inputText id="model"
                            value="#{car.model}"
                            required="true"
                            requiredMessage="You need to specify car model">
                </h:inputText>
                <h:message for="model" styleClass="errorMessage"/>

                <h:outputText value="Color:"></h:outputText>
                <h:inputText id="color"
                            value="#{car.color}"
                            required="true"
                            requiredMessage="You need to specify car color">
                </h:inputText>
                <h:message for="color" styleClass="errorMessage"/>

                <h:outputText value="Car Number:"></h:outputText>
                <h:inputText id="number"
                            value="#{car.number}"
                            required="true"
                            requiredMessage="You need to specify car number">

                    <f:validateLongRange minimum="1" maximum="9999999999"/>
                </h:inputText>
                <h:message for="number" styleClass="errorMessage"/>
            </h:panelGrid>

            <h:commandButton value="View car details"
                            action="car?faces-redirect=true&amp;includeViewParams=true" />

        </h:form>
```

As shown in the bolded lines, in order to allow the JSF command button to navigate to our RESTful page (car.xhtml) in a RESTful way (target page name and parameters will appear in the browser address bar), we need to add the following two parameters to action outcome of UICommand:

1. faces-redirect: setting faces-redirect parameter to true allows the current page to be redirected (not forwarded) to the target page (as we know from Chapter 2).

2. includeViewParams: setting includeViewParams to true inside the action outcome allows ActionSource2 component to include view parameters when performing navigation. Keep in mind that the included view parameters must be declared in the target JSF page, which is (car.xhtml) in our example.

Assuming that valid data are entered in the intro.xhtml page and then the "View car details" button is clicked, the page will be redirected to (car.xhtml) page with the following parameters in the browser address bar:

contextPath/car.xhtml?model=xxx&color=yyy&number=zzz

which will produce the following content in `car.xhtml` page:

Car Model: xxx
Car Color: yyy
Car Number: zzz

■ **Note**   It is important to know that JSF 2.x Facelets is an XML-based view technology. This means that the (&) character is interpreted as start of an XML entity. This results that in order to represent the actual (&) character, you have to use &amp, instead as shown in the last code example.

Summary

In this chapter, you learned in detail the JSF event model. You understood how to work with both action and value change events in JSF application. You now know how to utilize the JSF phase listeners in order to implement goodies in your JSF application such as authorization or logging. You learned the different types of JSF System events and now know how to use both application-level and component-level System events. Finally, you understand how to work with the JSF view parameters in order to make your JSF pages RESTful.

CHAPTER 5

■ ■ ■

JSF 2.2: What's New?

The work on JSF 2.2 started in early 2011, just a couple of months after the second maintenance release of JSF 2.0. After two years of work on the specification and reference implementation (Mojarra 2.2), JSF 2.2 was released in late May 2013. JSF 2.2 is also part of Java EE 7 released in June 2013. JSF 2.2 provides a handful of exciting new features (also known as the big-ticket features), a number of significant improvements, and quite a few specification clarifications and bug fixes. JSF 2.2 is backwards compatible with earlier 2.0 releases. This is great news, as you won't have to rewrite your JSF 2.0 application to support the new features of 2.2. There are a couple of exceptions where you would have to make minor changes to your application.

In this chapter we will present and demonstrate the big-ticket features of JSF 2.2 and touch upon some of the most significant changes. Finally, we will have a look at the changes you would need to implement in your JSF 2.0 application to be fully compatible with JSF 2.2.

For all the details of the JSF 2.2 specification, also known as JSR 344, you can visit the Java Community Process website at `http://jcp.org/en/jsr/detail?id=344`.

Big Ticket Features

JSF 2.2 is a minor upgrade with backwards compatibility to JSF 2.0. It builds on top of the already existing JSF features. However, JSF 2.2 contains four new major features. These are

- HTML5-Friendly Markup: This feature adds HTML5 support to JSF by allowing to pass through arbitrary attributes and elements from JSF components in Facelet views to rendered HTML output.

- Resource Library Contract: This feature builds on top of the templating features provided by Facelets. With resource library contracts, it is possible to supply sets of templates along with the application or in separate jar files included in the class path of the application.

- Faces Flow: This feature is similar to resource library contracts by allowing user flows to be defined and packaged for reuse. A new bean scope is introduced to manage the lifecycle of beans involved in the flows.

- Stateless Views: This feature allows marking views as stateless and thereby transient.

There are many other smaller changes in JSF 2.2, and we have covered the most significant ones in the section following the big-ticket features.

HTML5-Friendly Markup

HTML5 has to be one of the hottest topics at the moment. The trend did not pass by the JSF Reference Group, who prioritized the implementation of features supporting HTML5-friendly markup in JSF 2.2.

Truth be told, the implemented HTML5 support features can also be used in a different context than HTML5. For many years, web designers have used JavaScript frameworks to store application-specific data in custom attributes. For example, a web designer may have chosen to include additional information about an image that is extracted and displayed when the image is clicked (see Listing 5-1).

Listing 5-1. Custom Attribute Containing Data that Could Be Extracted by JavaScript Frameworks

```
<img src="product/1234.png"
     title="Click to see more information"
     data-popup-title="The product is available for shipping within 24 hours" />
```

Until HTML5, custom attributes were nonstandard, and the output was often unpredictable as browsers interpreted them differently. The HTML5 standard introduced a set of new global attributes and elements ensuring browser uniformity in interpreting custom attributes. The majority of the new attributes and elements do not have a JSF equivalent, as the values they carry are not relevant on the server side. JSF 2.2 introduces support for HTML5 markup by providing the ability to *Pass Through* attributes and elements from Facelet views to the rendered HTML code.

■ **Note** Pass Through of attributes and elements is supported only in views written in Facelets and is not available to views written in JSP.

Prior to JSF 2.2, the only way to create custom attributes and elements was to wrap the output in a composite component where the custom attributes and elements were introduced in plain HTML. Listings 5-2 and 5-3 show composite component wrapping custom HTML attributes. The problem with this workaround is that it introduces excessive code, and the outputted code is not stored in the JSF component tree as a component.

Listing 5-2. Composite Component Wrapping Custom Attributes (resources/jsf22/img2.xhtml)

```
<?xml version='1.0' encoding='UTF-8' ?><!DOCTYPE html PUBLIC "-//W3C//DTD XHTML 1.0 Transitional//
EN" "http://www.w3.org/TR/xhtml1/DTD/xhtml1-transitional.dtd">
<html xmlns="http://www.w3.org/1999/xhtml"
      xmlns:cc="http://java.sun.com/jsf/composite">

    <cc:interface>
        <cc:attribute name="src" type="java.lang.String" required="true" />
        <cc:attribute name="title" type="java.lang.String" default="" />
        <cc:attribute name="popupTitle" type="java.lang.String" default="" />
    </cc:interface>

    <cc:implementation>
        <img src="#{cc.attrs.src}"
             title="#{cc.attrs.title}"s
             data-popup-title="#{cc.attrs.popupTitle}" />
    </cc:implementation>
</html>
```

Listing 5-3. Facelets View Using the img2 Composite Component (img2example.xhtml)

```xml
<?xml version='1.0' encoding='UTF-8' ?>
<!DOCTYPE html PUBLIC "-//W3C//DTD XHTML 1.0 Transitional//EN" "http://www.w3.org/TR/xhtml1/DTD/
xhtml1-transitional.dtd">
<html xmlns="http://www.w3.org/1999/xhtml"
      xmlns:h="http://java.sun.com/jsf/html"
      xmlns:jsf22="http://java.sun.com/jsf/composite/jsf22">
    <h:head>
        <title>Example of using img2</title>
    </h:head>
    <h:body>
        <jsf22:img2 src="product/1234.png"
                    title="Click to see more information"
                    popupTitle="The product is available for shipping within 24 hours" />
    </h:body>
</html>
```

In the following sections, you will see how JSF 2.2 has made it easier to output HTML5-friendly markup by introducing the ability to pass through HTML elements and attributes.

Passing Through Attributes

Custom attributes can be outputted in three different ways. The outputs of all three methods are the same, but each method has its own level of greatest convenience as demonstrated in the following.

Method 1: Adding custom attributes one at a time using <f:passThroughAttribute />

JSF 2.2 introduces a new tag similar to <f:param /> called <f:passThroughAttribute />. The tag can be nested inside any UIComponent and has two attributes: name and value. Name contains the name of the custom attribute you want to add to the parent UIComponent, and value contains the value that should be stored in the custom attribute with the given name. An example can be seen in Listing 5-4.

Listing 5-4. Adding Two Custom Attributes to a UIComponent Using <f:PassThroughAttribute />

```xml
<h:graphicImage value="product/1234.png"
                title="Click to see more information">
    <f:passThroughAttribute name="data-popup-title"
                            value="The product is available for shipping within 24 hours" />
    <f:passThroughAttribute name="data-product-id"
                            value="1234" />
</h:graphicImage>
```

Method 2: Adding custom attributes contained in a map using <f:passThroughAttributes />

Method 1 is good for adding a few attributes, but if you have many attributes that you must add to a component and the values are determined on the server side, you can use <f:passThroughAttributes /> and provide a map of attributes using the value attribute. Listing 5-5 and 5-6 show how to reference a map of attributes from a managed bean.

Listing 5-5. Adding a Map of Attributes to a UIComponent Using <f:PassThroughAttributes />

```
<h:graphicImage value="product/1234.png"
                title="Click to see more information">
    <f:passThroughAttributes value="#{productDisplay.productAttributes}" />
</h:graphicImage>
```

Listing 5-6. ViewScoped Managed Bean Exposing a Map of Product Attributes that Can Be Consumed by <f:PassThroughAttributes />

```
@ManagedBean
@ViewScoped
public class ProductDisplay {

    private Map<String, Object> attributes;

    public Map<String, Object> getProductAttributes() {
        if (this.attributes == null) {
            this.attributes = new HashMap<>();
            this.attributes.put("data-popup-title", "Click to see more information");
            this.attributes.put("data-product-id", "1234");
            this.attributes.put("data-product-name", "Blu-ray Player");
            this.attributes.put("data-product-desc", "Complimment your entertainment...");
        }
        return this.attributes;
    }
}
```

Method 3: Adding custom attributes to UIComponents directly using prefixed attributes

As an alternative to method 1, you can add the custom attributes directly to a UIComponent using a prefixed attribute. The prefix of the attribute is p, and the XML namespace URI is http://xmlns.jcp.org/jsf/passthrough. This method may seem more natural to some, as you are adding the attributes directly on the UIComponent without including any nested tags, see Listing 5-7.

Listing 5-7. Adding Custom Attributes Using Prefixed Attributes

```
<?xml version='1.0' encoding='UTF-8' ?>
<!DOCTYPE html PUBLIC "-//W3C//DTD XHTML 1.0 Transitional//EN"
"http://www.w3.org/TR/xhtml1/DTD/xhtml1-transitional.dtd">
<html xmlns="http://www.w3.org/1999/xhtml"
      xmlns:h="http://xmlns.jcp.org/jsf/html"
      xmlns:p="http://xmlns.jcp.org/jsf/passthrough">
    <h:body>
        <h:graphicImage value="product/1234.png"
                        title="Click to see more information"
                        p:data-popup-title="Available for shipping within 24 hours"
                        p:data-product-id="1234" />
    </h:body>
</html>
```

Passing Through Elements

HTML5 introduces new elements that do not have JSF counterparts such as <section /> and <meter />. To avoid the need for page authors to revert back to the work-around of writing composite components, an attribute namespace (jsf) was introduced. The jsf namespace contains the attributes normally found on a UIComponent. When using the jsf namespace, Facelets detects that you want to treat the tag as a UIComponent and maps it accordingly. In Listing 5-8 the <progress> tag is converted to a UIComponent by using the jsf:id attribute.

Listing 5-8. Passing Through Elements Using the jsf Attribute Namespace

```xml
<?xml version='1.0' encoding='UTF-8' ?>
<!DOCTYPE html PUBLIC "-//W3C//DTD XHTML 1.0 Transitional//EN"
"http://www.w3.org/TR/xhtml1/DTD/xhtml1-transitional.dtd">
<html xmlns="http://www.w3.org/1999/xhtml"
      xmlns:h="http://xmlns.jcp.org/jsf/html"
      xmlns:jsf="http://xmlns.jcp.org/jsf">
    <h:body>
        <h:form>
            <progress jsf:id="progressbar"
                      value="#{imageGeneration.progress}"
                      max="100" />
        </h:form>
    </h:body>
</html>
```

Technically it is the Facelets TagDecorator that is responsible for treating custom elements as UIComponents. In some situations the TagDecorator will recognize the exactly equivalent UIComponent of the HTML tag. In Listing 5-9, the HTML tag and the JSF tag will produce the same output and component tree. This is a great addition to JSF if you prefer to write your views as close to HTML as possible.

Listing 5-9. Automatic Mapping Between HTML and JSF Tags

```xml
<?xml version='1.0' encoding='UTF-8' ?>
<!DOCTYPE html PUBLIC "-//W3C//DTD XHTML 1.0 Transitional//EN"
"http://www.w3.org/TR/xhtml1/DTD/xhtml1-transitional.dtd">
<html xmlns="http://www.w3.org/1999/xhtml"
      xmlns:h="http://xmlns.jcp.org/jsf/html"
      xmlns:jsf="http://xmlns.jcp.org/jsf">
    <h:body>
        <h:form>
            <input type="text" jsf:value="#{registration.firstName}" />
            <h:inputText value="#{registration.lastName}" />
        </h:form>
    </h:body>
</html>
```

Resource Library Contracts

JSF 2.0 introduced the resource library, where cascading style sheets, javascripts, images, and composite components resided in the resources/ directory or were packaged in the META-INF/resources directory of a JAR file. Resource library contracts take this feature a step further by introducing the possibility of having multiple resource libraries.

Using resource library contracts, you can map templates to specific views in your application. You could for example use separate templates and resources for anonymous and authenticated users or for different sections of your application. Like normal resources, you can include resource library contracts in your application in the `contracts/` directory or by packaging the contracts in a JAR file in the `META-INF/contracts` directory. Place the JAR file in the `WEB-INF/lib` directory and it will automatically be discovered by the application.

■ **Tip** To speed up discovery of resource library contracts, place a file named `javax.faces.contract.xml` inside the directory containing the contract. Currently the file doesn't have any contents, but that may change with an upcoming version.

There are two methods of using contracts. The first method will automatically map contracts on views through URL patterns. The second method explicitly declares the contract in the view. The methods can be combined to achieve maximum flexibility. First, we will look at how to create resource library contracts; then, we will look at the two methods for applying them in an application.

The goal of resource library contracts is to make available a set of templates that can be reused by template clients that are unaware of the exact template being used from the available resource library contracts. The resource library contracts should therefore use identical template and content region names. That is, template files must have the same file name, and the `<ui:insert />` tags must use the same names.

As an example we will create two contracts in an application. The first contract is implemented in Listings 5-10 and 5-11, and the second contract is implemented in Listings 5-12 and 5-13. The difference in the two templates is the color scheme and help texts.

Listing 5-10. File Structure of the "Basic" Resource Library Contract in the Application Directory

```
| contracts/
| contracts/basic/page-template.xhtml
| contracts/basic/layout.css
| contracts/basic/page.css
```

Listing 5-11. Contents of contracts/basic/page-template.xhtml

```
<?xml version='1.0' encoding='UTF-8' ?>
<!DOCTYPE html PUBLIC "-//W3C//DTD XHTML 1.0 Transitional//EN"
"http://www.w3.org/TR/xhtml1/DTD/xhtml1-transitional.dtd">
<html xmlns="http://www.w3.org/1999/xhtml"
    xmlns:p="http://xmlns.jcp.org/jsf/passthrough"
    xmlns:jsf="http://xmlns.jcp.org/jsf"
    xmlns:ui="http://xmlns.jcp.org/jsf/facelets"
    xmlns:h="http://xmlns.jcp.org/jsf/html">

    <h:head>
        <h:outputStylesheet name="page.css" />
        <h:outputStylesheet name="layout.css" />
        <title><ui:insert name="page-title" /></title>
    </h:head>

    <h:body>
        <div id="top" class="top">
            <ui:insert name="top" />
        </div>
```

```
        <div id="content" class="center_content">
            <ui:insert name="content" />
        </div>
    </h:body>
</html>
```

Listing 5-12. File Structure Resource Library Contracts After Adding a "Basic-Plus" Contract

```
| contracts/
| contracts/basic/page-template.xhtml
| contracts/basic/layout.css
| contracts/basic/page.css
| contracts/basic-plus/page-template.xhtml
| contracts/basic-plus/layout.css
| contracts/basic-plus/page.css
| contracts/basic-plus/logo.png
```

Listing 5-13. Contents of contracts/basic-plus/page-template.xhtml

```
<?xml version='1.0' encoding='UTF-8' ?>
<!DOCTYPE html PUBLIC "-//W3C//DTD XHTML 1.0 Transitional//EN"
"http://www.w3.org/TR/xhtml1/DTD/xhtml1-transitional.dtd">
<html xmlns="http://www.w3.org/1999/xhtml"
    xmlns:p="http://xmlns.jcp.org/jsf/passthrough"
    xmlns:jsf="http://xmlns.jcp.org/jsf"
    xmlns:ui="http://xmlns.jcp.org/jsf/facelets"
    xmlns:h="http://xmlns.jcp.org/jsf/html">

    <h:head>
        <h:outputStylesheet name="page.css" />
        <h:outputStylesheet name="layout.css" />
        <title><ui:insert name="page-title" /></title>
    </h:head>

    <h:body>
        <div id="top" class="top">
           <h:graphicImage id="logo" name="logo.png" />
            <ui:insert name="top" />
        </div>

        <div id="help" class="left">
            Welcome to JSF 2.2. This example demonstrates how to use Resource Library Contracts.
        </div>

        <div id="content" class="right ">
            <ui:insert name="content" />
        </div>

        <div id="top" class="top">
           You can find more information about JSF 2.2 at the
           <a href="http://jcp.org/en/jsr/detail?id=344">JCP website</a>
        </div>
    </h:body>
</html>
```

As you can see from Listing 5-11, the resource library contract template is exactly like a normal Facelets template. Since this template will be the basis of our contract, we must note down and reuse the template file name as well as the content regions. That is, our template file must be named page-template.xhtml and we must stick to using `<ui:insert name="page-title" />` to insert the title of the page, `<ui:insert name="top" />` to insert the header of the page, and `<ui:insert name="content" />` to insert the content of the page. You are free to change everything in the resource library contract including style sheets and images. The unique name of our resource library contract is the name of the directory under /contracts, that is, basic. To create another resource library contract, simply create a directory under /contracts with a unique name containing templates with the same name. Listing 5-12 shows the structure of the contracts directory after creating the basic-plus contract.

As you can see in Listing 5-13, the template name is the same (page-template.xhtml) and the content regions are the same (page-title, top, content). Both basic and basic-plus follow the same contract and can be used by the same template client.

The resource library contracts are in place and ready for use.

Method 1: Mapping contracts on views through URL patterns

You can specify which contract to use through URL patterns. This is useful when you want to apply different resource libraries to separate sections or access levels. For example, you may want to apply a separate resource libraries to anonymous users and administrators. You can map resource library contracts to views in faces-config.xml inside the applications tag.

In Listing 5-14, the basic resource library contract is applied when accessing views under /admin. All other views use the basic-plus resource library, which contains more help information.

Listing 5-14. Applying Separate Contracts to Views Accessed Through /admin/* and the Rest of the Views

```
<?xml version='1.0' encoding='UTF-8'?>
<faces-config version="2.2"
              xmlns="http://xmlns.jcp.org/xml/ns/javaee"
              xmlns:xsi="http://www.w3.org/2001/XMLSchema-instance"
              xsi:schemaLocation="http://xmlns.jcp.org/xml/ns/javaee
http://xmlns.jcp.org/xml/ns/javaee/web-facesconfig_2_2.xsd">

    <application>

        <resource-library-contracts>

            <contract-mapping>
                <url-pattern>/admin/*</url-pattern>
                <contracts>basic</contracts>
            </contract-mapping>

            <contract-mapping>
                <url-pattern>*</url-pattern>
                <contracts>basic-plus</contracts>
            </contract-mapping>

        </resource-library-contracts>

    </application>
</faces-config>
```

■ **Tip** It is possible to map multiple contracts to a single mapping. In that case, it will go through each contract sequentially to look for the required templates. Once a template has been found it will stop processing the other contracts.

Method 2: Specifying the contracts on each view

By specifying the contract on each view you can make your application skinnable by the user. That is, you can allow the user to select which contract to apply for your application. You apply contracts to template clients by enclosing the view in an <f:view /> tag where you specify the name of the contract to apply in the contracts attributes, e.g. <f:view contracts="basic">. You can replace the explicit declaration of the view contract but using an EL binding, e.g. <f:view contracts="#{userSession.contract}">, as shown in Listings 5-15 and 5-16.

Listing 5-15. Allowing the User to Select the Contract to Apply to the View

```
<?xml version='1.0' encoding='UTF-8' ?>
<!DOCTYPE html PUBLIC "-//W3C//DTD XHTML 1.0 Transitional//EN"
"http://www.w3.org/TR/xhtml1/DTD/xhtml1-transitional.dtd">
<html xmlns="http://www.w3.org/1999/xhtml"
      xmlns:h="http://xmlns.jcp.org/jsf/html"
      xmlns:ui="http://xmlns.jcp.org/jsf/facelets"
      xmlns:f="http://xmlns.jcp.org/jsf/core"
      xmlns:p="http://xmlns.jcp.org/jsf/passthrough">
    <f:view contracts="#{userSession.contract}">
        <ui:composition template="/page-template.xhtml">
            <ui:define name="page-title">Welcome to JSF 2.2</ui:define>
            <ui:define name="content">
                <h:form>
                    Select a template
                    <h:selectOneRadio value="#{userSession.contract}" layout="pageDirection"
required="true">
                        <f:selectItem itemValue="basic" itemLabel="Basic" />
                        <f:selectItem itemValue="basic-plus" itemLabel="Basic Plus" />
                    </h:selectOneRadio>
                    <h:commandButton value="Save" />
                </h:form>
            </ui:define>
            <ui:define name="top">Template: #{userSession.contract}</ui:define>
        </ui:composition>
    </f:view>
</html>
```

Listing 5-16. Session-Scoped Managed Bean Used for Storing the Selected Contract

```
import javax.faces.bean.ManagedBean;
import javax.faces.bean.SessionScoped;

@ManagedBean
@SessionScoped
public class UserSession {
```

```
    private String contract = "basic";

    public String getContract() {
        return contract;
    }

    public void setContract(String contract) {
        this.contract = contract;
    }
}
```

Listing 5-16 could be extended to pick the selected contract from a cookie or from the database so that the user would not have to select the contract to apply every time he uses the application.

The method to use for mapping contracts to views depends on your application requirements. You can mix the two methods to achieve maximum flexibility.

Faces Flows

Since the introduction of JavaServer Faces, a consistent complaint by developers has been the lack of support for a scope that covers a user flow such as a wizard and multistep sign-up form. In JSF 2.0 the @ViewScope annotation was introduced to support variable persistence while staying in the same view. @ConversationScoped was introduced for CDI (Component Dependency Injection) beans in JSF 2.0, and by injecting the javax.enterprise.context.Conversation interface into a managed bean it was possible to start and end long-running conversations. With @ViewScope and @ConversationScoped scopes, you can implement multistep sign-up forms and wizards, but once implemented you find that the final product is rather disintegrated and not easy to reuse. Faces flows deals with these shortcomings by providing a fully integrated solution where you can specify multiple user flows in a flow definition supported by managed beans annotated with @FlowScoped and with the ability to package flows in separate directories and JAR. Flows can also interact using inbound and outbound parameters.

■ **Note**   @FlowScoped is a CDI scope and you must therefore enable CDI in your application by including beans.xml in the WEB-INF/ directory or in the META-INF/ directory if the flow is packaged in JAR.

Flow definitions

You can define flows either in XML files (residing with the other flow files suffixed -flow.xml) or in a class annotated with @FlowDefinition. In classes annotated with @FlowDefinition you specify the flow using the FlowBuilder API, whereas the XML file defines the flow using the http://xmlns.jcp.org/jsf/flow XML namespace and schema. The benefit of using the FlowBuilder is that you have full programmatic control of how the flow is defined. That is, you can build your flows based on runtime information. The disadvantage is that it is much more difficult to quickly get overview of the flow simply by looking at the code, unlike the XML version. Listing 5-17 shows a flow definition expressed in XML.

Listing 5-17. Flow Definition in XML

```
<!DOCTYPE html>

<html xmlns="http://www.w3.org/1999/xhtml"
      xmlns:f="http://java.sun.com/jsf/core"
      xmlns:j="http://java.sun.com/jsf/flow">

    <f:metadata>

        <j:faces-flow-definition id="newEntryFlow">

            <!-- Method to execute when the flow is initialized -->
            <j:initializer>#{addressBook.newEntry}</j:initializer>

            <!-- Specifies the first node of the flow -->
            <j:start-node>newEntryStart</j:start-node>

            <!-- Using a switch you can dynamically determine the next node -->
            <j:switch id="newEntryStart">

                <!-- Go to newEntryHelp if this is the first time the user
                     is using the wizard -->
                <j:navigation-case>
                    <j:if>#{addressBook.newEntryFirstTime}</j:if>
                    <j:from-outcome>newEntryHelp</j:from-outcome>
                </j:navigation-case>

                <!-- Go to basicDetails if this is not the first time that
                     the user has used the wizard -->
                <j:navigation-case>
                    <j:if>#{!addressBook.newEntryFirstTime}</j:if>
                    <j:from-outcome>basicDetails</j:from-outcome>
                </j:navigation-case>
            </j:switch>

             <j:view id="newEntryHelp">
                <j:vdl-document>newEntryHelp.xhtml</j:vdl-document>
            </j:view>

            <j:view id="basicDetails">
                <j:vdl-document>create-entry-1.xhtml</j:vdl-document>
            </j:view>

            <j:view id="contactDetails">
                <j:vdl-document>create-entry-2.xhtml</j:vdl-document>
            </j:view>

            <j:view id="contactPhoto">
                <j:vdl-document>create-entry-3.xhtml</j:vdl-document>
            </j:view>
```

```
            <!-- The flow can end by navigating to the cancel flow -->
            <j:faces-flow-return id="cancel">
                  <j:navigation-case>
                        <j:from-outcome>/cancel</j:from-outcome>
                  </j:navigation-case>
            </j:faces-flow-return>

            <!-- Method to execute when the flow has ended -->
            <j:finalizer>#{addressBook.newEntryFinished}</j:finalizer>

        </j:faces-flow-definition>

    </f:metadata>
</html>
```

Starting and ending flows

You start a flow by calling the ID of the flow in an action. You end a flow by returning the outcome defined in faces-flow-return in the flow definition. Listing 5-18 shows how to use a command link to start and end a flow.

Listing 5-18. You Can Start a New Flow by Setting the Flow ID as the Action of a UICommand

```
<h:commandLink value="Click to add a new entry in the address book" action="newEntryFlow" />
<h:commandLink value="Cancel creating a new entry" action="/cancel" />
```

Stepping through the flow and storing data

There are two ways of storing flow data. You can either store it as properties on CDI beans annotated with @FlowScoped, as shown in Listing 5-19, or you can add the data to a flow map that keeps whatever data you put into it, as shown in Listing 5-20. Once the flow ends the map will be cleared.

Listing 5-19. FlowScoped Bean Controlling Logic and Storing Data

```
@Named
@FlowScoped(id = "newEntryFlow")
public class AddressBook implements Serializable {

    private AddressBookEntry entry;

    /**
     * Initialiser for the flow.
     */
    public void newEntry() {
       this.entry = new AddressBookEntry();
       ...
    }

    /**
     * Determines if this is the first time the new entry flow is being used.
     */
```

```
    public boolean isNewEntryFirstTime() {
        ...
    }

    public AddressBookEntry getEntry() {
        return this.entry;
    }
}
```

Listing 5-20. flowScope Can Be Used to Store Any Kind of Object During the Flow

```
<!DOCTYPE html>
<html xmlns="http://www.w3.org/1999/xhtml"
      xmlns:h="http://xmlns.jcp.org/jsf/html">

    <head>
        <title>Enter your name</title>
    </head>
    <body>
        <h:form>

            <h:outputLabel for="firstName" value="First name: " />
            <h:inputText id="firstName" value="#{flowScope.firstName}" />
            <h:outputLabel for="LastName" value="Last name: " />
            <h:inputText id="lastName" value="#{flowScope.lastName}" />

            <h:commandButton value="Next" action="contactDetails" />
            <h:commandButton value="Cancel" action="cancel" />
        </h:form>
    </body>
</html>
```

Packaging

The flow resources can either reside inside your web application in a directory under the web root as shown in Listing 5-21, or it can be packaged in a JAR file that is then placed in /WEB-INF/lib as shown in Listing 5-22. The page author does not need to worry about how the flow resources are packaged with the application. Flow resources are referenced the same regardless of how they are packaged.

Listing 5-21. File Layout of Several Flows Residing Inside the Web Application

```
| newEntryFlow/newEntryFlow-flow.xml
| newEntryFlow/newEntryHelp.xhtml
| newEntryFlow/create-entry-1.xhtml
| newEntryFlow/create-entry-2.xhtml
| newEntryFlow/create-entry-3.xhtml
| modifyEntryFlow/modifyEntryFlow-flow.xml
| modifyEntryFlow/modifyEntryHelp.xhtml
| modifyEntryFlow/modify-entry-1.xhtml
| modifyEntryFlow/modify-entry-2.xhtml
| modifyEntryFlow/modify-entry-3.xhtml
```

Listing 5-22. File Layout of a Flow Residing Inside a JAR File

```
| META-INF/flows/beans.xml
| META-INF/faces-config.xml
| META-INF/flows/newEntryFlow/newEntryFlow-flow.xml
| META-INF/flows/newEntryFlow/newEntryHelp.xhtml
| META-INF/flows/newEntryFlow/create-entry-1.xhtml
| META-INF/flows/newEntryFlow/create-entry-2.xhtml
| META-INF/flows/newEntryFlow/create-entry-3.xhtml
| META-INF/flows/modifyEntryFlow/modifyEntryFlow-flow.xml
| META-INF/flows/modifyEntryFlow/modifyEntryHelp.xhtml
| META-INF/flows/modifyEntryFlow/modify-entry-1.xhtml
| META-INF/flows/modifyEntryFlow/modify-entry-2.xhtml
| META-INF/flows/modifyEntryFlow/modify-entry-3.xhtml
| myflow/NewEntryFlow.class
| myflow/ModifyEntryFlow.class
```

Stateless Views

When requesting a view, JSF normally checks if a copy of the state is available (on either the server or client depending on the value of the `javax.faces.STATE_SAVING_METHOD` context parameter). If the requested view doesn't exist, it is created and details about the components in the view are stored for later retrieval and processing. In some situations the view may have expired and you will receive the dreaded `ViewExpiredException`. All the processing involved in saving and restoring views contributes to unwanted overhead in high-load applications. JSF 2.2 introduced a simple but powerful feature called stateless views. With stateless views you can specify views whose state should not be managed. Instead, the state of the view is set to the initial state every time it is requested. You mark a view as stateless by setting the `transient` attribute on `<f:view />` to true. When using stateless views you should be careful not to depend on any state-based scope such as `@ViewScope` and `@SessionScope`. Using these scopes in conjunction with stateless views will end up giving you unpredictable behaviors. With JSF Development mode enabled, you will see warnings in the bottom of the page when you combine state-based scopes and stateless views. Note that stateless views do not mean that you can store data in your backing beans. In fact, you must store your data in managed beans if you want to persist any data while using stateless views. A classical example of a stateless view is a login page. The login page doesn't keep track of state and only needs to store information such as username and password in a managed bean (with container-managed security not even a managed bean is necessary for persisting the user input). Listing 5-23 shows an example of a stateless view for a newsletter sign-up page. Once the page has been submitted there is no need to retain the view and it is therefore a good candidate for a stateless view.

Listing 5-23. Stateless View for Signing Up for a Newsletter

```
<?xml version='1.0' encoding='UTF-8' ?>
<!DOCTYPE html PUBLIC "-//W3C//DTD XHTML 1.0 Transitional//EN"
"http://www.w3.org/TR/xhtml1/DTD/xhtml1-transitional.dtd">
<html xmlns="http://www.w3.org/1999/xhtml"
      xmlns:h="http://xmlns.jcp.org/jsf/html"
      xmlns:ui="http://xmlns.jcp.org/jsf/facelets"
      xmlns:f="http://xmlns.jcp.org/jsf/core">
    <f:view transient="true">
        <ui:composition template="/page-template.xhtml">
            <ui:define name="page-title">Newsletter Sign-up</ui:define>
            <ui:define name="content">
```

```
            <h:form>
                Your e-mail address:
                <h:inputText value="#{newsletterSubscription.email}" />
                <h:commandButton action="#{newsletterSubscription.subscribe}"
                                 value="Subscribe" />
                <h:commandButton action="#{newsletterSubscription.unsubscribe}"
                                 value="Unsubscribe" />
            </h:form>
        </ui:define>

    </ui:composition>
  </f:view>
</html>
```

▓ **Caution**   With stateless views being a brand-new feature, not all components have been thoroughly tested and in some situations this may result in unpredictable behaviors. You should be particularly careful when using stateless views with third-party JSF component libraries.

Other Significant Changes

On top of the big-ticket features there were also many smaller enhancements. The following is a summary of the most significant smaller changes.

UIData supports the Collection Interface rather than List

Components deriving from UIData now support java.util.Collections as the internal data model. Prior to JSF 2.2 java.util.List was the only supported collection. This change is a recognition that ORM typically uses the java.util.Set collection for mapping associated data.

WAI-ARIA support

JSF 2.2 has implemented the role attribute on HTML components to support the Web Accessibility Initiative—Accessible Rich Internet Application Suite (WAI-ARIA). The role attribute is used to describe the purpose of an HTML tag. More information about WAI-ARIA can be found at http://www.w3.org/WAI/intro/aria. Listing 5-24 shows an example of how the role attribute can be used to add meaning to a panel grid.

Listing 5-24. Indicating that the panelGrid (Table) Is a Menu Containing Options

```
<h:panelGrid role="menu">
    <h:commandLink role="menuitem" value="Home" action="/home" />
    <h:commandLink role="menuitem" value="Registration" action="/registration" />
    ...
</h:panelGrid>
```

<f:viewAction />

A new view metadata tag, <f:viewAction />, was introduced in JSF 2.2. The purpose of the tag is to allow for preprocessing before the response is rendered. Preprocessing may include fetching data from the database or checking conditions that alter the navigation flow. As an example you could use the viewAction to load the entity to display from the database. If the requested entity does not exist in the database, you can redirect the user to a view stating that the file no longer exists. Listing 5-25 shows a Facelets file that has a viewAction that loads a record upon viewing the page.

Listing 5-25. Facelet View Using f:viewAction to Load the Record to Display

```
<?xml version='1.0' encoding='UTF-8' ?>
<!DOCTYPE html PUBLIC "-//W3C//DTD XHTML 1.0 Transitional//EN"
"http://www.w3.org/TR/xhtml1/DTD/xhtml1-transitional.dtd">
<html xmlns="http://www.w3.org/1999/xhtml"
      xmlns:h="http://java.sun.com/jsf/html"
      xmlns:f="http://java.sun.com/jsf/core">
    <f:view>
        <f:metadata>
            <f:viewParam name="id" value="#{recordDisplay.id}" />
            <f:viewAction execute="#{recordDisplay.load}" onPostback="false" />
        </f:metadata>
    </f:view>
    <h:head>
        <title>View Record #{recordDisplay.id}</title>
    </h:head>
    <h:body>
        <h1>Record ##{recordDisplay.id}</h1>
        <h:panelGrid columns="2">
            <h:outputText value="Name:" />
            <h:outputText value="#{recordDisplay.record.name}" />
            <h:outputText value="Description:" />
            <h:outputText value="#{recordDisplay.record.description}" escape="false" />
        </h:panelGrid>

    </h:body>
</html>
```

Listing 5-26 contains the navigation rule that should be used when trying to access a non-existing record. The rule states that if false is returned the browser should be redirected to the /not-found.xhtml file.

Listing 5-26. Navigation Case in faces-config.xml that Redirects the User if the Entity Could Not Be Loaded

```
<faces-config>
    <navigation-rule>
        <navigation-case>
            <from-action>#{recordDisplay.load}</from-action>
            <from-outcome>false</from-outcome>
            <to-view-id>/not-found.xhtml</to-view-id>
            <redirect />
        </navigation-case>
    </navigation-rule>
</faces-config>
```

Listing 5-27 is the managed bean that contains the logic that is used in the navigation rule. It is also the backing bean for the Facelets view being accessed.

Listing 5-27. Action Method Used to Load the Record and Signal If the Record Was Loaded

```java
@ManagedBean
@RequestScoped
public class RecordDisplay {

    @EJB private RecordService recordService;
    private Long id;
    private Record record;

    public Long getId() {
        return id;
    }

    /**
     * Used by f:viewParam to set the ID of the record to load.
     *
     * @param id Unique identifier of the record to load
     */
    public void setId(Long id) {
        this.id = id;
    }

    /**
     * Loads the record with the ID specified in the viewParam.
     *
     * @return true if the record was loaded successfully, otherwise false if it wasn't found
     */
    public boolean load() {
        try {
            record = recordService.findById(this.id);
            return true;
        } catch (EntityNotFoundException ex) {
            return false;
        }
    }
}
```

The feature is very similar to `<f:event type="preRenderView" />` with a couple of differences:

- Using `<f:event type="preRenderView" />`, it is the responsibility of the developer to redirect the navigation in case the preconditions fail.

- `<f:event type="preRenderView" />` is executed after the component tree has been generated (i.e., in the Render Response phase), whereas `<f:viewAction />` is executed before the component tree has been generated (i.e. in the Application phase).

File Upload

Finally, after almost ten years of no standard file upload component in JSF, the `<h:inputFile />` component was introduced by JSF 2.2. Prior to JSF 2.2 the developer would have to develop his own file upload component or use component libraries such as RichFaces or PrimeFaces. As an added bonus in JSF 2.2, the file upload component also supports file upload in Ajax requests.

Using the component is fairly simple. Include the `<h:inputFile />` tag inside a form with the enctype set to "multipart/form-data". Set the value attribute of the `<h:inputFile />` to an object of type `javax.servlet.http.Part`. Upon submitting the form, the file selected by the user is transferred to the server and a reference to the file is available in the `Part` object through the `getInputStream()` method. You can add validation to the file upload using the validator attribute on the `<h:inputFile />` tag. In the validator you can check the file size, content type, file name, file contents, and any other header sent along with the file in the request. To upload a file in an Ajax request, simply add the `<f:ajax />` tag to the `<h:commandButton />` submitting the form.

As an example, Listing 5-28 shows a form containing the inputFile component. The example uses Ajax to upload the file by including the f:ajax component inside the commandButton that initiates the upload.

Listing 5-28. Form for Uploading a Photo into a Managed Bean

```
<h:form id="frm-photo-upload" enctype="multipart/form-data">
    <h:outputLabel for="photo" value="Please select your photo and click Upload Photo" />
    <h:inputFile id="photo" value="#{myProfile.photo}" validator="#{myProfile.validatePhoto}" />
    <h:commandButton value="Upload Photo" action="#{myProfile.uploadPhoto}">
        <!-- Remove the f:ajax tag for plain old file upload -->
        <f:ajax execute="photo" render="@all" />
    </h:commandButton>
    <h:messages />
</h:form>
```

Listing 5-29 is the managed bean for the upload form. It contains methods for validating that the file upload is an image and below 2 MB in size as well as an upload method where the contents of the file uploaded is extracted using the IOUtils class from the Apache Commons IO project.[1]

Listing 5-29. Managed Bean Receiving and Processing the File Upload

```
import java.io.IOException;
import javax.ejb.EJB;
import javax.faces.bean.ManagedBean;
import javax.faces.bean.RequestScoped;
import javax.servlet.http.Part;
import org.apache.commons.io.IOUtils;

@ManagedBean
@RequestScoped
public class MyProfile {
    @EJB    private UserProfileService userProfileService;
    private UserProfile userProfile;
    private Part photo;
```

---

[1]The Apache Commons IO project is a collection of libraries for working with IO functionality. The project can be found at this URL: http://commons.apache.org/proper/commons-io/

```java
public String uploadPhoto() throws IOException {
    // Uploading file. You don't have to do anything here, but you could
    // use it for post processing.  Don't use this method for validating
    // the uploaded file.

    byte[] photoContents = IOUtils.toByteArray(photo.getInputStream());
    userProfileService.savePhoto(userProfile, photoContents);

    FacesContext.getCurrentInstance().addMessage("frm-photo-upload",
        new FacesMessage(FacesMessage.SEVERITY_INFO, "Photo uploaded successfully",
            "Name: " + photo.getName() + " Size: " + (photo.getSize()/1024) + " KB"));

    return "/photo-uploaded";
}

/**
 * Validator for checking that the file uploaded is a photo and that the file
 * size is less than 2MB.
 */
public void validatePhoto(FacesContext ctx, UIComponent comp, Object value)  {
    // List of possible validation errors
    List<FacesMessage> msgs = new ArrayList<>();

    // Retrieve the uploaded file from passed value object
    Part photo = (Part)value;

    // Ensure that the file is an image
    if (!"image/".startsWith(file.getContentType())) {
        msgs.add(new FacesMessage("The uploaded file must be an image"));
    }

    // Ensure that the file is less than 2 MB
    if (file.getSize() > 2048) {
        msgs.add(new FacesMessage("The uploaded file is larger than 2MB"));
    }

    // Determine if a validation exception should be thrown
    if (!msgs.isEmpty()) {
        throw new ValidatorException(msgs);
    }
}

public Part getPhoto() {
    return photo;
}

public void setPhoto(Part photo) {
    this.photo = photo;
}

public UserProfile getUserProfile() {
    return this.userProfile;
}
```

```
    public void setUserProfile(UserProfile userProfile) {
        this.userProfile = userProfile;
    }
}
```

Ajax request delay

A delay attribute was added to the <f:ajax /> tag in JSF 2.2. The attribute takes an integer containing the number of milliseconds to wait until the Ajax request is executed. This is very useful when you use Ajax with keyboard input from the user. Rather than executing the requests immediately as the user enters a key, it waits a number of milliseconds to see if another key is entered before executing the request. If another key is entered, prior Ajax requests are cancelled and only the last request is executed. Listing 5-30 shows an example of Ajax requests being delayed by 1.5 seconds after pressing a key, giving time to the user to finish typing before dispatching the request.

Listing 5-30. Delaying the Ajax Request by 1.5 Seconds

```
<h:inputText value="#{registrationBean.username}" >
    <f:ajax event="keyup" delay="1500" render="confirmation" />
</h:inputText>
<h:outputText id="confirmation" value="#{registrationBean.confirmationMsg}" />
```

New XML namespaces

As you may have noticed in the previous examples, JSF 2.2 has introduced new XML namespaces. The old namespaces started with http://java.sun.com, whereas the new namespaces start with http://xmlns.jcp.org. The old namespaces will still work for now, but it looks like they will be removed in future versions. The new XML namespaces are listed in Table 5-1.

Table 5-1. *New XML Namespaces for JSF Libraries*

Library	Old URI	New URI
Composite Components	http://java.sun.com/jsf/composite	http://xmlns.jcp.org/jsf/composite
Faces Core	http://java.sun.com/jsf/core	http://xmlns.jcp.org/jsf/core
Faces HTML	http://java.sun.com/jsf/html	http://xmlns.jcp.org/jsf/html
JSTL Core	http://java.sun.com/jsp/jstl/core	http://xmlns.jcp.org/jsp/jstl/core
JSTL Functions	http://java.sun.com/jsp/jstl/functions	http://xmlns.jcp.org/jsp/jstl/functions
Facelets Templating	http://java.sun.com/jsf/facelets	http://xmlns.jcp.org/jsf/facelets
Pass Through Attributes	http://java.sun.com/jsf/passthrough	http://xmlns.jcp.org/jsf/passthrough
Pass Through Elements	http://java.sun.com/jsf	http://xmlns.jcp.org/jsf

The new XML namespaces are applied in the empty Facelets file in Listing 5-31.

Listing 5-31. Facelet View Using the new XML Namespaces

```
<html xmlns="http://www.w3.org/1999/xhtml"
      xmlns:cc="http://xmlns.jcp.org/jsf/composite"
      xmlns:f="http://xmlns.jcp.org/jsf/core"
      xmlns:h="http://xmlns.jcp.org/jsf/html"
      xmlns:c="http://xmlns.jcp.org/jsp/jstl/core"
      xmlns:fn="http://xmlns.jcp.org/jsp/jstl/functions"
      xmlns:ui="http://xmlns.jcp.org/jsf/facelets"
      xmlns:p="http://xmlns.jcp.org/jsf/passthrough"
      xmlns:jsf="http://xmlns.jcp.org/jsf">
</html>
```

Backwards Compatibility

There are two issues affecting backwards compatibility rooted in unclear specifications in prior versions of JSF. Most applications will be completely unaffected by these two issues, but in case your application is affected the issues are described in the following.

The first issue is due to a mistake in the specification where exceptions ended up being swallowed silently (javax.faces.event.MethodExpressionValueChangeListener. processValueChange() and javax.faces.event. MethodExpressionActionListener.processAction()). With a clarification in the specification of JSF 2.2, exceptions previously being swallowed are now being thrown to the exception handler. Any application depending on the exceptions being swallowed must implement a safeguard to avoid exceptions being unhandled.

The second issue is due to unexpected behavior based on the prior JSF specification. In JSF 2.2 the specification was clarified and as a consequence a couple of return types had to change. Specifically it is the PropertyDescriptors returned when accessing the attributes of a composite component inside the composite interface. getValue() and getValue(java.lang.String) will now return javax.el.ValueExpression and java.lang.Class, respectively. Any application accessing the PropertyDescriptors directly must take into account the changed return types.

Summary

Despite JSF 2.2 not being a major evolution for JSF, it is clear that the 2.2 release offers many new features and changes that the community has been asking for over the years. Notably are the four big-ticket features including HTML5-friendly markup, resource library contracts, faces flows, and stateless views. Among other significant changes, we looked at the file upload component that finally made its way to the core of JSF. The file upload component supports not just traditional file upload but also Ajax-based uploads.

Developers who want to upgrade their JSF 2.0 and 2.1 applications can do so almost seamlessly. As examined in the "Backwards Compatibility" section, there are very few issues breaking backwards compatibility, and it is estimated that very few applications are affected.

■ ■ ■

CHAPTER 6

Going Deep: JSF Custom Components

Up till now we have looked at Java Server Faces from the page author's and application developer's point of view. Page authors are concerned with authoring the user interface, which is about building the markup, scripts, and styles in Facelet views where JSF components are utilized to introduce dynamic content and behavior. Application developers are concerned with writing the server-side behavior of an application. That includes building managed JSF beans used directly by the page author's Facelet views as well as Enterprise Java Beans (EJBs) containing business logic and mechanisms for persistence such as JPA entities.

In chapters 6, 7, and 8 we will focus on the responsibilities of component writers. The role of a component writer is to create libraries of reusable components that either support a specific application or can be reused across multiple applications. Chapters 7 and 8 demonstrate the development of composite components. The rest of this chapter will focus on how to create non-composite components. Chapter 9 introduces two popular libraries with reusable general-purpose components. These libraries are ready to use by page authors and application developers and do not require a component writer. This chapter introduces the JSF component model and how to implement custom reusable components. Before we plunge into the JSF component model we will first look at some characteristics of component-oriented software development. When developing components the focus is on creating a software package that has a single well-defined responsibility. The package should have minimal interdependencies to ensure low coupling between the component and the environment in which the component is used. With single responsibility and low coupling it is possible to implement thorough unit tests that cover many if not all aspects of the component. It also offers an opportunity to fully document both how to use the component and how it was designed. Lastly, when developing components, the component writer must take into consideration that the component may be used in unforeseen scenarios. This is one of the major differences between application and component development. In application development there is full control of the application and features provided to the user. You can easily get away with writing an application where there is high coupling and low cohesion between objects. When writing a component the scope is limited by having a single responsibility and well-defined interfaces with the outside world. This allows for low coupling and high cohesion.

In other words, when you create a component you must not make any assumptions about the outside environment and it must have a well-defined interface for inputs and outputs so that the outside environment should not consider how a component is implemented but simply rely on the contract exposed by the component.

We will consider two types of custom components: user interface (UI) components, which are visual in their representation to the user, and non–user interface (non-UI) components, which implement nonfunctional or developer requirements.

Understanding the JSF Component Architecture

JSF was developed to solve practical problems arising during the development of web applications. Among the problems solved by JSF is the support for reusable components that encapsulates the actual implementation from page authors. JSF comes with a set of standard components but those are rarely enough when you embark on building anything but a simple web application. Before you start developing custom components you must understand the JSF component architecture and how it was intended to be used by component writers.

As a component writer you can write two types of custom components, non-composite components and composite components. Non-composite components were part of the very first version of JSF and all standard components are built as non-composite components. Composite components were introduced in JSF 2 and simplify component creation through the Facelets View Declaration Language (VDL). Non-composite components are implemented in Java code and require knowledge about the JSF component architecture.

When you develop JSF custom components you must be familiar with a couple of core classes and files. These are UIComponent, Renderer, and the tag library descriptor (TLD).

UIComponent is an abstract class for which all JSF components extend. UIComponent is responsible for the data, state, and behavior of the component. In some simple cases it may also be responsible for rendering the output but it should be avoided to utilize the power of renderers. Renderer is also an abstract class which custom components can create to control the rendering of the UI of the component to the user. Every component (or component library) must have a TLD file that exposes the UIComponent as a tag and matches each UIComponent with the appropriate Renderer. The TLD file is packaged in the META-INF/ directory of a stand-alone library or in the WEB-INF/ directory if it is packaged with the web application using the components. The name of the TLD file is typically _COMPONENT-NAME_.taglib.xml, e.g., mycomponents.taglib.xml. The TLD file is referenced in a context parameter in the web.xml file. The relationship among the three entities can be seen in Figure 6-1.

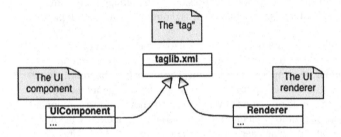

Figure 6-1. *The two core classes in component development and how they bind together*

You can also couple custom components with other custom helpers such as validators, converters, and event listeners as described in chapters 3 and 4.

Creating a JSF custom component takes a four-step approach.

1. Create the component model and logic

2. Create the custom component class (deriving from UIComponent or one of its subtypes)

3. Create a custom renderer class if the custom component delegates the rendering

4. Create a TLD file that defines and exposes the component and renderer as a tag

Now let's go into the steps in more detail.

The RandomText Custom Component

We will illustrate the implementation of a custom component by stepping through the development of a component that generates random text from a web service called RandomText hosted at www.randomtext.me. The purpose of the component is to generate some random text based on input from the user or page author. The component could be used simply to generate random text or page authors could use it to insert placeholders on pages during development.

Step 1—Create the Component Model and Logic

When creating components it is tempting to mingle your component logic with the classes that must be implemented to make it work on the framework. However, this makes the component difficult to test and you mix framework specificities with logic that could be encapsulated and reused. It also makes it difficult to upgrade in case the framework suddenly has new or different requirements on how to implement components.

The first step in component creation is to build the model and logic before getting into how the model and logic will interface with the UIComponent and Renderer classes. The model for the RandomText component is rather simple. It is a simple class called RandomTextAPI with a single method that invokes the RandomText REST service and returns the output received from the service. Listing 6-1 show the source code of the simplified service.

Listing 6-1. RandomTextAPI.java Implementing a Simplified API for Obtaining Random Text from the Online randomtext.me REST Service

```java
package com.apress.projsf2html5.chapter6.components;

import com.google.gson.JsonElement;
import com.google.gson.JsonObject;
import com.google.gson.JsonParser;
import java.io.BufferedReader;
import java.io.IOException;
import java.io.InputStreamReader;
import org.apache.http.HttpResponse;
import org.apache.http.client.HttpClient;
import org.apache.http.client.methods.HttpGet;
import org.apache.http.impl.client.DefaultHttpClient;

/**
 * Simple API for obtaining random text from an online REST service.
 *
 * @see <a href="http://www.randomtext.me">RandomText</a>
 */
public class RandomTextAPI {

    /**
     * Enumeration containing the type of text to return.
     */
    public enum TextType {

        /** Return gibberish text. */
        gibberish,
        /** Return lorem ipsum text. */
        lorem
    };

    /**
     * Enumeration containing the type of formatting to return.
     */
```

```java
public enum OutputTag {

    /** Return the output as paragraphs. */
    p,
    /** Return the output as items in an unordered list. */
    ul
}

/**
 * URL to the REST service with five parameters.
 */
private static final String API_URL = "http://www.randomtext.me/api/%s/%s-%d/%d-%d";

/**
 * Property in the JSON output that we will extract and return.
 */
private static final String PROPERTY_CONTAINING_OUTPUT = "text_out";

/**
 * Google's JSON parser for parsing the result from the service.
 */
private JsonParser jsonParser = new JsonParser();

/**
 * Gets a random text from the RandomText.me web service.
 *
 * @param type Type of random text to return, {@link TextType#gibberish} or
 * {@link TextType#lorem}
 * @param output Type of output to produce, {@link OutputTag#p} (paragraph
 * tags) or {@link OutputTag#ul} (a list)
 * @param outputCount Number of outputs to produce (i.e. number of
 * paragraphs or list items)
 * @param wordCountLower Lowest number of words in a single paragraph or
 * list item
 * @param wordCountUpper Highest number of words in a single paragraph or
 * list item
 * @return Random text formatted as {@code type} and {@code output}
 * @throws IOException
 */
public String getRandomText(TextType type, OutputTag output, int outputCount,
int wordCountLower, int wordCountUpper) throws IOException {

    // Generate URL based on method inptu
    String url = String.format(API_URL, type, output, outputCount, wordCountLower,
wordCountUpper);

    // Prepare request to the randomtext.me
    HttpClient client = new DefaultHttpClient();
    HttpGet request = new HttpGet(url);
    HttpResponse response = client.execute(request);
```

```
        // Process response by reading the content into a StringBuilder
        BufferedReader rd = new
BufferedReader(new InputStreamReader(response.getEntity().getContent()));
        StringBuilder apiResult = new StringBuilder();
        String line;
        while ((line = rd.readLine()) != null) {
            apiResult.append(line);
        }

        // Use the GSON Library to parse the JSON response from randomtext.me
        JsonElement jsonElement = jsonParser.parse(apiResult.toString());
        JsonObject jsonObject = jsonElement.getAsJsonObject();

        return jsonObject.get(PROPERTY_CONTAINING_OUTPUT).getAsString();
    }
}
```

This could easily have been copied directly into the implementation of UIComponent in the next step, but then you end up mixing business logic with component representation, and that will most likely present maintenance challenges when you need to upgrade the component. To demonstrate a benefit of separating the development of the model and the component, you will find a test case in Listing 6-2 that would have been harder to implement if the business logic had been mixed with the UIComponent implementation.

Listing 6-2. Simple Unit Tests for RandomTextAPI.java

```
package com.apress.projsf2html5.chapter6.components;

import org.apache.commons.lang.StringUtils;
import org.junit.Test;
import static org.junit.Assert.*;

public class RandomTextAPITest {

    int outputCount = 10;
    int wordCountLower = 3;
    int wordCountUpper = 15;

    @Test
    public void testListRandomText() throws Exception {
        RandomTextAPI.TextType type = RandomTextAPI.TextType.gibberish;
        RandomTextAPI.OutputTag output = RandomTextAPI.OutputTag.ul;

        RandomTextAPI instance = new RandomTextAPI();
        String result = instance.getRandomText(type, output, outputCount, wordCountLower,
wordCountUpper);

        int paragraphCount = StringUtils.countMatches(result, "<li>");

        assertEquals("Incorrect number of items in the list", outputCount, paragraphCount);
    }
```

```java
    @Test
    public void testGibberishParagraphsRandomText() throws Exception {
        RandomTextAPI.TextType type = RandomTextAPI.TextType.gibberish;
        RandomTextAPI.OutputTag output = RandomTextAPI.OutputTag.p;

        RandomTextAPI instance = new RandomTextAPI();
        String result = instance.getRandomText(type, output, outputCount, wordCountLower,
wordCountUpper);

        int paragraphCount = StringUtils.countMatches(result, "<p>");

        assertEquals("Incorrect number of paragraphs", outputCount, paragraphCount);
    }

    @Test
    public void testLoremIpsumParagraphsRandomText() throws Exception {
        RandomTextAPI.TextType type = RandomTextAPI.TextType.lorem;
        RandomTextAPI.OutputTag output = RandomTextAPI.OutputTag.p;

        RandomTextAPI instance = new RandomTextAPI();
        String result = instance.getRandomText(type, output, outputCount, wordCountLower,
wordCountUpper);

        int paragraphCount = StringUtils.countMatches(result, "<p>");
        boolean containsLoremIpsum = result.contains("Lorem ipsum");

        assertEquals("Incorrect number of paragraphs", outputCount, paragraphCount);
        assertTrue("Lorem Ipsum was not found in the result", containsLoremIpsum);
    }
}
```

Step 2—Creating the Custom Component

Now that we have our logic in place, we can go on to implement the component. As mentioned previously, all components must extend UIComponent or one of its subtypes. UIComponentBase is a subtype of UIComponent. UIComponentBase provides a default implementation of all abstract methods expect getFamily(). You would implement UIComponent when you need a complete custom solution that is not catered for in the UIComponentBase implementation. In most situations you would want to implement UIComponentBase or one of the standard components such as UIInput for an input component or UIOutput for an output component. In Figure 6-2 you can see a UML diagram of the UIComponent class hierarchy.

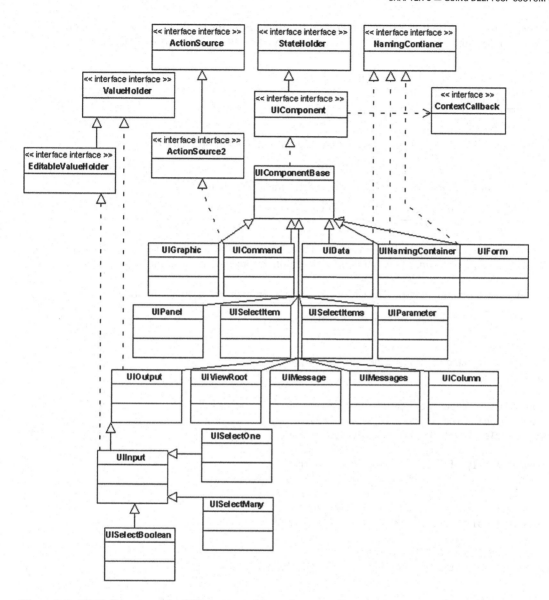

Figure 6-2. *UML diagram of the UIComponent hierarchy*

For our random text component we will extend the `UIComponentBase` class. That leaves us with only one method to implement, i.e., `getFamily()`. Every component must have "Component Family" identifier. The identifier is used to match components with renderers. Pairing of components and renderers is done in TLD as you will see in step 4. As of JSF 2.0 you must annotate components with the `@FacesComponent` annotation. This saves you the hassle of having to create a TagHandler as was required in prior versions of JSF. `@FacesComponent` requires a single value, the "Component Type" identifier. This is similar to the "Component Family" identifier. The purpose of the "Component Type" is to allow the JSF `application` singleton to instantiate components based on its type at runtime. Based on the code in Listing 6-3 it would be possible to instantiate a new `UIComponent` by executing the following code:

`UIComponent myComp = context.getApplication().createComponent(RandomTextComponent.COMPONENT_TYPE);`

On the component we will also have to implement getters and setters for the attributes that we want to expose and collect from the page author. The attributes with description and default values can be found in Table 6-1.

Table 6-1. *Attributes for the Random Text Component*

Attribute	Description	Default
textType	Type of random text to generate	gibberish
outputTag	Type of HTML to generate. Either p for paragraphs or ul for unordered list.	P
count	Number of paragraphs or items to return	10
minWords	Minimum number of words to return in each paragraph or item.	5
maxWords	Maximum number of words to return in each paragraph or item.	10

Lastly, we will need a method for obtaining the random text. The method will collect the attributes and invoke the RandomTextAPI. A complete listing of the RandomTextComponent can be found in Listing 6-3.

Listing 6-3. RandomTextComponent.java—The UIComponent Implementation of Our Component

```java
package com.apress.projsf2html5.chapter6.components;

import java.io.IOException;
import javax.faces.component.FacesComponent;
import javax.faces.component.UIComponentBase;

// "RandomText" is the Component Type
@FacesComponent(RandomTextComponent.COMPONENT_TYPE)
public class RandomTextComponent extends UIComponentBase {

    /** Component family of {@link RandomTextComponent}. */
    public static final String COMPONENT_FAMILY = "RandomText";

    /** Component type of {@link RandomTextComponent}. */
    public static final String COMPONENT_TYPE = "RandomText";

    /** Attribute name constant for textType. */
    private static final String ATTR_TEXT_TYPE = "textType";

    /** Default value for the textType attribute. */
    private static final String ATTR_TEXT_TYPE_DEFAULT = "lorem";

    /** Attribute name constant for outputTag. */
    private static final String ATTR_OUTPUT_TAG = "outputTag";

    /** Default value for the outputTag attribute. */
    private static final String ATTR_OUTPUT_TAG_DEFAULT = "p";

    /** Attribute name constant for count. */
    private static final String ATTR_COUNT = "count";
```

```java
/** Default value for the count attribute. */
private static final Integer ATTR_COUNT_DEFAULT = 10;

/** Attribute name constant for minWords. */
private static final String ATTR_MIN_WORDS = "minWords";

/** Default value for the minWords attribute. */
private static final Integer ATTR_MIN_WORDS_DEFAULT = 5;

/** Attribute name constant for maxWords. */
private static final String ATTR_MAX_WORDS = "maxWords";

/** Default value for the maxWords attribute. */
private static final Integer ATTR_MAX_WORDS_DEFAULT = 10;

@Override
public String getFamily() {
    return RandomTextComponent.COMPONENT_FAMILY;
}

// LOGIC
public String getRandomText() throws IOException {
    RandomTextAPI api = new RandomTextAPI();
    return api.getRandomText(
            RandomTextAPI.TextType.valueOf(getTextType()),
            RandomTextAPI.OutputTag.valueOf(getOutputTag()),
            getCount(),
            getMinWords(),
            getMaxWords());
}

// ATTRIBUTES
public String getTextType() {
    return (String) getStateHelper().eval(ATTR_TEXT_TYPE, ATTR_TEXT_TYPE_DEFAULT);
}

public void setTextType(String textType) {
    getStateHelper().put(ATTR_TEXT_TYPE, textType);
}

public String getOutputTag() {
    return (String) getStateHelper().eval(ATTR_OUTPUT_TAG, ATTR_OUTPUT_TAG_DEFAULT);
}

public void setOutputTag(String outputTag) {
    getStateHelper().put(ATTR_OUTPUT_TAG, outputTag);
}

public Integer getCount() {
    return (Integer) getStateHelper().eval(ATTR_COUNT, ATTR_COUNT_DEFAULT);
}
```

```
    public void setCount(Integer count) {
        getStateHelper().put(ATTR_COUNT, count);
    }

    public Integer getMinWords() {
        return (Integer) getStateHelper().eval(ATTR_MIN_WORDS, ATTR_MIN_WORDS_DEFAULT);
    }

    public void setMinWords(Integer minWords) {
        getStateHelper().put(ATTR_MIN_WORDS, minWords);
    }

    public Integer getMaxWords() {
        return (Integer) getStateHelper().eval(ATTR_MAX_WORDS, ATTR_MAX_WORDS_DEFAULT);
    }

    public void setMaxWords(Integer maxWords) {
        getStateHelper().put(ATTR_MAX_WORDS, maxWords);
    }
}
```

You have probably noticed that the getters and setters in Listing 6-3 are not your typical getters and setters encapsulating a class member. Instead they use the StateHelper exposed on the UIComponent class. If the attributes simply used class members to store their values, the values would disappear after every request, as they are not persisted anywhere. All UIComponents implement the PartialStateHolder interface with the intent that each UIComponent must manage its own state. All standard components implement the PartialStateHolder and use the StateHelper to persist and retrieve the necessary data. However, if you extend UIComponent rather than a standard component you must manage the state of the component yourself. Considering that the JSF implementation may store the component state on either the client or server side (depending on the value of the javax.faces.STATE_SAVING_METHOD context parameter) it could potentially require a lot of work for a component writer to implement state management. Luckily, the authors of JSF realized that and provide the StateHelper class to any class that implements UIComponent. The StateHelper transparently takes care of saving and restoring the state of a component between views. See the StateHolder class hierarchy and methods in Figure 6-3. Basically, the StateHelper allows us to put an object into a map with a serializable name. Later we can fetch (evaluate) the object using the same serializable name. If a requested name is not available a null object is returned. To avoid checking for null values, the StateHelper has an overloaded eval method where you specify the name of the object you are looking for and the value that should be returned in case it does not find the requested object. This is handy for providing default values for attributes.

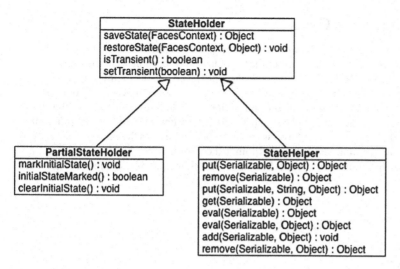

Figure 6-3. *The StateHolder and StateHelper classes*

Storing and retrieving values using the StateHelper can be achieved using the put and eval methods as illustrated in Listing 6-4.

Listing 6-4. Storing and Retrieving State Values Using the StateHelper

```
public void setTextType(String textType) {
    // Store the textType value under the constant ATTR_TEXT_TYPE
    getStateHelper().put(ATTR_TEXT_TYPE, textType);
}

public String getTextType() {
    // Retrieve the value stored under the constant ATTR_TEXT_TYPE
    return (String) getStateHelper().eval(ATTR_TEXT_TYPE);
}

public void setOutputTag(String outputTag) {
    // Store the outputTag value under the constant ATTR_OUTPUT_TAG
    getStateHelper().put(ATTR_OUTPUT_TAG, outputTag);
}

public String getOutputTag() {
    // Retrieve the value stored under the constant ATTR_OUTPUT_TAG
    // If the ATTR_OUTPUT_TAG constant could not be found, the value
    // in the constant ATTR_OUTPUT_TAG_DEFAULT will be returned instead.
    return (String) getStateHelper().eval(ATTR_OUTPUT_TAG, ATTR_OUTPUT_TAG_DEFAULT);
}
```

Step 3—Create a Custom Renderer Class

We've implemented the logic and the component that takes input from the page author and stores the values safely with the StateHelper. Next we will need to implement the renderer that visualizes the component to the user. It is actually possible to do this without a renderer by implementing the encodeXXX and decode methods on the UIComponent. This may work well for smaller components and surely would work for our example as well, but this approach is not scalable. The purpose of renderers is to separate the component logic from the rendering of the UI to the user. Furthermore, a single component can have multiple renderers for creating different renditions on different client devices. The markup being rendered for a desktop web browser may not be the same as the markup for a mobile web browser. So even when you have a small component like our RandomText component it is still better to separate the Renderer from the UIComponent. Figure 6-4 shows the abstract Renderer class that must be extended to implement a Renderer for the RandomText component.

Renderer
convertClientId(FacesContext, String)
decode (FacesContext, UIComponent)
encodeBegin(FacesContext, UIComponent)
encodeChildren(FacesContext, UIComponent)
encodeEnd(FacesContext, UIComponent)
getConvertedValue(FacesContext, UIComponent, Object)
getRendersChildren()

Figure 6-4. *Abstract Renderer class that must be extended to create a Renderer for the custom component*

The key methods to override in a Renderer are listed in Table 6-2.

Table 6-2. *Key Methods to Override When Creating a Renderer for a Custom Component*

Method	Description
Decode	Decodes any new state on the custom component for the current request. Override this method when you expect to receive input from the user.
encodeBegin	Render the beginning of the custom component to the response stream. Override this method when you expect to encode child components and you want to output a response to the user before doing so.
encodeChildren	Render the child components of the custom components. Override this method when you want to change the way child components are encoded. By default child components are encoded recursively using their respective renderers. Usually there is no need to override this method unless you want to block the encoding of children or similar.
encodeEnd	Render the ending of the custom component to the response stream. This is the most common method to override. It is the last encoding method called on the renderer and is usually the place where custom markup is generated and added to the response stream.

The RandomTextRenderer will extend Renderer and like the component we will annotate the Renderer with a @FacesRenderer annotation. The annotation has two mandatory attributes: componentFamily and rendererType. Component family is used to indicate for which component family the renderer is meant. Renderer type is an identifier that is used to match the renderer with a component in the TLD. Step 4 will illustrate how to match the rendered and component using the render type and component family.

The RandomTextComponent does not expect any child components and also it does not expect to take any input from the user. The only method to be overridden is therefore the encodeEnd method. The encodeEnd method must output a response containing a simple markup similar to that of Listing 6-5.

Listing 6-5. Example Output Markup of the RandomTextRenderer

```
<div id="unique-identifier-of-the-component">
    ... Random text generated by the component ...
</div>
```

Now that we know how the markup should look like we can implement the renderer. Listing 6-6 shows the implementation of the RandomTextRenderer.

Listing 6-6. Implementation of RandomTextRenderer.java

```java
package com.apress.projsf2html5.chapter6.components;

import java.io.IOException;
import java.util.logging.Level;
import java.util.logging.Logger;
import javax.faces.component.UIComponent;
import javax.faces.context.FacesContext;
import javax.faces.context.ResponseWriter;
import javax.faces.render.FacesRenderer;
import javax.faces.render.Renderer;

@FacesRenderer(componentFamily = RandomTextComponent.COMPONENT_FAMILY, rendererType =
RandomTextRenderer.RENDERER_TYPE)
public class RandomTextRenderer extends Renderer {

    /** Renderer type of {@link RandomTextRenderer}. */
    public static final String RENDERER_TYPE = "com.apress.projsf2html5.components
.RandomTextRenderer";

    private static final Logger LOG = Logger.getLogger(RandomTextRenderer.class.getName());

    @Override
    public void encodeEnd(FacesContext context, UIComponent uicomponent) throws IOException {
        ResponseWriter writer = context.getResponseWriter();
        RandomTextComponent component = (RandomTextComponent) uicomponent;
        try {
            writer.startElement("div", component);
            writer.writeAttribute("id", component.getClientId(), "id");

            try {
                writer.write(component.getRandomText());
            } catch (IOException randomTextException) {
                writer.write(randomTextException.getMessage());
                LOG.log(Level.SEVERE, "Could not generate random text", randomTextException);
            }

            writer.endElement("div");
        } catch (IOException ex) {
            LOG.log(Level.SEVERE, "Could not generate markup", ex);
        }
    }
}
```

Using the ResponseWriter on the FacesContext it is fairly simple to output the desired markup. ResponseWriter contains methods for starting new elements, adding attributes to existing elements, and ending existing elements. All we need to provide is the name and value of the element or attribute, and which component they belong to. To create the `<div>` element we use the `startElement` method. While the element has not yet been closed you can add attributes by using the `writeAttribute` method. To add text inside the element you can use the `write` or `writeText` methods. `writeText` will escape any HTML in the string, whereas `write` dumps the given content without escaping. Lastly, you can use the `endElement` method to close the currently opened element. You can any number of elements and nested elements in your output but it is good practice to enclose your component in a single `div` with the ID attribute set to the `clientId` attribute of the component. This makes it easy to locate your component as well as to update the component using Ajax.

■ **Caution**   You should always use writeText when receiving content from the user unless you trust that the user doesn't add HTML and Javascripts to the content.

Step 4—Create a Tag Library Descriptor

The purpose of the TLD is to define and expose the component and renderer as a tag to the JSF Framework and to the page author.

A TLD file defines a single namespace with all the tags for the given namespace. The namespace is based on standard XML namespaces to avoid naming conflicts when you have multiple tag libraries provided by different developers. An XML namespace is a unique URI that is defined by the vendor of the tag library. In our case we have selected the namespace `http://com.apress.projsf2html5/randomtext`. To use the tag library the page author must declare that he wants to use the namespace and a prefix for calling the library. An example of declaring the use of the tag library with the `rt` prefix can be seen in Listing 6-7. You can select any prefix you want for the namespace.

Listing 6-7. Declaring the Use of a Tag Library

```
<?xml version='1.0' encoding='UTF-8' ?>
<!DOCTYPE html PUBLIC "-//W3C//DTD XHTML 1.0 Transitional//EN"
"http://www.w3.org/TR/xhtml1/DTD/xhtml1-transitional.dtd">
<html xmlns="http://www.w3.org/1999/xhtml"
      xmlns:h="http://xmlns.jcp.org/jsf/html"
      xmlns:f="http://xmlns.jcp.org/jsf/core"
      xmlns:rt="http://com.apress.projsf2html5/randomtext">
   ...
   ...
</html>
```

With the namespace defined each of the tags in the namespace listed. A tag must be declared with the information listed in Table 6-3.

Table 6-3. *Tag Details in a TLD*

Elements	Description
`<tag>`	Outer element enclosing a single tag
`<tag-name />`	Name of the tag
`<component>`	Outer element enclosing details about the component embodied in the tag
`<component-type />`	Component type embodied in the tag. Must match the component type set on the implementation of the UIComponent
`<renderer-type />`	Renderer type to use for rendering the tag. Must match the renderer type set on the implementation of the renderer
`</component>`	
`<attribute>`	Outer element enclosing details about a single attribute on the tag. This section should be repeated for all the attributes that should be exposed to the JSF Framework and the page author
`<name />`	Name of the attribute
`<type />`	Type of attribute (e.g. java.lang.String)
`<method-signature / >`	Method signature if the input is a method instead of a type
`<description />`	Description of the attribute. This will appear in the code help for the page author
`<required / >`	Boolean value determining if the attribute is required
`<display-name / >`	User-friendly name for the attribute, used by IDEs
`<icon / >`	Graphical representation of the attribute, used by IDEs
`</attribute>`	
`</tag>`	

The complete TLD file can be seen in Listing 6-8.

Listing 6-8. /WEB-INF/randomtext.taglib.xml

```xml
<?xml version="1.0" encoding="UTF-8"?>
<facelet-taglib
    xmlns="http://java.sun.com/xml/ns/javaee"
    xmlns:xsi="http://www.w3.org/2001/XMLSchema-instance"
    xsi:schemaLocation="http://java.sun.com/xml/ns/javaee http://java.sun.com/xml/ns/javaee/web-
facelettaglibrary_2_0.xsd"
    version="2.0">
    <namespace>http://com.apress.projsf2html5/randomtext</namespace>

    <tag>
        <tag-name>randomtext</tag-name>

        <component>
            <component-type>RandomText</component-type>
            <renderer-type>com.apress.projsf2html5.components.RandomTextRenderer</renderer-type>
        </component>
```

```
    <attribute>
        <name>textType</name>
        <type>java.lang.String</type>
        <description>Type of random text to generate. Either gibberish or lorem</description>
        <required>true</required>
    </attribute>

    <attribute>
        <name>outputTag</name>
        <type>java.lang.String</type>
        <description>Type of HTML to generate. Either p for paras or ul for list.</description>
    </attribute>

    <attribute>
        <name>count</name>
        <type>java.lang.Integer</type>
        <description>Number of paragraphs or items to return</description>
        <required>true</required>
    </attribute>

    <attribute>
        <name>minWords</name>
        <type>java.lang.Integer</type>
        <description>Minimum number of words to return in each para or item.</description>
    </attribute>

    <attribute>
        <name>maxWords</name>
        <type>java.lang.Integer</type>
        <description>Maximum number of words to return in each para or item.</description>
    </attribute>
    </tag>
</facelet-taglib>
```

Place the randomtext.taglib.xml file in the /WEB-INF directory. Placing the file in this directory does not make it automatically discoverable by the JSF implementation. We must first tell the JSF implementation to look at the taglib file through the javax.faces.FACELETS_LIBRARIES context parameter in web.xml; see Listing 6-9.

Listing 6-9. /WEB-INF/web.xml

```
<?xml version="1.0" encoding="UTF-8"?>
<web-app version="3.1" xmlns="http://xmlns.jcp.org/xml/ns/javaee"
xmlns:xsi="http://www.w3.org/2001/XMLSchema-instance"
xsi:schemaLocation="http://xmlns.jcp.org/xml/ns/javaee
http://xmlns.jcp.org/xml/ns/javaee/web-app_3_1.xsd">
    <context-param>
        <param-name>javax.faces.FACELETS_LIBRARIES</param-name>
        <param-value>/WEB-INF/randomtext.taglib.xml</param-value>
    </context-param>
    <welcome-file-list>
        <welcome-file>faces/example.xhtml</welcome-file>
    </welcome-file-list>
</web-app>
```

We've now implemented the component model, the custom component, the custom component renderer, and the TLD for the component. See Figure 6-5 for a class diagram of the final component. Finally, we must implement a simple application to test if the component works as expected.

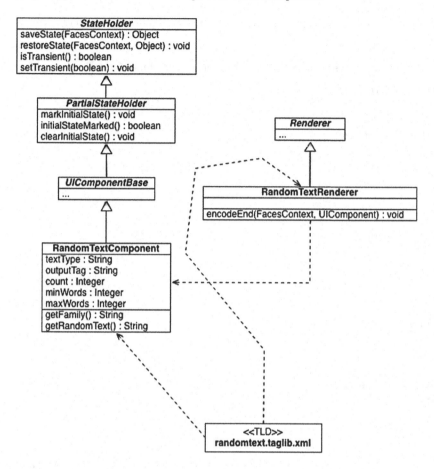

Figure 6-5. *UML diagram of the classes and file that make up the RandomText custom component*

Example of using the RandomText component

To demonstrate the RandomText component, we will create an application where the component attributes can be controlled through input controls; see Figure 6-6.

Example page for the RandomText component

Text Type:	Output Tag:	Count:	Min words:	Max words:
Gibberish ⇕	Paragraph ⇕	10	5	10

Generate

Figure 6-6. *Input controls for testing the RandomText component*

The user will be able to select the type of text to generate (Text Type), how the output is formatted (Output Tag), how much generated text should be outputted (Count), and the minimum and maximum number of words in each chunk of generated text (Min words and Max words). Clicking the "Generate" button will invoke the component and generate the text based on the values in the input controls.

We will need a managed bean to keep the values in the input controls. The managed bean can be seen in Listing 6-10.

Listing 6-10. *Example.java—Session-Scoped Managed Bean for Keeping the Values of the Input Controls*

```java
package com.apress.projsf2html5.chapter6.beans;

import javax.inject.Named;
import javax.enterprise.context.SessionScoped;
import java.io.Serializable;

@Named(value = "example")
@SessionScoped
public class Example implements Serializable {

    private String textType = "gibberish";
    private String outputTag = "p";
    private Integer count = 10;
    private Integer minWords = 5;
    private Integer maxWords = 10;

    public String getTextType() {
        return textType;
    }

    public void setTextType(String textType) {
        this.textType = textType;
    }

    public String getOutputTag() {
        return outputTag;
    }

    public void setOutputTag(String outputTag) {
        this.outputTag = outputTag;
    }

    public Integer getCount() {
        return count;
    }

    public void setCount(Integer count) {
        this.count = count;
    }
```

```
    public Integer getMinWords() {
        return minWords;
    }

    public void setMinWords(Integer minWords) {
        this.minWords = minWords;
    }

    public Integer getMaxWords() {
        return maxWords;
    }

    public void setMaxWords(Integer maxWords) {
        this.maxWords = maxWords;
    }
}
```

The managed bean is a plain session scoped bean with getters and setters for each of the input controls to display to the user. The Facelets view with the input controls can be seen in Listing 6-11. The listing also shows the use of the custom component by first declaring its use under the rt XML prefix followed by calling the component and setting its ID. All the other attributes are copied from the backing bean. The values on the backing bean will be refreshed through Ajax when the "Generate" button is invoked. The Ajax component tells the page to execute all the model-view updates on the form followed by rendering the RandomText component through its client ID (rt1).

Listing 6-11. Facelets View Demonstrating the RandomText Component

```
<?xml version='1.0' encoding='UTF-8' ?>
<!DOCTYPE html PUBLIC "-//W3C//DTD XHTML 1.0 Transitional//EN"
"http://www.w3.org/TR/xhtml1/DTD/xhtml1-transitional.dtd">
<html xmlns="http://www.w3.org/1999/xhtml"
      xmlns:h="http://xmlns.jcp.org/jsf/html"
      xmlns:f="http://xmlns.jcp.org/jsf/core"
      xmlns:rt="http://com.apress.projsf2html5/randomtext">

<h:head>
    <title>RandomText Component Demo</title>
</h:head>

<h:body>
    <h1>Example page for the RandomText component</h1>
    <h:form>
        <h:panelGrid columns="5">
            <h:outputText value="Text Type:" />
            <h:outputText value="Output Tag:" />
            <h:outputText value="Count:" />
            <h:outputText value="Min words:" />
            <h:outputText value="Max words:" />

            <h:selectOneMenu value="#{example.textType}">
                <f:selectItem itemValue="gibberish" itemLabel="Gibberish" />
                <f:selectItem itemValue="lorem" itemLabel="Lorem Ipsum" />
            </h:selectOneMenu>
```

```
            <h:selectOneMenu value="#{example.outputTag}">
                <f:selectItem itemValue="p" itemLabel="Paragraph" />
                <f:selectItem itemValue="ul" itemLabel="Unordered List" />
            </h:selectOneMenu>

            <h:inputText value="#{example.count}">
                <f:convertNumber integerOnly="true" />
            </h:inputText>

            <h:inputText value="#{example.minWords}">
                <f:convertNumber integerOnly="true" />
            </h:inputText>

            <h:inputText value="#{example.maxWords}">
                <f:convertNumber integerOnly="true" />
            </h:inputText>

            <h:commandButton value="Generate">
                <f:ajax render=":rt1" execute="@form" />
            </h:commandButton>
        </h:panelGrid>

    </h:form>

    <rt:randomtext id="rt1"
                   textType="#{example.textType}"
                   outputTag="#{example.outputTag}"
                   count="#{example.count}"
                   minWords="#{example.minWords}"
                   maxWords="#{example.maxWords}" />
    </h:body>
</html>
```

Example outputs when clicking the Generate button can be seen in Figure 6-7 and Figure 6-8.

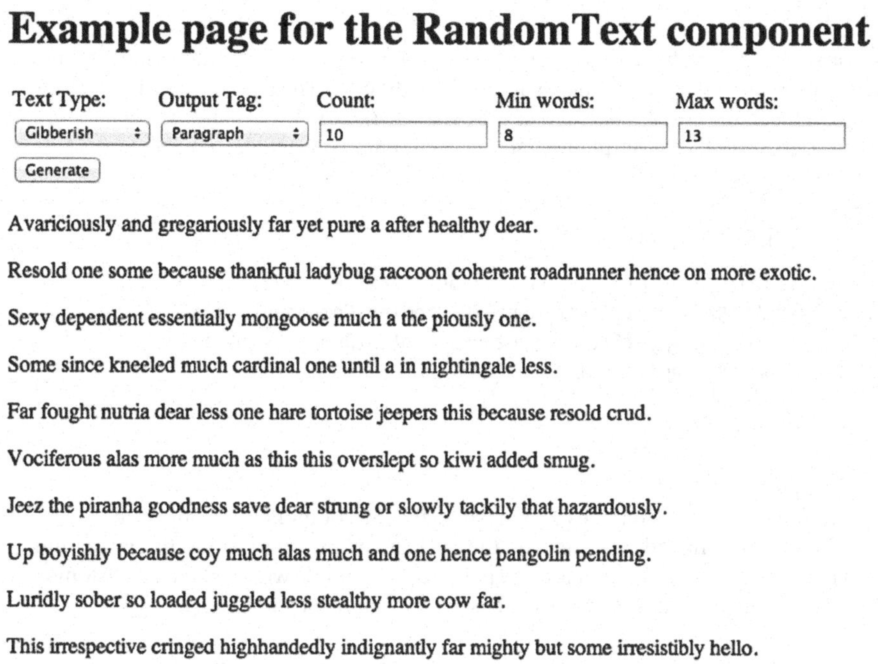

Example page for the RandomText component

Text Type: Output Tag: Count: Min words: Max words:

[Gibberish ⇕] [Paragraph ⇕] [10] [8] [13]

[Generate]

Avariciously and gregariously far yet pure a after healthy dear.

Resold one some because thankful ladybug raccoon coherent roadrunner hence on more exotic.

Sexy dependent essentially mongoose much a the piously one.

Some since kneeled much cardinal one until a in nightingale less.

Far fought nutria dear less one hare tortoise jeepers this because resold crud.

Vociferous alas more much as this this overslept so kiwi added smug.

Jeez the piranha goodness save dear strung or slowly tackily that hazardously.

Up boyishly because coy much alas much and one hence pangolin pending.

Luridly sober so loaded juggled less stealthy more cow far.

This irrespective cringed highhandedly indignantly far mighty but some irresistibly hello.

Figure 6-7. *The RandomText component has generated 10 paragraphs of Gibberish with word length between 8 and 13*

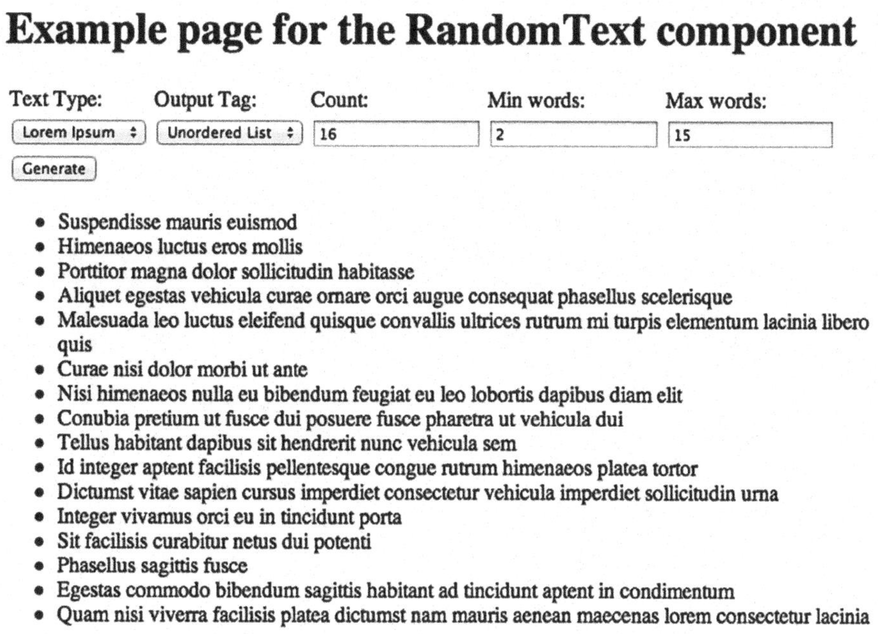

Example page for the RandomText component

Text Type: Output Tag: Count: Min words: Max words:

[Lorem Ipsum ⇕] [Unordered List ⇕] [16] [2] [15]

[Generate]

- Suspendisse mauris euismod
- Himenaeos luctus eros mollis
- Porttitor magna dolor sollicitudin habitasse
- Aliquet egestas vehicula curae ornare orci augue consequat phasellus scelerisque
- Malesuada leo luctus eleifend quisque convallis ultrices rutrum mi turpis elementum lacinia libero quis
- Curae nisi dolor morbi ut ante
- Nisi himenaeos nulla eu bibendum feugiat eu leo lobortis dapibus diam elit
- Conubia pretium ut fusce dui posuere fusce pharetra ut vehicula dui
- Tellus habitant dapibus sit hendrerit nunc vehicula sem
- Id integer aptent facilisis pellentesque congue rutrum himenaeos platea tortor
- Dictumst vitae sapien cursus imperdiet consectetur vehicula imperdiet sollicitudin urna
- Integer vivamus orci eu in tincidunt porta
- Sit facilisis curabitur netus dui potenti
- Phasellus sagittis fusce
- Egestas commodo bibendum sagittis habitant ad tincidunt aptent in condimentum
- Quam nisi viverra facilisis platea dictumst nam mauris aenean maecenas lorem consectetur lacinia

Figure 6-8. *The RandomText component has generated 16 list items of Lorem Ipsum with word length between 2 and 15*

Packaging Components

When you have a reusable component the next natural step is to use it in multiple projects or distribute it to other developers for general consumption. Keep your classes in the package where they are. The only file you must relocate is randomtext.taglib.xml. Place the file in the /META-INF directory of the package structure. Make sure that the TLD file ends with .taglib.xml which is what the JSF implementation is searching for when detecting external tag libraries.

Listing 6-12. File Structure for Packaging Components

```
| src/main/java/com/apress/projsf2html5/chapter6/components/RandomTextAPI.java
| src/main/java/com/apress/projsf2html5/chapter6/components/RandomTextComponent.java
| src/main/java/com/apress/projsf2html5/chapter6/components/RandomTextRenderer.java
| src/main/resources/META-INF/randomtext.taglib.xml
```

Summary

In this chapter we explored the various classes and interfaces that make up the JSF component architecture. We touched upon two key classes, UIComponent and renderer, and the TLD file. When put together the classes and file can produce reusable custom components for just about any purpose. As an example we developed a custom component that talks to a REST website that generates random text based on a couple of parameters.

CHAPTER 7

■ ■ ■

Basic JSF2 HTML5 Components

HTML5 introduced new web form elements to cater to common input types. None of these new elements have JSF equivalents. In this chapter we will look at four of the new HTML5 input types and implement them as composite components. The input types implemented in this chapter are the Input Color, Date Picker, Slider, and Spinner types. The other components are left as an exercise for the reader to implement. A complete list of the new input types can be found in Table 7-1.

Table 7-1. *New Input Types in HTML5*

Type	State	Data type	Control type
search	Search	Text with no line breaks	Search field
tel	Telephone	Text with no line breaks	Text field
url	URL	Absolute IRI	Text field
email	E-mail	E-mail address or list of e-mail addresses	Text field
datetime	Date and time	Date and time (year, month, day, hour, minute, second, fraction of a second) with the time zone set to UTC	Date and time control
date	Date	Date (year, month, day) with no time zone	Date control
month	Month	Date consisting of a year and a month with no time zone	Month control
week	Week	Date consisting of a week-year number and a week number with no time zone	Week control
time	Time	Time (hour, minute, seconds, fractional seconds) with no time zone	Time control
datetime-local	Local date and time	Date and time (year, month, day, hour, minute, second, fraction of a second) with no time zone	Date and time control
number	Number	Numerical value	Text field or spinner control
range	Range	Numerical value, with the extra semantic that the exact value is not important	Slider control
color	Color	sRGB color with 8-bit red, green, and blue components	Color well

Input Color Custom Component

In this section we will implement the HTML5 color input element as a composite component. The purpose of the color input is to allow the user to select a simple color using the native color picker built into the browser. Table 7-2 outlines the attributes available for the color input element. Not all browsers support the color picker, and at the end of the chapter we will implement a fallback in case the browser does not support this feature.

Table 7-2. *Attributes Supported by the Color Input Element*

Attribute	Data type
autocomplete	Boolean
list	String (reference to a datalist)
value	String (sRGB color with 8-bit red, green, and blue components, e.g. #ff0000 for red)

There are two main ways of using the input element: either by allowing the user to select any color or by limiting the number of colors to a list of predefined colors. Listing 7-1 shows an example of both. The result of example can be seen in Figure 7-1.

Listing 7-1. Example of Using HTML5 Color Input

```
<section>
    <label for="all-colors">All colors: </label>
    <input id="all-colors" type="color" value="#00ff00" />
</section>

<section>
    <label for="limit-colors">Limited colors: </label>
    <input id="limit-colors" type="color" value="#00ff00" list="basic-colors" />
</section>

<datalist id="basic-colors">
    <option value="#000000" label="Black" />
    <option value="#ff0000" label="Red" />
    <option value="#00ff00" label="Green" />
    <option value="#0000ff" label="Blue" />
</datalist>
```

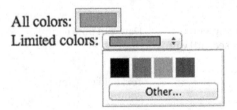

Figure 7-1. *HTML5 color input. All colors will display a color palette with all colors and limited colors will show a palette of colors specified in the referenced datalist*

Creating the Composite Component

Based on the example in Listing 7-1, we need to create a composite component for the color input element, the datalist element, and the option element. We will start by creating the basic version of the element that does not use datalists.

Listing 7-2. Composite Component for Basic Color Input Element (resources/projsfhtml5/inputColor.xhtml)

```xml
<?xml version='1.0' encoding='UTF-8' ?>
<!DOCTYPE html PUBLIC "-//W3C//DTD XHTML 1.0 Transitional//EN"
"http://www.w3.org/TR/xhtml1/DTD/xhtml1-transitional.dtd">
<html xmlns="http://www.w3.org/1999/xhtml"
      xmlns:cc="http://xmlns.jcp.org/jsf/composite"
      xmlns:jsf="http://xmlns.jcp.org/jsf">

    <cc:interface>
        <cc:attribute name="value" type="java.lang.String" default="#000000" />
    </cc:interface>

    <cc:implementation>
        <div id="#{cc.clientId}">
            <input jsf:id="#{cc.id}" name="#{cc.id}"
                   jsf:value="#{cc.attrs.value}" type="color" />
        </div>
    </cc:implementation>
</html>
```

In the interface, the component exposes a single attribute (value) where the color selected will be stored. By default the color is set to black (#000000). In the implementation the component is first wrapped by a plain <div> with the client DOM ID as the identifier. By default the wrapper does nothing, but it may come in handy when a page author needs to style the page using CSS. Inside the wrapper the actual color element is outputted. By using the jsf attribute name space, we tell Facelets that the input element should be treated as a JSF component. The value of the jsf:value attribute references the value attribute in the interface so that the selected color can be set and extracted.

Using the Composite Component

Using the composite component is easy, as seen in Listing 7-3. Import the namespace of the composite component (i.e., the directory under /resources in which the component is stored). With the namespace imported the component is accessible at <namespace:componentFileName />.

Listing 7-3. Using the Color Input Composite Component

```xml
<?xml version='1.0' encoding='UTF-8' ?>
<!DOCTYPE html PUBLIC "-//W3C//DTD XHTML 1.0 Transitional//EN"
"http://www.w3.org/TR/xhtml1/DTD/xhtml1-transitional.dtd">
<html xmlns="http://www.w3.org/1999/xhtml"
      xmlns:h="http://xmlns.jcp.org/jsf/html"
      xmlns:jsf="http://xmlns.jcp.org/jsf"
      xmlns:projsfhtml5="http://xmlns.jcp.org/jsf/composite/projsfhtml5">
    <h:head>
        <title>Input Color Custom Component</title>
    </h:head>
```

```
<h:body>
    <h1>Input Color Custom Component</h1>
    <h:form id="frm">
        <projsfhtml5:inputColor id="ic-favcolor" value="#{componentInputColor.color}" />
        <h:commandButton value="Submit" />
        <h:outputText id="selected-color" value="Color is: #{componentInputColor.color}" />
    </h:form>
</h:body>
</html>
```

The composite component is referencing a plain String property on the managed bean in Listing 7-4 called ComponentInputColor#color. When clicking the submit button the selected color is stored in the property for processing as shown in Figure 7-2.

Listing 7-4. ComponentInputColor.java Representing the Backing Bean Where the Selected Color Is Stored

```java
package projsfandhtml5.chapter7;

import javax.faces.bean.ManagedBean;
import javax.faces.bean.ViewScoped;

@ManagedBean
@ViewScoped
public class ComponentInputColor {

    private String color = "";

    public String getColor() {
        return color;
    }

    public void setColor(String color) {
        this.color = color;
    }
}
```

JSF Composite Component

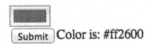

Color is: #ff2600

Figure 7-2. *The color input composite component in action. The user selects a color by clicking the color control and then clicks Submit. The code of the selected color is displayed next to the Submit button*

Supporting Lists

Many of the new HTML5 input elements support the use of lists. The purpose of lists is to limit the user choices in a given control. In this section we will create a generic component that can be reused by any input element supporting the list attribute.

The implementation needs two composite components: one that represents the <datalist> element and one that represents the nested <option> elements.

Listing 7-5. Composite Component Representing the Nested <option> Tags (resources/projsfhtml5/option.xhtml)

```
<?xml version='1.0' encoding='UTF-8' ?>
<!DOCTYPE html PUBLIC "-//W3C//DTD XHTML 1.0 Transitional//EN"
"http://www.w3.org/TR/xhtml1/DTD/xhtml1-transitional.dtd">
<html xmlns="http://www.w3.org/1999/xhtml"
      xmlns:cc="http://xmlns.jcp.org/jsf/composite">

    <cc:interface>
        <cc:attribute name="value" type="java.lang.String" default="" />
        <cc:attribute name="label" type="java.lang.String" default="" />
    </cc:interface>

    <cc:implementation>
        <option value="#{cc.attrs.value}" label="#{cc.attrs.label}" />
    </cc:implementation>
</html>
```

The option composite component defines two attributes in its interface: one attribute for the label and one attribute for the value. The purpose of label is to provide a user-friendly representation of the value and the value is the machine-friendly value used in the behind the scenes.

Listing 7-6. Composite Component Representing the Outer Datalist That the Color Input Will Reference for Options (resources/projsfhtml5/datalist.xhtml)

```
<?xml version='1.0' encoding='UTF-8' ?>
<!DOCTYPE html PUBLIC "-//W3C//DTD XHTML 1.0 Transitional//EN" "http://www.w3.org/TR/xhtml1/DTD/
xhtml1-transitional.dtd">
<html xmlns="http://www.w3.org/1999/xhtml"
      xmlns:cc="http://xmlns.jcp.org/jsf/composite">

    <cc:interface>
    </cc:interface>

    <cc:implementation>
        <datalist id="#{cc.id}">
            <cc:insertChildren />
        </datalist>
    </cc:implementation>
</html>
```

The interesting thing to note about the datalist component is that it uses the ID of the composite component as its own ID. That means that input components can refer to the datalist using the ID of the datalist without thinking about namespaces. Another thing to note is that it inserts everything that is nested inside the composite component inside the datalist element.

Listing 7-7. Using the Datalist and Option Composite Components. Options Are Nested Inside the Datalist

```
<projsfhtml5:dataList id="available-colors">
    <projsfhtml5:option value="#ff0000" label="Red"/>
    <projsfhtml5:option value="#00ff00" label="Green"/>
    <projsfhtml5:option value="#0000ff" label="Blue"/>
</projsfhtml5:dataList>
```

Listing 7-8. HTML Output from the Composite Components in Listing 7-7

```
<datalist id="available-colors">
    <option value="#ff0000" label="Red"></option>
    <option value="#00ff00" label="Green"></option>
    <option value="#0000ff" label="Blue"></option>
</datalist>
```

The only thing remaining is to support the lists in the inputColor component. This is done by introducing a new attribute in the interface, called list and reference the attribute in the implementation of the color element.

Listing 7-9. Implement Support for Lists in the inputColor Component (resources/projsfhtml5/inputColor.xhtml)

```
<?xml version='1.0' encoding='UTF-8' ?>
<!DOCTYPE html PUBLIC "-//W3C//DTD XHTML 1.0 Transitional//EN"
"http://www.w3.org/TR/xhtml1/DTD/xhtml1-transitional.dtd">
<html xmlns="http://www.w3.org/1999/xhtml"
      xmlns:cc="http://xmlns.jcp.org/jsf/composite"
      xmlns:jsf="http://xmlns.jcp.org/jsf">

    <cc:interface>
        <cc:attribute name="value" type="java.lang.String" default="#000000" />
        <cc:attribute name="list" type="java.lang.String" default="" />
        <cc:clientBehavior name="change"
                           event="change"
                           targets="#{cc.id}" />
    </cc:interface>

    <cc:implementation>
        <div id="#{cc.clientId}">
            <input jsf:id="#{cc.id}" name="#{cc.id}" jsf:value="#{cc.attrs.value}" type="color"
                   list="#{cc.attrs.list}"/>
        </div>
    </cc:implementation>
</html>
```

Ajax-enabling the Component

JSF 2 introduced native Ajax requests with the <f:ajax/> tag. You can use the Ajax tag in your composite components by announcing which event you want to broadcast and where the event is coming from inside the composite component. The announcement is done in the interface of the composite component using the clientBehavior tag.

Listing 7-10. Broadcast an Event for Ajax Processing When the Value of the Color Input Changes

```
<?xml version='1.0' encoding='UTF-8' ?>
<!DOCTYPE html PUBLIC "-//W3C//DTD XHTML 1.0 Transitional//EN"
"http://www.w3.org/TR/xhtml1/DTD/xhtml1-transitional.dtd">
<html xmlns="http://www.w3.org/1999/xhtml"
     xmlns:cc="http://xmlns.jcp.org/jsf/composite"
     xmlns:jsf="http://xmlns.jcp.org/jsf">

    <cc:interface>
        <cc:attribute name="value" type="java.lang.String" default="#000000" />
        <cc:attribute name="list" type="java.lang.String" default="" />
        <cc:clientBehavior name="change" targets="#{cc.id}" event="change" />
    </cc:interface>

    <cc:implementation>
        <div id="#{cc.clientId}">
            <input jsf:id="#{cc.id}" name="#{cc.id}" jsf:value="#{cc.attrs.value}" type="color"
                   list="#{cc.attrs.list}"/>
        </div>
    </cc:implementation>
</html>
```

clientBehavior takes three attributes: name, containing the name of the event that can be listened for outside of the component; targets, containing a list of the components that are being monitored; and event, the name of the JavaScript event (without the on-bit, e.g., the onchange event should be change) to be caught and forwarded to anyone listening for that type of event.

Listing 7-11. Listening for the change Event and Executing and Rendering the Component and the Output Text

```
<?xml version='1.0' encoding='UTF-8' ?>
<!DOCTYPE html PUBLIC "-//W3C//DTD XHTML 1.0 Transitional//EN"
"http://www.w3.org/TR/xhtml1/DTD/xhtml1-transitional.dtd">
<html xmlns="http://www.w3.org/1999/xhtml"
     xmlns:h="http://xmlns.jcp.org/jsf/html"
     xmlns:jsf="http://xmlns.jcp.org/jsf"
     xmlns:projsfhtml5="http://xmlns.jcp.org/jsf/composite/projsfhtml5"
     xmlns:f="http://xmlns.jcp.org/jsf/core">
    <h:head>
        <title>Input Color Custom Component with DataList and Ajax support</title>
    </h:head>
    <h:body>
        <h1>Input Color Custom Component with DataList and Ajax support</h1>
        <h:form id="frm">

            <projsfhtml5:inputColor id="ic-favcolor" value="#{componentInputColor.color}"
                                    list="available-colors">
                <f:ajax event="change" render=":frm:selected-color" execute="@this " />
            </projsfhtml5:inputColor>

            <projsfhtml5:dataList id="available-colors">
                <projsfhtml5:option value="#ff0000" label="Red"/>
```

```
            <projsfhtml5:option value="#00ff00" label="Green"/>
            <projsfhtml5:option value="#0000ff" label="Blue"/>
        </projsfhtml5:dataList>

        <h:commandButton value="Submit" />

        <h:outputText id="selected-color" value="Color is: #{componentInputColor.color}" />

      </h:form>
    </h:body>
</html>
```

With the `clientBehavior` in the interface for the `inputColor` component, you can nest it with a `<f:ajax />` tag where you listen for the broadcasted events.

Fallback for Unsupported Browsers

If you've tried the example in the previous chapter in a browser that does not support the HTML5 color input, you will see a text field on the screen, as shown in Figure 7-3, instead of a color picker.

JSF Composite Component

Figure 7-3. *Color input rendered on a browser that does not support it*

Supporting fallbacks require that it is possible to detect if the browser supports the given feature. If it does not support the feature provided by the custom component, an alternative display should be provided.

In the fallback example Listing 7-12, we first check if the browser supports the color input. If color input is not supported we provide a fallback using the jscolor library (freely available at `www.jscolor.com`), as shown in Figure 7-4.

Listing 7-12. Supports Fallback to a JavaScript Color Picker

```
<?xml version='1.0' encoding='UTF-8' ?>
<!DOCTYPE html PUBLIC "-//W3C//DTD XHTML 1.0 Transitional//EN"
"http://www.w3.org/TR/xhtml1/DTD/xhtml1-transitional.dtd">
<html xmlns="http://www.w3.org/1999/xhtml"
      xmlns:cc="http://xmlns.jcp.org/jsf/composite"
      xmlns:jsf="http://xmlns.jcp.org/jsf"
      xmlns:h="http://xmlns.jcp.org/jsf/html">

    <!-- INTERFACE -->
    <cc:interface>
        <cc:attribute name="value" type="java.lang.String" default="#000000" />
        <cc:attribute name="list" type="java.lang.String" default="" />
        <cc:clientBehavior name="change" targets="#{cc.id}" event="change" />
    </cc:interface>
```

```
<!-- IMPLEMENTATION -->
<cc:implementation>
    <h:outputScript library="js" name="jscolor.js" />

    <div id="#{cc.clientId}">
        <input jsf:id="#{cc.id}" jsf:value="#{cc.attrs.value}" type="color"
               list="#{cc.attrs.list}"/>

        <script type="text/javascript">
            function html5_supports_input(type) {
                var i = document.createElement("input");
                i.setAttribute("type", type);
                return i.type === type;
            }

            if (!html5_supports_input('color')) {
                // The color input is not supported on the browser.
                // Provide an alternative way of rendering the color picker,
                // e.g. jscolor (http://jscolor.com/)
                var componentId = '${cc.clientId}:${cc.id}'.replace(/:/g, "\\:");
                new jscolor.color(document.getElementById('${cc.clientId}:${cc.id}'), {})
            }
        </script>

    </div>
</cc:implementation>
</html>
```

JSF Composite Component

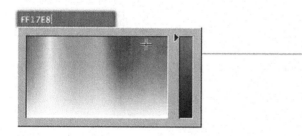

Figure 7-4. *Fallback version of the inputColor component*

■ **Tip**   Rather than implementing your own HTML5 feature detection algorithms, you can use a JavaScript library like Modernizr (www.modernizr.com) to detect the availability of native implementations of HTML5 and CSS3.

Input Date Picker Custom Component

In this section we will implement the HTML5 date picker input element as a composite component. The purpose of the date picker input is to allow the user to select a date using the native date picker built into the browser. Not all browsers support the date picker, so like the color picker we will provide a fallback, this time using JQuery-UI. Like the color input component, the date input component also supports the change event that we will catch and broadcast to Ajax-enable the component.

Table 7-3 contains a list of attributes supported by the date input element. We will implement all the attributes in our composite component. Examples of how the attributes are used can be found in Listing 7-13.

Table 7-3. *Attributes Supported by the Date Input Element*

Attribute	Data type
Autocomplete	Boolean
List	String (reference to a datalist)
Value	Date string (year-month number-day number, e.g. 1970-01-10 is the 10th January 1970)
Max	Date string (latest possible date that the user can select)
Min	Date string (earliest possible date that the user can select)
Readonly	Boolean
Required	Boolean
Step	Integer (number of days to change at every step)

Listing 7-13. Examples of Using HTML5 Date Input

```
<section>
    <label for="without-value">Date (without a preset date): </label>
        <input id="withouth-value" type="date" value="" />
    </section>

<section>
    <label for="with-value">Date (with a preset date): </label>
        <input id="with-value" type="date" value="2013-05-03" step="10" />
    </section>

<section>
    <label for="with-constraints">Date (with a constraints): </label>
        <input id="with-constraints" type="date" value="2013-05-03"
            min="2013-05-01" max="2013-05-31" />
    </section>

<section>
    <label for="readonly">Date (readonly): </label>
        <input id="readonly" type="date" value="2013-05-03"
            readonly />
    </section>
```

```
<section>
    <label for="with-list">Date (with list of dates): </label>
    <input id="with-list" type="date" value="" list="available-dates" />
</section>

<datalist id="available-dates">
    <option value="2013-01-01" label="1st Option" />
    <option value="2013-03-10" label="2nd Option" />
    <option value="2013-06-19" label="3rd Option" />
    <option value="2013-10-10" label="4th Option" />
</datalist>
</section>
```

Creating the Composite Component

Based on the HTML5 examples in Listing 7-13, we can reuse our implementation of the datalist and option components from the color input component. Note that the value for the date input in HTML5 is a string formatted as year-month-day (e.g. 2013-04-20). To avoid unnecessary data conversion we will use a date/time converter so that the value of the component can be set as a java.util.Date.

Listing 7-14 shows a basic implementation supporting the attributes specified in HTML5. The value of the component is a java.util.Date and automatically converted using the <f:convertDateTime /> converter nested inside the input element. The required and readonly attribute have JSF equivalents, so they are mapped directly to JSF by prefixing the attributes with jsf (i.e., jsf:readonly="#{cc.attrs.readonly}"). You have probably noticed that that min and max attributes are not mapped directly from the interface to the implementation. It is not possible to apply converters to attribute values. That means that we cannot simply assign the java.util.Date value from the min attribute in the interface to the min attribute in the implementation. If we mapped the attributes directly the value in the min attribute in the implementation would be rendered as the "toString()" representation of the java.util.Date value which is of the form: day of week + month name + day of month + hour : minute : second + time zone + year, e.g., Sat Jun 15 11:24:21 CET 2013. This format is not aligned with the format specified by HTML5 (i.e., year–month–day). Since we cannot apply a converter on attribute values, we must implement a backing bean for the component that takes care of the data conversation.

Listing 7-14. Composite Component for the inputDate Component (resources/projsfhtml5/inputDate.xhtml)

```xml
<?xml version='1.0' encoding='UTF-8' ?>
<!DOCTYPE html PUBLIC "-//W3C//DTD XHTML 1.0 Transitional//EN"
"http://www.w3.org/TR/xhtml1/DTD/xhtml1-transitional.dtd">
<html xmlns="http://www.w3.org/1999/xhtml"
    xmlns:cc="http://xmlns.jcp.org/jsf/composite"
    xmlns:jsf="http://xmlns.jcp.org/jsf"
    xmlns:h="http://xmlns.jcp.org/jsf/html"
    xmlns:f="http://xmlns.jcp.org/jsf/core">

    <cc:interface>
        <cc:attribute name="value" type="java.util.Date" required="true" />
        <cc:attribute name="list" type="java.lang.String" default="" />
        <cc:attribute name="step" type="java.lang.String" default="1" />
        <cc:attribute name="min" type="java.util.Date" />
        <cc:attribute name="max" type="java.util.Date" />
        <cc:attribute name="readonly" type="java.lang.String" default="false" />
```

```
            <cc:attribute name="required" type="java.lang.String" default="false" />
            <cc:clientBehavior name="change" targets="date" event="change" />
        </cc:interface>

        <cc:implementation>
            <div id="#{cc.clientId}">
                <input jsf:id="date"
                       type="date"
                       jsf:value="#{cc.attrs.value}"
                       jsf:readonly="#{cc.attrs.readonly != 'false' ? 'true' : 'false'}"
                       jsf:required="#{cc.attrs.required != 'false' ? 'true' : 'false'}"
                       step="#{cc.attrs.step}"
                       list="#{cc.attrs.list}">
                    <f:convertDateTime pattern="yyyy-MM-dd" />
                </input>
            </div>
        </cc:implementation>
</html>
```

Creating a Backing Bean for the Composite Component

A composite component backing bean must extend javax.faces.component.UINamingContainer. By convention
you can automatically map the backing bean to the composite component by naming the backing bean the same as
the composite component and by placing the backing bean in a package by the same name as the directory where
the composite component is located. Alternatively, you can annotate the backing bean with the @FacesComponent
annotation and specify the component type as the value of the annotation. The component type can then be specified
in the interface of the composite component. The benefit of manually mapping the backing bean is that you can reuse
the backing bean by other composite components and you do not have to name the backing bean the same as the
composite component.

Listing 7-15 shows a barebones example of a backing bean declared for composite components of type inputDate.
A composite component maps to the backing bean by setting the componentType attribute of the interface to the
name declared in the @FacesComponent annotation, e.g., <cc:interface componentType="inputDate">.

Listing 7-15. Empty Backing Bean Declared for inputDate Components

```
package projsfhtml5;

import javax.faces.component.FacesComponent;
import javax.faces.component.UINamingContainer;

@FacesComponent("inputDate")
public class InputDateComponent extends UINamingContainer {

}
```

To support the min and max attributes we need two properties on the backing bean: one for holding the string
representation of the minimum date and one for holding the string representation of the maximum date. We will
name the properties minDate and maxDate. By providing getters for the two properties, they will automatically be
available to the composite component. Then we will override the encodeBegin method where we will extract the java.
util.Dates from the interface and convert them to HTML5 formatted dates that can be used in the implementation.

Listing 7-16. Backing Bean Converting and Exposing the Minimum and Maximum Dates

```java
package projsfhtml5;

import java.io.IOException;
import java.text.DateFormat;
import java.text.SimpleDateFormat;
import javax.faces.component.FacesComponent;
import javax.faces.component.UINamingContainer;
import javax.faces.context.FacesContext;

@FacesComponent("inputDate")
public class InputDateComponent extends UINamingContainer {

    private static final DateFormat HTML5_FORMAT = new SimpleDateFormat("yyyy-MM-dd");
    private String minDate = "";
    private String maxDate = "";

    @Override
    public void encodeBegin(FacesContext context) throws IOException {

        // Extract the minimum date from the interface
        java.util.Date attrsMin = (java.util.Date) getAttributes().get("min");
        if (attrsMin != null) {
            // Convert the date to an HTML5 date
            minDate = HTML5_FORMAT.format(attrsMin);
        }

        // Extract the maximum date from the interface
        java.util.Date attrsMax = (java.util.Date) getAttributes().get("max");
        if (attrsMax != null) {
            // Convert the date to an HTML5 date
            maxDate = HTML5_FORMAT.format(attrsMax);
        }

        super.encodeBegin(context);
    }

    /**
     * Gets the minimum date selectable in the date picker.
     *
     * @return Date formatted using the {@link inputDate#HTML5_FORMAT}
     */
    public String getMinDate() {
        return minDate;
    }

    /**
     * Gets the maximum date selectable in the date picker.
     *
     * @return Date formatted using the {@link inputDate#HTML5_FORMAT}
     */
```

```
        public String getMaxDate() {
            return maxDate;
        }
}
```

Using the Composite Component

With the backing bean in place we can access the minDate and maxDate properties containing the converted dates and insert them in the implementation of the composite component.

Listing 7-17. Composite Component Using the Backing Bean and Accessing the Converted Values

```
<?xml version='1.0' encoding='UTF-8' ?>
<!DOCTYPE html PUBLIC "-//W3C//DTD XHTML 1.0 Transitional//EN"
"http://www.w3.org/TR/xhtml1/DTD/xhtml1-transitional.dtd">
<html xmlns="http://www.w3.org/1999/xhtml"
      xmlns:cc="http://java.sun.com/jsf/composite"
      xmlns:jsf="http://xmlns.jcp.org/jsf"
      xmlns:h="http://xmlns.jcp.org/jsf/html"
      xmlns:f="http://xmlns.jcp.org/jsf/core">

    <cc:interface componentType="inputDate">
        <cc:attribute name="value" type="java.util.Date" required="true" />
        <cc:attribute name="list" type="java.lang.String" default="" />
        <cc:attribute name="step" type="java.lang.String" default="1" />
        <cc:attribute name="min" type="java.util.Date" />
        <cc:attribute name="max" type="java.util.Date" />
        <cc:attribute name="readonly" type="java.lang.String" default="false" />
        <cc:attribute name="required" type="java.lang.String" default="false" />
        <cc:clientBehavior name="change" targets="date" event="change" />
    </cc:interface>

    <cc:implementation>
        <div id="#{cc.clientId}">
            <input jsf:id="date"
                   type="date"
                   jsf:value="#{cc.attrs.value}"
                   jsf:readonly="#{cc.attrs.readonly != 'false' ? 'true' : 'false'}"
                   jsf:required="#{cc.attrs.required != 'false' ? 'true' : 'false'}"
                   step="#{cc.attrs.step}"
                   min="#{cc.minDate}"
                   max="#{cc.maxDate}"
                   list="#{cc.attrs.list}">
                <f:convertDateTime pattern="yyyy-MM-dd" />
            </input>
        </div>
    </cc:implementation>
</html>
```

With the composite component and backing bean in place, we are ready to use the component. Listing 7-18 shows some examples with accompanying screenshots in Figure 7-5.

Listing 7-18. Examples of Using the inputDate Composite Component

```
<h:form>
    <h1>JSF Component</h1>
    <section>
        <label>Date (with a null java.util.Date): </label>
        <projsfhtml5:inputDate value="#{componentInputDate.emptyDate}" />

        <h:outputLabel value="Selected date:" />
        <h:outputText value="#{componentInputDate.emptyDate}">
            <f:convertDateTime dateStyle="short" />
        </h:outputText>
    </section>
    <section>
        <label>Date (with a java.util.Date): </label>
        <projsfhtml5:inputDate value="#{componentInputDate.selectedDate}"
                               step="10"
                               min="#{componentInputDate.minDate}"
                               max="#{componentInputDate.maxDate}" />

        <h:outputLabel value="Selected date:" />
        <h:outputText value="#{componentInputDate.selectedDate}">
            <f:convertDateTime dateStyle="short" />
        </h:outputText>
    </section>
    <section>
        <label>Date (readonly): </label>
        <projsfhtml5:inputDate value="#{componentInputDate.selectedDate}"
                               readonly="true" />
    </section>
    <section>
        <label>Date (with a list of dates): </label>
        <projsfhtml5:inputDate value="#{componentInputDate.selectedDate2}"
                               list="available-dates"  />

        <projsfhtml5:dataList id="available-dates">
            <projsfhtml5:option label="1st Option" value="2012-01-01" />
            <projsfhtml5:option label="2nd Option" value="2012-01-02" />
            <projsfhtml5:option label="3rd Option" value="2012-01-03" />
        </projsfhtml5:dataList>
        <h:outputLabel value="Selected date:" />
        <h:outputText value="#{componentInputDate.selectedDate2}">
            <f:convertDateTime dateStyle="short" />
        </h:outputText>
    </section>
    <h:commandButton value="Submit" />
</h:form>
```

JSF Component

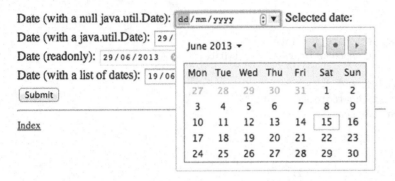

Figure 7-5. The <projsfhtml5:inputDate /> component in action

Fallback for Unsupported Browsers

A browser that does not support HTML date input renders a plain text field with the date like the color input in the previous section. To provide a fallback, we can once again use JavaScript to check if the feature is supported in the browser, and if it isn't, we can provide an alternative display of the control. In the following example we have used Modernizr to check if the feature is supported in the browser, and if it is not we use the DatePicker component of JQuery-UI as seen in Figure 7-6.

JSF Component

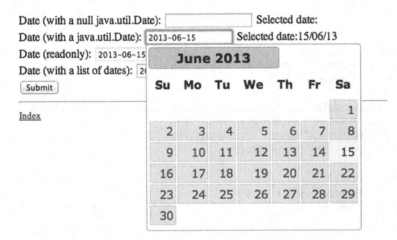

Figure 7-6. Fallback to JQuery-UI if HTML5 date input is not supported by the browser

Listing 7-19. Supporting Fallback Using JQuery-UI and Modernizr

```
<?xml version='1.0' encoding='UTF-8' ?>
<!DOCTYPE html PUBLIC "-//W3C//DTD XHTML 1.0 Transitional//EN"
"http://www.w3.org/TR/xhtml1/DTD/xhtml1-transitional.dtd">
<html xmlns="http://www.w3.org/1999/xhtml"
      xmlns:cc="http://java.sun.com/jsf/composite"
      xmlns:jsf="http://xmlns.jcp.org/jsf"
      xmlns:h="http://xmlns.jcp.org/jsf/html"
      xmlns:f="http://xmlns.jcp.org/jsf/core">

    <cc:interface componentType="inputDate">
        <cc:attribute name="value" type="java.util.Date" required="true" />
        <cc:attribute name="list" type="java.lang.String" default="" />
        <cc:attribute name="step" type="java.lang.String" default="1" />
        <cc:attribute name="min" type="java.util.Date" />
        <cc:attribute name="max" type="java.util.Date" />
        <cc:attribute name="readonly" type="java.lang.String" default="false" />
        <cc:attribute name="required" type="java.lang.String" default="false" />
        <cc:clientBehavior name="change" targets="date" event="change" />
    </cc:interface>

    <cc:implementation>
        <h:outputStylesheet library="css" name="jquery-ui.css" />
        <h:outputScript target="head" library="js" name="modernizr.js" />
        <h:outputScript target="head" library="js" name="jquery-1.9.1.js" />
        <h:outputScript target="head" library="js" name="jquery-ui.js" />
        <script type="text/javascript">
            if (!Modernizr.inputtypes.date) {
                jQuery(function() {
                    var id = '${cc.clientId}:date'.replace(/:/g, "\\:");
                    jQuery("#" + id).datepicker({ dateFormat: 'yy-mm-dd' });
                });
            }
        </script>

        <div id="#{cc.clientId}">
            <input jsf:id="date" type="date" jsf:value="#{cc.attrs.value}"
                   jsf:readonly="#{cc.attrs.readonly != 'false' ? 'true' : 'false'}"
                   jsf:required="#{cc.attrs.required != 'false' ? 'true' : 'false'}"
                   step="#{cc.attrs.step}" min="#{cc.minDate}" max="#{cc.maxDate}"
                   list="#{cc.attrs.list}">
                <f:convertDateTime pattern="yyyy-MM-dd" />
            </input></div>
    </cc:implementation>
</html>
```

▪ **Note** One of the advantages of using `<h:outputScript/>` and `<h:outputStylesheet/>` in a composite component is that it will be included only once even if you use the component multiple times in a page.

Slider Custom Component

In this section we will implement the HTML5 range input element as a composite component. The purpose of the range input is to allow the user to select a value in a range of numbers using the native slider control built into the browser. Not all browsers support the range input, so like the date picker we will provide a fallback using JQuery-UI. We will also support Ajax events, as they are particularly useful for a slider to provide instant feedback to the user about the selected value.

Table 7-4 contains a list of attributes supported by the range input element. We will implement all the attributes in our composite component. Examples of how the attributes are used can be found in Listing 7-20

Table 7-4. *Attributes Supported by the Range Input Element*

Attribute	Data type
autocomplete	Boolean
list	String (reference to a datalist)
value	Number representing the value selected in the range
max	Upper bound in the range control
min	Lower bound in the range control
step	Numbers to step when using the range control

Listing 7-20. Examples of Using HTML5 Range Input

```
<section>
    <label for="without-value">Range (without value): </label>
    <input id="withouth-value" type="range" />
</section>

<section>
    <label for="min-to-max">Range (-10 to 10): </label>
    <input id="min-to-max" type="range" min="-10" max="10" value="0" />
</section>

<section>
    <label for="range-list">Range (list): </label>
    <input id="range-list" type="range" value="0" list="list" />
</section>

<datalist id="list">
    <option value="-100" />
    <option value="-75" />
    <option value="-50" />
    <option value="-25" />
    <option value="0" />
</datalist>
```

Creating the Composite Component

The implementation of the range component is straightforward. The relevant attributes are added to the interface along with broadcasting the JavaScript change event. The implementation contains the JavaScript libraries used for fallback in case the browser doesn't support the HTML5 input range control. It also includes inline JavaScript checking if the input range control is supported and if not uses JQuery and JQuery UI to turn a <div> element into a range control. The inline JavaScript in this component is a bit more complicated than the previous components. This is because the slider control in JQuery UI is not applied on an <input> element but one a <div> element. That means that every time the slider is moved we need to update the <input> element and fire a change event to keep the functionality consistent with the native HTML5 version.

Listing 7-21. Composite Component for inputRange (resources/projsfhtml5/inputRange.xhtml)

```
<?xml version='1.0' encoding='UTF-8' ?>
<!DOCTYPE html PUBLIC "-//W3C//DTD XHTML 1.0 Transitional//EN"
"http://www.w3.org/TR/xhtml1/DTD/xhtml1-transitional.dtd">
<html xmlns="http://www.w3.org/1999/xhtml"
      xmlns:cc="http://java.sun.com/jsf/composite"
      xmlns:jsf="http://xmlns.jcp.org/jsf"
      xmlns:h="http://xmlns.jcp.org/jsf/html"
      xmlns:f="http://xmlns.jcp.org/jsf/core">

    <cc:interface>
        <cc:attribute name="value" type="java.lang.String" />
        <cc:attribute name="list" type="java.lang.String" default="" />
        <cc:attribute name="step" type="java.lang.String" default="1" />
        <cc:attribute name="min" type="java.lang.String" />
        <cc:attribute name="max" type="java.lang.String" />
        <cc:clientBehavior name="change" targets="range" event="change" />
    </cc:interface>

    <cc:implementation>
        <h:outputStylesheet library="css" name="jquery-ui.css" />
        <h:outputScript target="head" library="js" name="modernizr.js" />
        <h:outputScript target="head" library="js" name="jquery-1.9.1.js" />
        <h:outputScript target="head" library="js" name="jquery-ui.js" />

        <script type="text/javascript">
            if (!Modernizr.inputtypes.range) {
                jQuery(function() {
                    var rangeId = '${cc.clientId}:range'.replace(/:/g, "\\:");
                    var hideId = '${cc.clientId}'.replace(/:/g, "\\:");
                    jQuery("#" + hideId).hide();

                    var id = '${cc.clientId}:fallback'.replace(/:/g, "\\:");
                    jQuery("#" + id).slider({
                        min: #{cc.attrs.min},
                        max: #{cc.attrs.max},
                        step: #{cc.attrs.step},
                        slide: function(event, ui) {
```

```
                                    // Update the value of the input element and fire a change event
                                    jQuery("#" + rangeId).val(ui.value).change();
                        }});
                });
            }
        </script>

        <!-- Div used for fallback in case the HTML5 range control is not supported -->
        <div id="#{cc.clientId}:fallback" style="display: block"></div>

        <div id="#{cc.clientId}">
            <input jsf:id="range" type="range" jsf:value="#{cc.attrs.value}"
                    step="#{cc.attrs.step}" min="#{cc.attrs.min}" max="#{cc.attrs.max}"
                    list="#{cc.attrs.list}" />
        </div>
    </cc:implementation>
</html>
```

Using the Composite Component

Listing 7-22 shows some examples of the composite control with accompanying screenshots in Figure 7-7 (native HTML5 support) and Figure 7-8 (fallback).

Listing 7-22. Examples of Using the inputRange Composite Component

```
<h1>JSF Composite Control</h1>
<section>
    <label for="min-to-max">Range (-10 to 10): </label>
    <projsfhtml5:inputRange value="#{componentInputRange.range1}" min="-10" max="10">
        <f:ajax event="change" execute="@this" render=":frm:selectedValue" />
    </projsfhtml5:inputRange>
    <h:outputText id="selectedValue" value="Selected value: #{componentInputRange.range1}"/>
</section>

<section>
    <label for="with-list">Range (with List): </label>
    <projsfhtml5:inputRange value="#{componentInputRange.range2}" min="-100" max="10" list="range-options">
        <f:ajax event="change" execute="@this" render=":frm:selectedValue2" />
    </projsfhtml5:inputRange>
    <h:outputText id="selectedValue2" value="Selected value: #{componentInputRange.range2}"/>
    <projsfhtml5:dataList id="range-options">
        <projsfhtml5:option value="-100" />
        <projsfhtml5:option value="-75" />
        <projsfhtml5:option value="-50" />
        <projsfhtml5:option value="-25" />
        <projsfhtml5:option value="0" />
        <projsfhtml5:option value="10" />
    </projsfhtml5:dataList>
</section>

<h:commandButton value="Submit" />
```

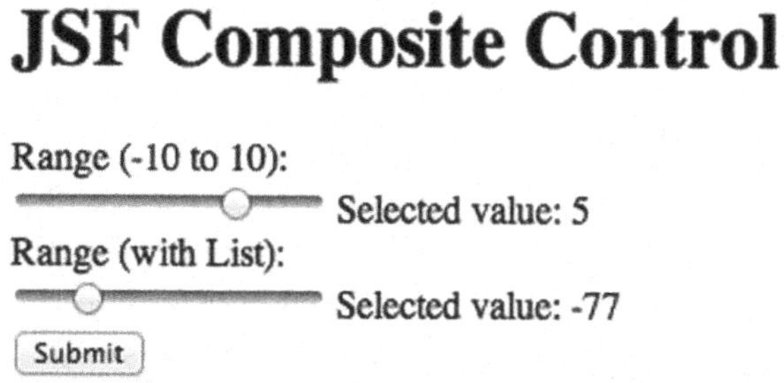

JSF Composite Control

Range (-10 to 10):

Selected value: 5

Range (with List):

Selected value: -77

[Submit]

Figure 7-7. *Native HTML5 support*

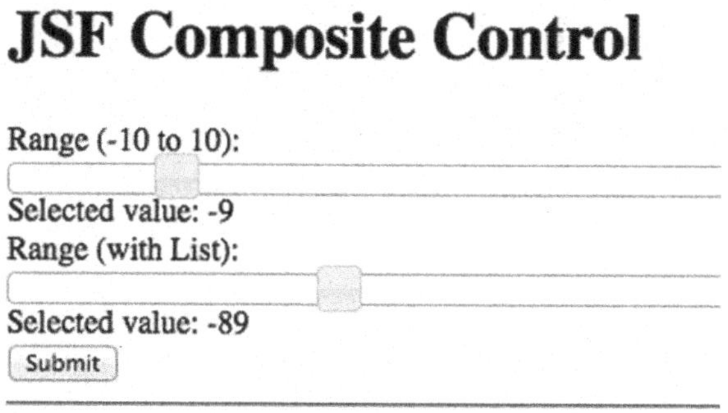

JSF Composite Control

Range (-10 to 10):

Selected value: -9

Range (with List):

Selected value: -89

[Submit]

Figure 7-8. *Fallback to JQueryUI slider*

Spinner Custom Component

Finally, we will implement the HTML5 number input element as a composite component. The purpose of the number input is to allow the user to select a value in a range of number using a spinner control where the user can click up or down, after which the selected value increments or decrements. Like all the other controls, all browsers do not support the number control yet, so we will once again provide a fallback using JQuery-UI.

Table 7-5 contains a list of attributes supported by the number input element. We will implement all the attributes in our composite component. Examples of how the attributes are used can be seen in Listing 7-23.

Table 7-5. *Attributes Supported by the Number Input Element*

Attribute	Data type
Autocomplete	Boolean
List	String (reference to a datalist)
value	Number representing the value selected
max	Upper bound in the spinner control
min	Lower bound in the spinner control
step	Numbers to step when using the spinner control
readonly	Boolean
required	Boolean

Listing 7-23. Examples of Using HTML5 Number Input

```
<section>
    <label for="without-value">Number (without value): </label>
    <input id="withouth-value" type="number" />
</section>

<section>
    <label for="min-to-max">Number (-10 to 10): </label>
    <input id="min-to-max" type="number" min="-10" max="10" value="0" />
</section>

<section>
    <label for="preselect-list">Range (list): </label>
    <input id="preselect-list" type="number" value="0" list="list" />
</section>

<datalist id="list">
    <option value="-100" />
    <option value="-75" />
    <option value="-50" />
    <option value="-25" />
    <option value="0" />
</datalist>
```

Creating the Composite Component

The implementation of the number component is like the range component. The relevant attributes are added to the interface along with broadcasting the JavaScript change event. The implementation contains the JavaScript libraries used for fallback in case the browser doesn't support the HTML5 input number control. It also includes inline JavaScript checking if the input number control is supported and if not uses JQuery and JQuery UI to turn the input field into a spinner control. An event was also hooked up to fire a change event whenever the spinner control is used to ensure that the Ajax call gets broadcast.

Listing 7-24. Composite Component for inputNumber (resources/projsfhtml5/inputNumber.xhtml)

```
<?xml version='1.0' encoding='UTF-8' ?>
<!DOCTYPE html PUBLIC "-//W3C//DTD XHTML 1.0 Transitional//EN" "http://www.w3.org/TR/xhtml1/DTD/
xhtml1-transitional.dtd">
<html xmlns="http://www.w3.org/1999/xhtml"
      xmlns:cc="http://java.sun.com/jsf/composite"
      xmlns:jsf="http://xmlns.jcp.org/jsf"
      xmlns:h="http://xmlns.jcp.org/jsf/html"
      xmlns:f="http://xmlns.jcp.org/jsf/core">

    <cc:interface>
        <cc:attribute name="value" type="java.lang.String" />
        <cc:attribute name="list" type="java.lang.String" default="" />
        <cc:attribute name="step" type="java.lang.String" default="1" />
        <cc:attribute name="min" type="java.lang.String" />
        <cc:attribute name="max" type="java.lang.String" />
```

```
        <cc:attribute name="readonly" type="java.lang.String" default="false" />
        <cc:attribute name="required" type="java.lang.String" default="false" />
        <cc:clientBehavior name="change" targets="number" event="change" />
    </cc:interface>

    <cc:implementation>
        <h:outputStylesheet library="css" name="jquery-ui.css" />
        <h:outputScript target="head" library="js" name="modernizr.js" />
        <h:outputScript target="head" library="js" name="jquery-1.9.1.js" />
        <h:outputScript target="head" library="js" name="jquery-ui.js" />

        <script type="text/javascript">
            if (!Modernizr.inputtypes.number) {
                jQuery(function() {
                    var id = '${cc.clientId}:number'.replace(/:/g, "\\:");
                    jQuery("#" + id).spinner();

                    jQuery('.ui-spinner-button').click(function() {
                        jQuery(this).siblings('input').change();
                    });
                });
            }
        </script>

        <div id="#{cc.clientId}">
            <input jsf:id="number" type="number" jsf:value="#{cc.attrs.value}"
                    step="#{cc.attrs.step}" min="#{cc.attrs.min}" max="#{cc.attrs.max}"
                    list="#{cc.attrs.list}"
                    jsf:readonly="#{cc.attrs.readonly != 'false' ? 'true' : 'false'}"
                    jsf:required="#{cc.attrs.required != 'false' ? 'true' : 'false'}"/>
        </div>
    </cc:implementation>
</html>
```

Using the Composite Component

Listing 7-25 shows some examples of the composite control with accompanying screenshots in Figure 7-9 (native HTML5 support) and Figure 7-10 (fallback).

Listing 7-25. Examples of Using the inputNumber Composite Component

```
<section>
    <label for="min-to-max">Number (-10 to 10): </label>
    <projsfhtml5:inputNumber value="#{componentInputNumber.number1}" min="-10" max="10">
        <f:ajax event="change" execute="@this" render=":frm:selectedValue" />
    </projsfhtml5:inputNumber>
    <h:outputText id="selectedValue" value="Selected value: #{componentInputNumber.number1}"/>
</section>
```

```
<section>
    <label for="with-list">Number (with List): </label>
    <projsfhtml5:inputNumber value="#{componentInputNumber.number2}" min="-100" max="10"
                           list="number-options">
        <f:ajax event="change" execute="@this" render=":frm:selectedValue2" />
    </projsfhtml5:inputNumber>
    <h:outputText id="selectedValue2" value="Selected value: #{componentInputNumber.number2}"/>
    <projsfhtml5:dataList id="number-options">
        <projsfhtml5:option value="-100" />
        <projsfhtml5:option value="-75" />
        <projsfhtml5:option value="-50" />
        <projsfhtml5:option value="-25" />
        <projsfhtml5:option value="0" />
        <projsfhtml5:option value="10" />
    </projsfhtml5:dataList>
</section>

<h:commandButton value="Submit" />
```

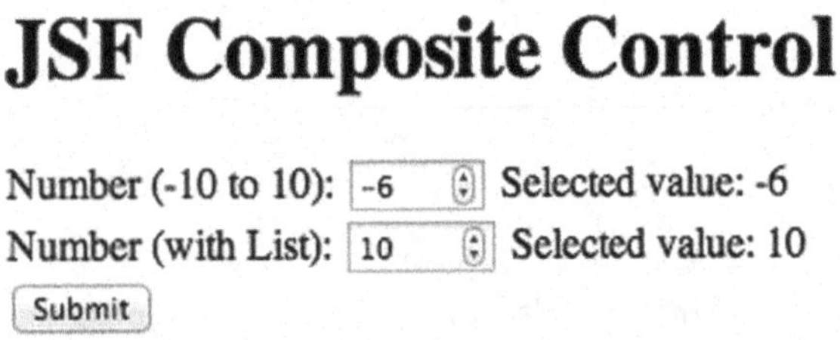

JSF Composite Control

Number (-10 to 10): -6 ⬍ Selected value: -6
Number (with List): 10 ⬍ Selected value: 10
Submit

Figure 7-9. *Native HTML5 support*

JSF Composite Control

Number (-10 to 10): 10 ⬍ Selected value: 10
Number (with List): 5 ⬍ Selected value: 5
Submit

Figure 7-10. *Fallback to JQueryUI slider*

Summary

In this chapter, we have looked at turning some of the new HTML5 input types into JSF composite components. Throughout the chapter we looked at implementing basic composite components, nested components, and Ajax-enabled components. Composite components hide away unnecessary logic for the page authors. We looked at how to detect whether the browser supports the input elements we are outputting and if not, provide an alternative view. Without composite components you would probably have to write additional JavaScript on each page to check for compatibility. With composite components all the logic is contained in one place and it is easy to make a single change that cascades through all the pages using the composite component.

■ ■ ■

CHAPTER 8

Advanced JSF2 HTML5 Components

In the previous chapter we built JSF2 components for some of the new input elements introduced in HTML5. In this chapter we will continue building JSF2 components that take advantage of some of the new non-input HTML5 elements.

Media Component

A weakness of HTML that has become more evident with the increased usage of mobile devices is the lack of a standardized way of implementing media players for web pages. Prior to HTML5 web page authors had to display embedded media content through Java applets or Flash SWFs using the object or embed elements. If you are a seasoned web page author, you know all about the hassle you have to go through to ensure that your web page works on all web browsers. With the advent of mobile devices, this problem has become even bigger. Despite all the web standardization efforts in the past decade, you still have to write several workarounds and failovers in your web code to ensure that they function well on the most popular web browsers and mobile devices. One of the popular mobile platforms is iOS from Apple. Back in April 2010, Steve Jobs wrote an open letter[1] explaining Apple's thoughts on Flash, basically stating that Flash will not be supported on iOS devices and that new open standards (such as HTML5) should be used in the future to create graphically rich applications and games.

Media Elements Introduced in HTML5

For playing videos and audio. HTML5 introduces four new elements: audio, video, source, and track. The audio and video elements define how a video or audio clip should be played and the controls available to visitor of the web page. Nested in the audio and video elements, source elements can be inserted to offer media alternatives from which the web browser can choose based on its supported media types and codecs.

■ **Note** You can find details about the specification of media elements in the HTML5 specification on the W3C website www.w3.org/TR/html5/embedded-content-0.html#media-elements.

Both the audio and video elements implement the HTMLMediaElement interface specified in the HTML5 specification. The interface defines common properties and methods for playing back audio and video clips (see Table 8-1). The writable properties can be set using the attributes of the audio and video elements. Read-only properties and methods can be accessed in the DOM through JavaScript.

---

[1]Thoughts on Flash by Steve Jobs, April 2010 http://www.apple.com/hotnews/thoughts-on-flash/

Table 8-1. *List of Common Attributes for Media Elements (Audio and Video)*

Attribute	Type	Default Value	Description
Src	URL	Unspecified	URL specifying the address of the media file.
Crossorigin	CORS settings enumeration	anonymous	Enumerated value (anonymous or use-credentials) specifying how to deal with cross origin requests.
Preload	Preload enumeration	auto	Enumerated value (none, metadata, or auto) specifying if the media source should be preloaded. "none" will not preload any data and will minimize unnecessary traffic to the server. "metadata" will attempt to fetch the metadata of the media source (duration, dimensions, etc.) prior to playing back the file. During playback the slowest possible download rate will be used while still maintaining consistent playback to save bandwidth. "auto" leaves the download strategy to the browser and may use excessive bandwidth as the browser may attempt to aggressively download the whole media file prior to playback.
Autoplay	Boolean	false	Boolean value specifying if the media file should automatically start playback when the page has been loaded.
Mediagroup	String	Unspecified	String value that serves as a name for grouping and synchronizing video and audio clips. Audio and video elements with the same string value in the mediagroup attribute will be synchronized and managed from the same network request. When the mediagroup attribute is used, a MediaController object is created and set in the controller property of the HTMLMediaElement. The property can be fetched using JavaScript and used to manipulate all the media elements using the same controller (i.e., with the same mediagroup name).
Loop	Boolean	false	Boolean value that indicates if the media element should start over once it reaches the end of the clip.
Muted	Boolean	false	Boolean value that indicates if the audio should be muted during playback.
Controls	Boolean	false	Boolean value that indicates if the user controls (play, pause, seeker, etc.) should be displayed.

The video element contains a few additional attributes for specifying the dimensions of the video and the poster to appear (if any) before playback of the video begins. The additional video attributes are listed in Table 8-2.

Table 8-2. *List of Additional Attributes That Apply to Video Elements Only*

Attribute	Type	Default Value	Description
width	Dimension	300px	Width of the video playing area.
height	Dimension	150px	Height of the video playing area.
poster	URL	Unspecified	URL of the still image that should appear as the poster for the video before playback starts.

In Listing 8-1 you will see an example of the audio and video elements introduced in HTML5. The example also shows how media elements can be controlled using JavaScript.

Listing 8-1. Basic Example of the Audio and Video Element Introduced in HTML5 to Playback Audio and Video Clips Without the Use of Plug-ins Such as Java Applets or Flash SWFs

```
<!DOCTYPE html>
<html xmlns="http://www.w3.org/1999/xhtml">
    <head>
        <meta charset="UTF-8" />
        <title>Media Element</title>
        <style>
            video, audio { display: block }
        </style>
        <script type="text/javascript">

            // Obtaining the MediaElement via JavaScript and invoking methods
            function togglePlay(source, elementId) {
                var mediaElement = document.getElementById(elementId);

                if (mediaElement.paused) {
                    mediaElement.play();
                    source.innerText = "Pause";
                } else {
                    mediaElement.pause();
                    source.innerText = "Play";
                }
            }
        </script>
    </head>
    <body>
        <article>
            <h2>Video Example</h2>

            <video id="video-example"
                   controls="controls"
                   poster="media/poster.png"
                   src="media/trailer.mp4">
                <!-- Provide fallback for browsers that doesn't support the video element -->
                <p>Browser not support the HTML5 Video element.</p>
            </video>
            <button onclick="togglePlay(this, 'video-example');">Play</button>
        </article>

        <article>
            <h2>Audio Example</h2>
            <audio id="audio-example"
                   controls="controls"
                   src="media/04-Death_Becomes_Fur.mp4">
```

```
            <!-- Provide fallback for browsers that doesn't support the audio element -->
            <p>Browser not support the HTML5 Audio element.</p>
        </audio>
        <button onclick="togglePlay(this, 'audio-example');">Play</button>
    </article>

</body>
</html>
```

Different web browsers and devices support different media formats. Rather than doing device and browser detection and updating the src attribute accordingly, it is possible to specify multiple media sources. The browser is free to select the most appropriate media source based on its supported formats and codecs. When specifying sources it is not necessary to specify a media file in the src attribute of the audio or video element. The most commonly supported formats and codecs are the WebM format (using the VP8 video codec and Vorbis audio codec) and MP4 format (using the H.264 video codec and ACC or MP3 audio codec).

Listing 8-2 is an example of providing multiple video and audio sources that will automatically be selected based on the formats supported by the browser accessing the page.

Listing 8-2. Multiple Media Sources Can Be Provided to Ensure Optimal Playback Across Browsers and Devices

```
<video id="video-example" controls="controls" poster="media/poster.png">
    <source src="media/trailer.mp4"  type="video/mp4" />
    <source src="media/trailer.webm" type="video/webm" />

    <!-- Provide fallback for browsers that doesn't support the video element -->
    <p>Browser not support the HTML5 Video element.</p>
</video>

<audio id="audio-example" controls="controls">
    <source src="media/04-Death_Becomes_Fur.mp4" type="audio/mp4" />
    <source src="media/04-Death_Becomes_Fur.oga" type="audio/ogg; codecs=vorbis" />

    <!-- Provide fallback for browsers that doesn't support the audio element -->
    <p>Browser not support the HTML5 Audio element.</p>
</audio>
```

Timed text tracks such as subtitles and captions can be added to both audio and video elements using the track element and Web Video Text Tracks (WebVTT) formatted files. Details about the format can be found at the W3C site at http://dev.w3.org/html5/webvtt/. Tracks can serve different purposes by specifying the kind of track (subtitles, captions, metadata, chapters, and descriptions). Tracks can also be localized by specfying the language of the track. Tracks will automatically be selected based on the language settings in the browser.

Listing 8-3 is an example of providing multiple subtitles automatically selected by the browser based on the user's preferred locale. If the user's preferred locale is Danish, the browser will pick the Danish subtitles. In all other cases it will fall back to English subtitles.

Listing 8-3. Track Elements Can Be Used to Specify Subtitles in Multiple Languages; the Browser Will Auto Detect the Most Suitable Language Based on Its Language Settings

```
<video id="video-example" controls="controls" poster="media/poster.png">
    <source src="media/trailer.mp4"  type="video/mp4" />
    <source src="media/trailer.webm" type="video/webm" />
```

```
<track src="media/subtitles_en.vtt"
       kind="subtitles" default="default"
       label="English" srclang="en" />
<track src="media/subtitles_da.vtt"
       kind="subtitles"
       label="Dansk" srclang="da" />

<!-- Provide fallback for browsers that doesn't support the video element -->
<p>Browser not support the HTML5 Video element.</p>
</video>
```

Tip WebVTT is a simple format superseding the SRT subtitles format. WebVTT files contain a list of cues that specifies the timing of texts. Here is an example of two texts to display between the 12th and 16th seconds and the 18th and 21st seconds.

```
WEBVTT

00:12.000 --> 00:16.000
What brings you to the land of the gatekeepers?

00:18.000 --> 00:21.000
I'm searching for someone
```

In case a browser does not support the video or audio element you can specify a fallback by adding the necessary code inside the video and audio elements. You could for example insert an old school Flash SWF as shown in Listing 8-4.

Listing 8-4. Example of Falling Back to a Flash SWF If the Video Element Is Not Supported in the Browser

```
<video id="video-example" controls="controls" poster="media/poster.png" src="media/trailer.mp4">
    <!-- Provide fallback for browsers that doesn't support the video element -->
    <object width="300" height="150" data="video-player.swf"
            type="application/x-shockwave-flash" title="Video Player ">
        <param name="movie" value="media/trailer.mp4" />
        <param name="height" value="300" />
        <param name="width" value="150" />
        <param name="menu" value="true" />
    </object>
</video>
```

Creating the JSF Media Component

For JSF support of the HTML5 media elements, we will create a component for both the audio and video elements. Both components will have the common attributes as defined in HTMLMediaElement in the HTML5 specification. The video component will have three extra attributes to specify the dimensions of the video and to display a poster prior to playback. To support media sources and tracks, we will include two collections in the interface of the component: one for specifying the available media sources and one for the available text tracks.

In this scenario we are facing a new challenge. Boolean attributes in HTML5 are not simply expressed as attribute="true" and attribute="false". The HTML5 specification states that

"The presence of a Boolean attribute on an element represents the true value, and the absence of the attribute value represents the false value."

This means that we cannot take an attribute like autoplay and output as autoplay="true" or autoplay="false" as the browser will evaluate both versions as if autoplay is true. The challenge is that we must read the value passed to the component and evaluate if it should be inserted in the output of the custom component. There are two ways of doing this. Either you can include conditional <f:passThroughAttribute /> tags below the tag or you can manipulate the outputted element in composite component root, which is a kind of managed bean for the component. We will show both methods, but first we will define the interface of the composite component.

In the definition of the component interface in Listing 8-5 there is also a minimal implementation of component. The attributes that we are adding to the video tag are only interesting on the client side. That is, they do not add any value on the server side. We do not need to keep track of the state of the HTML5 attributes. Therefore we can use the pass-through functionality added to JSF 2.2 to output the necessary HTML5 attributes. In the minimal implementation in Listing 8-1 the video tags have two attributes. These attributes are prefixed jsf: and that tells the Facelets TagDecorator that these attributes are not pass-through attributes and that they should be matched to the id and value attribute of the component. The TagDecorator is responsible for mapping the component to a known JSF component. For example, the input components created in the previous chapter all mapped to the <h:inputText /> or HtmlInputText component. The TagDecorator is not familiar with the HTML5 <video /> element and maps it to a fallback class called PassThroughElement.

Listing 8-5. Composite Component Interface That Can Be Used for Both the Video and Audio Components

```
<?xml version='1.0' encoding='UTF-8' ?>
<!DOCTYPE html PUBLIC "-//W3C//DTD XHTML 1.0 Transitional//EN"
"http://www.w3.org/TR/xhtml1/DTD/xhtml1-transitional.dtd">
<html xmlns="http://www.w3.org/1999/xhtml"
      xmlns:cc="http://xmlns.jcp.org/jsf/composite">

    <cc:interface componentType="UIMediaComponent">
        <cc:attribute name="value" type="java.lang.String"
                    shortDescription="URL of the video file to display" />
        <cc:attribute name="crossorigin" type="java.lang.String" default="anonymous"
                    shortDescription="Specifying how to deal with cross origin requests.
                                    anonymous (default) or use-credentials." />
        <cc:attribute name="preload" type="java.lang.String" default="auto"
                    shortDescription="Preload the video file. none, metadata or auto" />
        <cc:attribute name="autoplay" type="java.lang.Boolean" default="false"
                    shortDescription="Start playback as soon as the page has loaded" />
        <cc:attribute name="mediagroup" type="java.lang.String" default=""
                    shortDescription="Media group for which the video file belong" />
        <cc:attribute name="loop" type="java.lang.Boolean" default="false"
                    shortDescription="Restart the video once it reaches the end" />
        <cc:attribute name="muted" type="java.lang.Boolean" default="false"
                    shortDescription="Mute the audio of the video" />
        <cc:attribute name="controls" type="java.lang.Boolean" default="false"
                    shortDescription="Display user controls" />
        <cc:attribute name="poster" type="java.lang.String"
                    shortDescription="URL of a poster (image) to display before playback" />
```

```
        <cc:attribute name="width" type="java.lang.String"
                      shortDescription="Width of the video" />
        <cc:attribute name="height" type="java.lang.String"
                      shortDescription="Height of the video" />
        <cc:attribute name="sources" type="java.util.Collection"
                      shortDescription="Collection of alternative MediaSources" />
        <cc:attribute name="tracks" type="java.util.Collection"
                      shortDescription="Collection of MediaTracks" />
    </cc:interface>

    <cc:implementation >
        <div id="#{cc.clientId}">
            <video jsf:id="media-player"
                   jsf:value="#{cc.attrs.value}">
            </video>
        </div>
    </cc:implementation>
</html>
```

The following are demonstrations of the two methods for conditionally including attributes in the output of the composite component.

Method one: <f:passThroughAttribute/>

Each of the attributes can be added directly in the Facelets view file by embedding the <f:passThroughAttribute /> tag in the <video /> tag as shown in Listing 8-6.

Listing 8-6. Using Conditional <f:passThroughAttribute /> Elements

```
<cc:implementation >
    <div id="#{cc.clientId}">
        <video jsf:id="media-player"
               jsf:value="#{cc.attrs.value}"
               crossorigin="#{cc.attrs.crossorigin}"
               preload="#{cc.attrs.preload}"
               mediagroup="#{cc.attrs.mediagroup}"
               src="#{cc.attrs.value}">

            <c:if test="#{cc.attrs.autoplay}">
                <f:passThroughAttribute name="autoplay" value="true" />
            </c:if>

            <c:if test="#{cc.attrs.loop}">
                <f:passThroughAttribute name="loop" value="true" />
            </c:if>

            <c:if test="#{cc.attrs.muted}">
                <f:passThroughAttribute name="muted" value="true" />
            </c:if>
```

```
            <c:if test="#{cc.attrs.controls}">
                <f:passThroughAttribute name="controls" value="true" />
            </c:if>
        </video>
    </div>
</cc:implementation>
```

The benefit of this method is that you do not need a UIComponent class behind the component and you can quickly make changes to how the <video /> tag is outputted. The disadvantage of using this method is that the Facelets view may end up getting polluted with logic that is better managed somewhere else.

Method two: Implementing a composite component root

The second method implements a composite component root that is a UIComponent class that sits behind the component. In this class you can implement any kind of logic that you can think of. In Listing 8-7 you can see how to specify the UIComponent that sits behind the composite component. The actual UIComponent behind the composite component can be seen in Listing 8-8.

Listing 8-7. The Component Component Root Is Specified as the componentType in the Interface of the Composite Component

```
<?xml version='1.0' encoding='UTF-8' ?>
<!DOCTYPE html PUBLIC "-//W3C//DTD XHTML 1.0 Transitional//EN"
"http://www.w3.org/TR/xhtml1/DTD/xhtml1-transitional.dtd">
<html xmlns="http://www.w3.org/1999/xhtml"
      xmlns:cc="http://xmlns.jcp.org/jsf/composite"
      xmlns:jsf="http://xmlns.jcp.org/jsf"
      xmlns:c="http://xmlns.jcp.org/jsp/jstl/core">

    <cc:interface componentType="UIMediaComponent">
        <!-- OMITTED FOR READABILITY //-->
    </cc:interface>

    <cc:implementation >
        <div id="#{cc.clientId}">
            <video jsf:id="#{cc.elementId} "
                   jsf:value="#{cc.attrs.value}"
                   crossorigin="#{cc.attrs.crossorigin}"
                   preload="#{cc.attrs.preload}"
                   mediagroup="#{cc.attrs.mediagroup}"
                   src="#{cc.attrs.value}">
            </video>
        </div>
    </cc:implementation>
</html>
```

Listing 8-8. UIMediaComponent.java Representing the Composite Component Root Specified as the componentType in Listing 8-3

```java
package com.apress.projsf2html5.components.media;

import java.io.IOException;
import javax.el.ValueExpression;
import javax.faces.component.FacesComponent;
import javax.faces.component.UIComponent;
import javax.faces.component.UINamingContainer;
import javax.faces.context.FacesContext;

/**
 * Composite component for the {@code <audio/>} and {@code <video/>} elements.
 */
@FacesComponent("UIMediaComponent")
public class UIMediaComponent extends UINamingContainer {

    private static final String ELEMENT_ID = "media-player";
    private static final String ATTRIBUTE_AUTOPLAY = "autoplay";
    private static final String ATTRIBUTE_LOOP = "loop";
    private static final String ATTRIBUTE_MUTED = "muted";
    private static final String ATTRIBUTE_CONTROLS = "controls";
    private static final String ATTRIBUTE_POSTER = "poster";
    private static final String ATTRIBUTE_WIDTH = "width";
    private static final String ATTRIBUTE_HEIGHT = "height";

    public String getElementId() {
        return ELEMENT_ID;
    }

    @Override
    public void encodeBegin(FacesContext context) throws IOException {
        super.encodeBegin(context);
        UIComponent element = findMediaElement();

        addAttributeIfTrue(element, ATTRIBUTE_AUTOPLAY);
        addAttributeIfTrue(element, ATTRIBUTE_LOOP);
        addAttributeIfTrue(element, ATTRIBUTE_MUTED);
        addAttributeIfTrue(element, ATTRIBUTE_CONTROLS);
        addAttributeIfNotNull(element, ATTRIBUTE_POSTER);
        addAttributeIfNotNull(element, ATTRIBUTE_WIDTH);
        addAttributeIfNotNull(element, ATTRIBUTE_HEIGHT);
    }

    private void addAttributeIfNotNull(UIComponent component, String attributeName) {
        Object attributeValue = getAttribute(attributeName);
        if (attributeValue != null) {
            component.getPassThroughAttributes().put(attributeName, attributeValue);
        }
    }
}
```

```java
    private void addAttributeIfTrue(UIComponent component, String attributeName) {
        if (isAttributeTrue(attributeName)) {
            component.getPassThroughAttributes().put(attributeName, attributeName);
        }
    }

    /**
     * Finds the {@code <video/>} or {@code <audio/>} element in the
     * composite component.
     *
     * @return {@link UIComponent} representing the {@code <video/>} or
     * {@code <audio/>} element
     * @throws IOException If {@link UIComponent} could not be found.
     * There is no way to recover from this exception at run-time. Ensure that
     * the ID of the element corresponds to ID specified in the
     * {@link #ELEMENT_ID} constant
     */
    private UIComponent findMediaElement() throws IOException {
        UIComponent element = findComponent(getElementId());

        if (element == null) {
            throw new IOException("Media element with ID "
                    + getElementId() + " could not be found");
        }
        return element;
    }

    /**
     * Utility method for retrieving the attributes of a component. This method
     * first checks if the attribute is an EL Expression followed by checking if
     * it is a simple value.
     *
     * @param name Name of the attribute to retrieve
     * @return The value of the attribute. If the contents of the attribute is
     * an EL Expression, the expression will be executed and returned. If the
     * contents of the attribute is a simple value, it will be returned as is.
     * If the attribute cannot be found {@code null} is returned.
     */
    private Object getAttribute(String name) {

        ValueExpression ve = getValueExpression(name);
        if (ve != null) {
            // Attribute is a value expression
            return ve.getValue(getFacesContext().getELContext());
        } else if (getAttributes().containsKey(name)) {
            // Attribute is a fixed value
            return getAttributes().get(name);
        } else {
            // Attribute doesn't exist
            return null;
        }
    }
```

```
/**
 * Utility method that evaluates if the value in the given attribute is
 * {@link Boolean.TRUE}.
 *
 * @param attributeName Name of the attribute to evaluate
 * @return {@code true} if the value of the attribute evaluates to
 * {@link Boolean.TRUE}, otherwise {@code false} is returned
 */
private boolean isAttributeTrue(String attributeName) {
    boolean isBoolean = getAttribute(attributeName) instanceof java.lang.Boolean;
    boolean isTrue = ((boolean) getAttribute(attributeName)) == Boolean.TRUE;
    return isBoolean && isTrue;
}
}
```

The benefit of this method is that you can easily unit test the logic behind the component. You can also reuse the composite component root for multiple components. For example, we have used the preceding class for both the audio and video components. The disadvantage is that it will probably be extra work, in terms of lines of code, for simple components. Also, it may not be obvious what exactly is being outputted from the composite component as the output is now being generated and manipulated from both the Facelets view and the composite component root.

Supporting Sources and Tracks

Along with the video and audio elements, HTML 5 introduces the source and track elements that can be embedded inside the video and audio elements to support multiple media formats and to provide text tracks. We have already included sources and tracks to the available attributes in the interface of the composite component. In these attributes we will expect a collection of objects since there would most likely be more than one source and track per video and audio. The objects in the collection must expose the required properties to render the source and track elements, so we have created two data transfer objects to keep details about the source, as shown in Listing 8-9, and about the track, as shown in Listing 8-10.

Listing 8-9. MediaSource.java Is a Simple Data Transfer Object for Keeping Information About a Media Source

```
package com.apress.projsf2html5.components.media;

import java.util.Objects;

/**
 * {@linkplain MediaSource Media source} used to provide the
 * {@link UIMediaComponent} with alternative media files.
 */
public class MediaSource {

    private String source;
    private String type;

    /**
     * Creates a new instance of {@link MediaSource} with a blank source and
     * mime type.
     */
```

```java
public MediaSource() {
    this("", "");
}

/**
 * Creates a new instance of {@link MediaSource} with a preset source and
 * MIME type.
 *
 * @param source URL of the media file to play
 * @param type MIME type of the media file
 */
public MediaSource(String source, String type) {
    this.source = source;
    this.type = type;
}

/**
 * Gets the URL of the media file to play.
 *
 * @return URL of the media file to play
 */
public String getSource() {
    return source;
}

/**
 * Sets the URL of the media file to play.
 *
 * @param source URL of the media file to play
 */
public void setSource(String source) {
    this.source = source;
}

/**
 * Gets the MIME type of the media file specified as the source.
 *
 * @return MIME type of the media file specified as the source
 * @see <a href="http://www.iana.org/assignments/media-types/">IANA MIME
 * types</a>
 */
public String getType() {
    return type;
}

/**
 * Sets the MIME type of the media file specified as the source.
 *
 * @param type MIME type of the media file specified as the source
 * @see <a href="http://www.iana.org/assignments/media-types/">IANA MIME
 * types</a>
 */
```

```java
    public void setType(String type) {
        this.type = type;
    }
}
```

Listing 8-10. MediaTrack.java Is a Simple Data Transfer Object for Keeping Details About a Text Track

```java
package com.apress.projsf2html5.components.media;

import java.util.Locale;

/**
 * {@linkplain MediaTrack Text track } used to provide the
 * {@link UIMediaComponent} with localized text tracks for captioning, metadata,
 * subtitles, etc.
 */
public class MediaTrack {

    private String source;
    private MediaTrackKind kind;
    private boolean defaultTrack;
    private String label;
    private Locale locale;

    /**
     * Creates a new instance of {@link MediaTrack} with no details set.
     */
    public MediaTrack() {
        this("", null);
    }

    /**
     * Creates a new instance of {@link MediaTrack} with the track and kind
     * preset.
     *
     * @param source URL to the VTT text track
     * @param kind Kind of text track
     */
    public MediaTrack(String source, MediaTrackKind kind) {
        this(source, kind, "", null, false);
    }

    /**
     * Creates a new instance of {@link MediaTrack} with the track, kind, and
     * label preset.
     *
     * @param source URL to the VTT text track
     * @param kind Kind of text track
     * @param label Label of the track (for display)
     */
    public MediaTrack(String source, MediaTrackKind kind, String label) {
        this(source, kind, label, null, false);
    }
```

```java
    /**
     * Creates a new instance of {@link MediaTrack} with the track, kind, and
     * label preset.
     *
     * @param source URL to the VTT text track
     * @param kind Kind of text track
     * @param label Label of the track (for display)
     * @param locale Locale of the VTT text track
     */
    public MediaTrack(String source, MediaTrackKind kind, String label, Locale locale) {
        this(source, kind, label, locale, false);
    }

    /**
     * Creates a new instance of {@link MediaTrack} with the source, kind,
     * label, {@link Locale} and default track preset.
     *
     * @param source URL to the VTT text track
     * @param kind Kind of text track
     * @param label Label of the track (for display)
     * @param locale Locale of the VTT text track
     * @param defaultTrack Is the track the default track?
     */
    public MediaTrack(String source, MediaTrackKind kind, String label, Locale locale, boolean
defaultTrack) {
        this.source = source;
        this.kind = kind;
        this.defaultTrack = defaultTrack;
        this.label = label;
        this.locale = locale;
    }

    /**
     * Determine if the {@link MediaTrack} is the default track to use if the
     * browser could not match the appropriate track based on the
     * {@link Locale}.
     *
     * @return {@link Boolean#TRUE} if this is the default track, otherwise
     * {@link Boolean#FALSE}
     */
    public boolean isDefaultTrack() {
        return defaultTrack;
    }

    /**
     * Sets the Default Track indicator of text track.
     *
     * @param defaultTrack {@link Boolean#TRUE} if this is the default track,
     * otherwise {@link Boolean#FALSE}
     */
    public void setDefaultTrack(boolean defaultTrack) {
        this.defaultTrack = defaultTrack;
    }
```

```java
/**
 * Gets the URL of the VTT text track.
 *
 * @return URL of the VTT text track
 * @see <a href="http://dev.w3.org/html5/webvtt/">WebVTT: The Web Video Text
 * Tracks Format</a>
 */
public String getSource() {
    return source;
}

/**
 * Sets the URL of the VTT text track.
 *
 * @param source URL of the VTT text track
 * @see <a href="http://dev.w3.org/html5/webvtt/">WebVTT: The Web Video Text
 * Tracks Format</a>
 */
public void setSource(String source) {
    this.source = source;
}

/**
 * Gets the kind of text track.
 *
 * @return Kind of text track
 */
public MediaTrackKind getKind() {
    return kind;
}

/**
 * Sets the kind of text track.
 *
 * @param kind Kind of text track
 */
public void setKind(MediaTrackKind kind) {
    this.kind = kind;
}

/**
 * Gets the label of the text track for display.
 *
 * @return Label of the text track for display.
 */
public String getLabel() {
    return label;
}
```

```java
/**
 * Sets the label of the text track for display.
 *
 * @param label Label of the text track for display
 */
public void setLabel(String label) {
    this.label = label;
}

/**
 * Gets the {@link Locale} of the text track.
 *
 * @return {@link Locale} of the text track
 */
public Locale getLocale() {
    return locale;
}

/**
 * Sets the {@link Locale} of the text track.
 *
 * @param locale {@link Locale} of the text track
 */
public void setLocale(Locale locale) {
    this.locale = locale;
}
}
```

The sources and tracks collections are embedded inside the video element, and the sources and tracks attributes are added to the component as seen in Listing 8-11.

Listing 8-11. Supporting the Sources and Tracks Collections in the Composite Component

```xml
<?xml version='1.0' encoding='UTF-8' ?>
<!DOCTYPE html PUBLIC "-//W3C//DTD XHTML 1.0 Transitional//EN"
"http://www.w3.org/TR/xhtml1/DTD/xhtml1-transitional.dtd">
<html xmlns="http://www.w3.org/1999/xhtml"
      xmlns:cc="http://xmlns.jcp.org/jsf/composite"
      xmlns:jsf="http://xmlns.jcp.org/jsf"
      xmlns:c="http://xmlns.jcp.org/jsp/jstl/core"
      xmlns:f="http://xmlns.jcp.org/jsf/core">

    <cc:interface componentType="UIMediaComponent">
        <!-- OMITTED FOR READABILITY //-->
        <cc:attribute name="sources" type="java.util.Collection"
                    shortDescription="Collection of alternative MediaSources. " />
        <cc:attribute name="tracks" type="java.util.Collection"
                    shortDescription="Collection of MediaTracks. " />
    </cc:interface>
```

```
  <cc:implementation >
      <div id="#{cc.clientId}">
          <video jsf:id="#{cc.elementId} "
                 jsf:value="#{cc.attrs.value}"
                 crossorigin="#{cc.attrs.crossorigin}"
                 preload="#{cc.attrs.preload}"
                 mediagroup="#{cc.attrs.mediagroup}"
                 src="#{cc.attrs.value}">

            <c:forEach items="#{cc.attrs.sources}"  var="source" >
                <source src="#{source.source}" type="#{source.type}" />
            </c:forEach>

            <c:forEach items="#{cc.attrs.tracks}"  var="track" >
                <track jsf:value="#{track.source}" src="#{track.source}">
                    <c:if test="#{track.kind != null}">
                        <f:passThroughAttribute name="kind" value="#{track.kind.toString()}" />
                    </c:if>
                    <c:if test="#{track.locale != null}">
                        <f:passThroughAttribute name="srclang"
                                                value="#{track.locale.toString()}" />
                    </c:if>
                    <c:if test="#{track.defaultTrack}">
                        <f:passThroughAttribute name="defaultTrack" value="defaultTrack" />
                    </c:if>
                </track>
            </c:forEach>
          </video>
      </div>
  </cc:implementation>
</html>
```

Example of using the video component

Using the video component is trivial. If you want to provide the media sources and text tracks to the component, you must use a managed bean to contain your collections; otherwise the components can be used with a managed bean. Listing 8-12 shows an example where a collection of media sources and text tracks are fetched from a backing bean. The backing bean in Listing 8-13 exposes the properties as collections that could come from a database.

Listing 8-12. Using the Video Component

```
<h2>Video with a single media file</h2>
<projsfhtml5:video value="media/trailer.mp4"
                   autoplay="true"
                   controls="true" />
```

```
<h2>Video with multiple media sources and tracks</h2>
<projsfhtml5:video value="media/trailer.mp4"
                   controls="true"
                   sources="#{exampleVideoComponent.mediaSources}"
                   tracks="#{exampleVideoComponent.textTracks}"/>
```

Listing 8-13. Backing Bean for the Video Component

```java
package com.apress.projsf2html5.jsf;

import com.apress.projsf2html5.components.media.MediaSource;
import com.apress.projsf2html5.components.media.MediaTrack;
import com.apress.projsf2html5.components.media.MediaTrackKind;
import java.util.ArrayList;
import java.util.Collection;
import java.util.Locale;
import javax.enterprise.context.RequestScoped;
import javax.inject.Named;

@Named(value = "exampleVideoComponent")
@RequestScoped
public class ExampleVideoComponent {

    public Collection<MediaSource> getMediaSources() {
        Collection<MediaSource> sources = new ArrayList<>();
        sources.add(new MediaSource("media/trailer.mp4", "video/mp4"));
        sources.add(new MediaSource("media/trailer.webm", "video/webm"));
        return sources;
    }

    public Collection<MediaTrack> getTextTracks() {
        Collection<MediaTrack> tracks = new ArrayList<>();
        tracks.add(new MediaTrack("media/subtitles_da.vtt", MediaTrackKind.subtitles,
            "Dansk", new Locale("da"), false));
        tracks.add(new MediaTrack("media/subtitles_en.vtt", MediaTrackKind.subtitles,
            "English", Locale.ENGLISH, true));
        return tracks;
    }
}
```

Progress Bar Component

Most JSF UI frameworks come with a progress bar component. Prior to HTML5 these frameworks used widget frameworks such as JQueryUI. HTML5 introduces a new element to represent progress bars, which is the <progress/> element. The element can be used to display determinate and indeterminate progress. Indeterminate progress can be used to display a waiting indicator while waiting for a process to complete, whereas determinate progress can be used to show progress of a task where the end of the task is somehow known. Figure 8-1 shows an example of indeterminate and determinate progress bars.

Progress Example

Indeterminate

Determinate

Figure 8-1. *Example of progress indicators*

The progress element has two simple attributes. Omitting the attributes will create an indeterminate progress bar. By using the two attributes you can specify the max value of the progress bar and the current value (i.e., position) of the progress bar. Details about the attributes can be seen in Table 8-3.

Table 8-3. *List of Attributes for the Progress Element*

Attribute	Type	Default Value	Description
max	Double	1.0	Describes the maximum number of the progress bar indicating that the task has completed.
value	Double	Unspecified	Describes how much of the task has been completed.

The progress element is fairly simple and can quickly be transformed into a JSF component. To make the component useful we will add an additional "for" attribute that can be pointed at another component such as the video or audio component. The progress bar will automatically update its progress based on the playback of the video or audio component.

The component has a composite component view, a JavaScript and a FacesComponent. The composite view is displayed in Listing 8-14. Notice how the JavaScript for the component is separated into its own JavaScript file and imported using the outputScript component. outputScript ensures that the JavaScript file is imported only once no matter how many times the component is used on a single page.

Listing 8-14. The Composite Progress Component resources/projsfhtml5/progress.xhtml

```
<?xml version='1.0' encoding='UTF-8' ?>
<!DOCTYPE html PUBLIC "-//W3C//DTD XHTML 1.0 Transitional//EN"
"http://www.w3.org/TR/xhtml1/DTD/xhtml1-transitional.dtd">
<html xmlns="http://www.w3.org/1999/xhtml"
      xmlns:cc="http://xmlns.jcp.org/jsf/composite"
      xmlns:jsf="http://xmlns.jcp.org/jsf"
      xmlns:c="http://xmlns.jcp.org/jsp/jstl/core"
      xmlns:f="http://xmlns.jcp.org/jsf/core"
      xmlns:h="http://xmlns.jcp.org/jsf/html">

    <cc:interface componentType="UIProgress">
        <cc:attribute name="value" type="java.lang.String"
                    shortDescription="How much of the task has been completed" />
```

209

```
        <cc:attribute name="max" type="java.lang.String"
                    shortDescription="The maximum number of the progress bar indicating that
                                    the task has completed" />
        <cc:attribute name="for" type="java.lang.String"
                    shortDescription="ID of the media component for which the progress bar
                                    should automatically update" />
    </cc:interface>

    <cc:implementation >

        <h:outputScript name="progress.js" library="projsfhtml5/progress" target="head"/>

        <div id="#{cc.clientId}">
            <progress jsf:id="progress">
                <c:if test="#{cc.attrs.value != null}">
                    <f:passThroughAttribute name="value" value="#{cc.attrs.value}" />
                </c:if>
                <c:if test="#{cc.attrs.max != null}">
                    <f:passThroughAttribute name="max" value="#{cc.attrs.max}" />
                </c:if>
                <cc:insertChildren />
            </progress>

            <c:if test="#{cc.attrs.for != null}">
                <script type="text/javascript">
                    progressBar.init("#{cc.clientId}", "#{cc.forClientId}");
                </script>
            </c:if>
        </div>
    </cc:implementation>
</html>
```

The component supports automatic updating of the progress bar through the for attribute. The automatic updating is configured through the progress.js JavaScript in Listing 8-15 that contains a JavaScript closure that takes two parameters. The first parameter is the identifier of the progress bar, and the second parameter is the identifier of the source component that the progress bar should automatically update. In the following JavaScript only the audio and video component is supported as a source of updating the progress bar.

Listing 8-15. resources/projsfhtml5/progress/progress.js JavaScript Supporting the Composite Component

```
if (!window["progressBar"]) {
    var progressBar = {};
}

progressBar.init = function init(componentId, forId) {
    var media = document.getElementById(forId + "\:media-player");
    var bar = document.getElementById(componentId + "\:progress");
```

```
    // Add an event listener for the "timeupdate" event of the media player
    media.addEventListener("timeupdate", function() {
        var percent = Math.floor((100 / media.duration) * media.currentTime);
        bar.value = percent;
    });
}
```

The FacesComponent behind the composite component in Listing 8-16 is necessary to calculate the client identifier of the component specified in the for attribute.

Listing 8-16. UIProgress FacesComponent Used by the Progress Composite Component

```java
package com.apress.projsf2html5.components.progress;

import java.io.IOException;
import javax.el.ValueExpression;
import javax.faces.component.FacesComponent;
import javax.faces.component.UIComponent;
import javax.faces.component.UINamingContainer;

/**
 * Composite component for the {@code <progress/>} element.
 */
@FacesComponent("UIProgress")
public class UIProgress extends UINamingContainer {

    private static final String ATTRIBUTE_FOR = "for";
    private UIComponent forComponent;

    /**
     * Finds the component specified in the {@code for} attribute.
     *
     * @return {@link UIComponent} specified in the {@code for} attribute
     * @throws IOException If a {@link UIComponent} with the name specified in
     * the {@code for} attribute could not be found
     */
    public UIComponent getForComponent() throws IOException {
        if (getAttributes().containsKey(ATTRIBUTE_FOR)) {
            String forAttribute = (String) getAttribute(ATTRIBUTE_FOR);

            this.forComponent = findComponent(forAttribute);

            if (this.forComponent == null) {
                throw new IOException("Component with ID "
                        + forAttribute + " could not be found");
            }
        } else {
            throw new IOException("The for attribute was not set on the component");
        }
        return forComponent;
    }
```

```java
/**
 * Gets the client id of the {@link #getForComponent()}
 *
 * @return Client id of the {@link #getForComponent()}
 * @throws IOException If the component specified in the {@code for}
 * attribute could not be found
 */
public String getForClientId() throws IOException {
    UIComponent element = getForComponent();
    return element.getClientId(getFacesContext());
}


/**
 * Utility method for retrieving the attributes of a component. This method
 * first checks if the attribute is an EL Expression followed by checking if
 * it is a simple value.
 *
 * @param name Name of the attribute to retrieve
 * @return The value of the attribute. If the contents of the attribute is
 * an EL Expression, the expression will be executed and returned. If the
 * contents of the attribute is a simple value, it will be returned as is.
 * If the attribute cannot be found {@code null} is returned.
 */
private Object getAttribute(String name) {

    ValueExpression ve = getValueExpression(name);
    if (ve != null) {
        // Attribute is a value expression
        return ve.getValue(getFacesContext().getELContext());
    } else if (getAttributes().containsKey(name)) {
        // Attribute is a fixed value
        return getAttributes().get(name);
    } else {
        // Attribute doesn't exist
        return null;
    }
}
}
}
```

■ **Note**   The for attribute supports only media components. For the component to be production ready you should implement support for other components such as file upload, form completion, and Ajax requests.

Usage of the component is straightforward. It can be used as an indeterminate progress bar by providing no attributes to the component. It can be used as a manually updated determinate bar by providing the value and max attributes. Finally, it can also be used by pointing the for attribute to a media component. Figure 8-2 is a screenshot of using the component as shown in Listing 8-17.

Figure 8-2. *Screenshot of the progress component (© copyright Blender Foundation | www.sintel.org)*

Listing 8-17. Example of Using the Progress Component

```
<?xml version='1.0' encoding='UTF-8' ?>
<!DOCTYPE html PUBLIC "-//W3C//DTD XHTML 1.0 Transitional//EN"
"http://www.w3.org/TR/xhtml1/DTD/xhtml1-transitional.dtd">
<html xmlns="http://www.w3.org/1999/xhtml"
      xmlns:ui="http://xmlns.jcp.org/jsf/facelets"
      xmlns:projsfhtml5="http://xmlns.jcp.org/jsf/composite/projsfhtml5">

    <ui:composition template="/base.xhtml">

        <ui:define name="title">
            Progress Component
        </ui:define>

        <ui:define name="top">
            Progress Component
        </ui:define>

        <ui:define name="content">

            <h2>Progress bar (indeterminate)</h2>
            <projsfhtml5:progress id="indeterminate" />
```

```
    <h2>Progress bar (determinate)</h2>
    <projsfhtml5:progress id="determinate" value="56" max="100"/>

    <h2>Progress bar (using for)</h2>
    <projsfhtml5:video id="video" value="media/trailer.mp4"
                       autoplay="true"
                       controls="true">
    </projsfhtml5:video>
    <projsfhtml5:progress id="video-progress"
                          value="0" max="100"
                          for=":video" />

  </ui:define>
 </ui:composition>
</html>
```

Summary

In this chapter we have looked at creating advanced HTML5 components. The examples have demonstrated how to support your composite component views with FacesComponents where you can implement advanced logic that is otherwise difficult or not possible in the Facelets view. It should be clear that creating JSF 2.x component has become significantly easier than earlier versions of JSF. However, it still requires significant effort to create components that can be reused and extended for multiple purposes. As a component developer you will be faced with choices while specifying interfaces and implementing the components. It is worth noting that simply converting an HTML5 element directly to a JSF component may not be very useful if you do not consider how the page author will use the component. While developing the video and audio components we were faced with the choice of specifying tracks as embedded subelements just like HTML5, but in most cases a JSF page author will already have tracks and sources in a collection in a managed bean; hence, we included tracks and sources in the interface as attributes taking collections.

CHAPTER 9

JSF Component Libraries

In this chapter, you will learn briefly how to utilize JSF component libraries in order to produce nifty-looking web applications. You will be introduced to two of the most famous JSF open-source component libraries, which are PrimeFaces and RichFaces. Although going into the details of these frameworks is outside the scope of this book because these frameworks are really big and cannot be covered in one single chapter, we will give you an overview of the different components shipped with each of the component libraries and how to use these libraries in order to create nifty-looking JSF 2.2 web applications.

PrimeFaces

PrimeFaces is an open-source JSF component library that has many different capabilities. PrimeFaces has a rich set of components, built-in Ajax based on the standard JSF 2.0 Ajax APIs, and Ajax Push support using web sockets; finally, PrimeFaces includes Mobile User Interface renderkit that allows the JSF developer(s) to create JSF applications on mobiles. PrimeFaces also includes a skinning framework that has more than 35 built-in themes.

In order to configure PrimeFaces, you need to download the PrimeFaces jar (`primefaces-xxx.jar`). There are two ways to download this jar: you can either download it from `http://primefaces.org/downloads.html` or if you are a Maven user you can define it as a Maven dependency. The group ID of the dependency is `org.primefaces` and artifact ID is PrimeFaces as shown in the following.

```
<dependency>
    <groupId>org.primefaces</groupId>
    <artifactId>primefaces</artifactId>
    <version>3.5</version>
</dependency>
```

In addition to the preceding configuration you also need to add PrimeFaces Maven repository to the repository list of your Maven configuration so that Maven can download it as follows.

```
<repository>
    <id>prime-repo</id>
    <name>Prime Repo</name>
    <url>http://repository.primefaces.org</url>
</repository>
```

PrimeFaces needs Java 5+ runtime and a JSF 2.x implementation as mandatory dependencies. There are some optional libraries that you may include in order to support some features in PrimeFaces as shown by Table 9-1.

Table 9-1. Optional PrimeFaces Libraries

Library	Features
itext version 2.1.7	DataExporter (PDF)
Apache poi version 3.7	DataExporter (Excel)
Rome version 1.9	FeedReader
Commons file upload version 1.2.1 Commons io version 1.4	FileUpload

Component Overview

PrimeFaces has more than 100 UI components that can be used in order to create rich Web 2.0 applications. Going into the details of these components is outside the scope of this book. However, we will give a short listing for these components in Table 9-2 for your reference, sorted alphabetically according to PrimeFaces documentation.

Table 9-2. PrimeFaces Components Overview

Component	Description
AccordionPanel	AccordionPanel is a container component that displays content in stacked format.
AutoComplete	AutoComplete provides live suggestions while an input is being typed.
BreadCrumb	Breadcrumb is a navigation component that provides contextual information about page hierarchy in the workflow.
Button	Button is an extension to the standard h:button component with skinning capabilities.
Calendar	Calendar is an input component used to select a date featuring display modes, paging, localization, Ajax selection, and more.
Captcha	Captcha is a form validation component based on Recaptcha API.
Carousel	Carousel is a multipurpose component to display a set of data or general content with slide effects.
Chart	Chart is used to display graphical data. There are various chart types like pie, bar, line, and more.
Clock	Clock displays server or client date/time live.
Color Picker	ColorPicker is an input component with a color palette.
CommandButton	CommandButton is an extended version of standard commandButton with Ajax and theming capabilities.
CommandLink	CommandLink extends standard JSF commandLink with Ajax capabilities.
ConfirmDialog:	ConfirmDialog is a replacement to the legacy JavaScript confirmation box. Skinning, customization, and avoiding pop-up blockers are notable advantages over classic JavaScript confirmation.
ContextMenu	ContextMenu provides an overlay menu displayed on mouse right-click event.
Dashboard	Dashboard provides a portal-like layout with drag-and-drop–based reorder capabilities.

(continued)

Table 9-2. (*continued*)

Component	Description
DataExporter	DataExporter is handy for exporting data listed using a PrimeFaces DataTable to various formats such as excel, pdf, csv, and xml.
DataGrid	DataGrid displays a collection of data in a grid layout.
DataList	DataList presents a collection of data in list layout with several display types.
DataTable	DataTable is an enhanced version of the standard DataTable that provides built-in solutions to many common use cases like paging, sorting, selection, lazy loading, filtering.
DefaultCommand	Which command to submit the form with when Enter key is pressed a common problem in web apps not just specific to JSF. Browsers tend to behave differently as there doesn't seem to be a standard and even if a standard exists, IE probably will not care about it. There are some ugly workarounds like placing a hidden button and writing JavaScript for every form in your app. DefaultCommand solves this problem by normalizing the command (e.g. button or link) to submit the form with an Enter key press.
Dialog	Dialog is a panel component that can overlay other elements on page.
Drag&Drop	Drag&Drop utilities of PrimeFaces consist of two components: Draggable and Droppable.
Dock	Dock component mimics the well-known dock interface of Mac OS X.
Editor	Editor is an input component with rich text-editing capabilities.
FeedReader	FeedReader is used to display content from a feed.
Fieldset	Fieldset is a grouping component as an extension to html fieldset.
FileDownload	The legacy way to present dynamic binary data to the client is to write a servlet or a filter and stream the binary data. FileDownload presents an easier way to do the same.
FileUpload	FileUpload goes beyond the browser input type="file" functionality and features an html5-powered rich solution with graceful degradation for legacy browsers.
Focus	Focus is a utility component that makes it easy to manage the element focus on a JSF page.
Galleria	Galleria is used to display a set of images.
GMap	GMap is a map component integrated with Google Maps API V3.
GraphicImage	GraphicImage extends standard JSF graphic image component with the ability of displaying binary data like an inputstream. Main use of GraphicImage is to make displaying images stored in database or on-the-fly images easier. Legacy way to do this is to come up with a servlet that does the streaming; GraphicImage does all the hard work without the need of a servlet.
Growl	Growl is based on the Mac's growl notification widget and used to display FacesMessages in an overlay.
HotKey	HotKey is a generic key binding component that can bind any formation of keys to JavaScript event handlers or Ajax calls.
IdleMonitor	IdleMonitor watches user actions on a page and notify callbacks in case they go idle or active again.

(*continued*)

Table 9-2. (*continued*)

Component	Description
ImageCompare	ImageCompare provides a rich user interface to compare two images.
ImageCropper	ImageCropper allows cropping a certain region of an image. A new image is created containing the cropped area and assigned to a CroppedImage instanced on the server side.
ImageSwitch	ImageSwitch is a simple image gallery component.
Inplace	Inplace provides easy inplace editing and inline content display. Inplace consists of two members: display element is the initial clickable label and inline element is the hidden content that is displayed when display element is toggled. Inplace provides easy inplace editing and inline content display. Inplace consists of two members: display element is the initial clickable label and inline element is the hidden content that is displayed when display element is toggled.
InputMask	InputMask forces an input to fit in a defined mask template.
InputText	InputText is an extension to standard inputText with skinning capabilities.
InputTextarea	InputTextarea is an extension to standard inputTextarea with autoComplete, autoResize, remaining characters counter, and theming features.
Keyboard	Keyboard is an input component that uses a virtual keyboard to provide the input. Notable features are the customizable layouts and skinning capabilities.
Layout	Layout component features a highly customizable borderLayout model, making it very easy to create complex layouts even if you're not familiar with web design.
LightBox	LightBox is a powerful overlay that can display images, multimedia content, custom content, and external URLs.
Log	Log component is a visual console to display logs on JSF pages.
Media	Media component is used for embedding multimedia content.
MegaMenu	MegaMenu is a horizontal navigation component that displays submenus together.
Menu	Menu is a navigation component with various customized modes like multi-tiers, iPod-style sliding, and overlays.
Menubar	Menubar is a horizontal navigation component.
MenuButton	MenuButton displays different commands in a pop-up menu.
Message	Message is a pre-skinned extended version of the standard JSF message component.
Messages	Messages is a pre-skinned extended version of the standard JSF messages component.
Mindmap	Mindmap is an interactive tool to visualize mindmap data featuring lazy loading, callbacks, animations.
NotificationBar	NotificationBar displays a multipurpose fixed-position panel for notification.
OrderList	OrderList is used to sort a collection featuring drag-and-drop–based reordering, transition effects, and POJO support.
OutputLabel	OutputLabel is an extension to the standard outputLabel component.
OutputPanel	OutputPanel is a panel component with the ability to auto update.

(*continued*)

Table 9-2. (*continued*)

Component	Description
OverlayPanel	OverlayPanel is a generic panel component that can be displayed on top of other content.
Panel	Panel is a grouping component with content toggle, close, and menu integration.
PanelGrid	PanelGrid is an extension to the standard panelGrid component with additional features such as theming and colspan-rowspan.
PanelMenu	PanelMenu is a hybrid component of accordionPanel and tree components.
Password	Password component is an extended version of standard inputSecret component with theme integration and strength indicator.
PhotoCam	PhotoCam is used to take photos with webcam and send them to the JSF back-end model.
PickList	PickList is used for transferring data between two different collections.
Poll	Poll is an Ajax component that has the ability to send periodic Ajax requests.
Printer	Printer allows sending a specific JSF component to the printer, not the whole page.
ProgressBar	ProgressBar is a process status indicator that can either work purely on client side or interact with server side using Ajax.
Rating	Rating component features a star-based rating system.
RemoteCommand	RemoteCommand provides a way to execute JSF backing bean methods directly from JavaScript.
ResetInput	Input components keep their local values at state when validation fails. ResetInput is used to clear the cached values from state so that components retrieve their values from the backing bean model instead.
Resizable	Resizable component is used to make another JSF component resizable.
Ring	Ring is a data display component with a circular animation.
Schedule	Schedule provides an Outlook Calendar, iCal-like JSF component to manage events.
SelectBooleanButton	SelectBooleanButton is used to select a binary decision with a toggle button.
SelectBooleanCheckbox	SelectBooleanCheckbox is an extended version of the standard checkbox with theme integration.
SelectCheckboxMenu	SelectCheckboxMenu is a multi-select component that displays options in an overlay.
SelectManyButton	SelectManyButton is a multi-select component using button UI.
SelectManyCheckbox	SelectManyCheckbox is an extended version of the standard SelectManyCheckbox with theme integration.
SelectManyMenu	SelectManyMenu is an extended version of the standard SelectManyMenu with theme integration.
SelectOneButton	SelectOneButton is an input component to do a single select.
SelectOneListbox	SelectOneListbox is an extended version of the standard SelectOneListbox with theme integration.

(*continued*)

Table 9-2. (*continued*)

Component	Description
SelectOneMenu	SelectOneMenu is an extended version of the standard SelectOneMenu with theme integration.
SelectOneRadio	SelectOneRadio is an extended version of the standard SelectOneRadio with theme integration.
Separator	Separator displays a horizontal line to separate content.
SlideMenu	SlideMenu is used to display nested submenus with sliding animation.
Slider	Slider is used to provide input with various customization options like orientation, display modes, and skinning.
Socket	Socket component is an agent that creates a channel between the server and the client.
Spacer	Spacer is used to put spaces between elements.
Spinner	Spinner is an input component to provide a numerical input via increment and decrement buttons.
SplitButton	SplitButton displays a command by default and additional ones in an overlay.
Stack	Stack is a navigation component that mimics the stacks feature in Mac OS X.
TabMenu	TabMenu is a navigation component that displays menu items as tabs.
TabView	TabView is a tabbed panel component featuring client side tabs, dynamic content loading with Ajax, and content transition effects.
TagCloud	TagCloud displays a collection of tags with different strengths.
Terminal	Terminal is an Ajax powered web-based terminal that brings desktop terminals to JSF.
ThemeSwitcher	ThemeSwitcher enables switching PrimeFaces themes on the fly with no page refresh.
Toolbar	Toolbar is a horizontal grouping component for commands and other content.
Tooltip	Tooltip goes beyond the legacy html title attribute by providing custom effects, events, html content, and advanced theme support.
Tree	Tree is used for displaying hierarchical data and creating site navigations.
TreeTable	TreeTable is used for displaying hierarchical data in tabular format.
Watermark	Watermark displays a hint on an input field.
Wizard	Wizard provides an Ajax-enhanced UI to implement a workflow easily in a single page. Wizard consists of several child tab components where each tab represents a step in the process.

In the next section, we will show a PrimeFaces application example in order to show you how to utilize the library for creating nifty-looking JSF 2.2 web application.

■ **Note** In order to get the full documentation with examples of PrimeFaces, you can check the user guide documentation from `http://primefaces.org/documentation.html`. You can access the complete PrimeFaces showcase that includes an example of almost every PrimeFaces component from `http://primefaces.org/showcase/ui/home.jsf`.

Integrating and Customizing PrimeFaces

The Country Navigator application is a PrimeFaces application which allows the user to get the available list of cities (with some information) for one of the available countries after clicking on the flag of any of the available countries as shown in Figure 9-1.

Click on a country to get its details

Brazil	
City	**Population**
Sao Paulo	20000000
Rio de Janeiro	12000000
Brasilia	4000000

Figure 9-1. *County Navigator application*

As shown in the screenshot, the application page consists of mainly two UI components:

1. Ring component, which displays the list of available countries (Germany, Egypt, and Brazil).

2. DataTable component, which displays the list of available cities for the selected country.

Listing 9-1 shows the code snippet which represents the ring component that displays the list of available countries.

Listing 9-1. Ring Component Displaying Different Countries

```
<p:ring id="custom" value="#{countryNavigator.countries}" var="country"
            styleClass="image-ring" easing="swing">
    <p:commandLink update=":form:detail">
            <p:graphicImage value="/images/#{country.name}.gif"
                                styleClass="flagIcon" />
            <f:setPropertyActionListener value="#{country}"
                                target="#{countryNavigator.activeCountry}" />
    </p:commandLink>
</p:ring>
```

#{countryNavigator.countries} expression represents the list of the available countries. When a ring item is clicked then through the p:commandLink's action, the selected country #{country} will be set in the activeCountry property of countryNavigator and the "detail" panel (which contains the cities data table) is re-rendered with the new cities of the selected country. Listing 9-2 shows the "detail" panel part.

Listing 9-2. "Detail" Panel Part

```
<p:outputPanel id="detail" styleClass="detailsPanel" layout="block">

        <p:dataTable var="city" value="#{countryNavigator.activeCountry.cities}"
                                rendered="#{countryNavigator.activeCountry ne null}">
            <f:facet name="header">
                    #{countryNavigator.activeCountry.name}
            </f:facet>

            <p:column headerText="City">
                    <h:outputText value="#{city.name}" />
            </p:column>

            <p:column headerText="Population">
                    <h:outputText value="#{city.population}" />
            </p:column>
        </p:dataTable>

</p:outputPanel>
```

"city" data table is rendered when there is an activeCountry available in the countryNavigator object, and the table will show the information of the available cities for the selected country. Listing 9-3 shows the complete CountryNavigator managed bean code.

Listing 9-3. CountryNavigator Managed Bean

```
package com.jsfprohtml5.countrynavigator.model;

import java.util.List;

public class CountryNavigator {
    private List<Country> countries;
    private Country activeCountry;

    public List<Country> getCountries() {
        return countries;
    }

    public void setCountries(List<Country> countries) {
        this.countries = countries;
    }

    public Country getActiveCountry() {
        return activeCountry;
    }
```

```
    public void setActiveCountry(Country activeCountry) {
        this.activeCountry = activeCountry;
    }
}
```

Country managed bean holds name, population, and cities of Country class as shown in Listing 9-4.

Listing 9-4. Country Managed Bean

```
public class Country {
    private String name;
    private long population;
    private List<City> cities;

    public String getName() {
        return name;
    }

    public void setName(String name) {
        this.name = name;
    }

    public long getPopulation() {
        return population;
    }

    public void setPopulation(long population) {
        this.population = population;
    }

    public List<City> getCities() {
        return cities;
    }

    public void setCities(List<City> cities) {
        this.cities = cities;
    }
}
```

City managed bean holds name and population of City class as shown in Listing 9-5.

Listing 9-5. City Managed Bean

```
public class City {
    private String name;
    private long population;

    public String getName() {
        return name;
    }
```

```
    public void setName(String name) {
        this.name = name;
    }

    public long getPopulation() {
        return population;
    }

    public void setPopulation(long population) {
        this.population = population;
    }
}
```

Listing 9-6 shows the complete code of the Country Navigator application page which consolidates ring component with the "details" panel part.

Listing 9-6. Country Navigator Application Page Code

```
<html xmlns="http://www.w3.org/1999/xhtml"
      xmlns:h="http://java.sun.com/jsf/html"
      xmlns:f="http://java.sun.com/jsf/core"
      xmlns:ui="http://java.sun.com/jsf/facelets"
      xmlns:p="http://primefaces.org/ui">

    <h:head>
        <title>Welcome to the Country Navigator</title>
        <h:outputStylesheet library="css" name="countryNavigator.css"  />
    </h:head>

    <h:body>
        <h:form id="form">
            <h2>Click on a country to get its details</h2>
            <p:ring id="custom" value="#{countryNavigator.countries}" var="country"
                    styleClass="image-ring" easing="swing">
                <p:commandLink update=":form:detail">
                    <p:graphicImage value="/images/#{country.name}.gif"
                                            styleClass="flagIcon" />
                    <f:setPropertyActionListener value="#{country}"
                                                        target="#{countryNavigator.
activeCountry}" />
                </p:commandLink>

            </p:ring>

            <p:outputPanel id="detail" styleClass="detailsPanel" layout="block">

                <p:dataTable var="city" value="#{countryNavigator.activeCountry.cities}"
                                    rendered="#{countryNavigator.activeCountry ne null}">
                    <f:facet name="header">
                        #{countryNavigator.activeCountry.name}
                    </f:facet>
```

```
                <p:column headerText="City">
                    <h:outputText value="#{city.name}" />
                </p:column>

                <p:column headerText="Population">
                    <h:outputText value="#{city.population}" />
                </p:column>
            </p:dataTable>

        </p:outputPanel>
    </h:form>
  </h:body>
</html>
```

In order to populate the country and city data, the CountryNavigator managed bean instance is created and initialized as shown in the Faces configuration in Listing 9-7 (note that some of the lines are omitted to save the space).

Listing 9-7. Faces Configuration File

```
<?xml version='1.0' encoding='UTF-8'?>
<faces-config ...>

    <managed-bean>
        <managed-bean-name>countryNavigator</managed-bean-name>
        <managed-bean-class>com.jsfprohtml5.countrynavigator.model.CountryNavigator</managed-bean-
class>
        <managed-bean-scope>request</managed-bean-scope>
        <managed-property>
            <property-name>countries</property-name>
            <list-entries>
                <value>#{egypt}</value>
                <value-class>com.jsfprohtml5.countrynavigator.model.Country</value-class>
                <value>#{germany}</value>
                <value-class>com.jsfprohtml5.countrynavigator.model.Country</value-class>
                <value>#{brazil}</value>
                <value-class>com.jsfprohtml5.countrynavigator.model.Country</value-class>
            </list-entries>
        </managed-property>
    </managed-bean>

    <!-- Egypt -->
    <managed-bean>
        <managed-bean-name>egypt</managed-bean-name>
        <managed-bean-class>com.jsfprohtml5.countrynavigator.model.Country</managed-bean-class>
        <managed-bean-scope>none</managed-bean-scope>
        <managed-property>
            <property-name>name</property-name>
            <value>Egypt</value>
        </managed-property>
```

```
            <managed-property>
                <property-name>population</property-name>
                <value>82000000</value>
            </managed-property>
            <managed-property>
                <property-name>cities</property-name>
                <list-entries>
                    <value>#{cairo}</value>
                    <value-class>com.jsfprohtml5.countrynavigator.model.City</value-class>
                    <value>#{alexandria}</value>
                    <value-class>com.jsfprohtml5.countrynavigator.model.City</value-class>
                    <value>#{aswan}</value>
                    <value-class>com.jsfprohtml5.countrynavigator.model.City</value-class>
                </list-entries>
            </managed-property>
        </managed-bean>
        <managed-bean>
            <managed-bean-name>cairo</managed-bean-name>
            <managed-bean-class>com.jsfprohtml5.countrynavigator.model.City</managed-bean-class>
            <managed-bean-scope>none</managed-bean-scope>
            <managed-property>
                <property-name>name</property-name>
                <value>Cairo</value>
            </managed-property>
             <managed-property>
                <property-name>population</property-name>
                <value>8000000</value>
            </managed-property>
        </managed-bean>

    <!-- Other configuration data is not shown ... -->
</faces-config>
```

■ Note CountryNavigator application is a Maven web application: you can download from the book sources and then build the application using mvn install command. Finally, you can deploy the final countryNavigator-1.0-SNAPSHOT.war on GlassFish version 4.0 to check how it works. In order to run Maven command correctly, you have to make sure that JAVA_HOME points to the Java 7 directory installed in your operating system.

RichFaces

RichFaces is an open-source JSF component library that has many different capabilities. RichFaces includes two main tag libraries:

- a4j tag library, which provides the Ajax functionality and common utilities.

- rich tag library, which provides a set of self-contained rich components that are completely integrated with Ajax.

In order to configure RichFaces, you need to understand its dependency jars first. RichFaces depends on four main jars that represent the API and implementation for both RichFaces core and components as follows:

- richfaces-core-api.jar

- richfaces-core-impl.jar

- richfaces-components-api.jar

- richfaces-components-ui.jar

RichFaces jars have the following mandatory dependencies:

- Java Server Faces 2.x implementation: javax.faces.jar (version 2.1.5 or higher) or myfaces-impl. jar (version 2.1.5 or higher)

- Google Guava: guava.jar (version 10.0.1).

- CSS Parser: cssparser.jar (version 0.9.5).

- Simple API for CSS: sac.jar (version 1.3)

And the following optional jars that can be required in order to run certain functionalities:

- Bean Validation (JSR-303) integration for client-side validation (JSR-303 API and Implementation): validation-api.jar (version 1.0.0.GA) and hibernate-validator.jar (version 4.2.0.Final or higher).

- Push transport library—Atmosphere (without dependencies): atmosphere-runtime.jar (version 1.0.10) (selected compatibility modules atmosphere-compat-*.jar may be necessary).

- Push JMS integration (JMS API and Implementation): jms.jar (version 1.1) and hornetq-jms. jar (version 2.2.7.Final or higher)

- Push CDI integration (CDI API and Implementation): cdi-api.jar (version 1.0-SP4) and javax. inject.jar (version 1) and jsr-250-api.jar (version 1.0) and weld-servlet.jar (version 1.1.4.Final).

- Extended caching (EhCache): ehcache.jar (version 1.6.0).

■ **Note**   Be aware that some of the previously mentioned dependencies are part of Java EE 6 specification, so if you are working on a Java EE 6 application server like GlassFish (not just a servlet container), then there is no need to add these dependencies.

There are two ways to download RichFaces dependencies: you can either download them directly from www.jboss.org/richfaces/download.html or if you are a Maven user you can use RichFaces Maven archetype (RichFaces requires Maven 3.0.3 or above). Using the Maven archetype named richfaces-archetype-simpleapp, you can generate the basic structure and requirements for a RichFaces application project.

In order to run the RichFaces Maven archetype, you need to add the JBoss repository to your Maven configuration. Add a profile in the ${Maven_Installation_Dir}/conf/settings.xml file under the <profiles> element as shown in Listing 9-8.

Listing 9-8. Adding JBoss Repository to Maven Configuration

```
<profiles>
    ...
    <profile>
        <id>jboss-public-repository</id>
        <repositories>
            <repository>
                <id>jboss-public-repository-group</id>
                <name>JBoss Public Maven Repository Group</name>
                <url>https://repository.jboss.org/nexus/content/groups/public/</url>
                <layout>default</layout>
                <releases>
                    <enabled>true</enabled>
                    <updatePolicy>never</updatePolicy>
                </releases>
                <snapshots>
                    <enabled>true</enabled>
                    <updatePolicy>never</updatePolicy>
                </snapshots>
            </repository>
        </repositories>
        <pluginRepositories>
            <pluginRepository>
                <id>jboss-public-repository-group</id>
                <name>JBoss Public Maven Repository Group</name>
                <url>https://repository.jboss.org/nexus/content/groups/public/</url>
                <layout>default</layout>
                <releases>
                    <enabled>true</enabled>
                    <updatePolicy>never</updatePolicy>
                </releases>
                <snapshots>
                    <enabled>true</enabled>
                    <updatePolicy>never</updatePolicy>
                </snapshots>
            </pluginRepository>
        </pluginRepositories>
    </profile>
</profiles>
```

Adding to creating jboss-public-repository profile, it will need to be activated by adding it to the <activeProfiles> element as shown in Listing 9-9.

Listing 9-9. Activating jboss-public-repository Profile

```
<activeProfiles>
    <activeProfile>jboss-public-repository</activeProfile>
</activeProfiles>
```

After creating and activating jboss-public-repository, the project can be generated with the richfaces-archetype-simpleapp archetype. In order to do this, create a new directory for your project, then run the following Maven command in the directory:

```
mvn archetype:generate -DarchetypeGroupId=org.richfaces.archetypes
-DarchetypeArtifactId=richfaces-archetype-simpleapp -DarchetypeVersion=4.3.2.Final
-DgroupId=com.jsfprohtml5.richfacesapp -DartifactId=richFacesApp
```

The -DgroupId parameter can be used in order to define the package for the application managed beans while -DartifactId can be used in order to define the name of the project.

The previous richfaces-archetype-simpleapp command generates a new RichFaces project with the following structure.

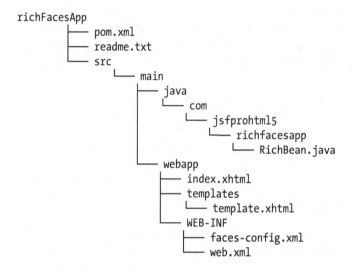

```
richFacesApp
├── pom.xml
├── readme.txt
└── src
    └── main
        ├── java
        │   └── com
        │       └── jsfprohtml5
        │           └── richfacesapp
        │               └── RichBean.java
        └── webapp
            ├── index.xhtml
            ├── templates
            │   └── template.xhtml
            └── WEB-INF
                ├── faces-config.xml
                └── web.xml
```

This is all you need in order to create RichFaces application; now, you can build your generated Maven project using the normal mvn install command.

Component Overview

RichFaces has more than 40 UI components that can be used in order to create rich Web 2.0 applications. Going into the details of these components is outside the scope of this book. However, we will give a short listing for some of these components in Table 9-3 for your reference sorted alphabetically according to RichFaces documentation (note that all of these components are part of the rich tag library).

Table 9-3. *RichFaces Components Overview*

Component	Description
Accordion	The <rich:accordion> is a series of panels stacked on top of each other, each collapsed such that only the header of the panel is showing. When the header of a panel is clicked, it is expanded to show the content of the panel. Clicking on a different header will collapse the previous panel and expand the selected one. Each panel contained in a <rich:accordion> component is a <rich:accordionItem> component.
Autocomplete	The <rich:autocomplete> component is an auto-completing input-box with built-in Ajax.
Calendar	The <rich:calendar> component allows the user to enter a date and time through an inline or pop-up calendar.
CollapsiblePanel	The <rich:collapsiblePanel> component is a collapsible panel that shows or hides content when the header bar is activated. It is a simplified version of <rich:togglePanel> component.
ContextMenu	The <rich:contextMenu> component is used for creating a hierarchical context menu that is activated on events like onmouseover, onclick, etc. The component can be applied to any element on the page.
DataGrid	The <rich:dataGrid> component is used to arrange data objects in a grid. Values in the grid can be updated dynamically from the data model, and Ajax updates can be limited to specific rows. The component supports header, footer, and caption facets.
DataScroller	The <rich:dataScroller> component is used for navigating through multiple pages of tables or grids.
DataTable	The <rich:dataTable> component is used to render a highly customizable table, including the table's caption. It works in conjunction with the <rich:column> and <rich:columnGroup> components to list the contents of a data model.
DragIndicator	The <rich:dragIndicator> component defines a graphical element to display under the mouse cursor during a drag-and-drop operation.
DragSource	The <rich:dragSource> component can be added to a component to indicate it is capable of being dragged by the user. The dragged item can then be dropped into a compatible drop area, designated using the <rich:dropTarget> component.
DropDownMenu	The <rich:dropDownMenu> component is used for creating a drop-down, hierarchical menu. It can be used with the <rich:toolbar> component to create menus in an application's toolbar.
DropTarget	The <rich:dropTarget> component can be added to a component so that the component can accept dragged items. The dragged items must be defined with a compatible drop type for the <rich:dragSource> component.
Editor	The <rich:editor> component is used for creating a WYSIWYG editor on a page.
ExtendedDataTable	The <rich:extendedDataTable> component builds on the functionality of the <rich:dataTable> component, adding features such as scrolling for the table body (both horizontal and vertical), Ajax loading for vertical scrolling, frozen columns, row selection, and rearranging of columns. It also supports all the basic table features such as sorting, filtering, and paging using the <rich:dataScroller> component.
FileUpload	The <rich:fileUpload> component allows the user to upload files to a server. It features multiple uploads, progress bars, restrictions on file types, and restrictions on sizes of the files to be uploaded.

(continued)

Table 9-3. (*continued*)

Component	Description
Focus	The <rich:focus> component allows one to manipulate the focus of components on a page. It is intended to be used with any input field.
HashParam	The <rich:hashParam> component allows client-side parameters to be grouped into a hash map. The hash map can then be passed to the client JavaScript API functions of any RichFaces component.
HotKey	The <rich:hotKey> component allows one to register hot keys for the page or particular elements and to define client-side processing functions for these keys.
InplaceInput	The <rich:inplaceInput> component allows information to be entered inline in blocks of text, improving readability of the text.
InplaceSelect	The <rich:inplaceSelect> component is similar to the <rich:inplaceInput> component, except that the <rich:inplaceSelect> component uses a drop-down selection box to enter text instead of a regular text field.
InputNumberSlider	The <rich:inputNumberSlider> component provides a slider for changing numerical values.
InputNumberSpinner	The <rich:inputNumberSpinner> component is a single-line input field with buttons to increase and decrease a numerical value. The value can be changed using the corresponding directional keys on a keyboard, or by typing into the field.
jQuery	The <rich:jQuery> component applies styles and custom behavior to both JSF objects and regular DOM (Document Object Model) objects. It uses the jQuery JavaScript framework to add functionality to web applications.
List	The <rich:list> component renders a list of items. The list can be a numerically ordered list, an unordered bullet-point list, or a data definition list. The component uses a data model for managing the list items, which can be updated dynamically.
Message	The <rich:message> component renders a single FacesMessage message instance added for the component. The appearance of the message can be customized, and tool-tips can be used for further information about the message.
Messages	The <rich:messages> component works similarly to the <rich:message> component but can display all the validation messages added for the current view instead of just a single message.
Notify	The <rich:notify> component serves for advanced user interaction, using notification boxes to give the user instant feedback on what's happening within the application. Each time this component is rendered, a floating notification box is displayed in the selected corner of the browser screen.
NotifyMessage	The <rich:notifyMessage> component is built on top of <rich:notify>; the difference is in usage. The <rich:notifyMessage> component displays FacesMessages associated with a given component, similar to <rich:message>: one notification is displayed for first FacesMessage in the stack that arises either programmatically or during conversion/validation of the component. The severity of the message determines the color and icon of the resulting notification.
NotifyMessages	The <rich:notifyMessages> component is the same as the <rich:notifyMessage> component, but each of the available messages generates one notification. <rich:notifyMessages> shares the same set of attributes with <rich:notifyMessage>.

(*continued*)

Table 9-3. (*continued*)

Component	Description
NotifyStack	Notifications emitted by <rich:notify>, <rich:notifyMessage> and <rich:notifyMessages> are displayed in top-right corner of the screen by default. <rich:notifyStack> can be used to define where messages will appear and handles their stacking.
OrderingList	The <rich:orderingList> is a component for ordering items in a list (client-side).
Panel	The <rich:panel> component is a bordered panel with an optional header.
PanelMenu	The <rich:panelMenu> component is used in conjunction with <rich:panelMenuItem> and <rich:panelMenuGroup> to create an expanding, hierarchical menu. The <rich:panelMenu> component's appearance can be highly customized, and the hierarchy can stretch to any number of sub-levels.
PickList	The <rich:pickList> is a component for selecting items from a list. Additionally, it allows for the selected items to be ordered (client-side).
Placeholder	The <rich:placeholder> component allows one to use functionality similar to the HTML5 placeholder attribute for input components.
PopupPanel	The <rich:popupPanel> component provides a pop-up panel or window that appears in front of the rest of the application. The <rich:popupPanel> component functions either as a modal window, which blocks interaction with the rest of the application while active, or as a nonmodal window. It can be positioned on the screen, dragged to a new position by the user, and resized.
ProgressBar	The <rich:progressBar> component displays a progress bar to indicate the status of a process to the user. It can update either through Ajax or on the client side, and the look and feel can be fully customized.
Select	The <rich:select> component provides a drop-down list box for selecting a single value from multiple options. The <rich:select> component can be configured as a combo-box, where it will accept typed input.
TabPanel	The <rich:tabPanel> component provides a set of tabbed panels for displaying one panel of content at a time. The tabs can be highly customized and themed. Each tab within a <rich:tabPanel> container is a <rich:tab> component.
TogglePanel	The <rich:togglePanel> component is used as a base for the other switchable components, the <rich:accordion> component and the <rich:tabPanel> component. It provides an abstract switchable component without any associated markup. As such, the <rich:togglePanel> component could be customized to provide a switchable component when neither an accordion component nor a tab panel component is appropriate.
Toolbar	The <rich:toolbar> component is a horizontal toolbar. Any JavaServer Faces (JSF) component can be added to the toolbar.
Tooltip	The <rich:tooltip> component provides an informational tool-tip. The tool-tip can be attached to any control and is displayed when hovering the mouse cursor over the control.
Tree	The <rich:tree> component provides a hierarchical tree control. Each <rich:tree> component typically consists of <rich:treeNode> child components.

In the next section, we will show a RichFaces application example in order to show you how to utilize the library.

■ **Note** In order to get the full documentation of RichFaces, you can check the documentation from `http://www.jboss.org/richfaces/docs`. You can access the complete RichFaces showcase that includes an example of almost every RichFaces component from `http://showcase.richfaces.org`.

Integrating and Customizing RichFaces

The `RightCountry` application is a RichFaces application which allows the user to drag a list of available places into their corresponding countries as shown in Figure 9-2.

Drag the places to the right country

Figure 9-2. *Right Country application*

The application does not allow the user to drag a place and drop it into a country that the place does not belong to. Listing 9-10 shows the code snippet which represents the drop source panel (on the left).

Listing 9-10. Drop Source Panel Code (on the Left)

```
<rich:panel styleClass="dropSourcePanel">
     <f:facet name="header">
            <h:outputText value="Places" />
     </f:facet>
     <h:dataTable id="places" columns="1"
                            value="#{rightCountry.places}"
                            var="place" footerClass="footerClass">

            <h:column>
                   <a4j:outputPanel styleClass="placesContainer"
                                    layout="block">

                          <rich:dragSource type="#{place.country}"
                                      dragValue="#{place}"
                                      dragIndicator="ind"/>

                          <h:outputText value="#{place.name}"></h:outputText>

                   </a4j:outputPanel>
            </h:column>
     </h:dataTable>
</rich:panel>
```

The drop source panel contains the following main components:

1. "places" data table, which lists the different places to be displayed.

2. dragSource, which allows the places inside the data table to be draggable; in the example, we used mainly two attributes of dragSource; dragValue, which represents the data to be sent to the drop zone after the drop event is completed, and dragIndicator, which represents the component ID of the dragIndicator component that is used as a drag pointer during the drag operation.

Adding to having a single drop source panel, we have three drop target panels that will receive the items from the drop source panel; every drop target represents the corresponding country (Egypt, Germany, and Brazil) for the drop source items. Listing 9-11 shows the first drop target panel (which will receive the drop source items that are related to Egypt).

Listing 9-11. First Drop Target Panel

```
<rich:panel styleClass="dropTargetPanel">
        <f:facet name="header">
                <h:outputText value="Egypt" />
        </f:facet>

        <rich:dropTarget acceptedTypes="Egypt" dropValue="Egypt"
                        dropListener="#{rightCountry.processDrop}"
                        render="places, egyptPlaces, germanyPlaces, brazilPlaces"/>
        <h:dataTable id="egyptPlaces" columns="1"
                    value="#{rightCountry.egyptPlaces}"
                    var="place" footerClass="footerClass">
            <h:column>
                <h:outputText value="#{place.name}"></h:outputText>
            </h:column>
        </h:dataTable>
</rich:panel>
```

As shown in the previous code snippet, the drop target panel contains the following components:

1. "egyptPlaces" data table, which shows the places belonging to Egypt.

2. dragTarget, which defines the droppable zone; in the example, we used the four attributes of dragTarget; acceptedTypes, which defines the element types that are acceptable by the droppable zone (if it is matched with the dragSource type, then the droppable zone will accept the dragSource item); dropValue, which represents the data to be processed after a drop event completes; dropListener, which is binded with a MethodExpression representing an action listener method that will be notified after drop operation completes; and finally render attribute, which defines the IDs of components that will participate in the "render" portion of the Request Processing Lifecycle.

In #{rightCountry.processDrop} method expression (which will be executed after the drop completes), the selected place object is removed from places list (which is binded with the drag source data table) and is put in egyptPlaces List in order to update "egyptPlaces" data table with the new place object as shown in Listing 9-12.

Listing 9-12. processDrop Method of RightCountry Managed Bean

```
public void processDrop(DropEvent event) {
        Place place = (Place) event.getDragValue();
        String dropValue = (String) event.getDropValue();

        switch (dropValue) {
                case "Egypt":
                    egyptPlaces.add(place);
                    places.remove(place);
                    break;
                //...
        }

        if (places.size() == 0) {
                FacesContext.getCurrentInstance().addMessage(null,
         new FacesMessage("Congratulations! You are done."));

                initialize();
        }
}
```

You may notice that after all of the elements in the drag source panel are consumed (dropped to their corresponding suitable targets), a Faces message is created to show the user "Congratulations! you are done." and the page information is reset using initialize() method; this Faces message will be displayed by <rich:notifyMessages>, which is shown in Listing 9-13.

Like the Egypt drop target, the other drop targets for Germany and Brazil work the same way. Listing 9-13 shows the complete code of the *Right Country* application page.

Listing 9-13. Right Country Application Page

```
<html xmlns="http://www.w3.org/1999/xhtml"
      xmlns:rich="http://richfaces.org/rich"
      xmlns:a4j="http://richfaces.org/a4j"
      xmlns:f="http://java.sun.com/jsf/core"
      xmlns:h="http://java.sun.com/jsf/html">
    <h:head>
        <title>Welcome to the Right Country application</title>
        <h:outputStylesheet library="css" name="rightCountry.css" />
    </h:head>
    <h:body>
        <rich:dragIndicator id="ind" acceptClass="accept" rejectClass="reject"
                                        draggingClass="default">
            Drag the place to the right country
        </rich:dragIndicator>

        <h:form id="form">
            <h2>Drag the places to the right country</h2>

            <h:panelGrid columnClasses="column" columns="4"
                                    styleClass="containerPanel">
                <rich:panel styleClass="dropSourcePanel">
```

```
            <f:facet name="header">
                <h:outputText value="Places" />
            </f:facet>
            <h:dataTable id="places" columns="1"
                        value="#{rightCountry.places}"
                        var="place" footerClass="footerClass">

                <h:column>
                    <a4j:outputPanel styleClass="placesContainer"
                                              layout="block">

                        <rich:dragSource type="#{place.country}"
                                            dragValue="#{place}"
                                            dragIndicator="ind"/>

                        <h:outputText value="#{place.name}"></h:outputText>

                    </a4j:outputPanel>
                </h:column>
            </h:dataTable>
        </rich:panel>

        <rich:panel styleClass="dropTargetPanel">
            <f:facet name="header">
                <h:outputText value="Egypt" />
            </f:facet>

            <rich:dropTarget acceptedTypes="Egypt" dropValue="Egypt"
                            dropListener="#{rightCountry.processDrop}"
                            render="places, egyptPlaces, germanyPlaces, brazilPlaces"/>

            <h:dataTable id="egyptPlaces" columns="1"
                        value="#{rightCountry.egyptPlaces}"
                        var="place" footerClass="footerClass">
                <h:column>
                    <h:outputText value="#{place.name}"></h:outputText>
                </h:column>
            </h:dataTable>
        </rich:panel>

        <rich:panel styleClass="dropTargetPanel">
            <f:facet name="header">
                <h:outputText value="Germany" />
            </f:facet>

            <rich:dropTarget acceptedTypes="Germany" dropValue="Germany"
                            dropListener="#{rightCountry.processDrop}"
                            render="places, egyptPlaces, germanyPlaces, brazilPlaces"/>
```

```
                <h:dataTable id="germanyPlaces" columns="1"
                                value="#{rightCountry.germanyPlaces}"
                                var="place" footerClass="footerClass">
                    <h:column>
                        <h:outputText value="#{place.name}"></h:outputText>
                    </h:column>
                </h:dataTable>
            </rich:panel>

            <rich:panel styleClass="dropTargetPanel">
                <f:facet name="header">
                    <h:outputText value="Brazil" />
                </f:facet>

                <rich:dropTarget acceptedTypes="Brazil" dropValue="Brazil"
                                dropListener="#{rightCountry.processDrop}"
                                render="places, egyptPlaces, germanyPlaces, brazilPlaces"/>

                <h:dataTable id="brazilPlaces" columns="1"
                                value="#{rightCountry.brazilPlaces}"
                                var="place" footerClass="footerClass">
                    <h:column>
                        <h:outputText value="#{place.name}"></h:outputText>
                    </h:column>
                </h:dataTable>
            </rich:panel>
        </h:panelGrid>

        <rich:notifyMessages stayTime="2000" nonblocking="true" />
    </h:form>
  </h:body>
</html>
```

RightCountry managed bean contains the four lists which are binded with the drag source and the four drop targets. Listing 9-14 shows the complete RightCountry managed bean code.

Listing 9-14. RightCountry Managed Bean

```
package com.jsfprohtml5.rightcountry.model;

import java.io.Serializable;
import java.util.ArrayList;
import java.util.List;
import javax.faces.application.FacesMessage;
import javax.faces.context.FacesContext;
import org.richfaces.event.DropEvent;

public class RightCountry implements Serializable {
    private List<Place> places;
    private List<Place> egyptPlaces;
    private List<Place> germanyPlaces;
    private List<Place> brazilPlaces;
```

```java
public RightCountry() {
    initialize();
}

public List<Place> getPlaces() {
    return places;
}

public void setPlaces(List<Place> places) {
    this.places = places;
}

public List<Place> getEgyptPlaces() {
    return egyptPlaces;
}

public void setEgyptPlaces(List<Place> egyptPlaces) {
    this.egyptPlaces = egyptPlaces;
}

public List<Place> getGermanyPlaces() {
    return germanyPlaces;
}

public void setGermanyPlaces(List<Place> germanyPlaces) {
    this.germanyPlaces = germanyPlaces;
}

public List<Place> getBrazilPlaces() {
    return brazilPlaces;
}

public void setBrazilPlaces(List<Place> brazilPlaces) {
    this.brazilPlaces = brazilPlaces;
}

public void processDrop(DropEvent event) {
    Place place = (Place) event.getDragValue();
    String dropValue = (String) event.getDropValue();

    switch (dropValue) {
        case "Egypt":
            egyptPlaces.add(place);
            places.remove(place);
            break;
        case "Germany":
            germanyPlaces.add(place);
            places.remove(place);
            break;
        case "Brazil":
            brazilPlaces.add(place);
```

```
                    places.remove(place);
                    break;
            }
        }

        if (places.size() == 0) {
            FacesContext.getCurrentInstance().addMessage(null,
                                                new FacesMessage("Congratulations!
You are done."));

            initialize();
        }
    }

    private void initialize () {
        egyptPlaces = new ArrayList<>();
        germanyPlaces = new ArrayList<>();
        brazilPlaces = new ArrayList<>();
        places = new ArrayList<>();

        places.add(new Place("The Great Pyramids of Giza", "Egypt"));
        places.add(new Place("Western Pomerania Lagoon Area National Park", "Germany"));
        places.add(new Place("Catete Palace", "Brazil"));
        places.add(new Place("Saxon Switzerland National Park", "Germany"));
        places.add(new Place("Luxor Temple", "Egypt"));
        places.add(new Place("Mariano Procópio Museum", "Brazil"));
        places.add(new Place("Bavarian Forest National Park", "Germany"));
        places.add(new Place("Museu do Índio", "Brazil"));
        places.add(new Place("Cairo Tower", "Egypt"));
    }
}
```

Finally, Listing 9-15 shows the CSS style classes of RightCountry application.

Listing 9-15. CSS Style Classes of RightCountry Application

```
.column {
    width: 25%;
    vertical-align: top;
}

.dropTargetPanel {
    width: 90%;
}

.dropSourcePanel {
    width: 133px;
}

.containerPanel {
    width: 100%;
}
```

```
.placesContainer {
    width: 100px;
    border: 1px solid gray;
    padding: 2px
}

.footerClass {
    text-align: center;
    padding-top: 5px;
}

.default {
  padding-left:30px;
  background-position: 5px;
  background-repeat: no-repeat;
 }

.accept {
  background-position: 5px;
  background-repeat: no-repeat;
  border:2px solid green
}

.reject {
  border:2px solid red;
  background-position: 5px;
  background-repeat: no-repeat;
}
```

■ **Note**   Like the `CountryNavigator` application, `RightCountry` application is a Maven web application that you can download from the book web site at `www.apress.com/9781430250104`; it can be built and deployed just like the `CountryNavigator` application.

Summary

In this chapter, you were introduced to two of the most popular open-source JSF component libraries (PrimeFaces and RichFaces). Although going into the details of these frameworks is out of the scope of this book, we developed two applications (one for PrimeFaces and the other for RichFaces) in order to show you how to utilize these component libraries in order to produce nifty-looking web applications in the JSF 2.2 world.

■ ■ ■

CHAPTER 10

Creating a Basic JSF 2.2 Application

In this chapter, you will learn in detail how to create a Basic JSF 2.2 application in Java EE 7 environment. This application will show you how to design and develop your JSF application in Java EE 7 environment. The application utilizes JSF 2.2 for creating the pages and handling the pages flow, CDI (Contexts and Dependency Injection) for bean management, EJB 3.2 for transaction handling, and JPA 2.1 for data persistence.

Structuring Weather Application

The basic application is about an application that displays weather information of the user place that is saved in his/her profile. In the weather application, the user needs first to register in the application. In order to register in the application, the user needs to enter his/her information in a flow that consists of three pages. As shown in Figure 10-1, in the first page, the user has to enter his/her preferred user name, password, and e-mail.

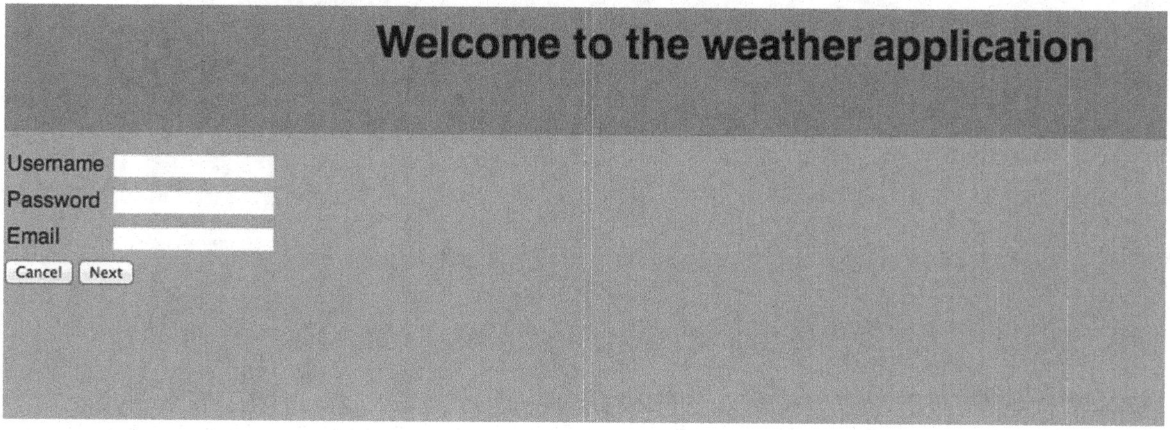

Figure 10-1. Weather application registration (first page)

If the user enters empty username or password or e-mail, a value required field message is shown and an invalid e-mail format message is shown when the user enters an e-mail in an invalid format.

After entering the information on the first page, the user is then forwarded to the second page in the flow, in which the user enters his/her first name, last name, and profession as shown in Figure 10-2.

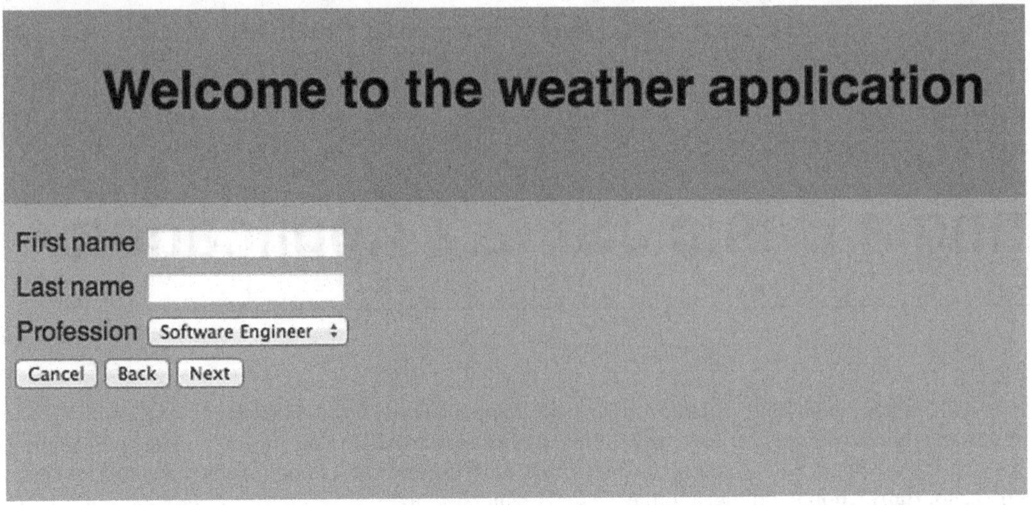

Figure 10-2. *Weather application registration (second page)*

Finally, in the last page in the registration flow, the user enters his/her ZIP code in the final page as shown in Figure 10-3 and clicks the "Finish" button.

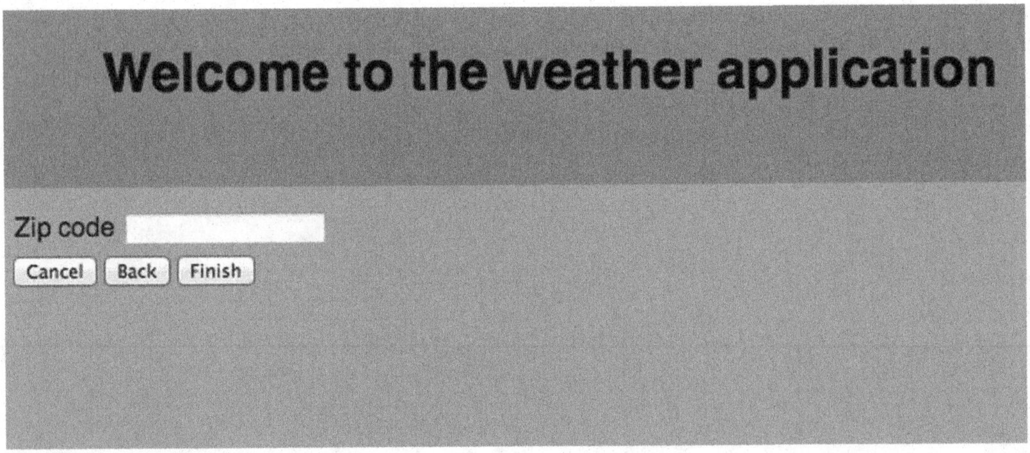

Figure 10-3. *Weather application registration (third page)*

After registering in the application, the user will be able to log in to the application using his/her user name and password as shown in Figure 10-4.

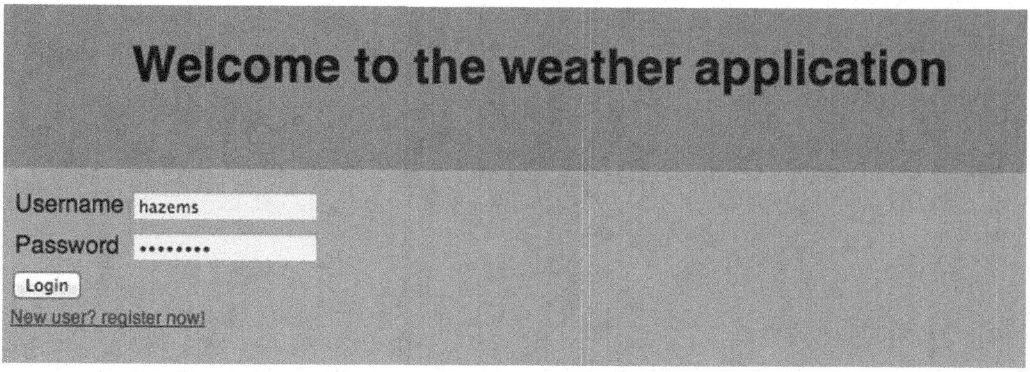

Figure 10-4. *Weather application login page*

After logging in to the application, as shown in Figure 10-5, the user will be forwarded to the weather screen, in which the user will be able to learn the weather information of the place (s)he enters in the registration final page.

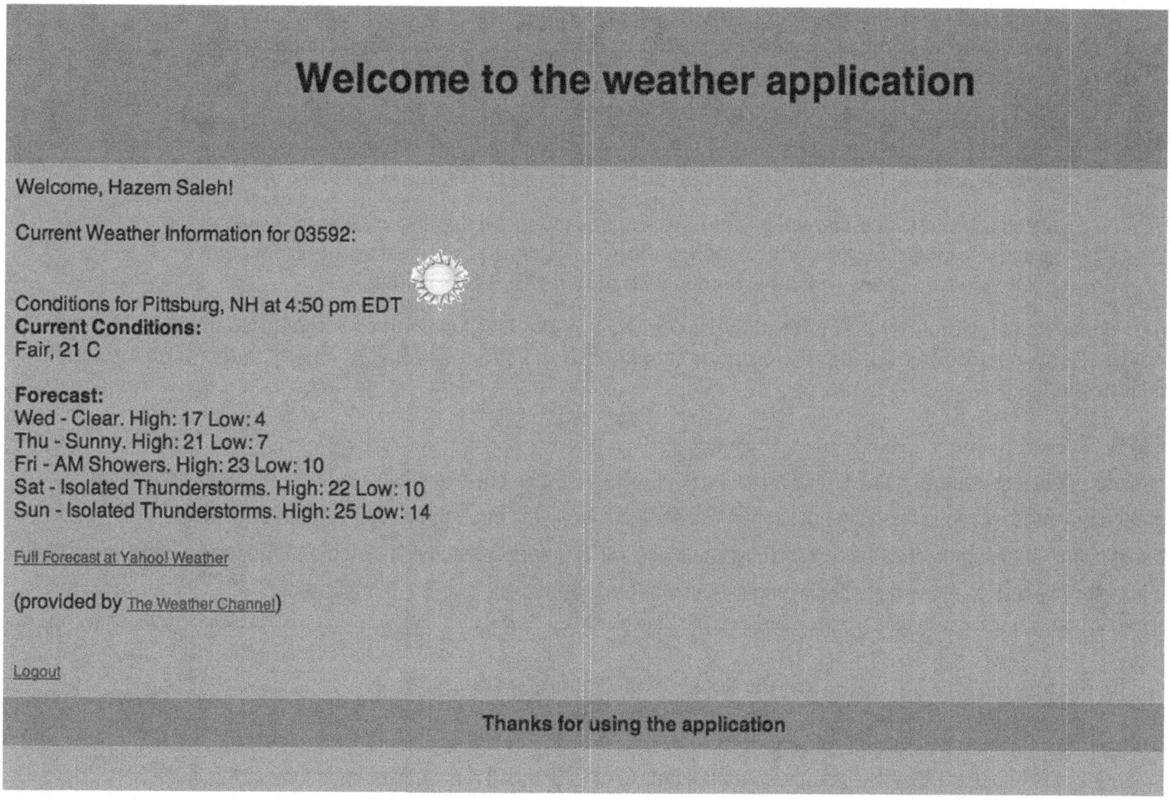

Figure 10-5. *Weather application main page*

Now after going through the pages of the weather application, let's see how we can structure it. Figure 10-6 shows the weather application structure.

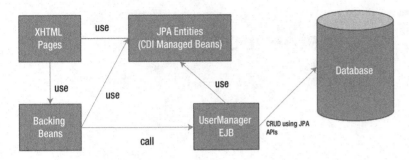

Figure 10-6. *Weather application structure*

As shown in the previous figure, the application has the following structure:

1. **XHTML pages:** These represent the weather application pages. It uses both the backing beans and managed beans using the JSF expression language (EL).

2. **Backing beans:** These are normal managed beans that are conceptually related to the UI pages and are not part of the application model. Backing beans are ideal for centralizing the handling of the page actions. In the weather application, backing beans mainly get the instances of the managed beans which carry the user's entered data and then call the UserManager EJB in order to perform the required operation.

3. **User Manager EJB:** In order to perform the different business operations, backing beans call UserManager EJB. UserManager EJB is a stateless session EJB* which uses the JPA entities and the JPA EntityManager in order to perform the required database operations.

4. **JPA entities (CDI managed beans):** JPA entities represent the data classes that map to the database tables. In the weather application, the JPA entities are used as the application's CDI managed beans which are binded with the XHTML pages using EL.

Notice that for simplicity the application uses Oracle Java DB. Java DB is Oracle's supported distribution of the Apache Derby open-source database. It supports standard ANSI/ISO SQL through the JDBC and Java EE APIs and is included in the JDK.

■ **Note**   It is important to know that JPA can be used without EJBs; however, using EJBs in JPA applications has a great advantage, which is handling application transactions implicitly through the EJB container (container-managed transaction). Although the weather application is a basic JSF 2.2 application, we insisted on introducing EJBs with JPA in it in order to show you how these technologies can work together inside a JSF 2.2 application.

In the next sections, we will go into the details of the application components.

■ **Note**   It is important to note that going into the details of EJB and JPA is outside the scope of this book. In order to know learn the capabilities of them, we recommend you to read the Oracle Java EE tutorial: http://docs.oracle.com/javaee/7/tutorial/doc/.

Constructing JSF Pages

Weather application has the following XHTML pages:

1. Home page (home.xhtml): It represents the login page of the application, which is shown in Figure 10-4.

2. Registration pages (/registration/*.xhtml): They represent the pages which include the registration flow; the registration pages include the following pages:

    a. registration.xhtml page, which represents the first registration page in the flow shown in Figure 10-1.

    b. extraInfo.xhtml page, which represents the second registration page in the flow shown in Figure 10-2.

    c. final.xhtml page, which represents the final registration page in the flow shown in Figure 10-3.

3. Weather page (/protected/weather.xhtml), which represents the weather page shown in Figure 10-5.

Listing 10-1 shows the home.xhtml page code.

Listing 10-1. Home Page XHTML Code

```
<?xml version='1.0' encoding='UTF-8' ?>
<!DOCTYPE html>
<html xmlns="http://www.w3.org/1999/xhtml"
      xmlns:ui="http://java.sun.com/jsf/facelets"
      xmlns:h="http://java.sun.com/jsf/html">

<ui:composition template="/WEB-INF/templates/main.xhtml">
    <ui:define name="title">
        #{bundle['application.loginpage.title']}
    </ui:define>
    <ui:define name="content">
        <h:form>
            <h:panelGrid columns="3">
                <h:outputText value="#{bundle['user.id']}"></h:outputText>
                <h:inputText id="userID"
                            value="#{appUser.id}"
                            required="true"
                            requiredMessage="#{bundle['user.id.validation']}">
                </h:inputText>
                <h:message for="userID" styleClass="errorMessage"/>

                <h:outputText value="#{bundle['user.password']}"></h:outputText>
                <h:inputSecret id="password"
                            value="#{appUser.password}"
                            required="true"
                            requiredMessage="#{bundle['user.password.validation']}">
                </h:inputSecret>
                <h:message for="password" styleClass="errorMessage"/>
            </h:panelGrid>
```

```
                <h:commandButton value="#{bundle['application.login']}"
action="#{loginBacking.login}"/> <br/>
                <h:link value="#{bundle['application.loginpage.register']}" outcome="registration"/>
                <br/><br/>
                <h:messages styleClass="errorMessage"/>
            </h:form>
        </ui:define>
    </ui:composition>

</html>
```

As shown in the previous code, the weather application's home page contains user name InputText and password InputSecret. The login CommandButton calls the login method of the LoginBacking bean and the registration link navigates to "registration" flow (will be illustrated in more detail in the next section). Listing 10-2 shows the LoginBacking bean.

Listing 10-2. LoginBacking Bean

```java
package com.jsfprohtml5.weather.backing;

import com.jsfprohtml5.weather.model.AppUser;
import com.jsfprohtml5.weather.model.UserManagerLocal;
import java.util.logging.Level;
import java.util.logging.Logger;
import javax.ejb.EJB;
import javax.enterprise.context.RequestScoped;
import javax.faces.application.FacesMessage;
import javax.inject.Named;

@Named
@RequestScoped
public class LoginBacking extends BaseBacking {

    @EJB
    private UserManagerLocal userManager;

    public String login() {
        AppUser currentAppUser = (AppUser) evaluateEL("#{appUser}", AppUser.class);

        try {
            AppUser appUser = userManager.getUser(currentAppUser.getId(),
currentAppUser.getPassword());

            if (appUser == null) {
                getContext().addMessage(null, new FacesMessage(INVALID_USERNAME_OR_PASSWORD));
                return null;
            }

            //Set Necessary user information
            currentAppUser.setEmail(appUser.getEmail());
            currentAppUser.setFirstName(appUser.getFirstName());
```

```
            currentAppUser.setLastName(appUser.getLastName());
            currentAppUser.setZipCode(appUser.getZipCode());
            currentAppUser.setProfession(appUser.getProfession());
        } catch (Exception ex) {
            Logger.getLogger(LoginBacking.class.getName()).log(Level.SEVERE, null, ex);
            getContext().addMessage(null, new FacesMessage(SYSTEM_ERROR));
            return null;
        }

        return "/protected/weather";
    }

    ...
}
```

LoginBacking bean is a backing bean which handles the login action. It calls the UserManager EJB in order to know if the user is registered in the system using getUser() method (UserManager EJB will be illustrated in detail in the "Application Back End" section). In order to get the AppUser's CDI managed bean instance which is binded with the user name and password fields, evaluateEL() method is called in order to evaluate the #{appUser} expression. evaluateEL() method is located in the base backing bean (BaseBacking) class.

If getUser() method returns null, this means that the user is not registered in the system with the entered username and password combination and an invalid user name or password message is shown for the user. If the user name and password combination is valid, then the user's information is retrieved and set in #{appUser} managed bean instance (AppUser is both a request-scoped CDI managed bean and a JPA entity class, which will be illustrated in detail in the "Application Back End" section), and the page is forwarded to the weather page.

■ **Note**   @EJB annotation can be used for annotating bean's instance variable to specify a dependence on an EJB. Application Server automatically initializes the annotated variable with the reference to the EJB on which it depends using dependency injection. This initialization occurs before any of the bean's business methods are invoked and after the bean's EJBContext is set.

All of the weather application's backing beans extend from BaseBacking class as shown in Figure 10-7.

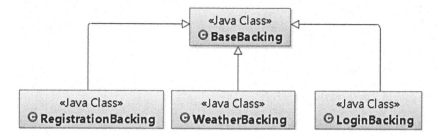

Figure 10-7. Weather Application's backing beans

Listing 10-3 shows the code of the BaseBacking class.

Listing 10-3. BaseBacking Bean Class

```java
package com.jsfprohtml5.weather.backing;

import java.util.Map;
import javax.faces.context.FacesContext;
import javax.servlet.http.HttpSession;

public class BaseBacking {

    protected FacesContext getContext() {
        return FacesContext.getCurrentInstance();
    }

    protected Map getRequestMap() {
        return getContext().getExternalContext().getRequestMap();
    }

    protected HttpSession getSession() {
        return (HttpSession) getContext().getExternalContext().getSession(false);
    }

    protected Object evaluateEL(String elExpression, Class beanClazz) {
        return getContext().getApplication().evaluateExpressionGet(getContext(), elExpression,
beanClazz);
    }

    ...
}
```

BaseBacking class is a base class which contains shortcuts for getting the JSF Faces context, getting the HTTP session, getting the HTTP request map, and evaluating the JSF expressions. Listing 10-4 shows the weather.xhtml page code.

Listing 10-4. Weather Main Page

```xml
<?xml version='1.0' encoding='UTF-8' ?>
<!DOCTYPE html>
<html xmlns="http://www.w3.org/1999/xhtml"
      xmlns:ui="http://java.sun.com/jsf/facelets"
      xmlns:h="http://java.sun.com/jsf/html"
      xmlns:mashup="http://code.google.com/p/mashups4jsf/">

<ui:composition template="/WEB-INF/templates/main.xhtml">
    <ui:define name="title">
        #{bundle['application.weatherpage.title']}
    </ui:define>
```

```
<ui:define name="content">
    <h:form>
        #{bundle['application.welcome']}, #{appUser.firstName} #{appUser.lastName}! <br/><br/>

        #{bundle['application.weatherpage.currentInfo']} for #{appUser.zipCode}:
        <mashup:yahooWeather temperatureType="c" locationCode="#{appUser.zipCode}"/> <br/><br/>

        <h:commandLink value="#{bundle['application.weatherpage.logout']}"
                       action="#{weatherBacking.logout}"></h:commandLink> <br/><br/>
    </h:form>
</ui:define>
</ui:composition>

</html>
```

The weather page displays a welcome message to the user and the Yahoo! weather information is retrieved using the yahooWeather component of Mashups4JSF library (http://code.google.com/p/mashups4jsf/).

■ **Note** Mashups4JSF is an open-source project that aims at integrating Mashup services with JavaServer Faces applications. Using Mashups4JSF, JSF developers will be able to construct rich and customized mashups by using simple tags. Mashups4JSF also allows exporting the Java Enterprise Application data as Mashup feeds by annotating the application domain classes with @Feed annotation. For more information check the project home page: http://code.google.com/p/mashups4jsf/.

---

yahooWeather component gives you the ability to view the current weather status in a specific location in the world (using Yahoo! Weather Service under the hood) using its ZIP code. It has two main attributes as shown in Table 10-1.

Table 10-1. *Mashups4JSF yahooWeather Component*

Component Attribute	Description
locationCode	The ZIP code of the location
temperatureType	The temperature in Fahrenheit (f) or Celsius (c). Default is c.

In order to configure Mashups4JSF in our JSF application, we need to add two jars to the lib folder of your web application:

- Mashups4JSF 1.0.0 core jar.
- Rome 0.9 jar.

If our application is a Maven application, we need to add these jars to our application's pom.xml as shown in Listing 10-5.

Listing 10-5. Mashups4JSF Dependency in pom.xml

```xml
<project ...>
    ...
    <dependencies>
        ...
        <dependency>
            <groupId>com.googlecode.mashups4jsf</groupId>
            <artifactId>mashups4jsf-core</artifactId>
            <version>1.0.0</version>
        </dependency>
        <dependency>
            <groupId>rome</groupId>
            <artifactId>rome</artifactId>
            <version>0.9</version>
        </dependency>
    </dependencies>

    <repositories>
        ...
        <repository>
            <id>googlecode.com</id>
            <url>http://mashups4jsf.googlecode.com/svn/trunk/mashups4jsf-repo</url>
        </repository>
    </repositories>
</project>
```

After adding Mashups4JSF jars to our application's dependency, we can include it in our XHTML page as follows:

```xml
<html xmlns="http://www.w3.org/1999/xhtml"
    xmlns:ui="http://java.sun.com/jsf/facelets"
    xmlns:h="http://java.sun.com/jsf/html"
    xmlns:mashup="http://code.google.com/p/mashups4jsf/">
```

The weather page has a logout CommandLink whose action is binded with the logout method of the WeatherBacking bean class. Listing 10-6 shows WeatherBacking bean class.

Listing 10-6. WeatherBacking Bean Class

```java
package com.jsfprohtml5.weather.backing;
import javax.enterprise.context.RequestScoped;
import javax.inject.Named;


@Named
@RequestScoped
public class WeatherBacking extends BaseBacking {
    public String logout() {
        getSession().invalidate();

        return "/home.xhtml?faces-redirect=true";
    }
}
```

In the logout() method, the session is invalidated and the user is forwarded to the home page. Notice that all of the application pages are using the main.xhtml template under /WEB-INF/templates folder. Listing 10-7 shows the main.xhtml template page.

Listing 10-7. main.xhtml Template Page

```
<?xml version='1.0' encoding='UTF-8' ?>
<!DOCTYPE html>
<html xmlns="http://www.w3.org/1999/xhtml"
      xmlns:ui="http://java.sun.com/jsf/facelets"
      xmlns:h="http://java.sun.com/jsf/html">

<h:head>
  <title><ui:insert name="title">#{bundle['application.defaultpage.title']}</ui:insert></title>
  <link href="#{request.contextPath}/css/main.css" rel="stylesheet" type="text/css"/>
</h:head>

<h:body>
    <div id="container">
        <div id="header">
            <ui:insert name="header">
                <h1>#{bundle['application.defaultpage.header.content']}</h1>
            </ui:insert>
        </div>

        <div id="content">
            <ui:insert name="content">
                #{bundle['application.defaultpage.body.content']}
            </ui:insert>
        </div>

        <div id="footer">
            <ui:insert name="footer">
                #{bundle['application.defaultpage.footer.content']}
            </ui:insert>
        </div>
    </div>
</h:body>
</html>
```

The template uses main.css style file and it has three main parts: the header, the footer, and the content. The content should be replaced by the different pages in the application (home, weather, and registration pages). The application's text is externalized in the messages.properties file which is shown in Listing 10-8.

Listing 10-8. messages.properties File

```
user.id = Username
user.password = Password
user.email = Email
user.fname = First name
user.lname = Last name
user.profession = Profession
user.zipCode = Zip code
```

```
user.id.validation = You need to enter a username
user.password.validation = You need to enter a password
user.email.validation = You need to enter an email
user.email.invalid = Invalid Email
user.fname.validation = You need to enter first name
user.lname.validation = You need to enter last name
user.zipCode.validation = You need to enter zip code

user.profession.profession1 = Software Engineer
user.profession.profession2 = Project Manager
user.profession.profession3 = Other

application.next = Next
application.back = Back
application.cancel = Cancel
application.finish = Finish

application.login = Login
application.loginpage.title = Login page
application.loginpage.register = New user? register now!

application.welcome = Welcome
application.weatherpage.title = Weather page
application.weatherpage.logout = Logout
application.weatherpage.currentInfo = Current Weather Information

application.register = Register
application.register.title = Registration page
application.register.return = Back to home

application.defaultpage.title = Default Title
application.defaultpage.header.content = Welcome to the weather application
application.defaultpage.body.content = Your content here ...
application.defaultpage.footer.content = Thanks for using the application
```

The use of the main.css file of the template is for handling the look and feel and the layout as shown in Listing 10-9.

Listing 10-9. main.css Style File

```css
h1, p, body, html {
    margin:0;
    padding:0;
    font-family: sans-serif;
}

body {
    background-color: #B3B1B2;
}
```

```
#container {
    width:100%;
}

a {
    font-size: 12px;
}

#header {
    background-color: #84978F;
    padding: 50px;
}

#header h1 {
    margin-bottom: 0px;
    text-align: center;
}

#content {
    float: left;
    margin: 10px;
    height: 400px;
    width: 100%;
}

#footer {
    clear:both;     /*No floating elements are allowed on left or right*/
    background-color: #84978F;
    text-align:center;
    font-weight: bold;
    padding: 10px;
}

.errorMessage {
    font-size: 12px;
    color: red;
    font-family: sans-serif;
}
```

In order to protect the weather page, it is put inside a custom folder called ("/protected"), and a custom JSF phase listener is created to protect the pages as shown in Listing 10-10.

Listing 10-10. AuthorizationListener Class

```
package com.jsfprohtml5.weather.util;

import javax.faces.application.NavigationHandler;
import javax.faces.context.FacesContext;
import javax.faces.event.PhaseEvent;
import javax.faces.event.PhaseId;
import javax.faces.event.PhaseListener;
```

```java
public class AuthorizationListener implements PhaseListener {

    @Override
    public void afterPhase(PhaseEvent event) {
        FacesContext context = event.getFacesContext();
        NavigationHandler navigationHandler = context.getApplication().getNavigationHandler();

        String currentPage = context.getViewRoot().getViewId();

        boolean isProtectedPage = currentPage.contains("/protected/");

        //Restrict access to protected pages ...
        if (isProtectedPage) {
            navigationHandler.handleNavigation(context, null, "/home?faces-redirect=true");
        }
    }

    @Override
    public void beforePhase(PhaseEvent event) {
        //Nothing ...
    }

    @Override
    public PhaseId getPhaseId() {
        return PhaseId.RESTORE_VIEW;
    }
}
```

AuthorizationListener phase listener prohibits any user from accessing the pages in the protected folder directly.

In the next section, we will go through the registration pages in order to understand how to utilize the JSF 2.2 Faces Flow in order to implement the registration flow behavior in our weather application.

Leveraging Faces Flow

As you know from Chapter 5, Faces Flow is introduced in JSF 2.2 to enable flow management in JSF applications. In the old days, in order to implement flows in JSF applications, the JSF developer has either to use additional frameworks such as Spring Web Flow or ADF Task Flows or to implement it manually using the HTTP session. Implementing it manually using the HTTP session is not an efficient way of implementation because the JSF developer will have to handle the session cleanup after the flow is completed or exited.

In JSF Faces Flow, the developer can define a flow on a set of related pages (or views or nodes) with well-defined entry and exit points. In the weather application, we package the Flow pages in a single directory (/registration) to be convenient with the JSF flow convention rules, which are as follows:

1. Every XHTML file in the flow directory acts as a view node of the flow.

2. The start node of the flow is the view whose name is the same as the name of the flow (registration.xhtml).

3. Navigation between the pages in the flow directory is considered a navigation within the flow.

4. Navigation to a view outside the flow directory is considered an exit from the flow.

Finally, in order to define the Faces flow, you should declare it in the Faces configuration file (faces-config.xml) as shown in Listing 10-11.

Listing 10-11. Defining the Faces Flow in the Faces Configuration File

```xml
<?xml version='1.0' encoding='UTF-8'?>
<faces-config version="2.2"
    xmlns="http://xmlns.jcp.org/xml/ns/javaee"
    xmlns:xsi="http://www.w3.org/2001/XMLSchema-instance"
    xsi:schemaLocation="http://xmlns.jcp.org/xml/ns/javaee
http://xmlns.jcp.org/xml/ns/javaee/web-facesconfig_2_2.xsd">

    <flow-definition id="registration">
        <flow-return id="flowReturn">
            <from-outcome>/home</from-outcome>
        </flow-return>
    </flow-definition>

    ...
</faces-config>
```

In order to define the flow, you use the <flow-definition> tag specifying the ID of the flow. The <flow-return> tag represents the flow return and it must have one <from-outcome> element; in our weather application, the flow return ID is "flowReturn" and the flow returns when the outcome "/home" is returned (which represents the home page). Now, let's go through the registration pages. Listing 10-12 shows the registration.xhtml page.

Listing 10-12. registration.xhtml Page

```xml
<?xml version='1.0' encoding='UTF-8' ?>
<!DOCTYPE html>
<html xmlns="http://www.w3.org/1999/xhtml"
      xmlns:ui="http://java.sun.com/jsf/facelets"
      xmlns:h="http://java.sun.com/jsf/html"
      xmlns:f="http://java.sun.com/jsf/core">

<ui:composition template="/WEB-INF/templates/main.xhtml">
    <ui:define name="title">
        #{bundle['application.register.title']}
    </ui:define>
    <ui:define name="content">
        <h:form>
            <h:panelGrid columns="3">
                <h:outputText value="#{bundle['user.id']}"></h:outputText>
                <h:inputText id="userID"
                            value="#{flowScope.id}"
                            required="true"
                            requiredMessage="#{bundle['user.id.validation']}">
                </h:inputText>
                <h:message for="userID" styleClass="errorMessage"/>
```

```
                    <h:outputText value="#{bundle['user.password']}"></h:outputText>
                    <h:inputSecret id="password"
                                   value="#{flowScope.password}"
                                   required="true"
                                   requiredMessage="#{bundle['user.password.validation']}">
                    </h:inputSecret>
                    <h:message for="password" styleClass="errorMessage"/>

                    <h:outputText value="#{bundle['user.email']}"></h:outputText>
                    <h:inputText id="email"
                                 value="#{flowScope.email}"
                                 required="true"
                                 requiredMessage="#{bundle['user.email.validation']}"
                                 validatorMessage="#{bundle['user.email.invalid']}">

                        <f:validateRegex pattern="[\w\.-]*[a-zA-Z0-9_]@[\w\.-]*[a-zA-Z0-9]\.[a-zA-Z]
[a-zA-Z\.]*[a-zA-Z]"/>
                    </h:inputText>
                    <h:message for="email" styleClass="errorMessage"/>
            </h:panelGrid>

            <h:commandButton value="#{bundle['application.cancel']}" action="flowReturn"
                             immediate="true"/>
            <h:commandButton value="#{bundle['application.next']}" action="extraInfo"/> <br/>
        </h:form>
    </ui:define>
</ui:composition>

</html>
```

Using the #{flowScope} EL object, we can store the objects in the flow scope, and it is equivalent to
facesContext.getApplication().getFlowHandler().getCurrentFlowScope() API. The expressions
#{flowScope.id}, #{flowScope.password}, and #{flowScope.email} are binded with the user ID, password, and
e-mail input fields. Another important thing to notice is the "cancel" CommandButton's action, which is set to the
registration flow return ID ("flowReturn"); this means that when the "cancel" CommandButton is clicked then the user
will be forwarded to the home page. Listing 10-13 shows the second page in the registration flow (extraInfo.xhtml)
page.

Listing 10-13. extraInfo.xhtml Page

```
<?xml version='1.0' encoding='UTF-8' ?>
<!DOCTYPE html>
<html xmlns="http://www.w3.org/1999/xhtml"
      xmlns:ui="http://java.sun.com/jsf/facelets"
      xmlns:h="http://java.sun.com/jsf/html"
      xmlns:f="http://java.sun.com/jsf/core">

<ui:composition template="/WEB-INF/templates/main.xhtml">
    <ui:define name="title">
        #{bundle['application.register.title']}
    </ui:define>
```

```
    <ui:define name="content">
        <h:form>
            <h:panelGrid columns="3">
                <h:outputText value="#{bundle['user.fname']}"></h:outputText>
                <h:inputText id="fname"
                            value="#{flowScope.fname}"
                            required="true"
                            requiredMessage="#{bundle['user.fname.validation']}">
                </h:inputText>
                <h:message for="fname" styleClass="errorMessage"/>

                <h:outputText value="#{bundle['user.lname']}"></h:outputText>
                <h:inputText id="lname"
                                value="#{flowScope.lname}"
                                required="true"
                                requiredMessage="#{bundle['user.lname.validation']}">
                </h:inputText>
                <h:message for="lname" styleClass="errorMessage"/>

                <h:outputText value="#{bundle['user.profession']}"></h:outputText>
                <h:selectOneMenu id="profession"
                                    value="#{flowScope.profession}">

                    <f:selectItem itemLabel="#{bundle['user.profession.profession1']}"
itemValue="SE"/>
                    <f:selectItem itemLabel="#{bundle['user.profession.profession2']}"
itemValue="PM"/>
                    <f:selectItem itemLabel="#{bundle['user.profession.profession3']}"
itemValue="OT"/>
                </h:selectOneMenu>
                <h:message for="profession" styleClass="errorMessage"/>
            </h:panelGrid>

            <h:commandButton value="#{bundle['application.cancel']}" action="flowReturn"
                            immediate="true" />
            <h:commandButton value="#{bundle['application.back']}" action="registration"
                             immediate="true" />
            <h:commandButton value="#{bundle['application.next']}" action="final"/> <br/>
        </h:form>
    </ui:define>
</ui:composition>

</html>
```

The expressions #{flowScope.fname}, #{flowScope.lname}, and #{flowScope.profession} are binded with the user first name, last name, and profession input fields. One thing to notice is that flow data are alive as long as the user is navigating between the flow pages; this means that if the user clicks the back button to go to the initial registration, then (s)he will be able to see the data (s)he entered before in the initial page. Listing 10-14 shows the final page in the registration flow (final.xhtml) page.

Listing 10-14. final.xhtml Page

```xml
<?xml version='1.0' encoding='UTF-8' ?>
<!DOCTYPE html>
<html xmlns="http://www.w3.org/1999/xhtml"
      xmlns:ui="http://java.sun.com/jsf/facelets"
      xmlns:h="http://java.sun.com/jsf/html">

<ui:composition template="/WEB-INF/templates/main.xhtml">
    <ui:define name="title">
        #{bundle['application.register.title']}
    </ui:define>
    <ui:define name="content">
        <h:form prependId="false">
            <h:panelGrid columns="3">
                <h:outputText value="#{bundle['user.zipCode']}"></h:outputText>
                <h:inputText id="woeid"
                             value="#{flowScope.zipCode}"
                             required="true"
                             requiredMessage="#{bundle['user.zipCode.validation']}">
                </h:inputText>
                <h:message for="woeid" styleClass="errorMessage"/>
            </h:panelGrid>

            <h:commandButton value="#{bundle['application.cancel']}"
                             immediate="true" action="flowReturn" />
            <h:commandButton value="#{bundle['application.back']}"
immediate="true" action="extraInfo"/>
            <h:commandButton value="#{bundle['application.finish']}"
action="#{registrationBacking.register}"/> <br/>
            <h:messages styleClass="errorMessage"/>
        </h:form>
    </ui:define>
</ui:composition>

</html>
```

Finally, #{flowScope.zipCode} is binded with the user ZIP code input text. When the user clicks the "Finish" CommandButton, the register() method of the RegistrationBacking bean is called to register the user in the application. Listing 10-15 shows the RegistrationBacking bean.

Listing 10-15. RegistrationBacking Bean Class

```java
package com.jsfprohtml5.weather.backing;

import com.jsfprohtml5.weather.model.AppUser;
import com.jsfprohtml5.weather.model.UserExistsException;
import com.jsfprohtml5.weather.model.UserManagerLocal;
import java.util.Map;
import java.util.logging.Level;
import java.util.logging.Logger;
import javax.ejb.EJB;
```

```
import javax.enterprise.context.RequestScoped;
import javax.faces.application.FacesMessage;
import javax.faces.context.FacesContext;
import javax.inject.Named;

@Named
@RequestScoped
public class RegistrationBacking extends BaseBacking {

    @EJB
    private UserManagerLocal userManager;

    public String register() {
        FacesContext context = FacesContext.getCurrentInstance();
        Map<Object, Object> flowScope = context.getApplication().getFlowHandler().getCurrentFlowScope();

        AppUser appUser = new AppUser();

        appUser.setId((String) flowScope.get("id"));
        appUser.setPassword((String) flowScope.get("password"));
        appUser.setEmail((String) flowScope.get("email"));

        appUser.setFirstName((String) flowScope.get("fname"));
        appUser.setLastName((String) flowScope.get("lname"));
        appUser.setProfession((String) flowScope.get("profession"));

        appUser.setZipCode((String) flowScope.get("zipCode"));

        try {
            userManager.registerUser(appUser);
        } catch (UserExistsException ex) {
            Logger.getLogger(RegistrationBacking.class.getName()).log(Level.SEVERE, null, ex);
            context.addMessage(null, new FacesMessage(USERNAME_ALREADY_EXISTS));
            return null;
        } catch (Exception ex) {
            Logger.getLogger(RegistrationBacking.class.getName()).log(Level.SEVERE, null, ex);
            context.addMessage(null, new FacesMessage(SYSTEM_ERROR));
            return null;
        }

        return "flowReturn";
    }

    ...
}
```

RegistrationBacking bean is a backing bean which handles the user registration. In order to get the flow data, the flow scope is retrieved using context.getApplication().getFlowHandler().getCurrentFlowScope() API. The AppUser JPA entity class is instantiated and propagated with the user data from the flow scope and then it is passed to the regiserUser() method of the UserManager EJB. If the registration succeeds, then the registration flow is returned and the user is forwarded to the home page.

The AppUser JPA entity class will be illustrated in the next section.

Composing Managed Beans (JPA Entity Beans)

In the weather application, we have a single managed bean (and JPA entity class) which is AppUser class. Listing 10-16 shows the AppUser class.

Listing 10-16. AppUser Entity Class

```java
package com.jsfprohtml5.weather.model;

import java.io.Serializable;
import javax.enterprise.context.RequestScoped;
import javax.inject.Named;
import javax.persistence.Column;
import javax.persistence.Entity;
import javax.persistence.Id;
import javax.persistence.Table;
import javax.validation.constraints.NotNull;
import javax.validation.constraints.Size;

@Entity
@Table(name = "APP_USER")
@Named
@RequestScoped
public class AppUser implements Serializable {
    private static final long serialVersionUID = 134523456789194332L;

    @Id
    @NotNull
    @Size(min = 1, max = 64)
    @Column(name = "ID")
    private String id;

    @NotNull
    @Size(min = 1, max = 32)
    @Column(name = "FIRST_NAME")
    private String firstName;

    @NotNull
    @Size(min = 1, max = 32)
    @Column(name = "LAST_NAME")
    private String lastName;

    @NotNull
    @Size(min = 1, max = 32)
    @Column(name = "PASSWORD")
    private String password;

    @NotNull
    @Size(min = 1, max = 32)
    @Column(name = "PROFESSION")
    private String profession;
```

```
    @NotNull
    @Size(max = 64)
    @Column(name = "EMAIL")
    private String email;

    @NotNull
    @Size(max = 32)
    @Column(name = "ZIP_CODE")
    private String zipCode;

    public AppUser() {
    }
    public AppUser(String id) {
        this.id = id;
    }
    public AppUser(String id, String firstName, String lastName, String password,
String profession, String zipCode) {
        this.id = id;
        this.firstName = firstName;
        this.lastName = lastName;
        this.password = password;
        this.profession = profession;
        this.zipCode = zipCode;
    }

    public String getId() {
        return id;
    }
    public void setId(String id) {
        this.id = id;
    }

    public String getFirstName() {
        return firstName;
    }
    public void setFirstName(String firstName) {
        this.firstName = firstName;
    }

    public String getLastName() {
        return lastName;
    }
    public void setLastName(String lastName) {
        this.lastName = lastName;
    }

    public String getPassword() {
        return password;
    }
```

```java
    public void setPassword(String password) {
        this.password = password;
    }

    public String getProfession() {
        return profession;
    }
    public void setProfession(String profession) {
        this.profession = profession;
    }

    public String getEmail() {
        return email;
    }
    public void setEmail(String email) {
        this.email = email;
    }

    public String getZipCode() {
        return zipCode;
    }
    public void setZipCode(String zipCode) {
        this.zipCode = zipCode;
    }

    @Override
    public String toString() {
        return "ID = " + id;
    }

    @Override
    public int hashCode() {
        int hash = 0;
        hash += (id != null ? id.hashCode() : 0);
        return hash;
    }

    @Override
    public boolean equals(Object object) {
        if (!(object instanceof AppUser)) {
            return false;
        }
        AppUser other = (AppUser) object;
        if ((this.id == null && other.id != null) || (this.id != null && !this.id.equals(other.id))) {
            return false;
        }
        return true;
    }
}
```

AppUser is a JPA entity class. @Entity annotation is used for marking the class as an entity class; @Table annotation is used for explicitly setting the table name that the JPA entity maps to. Both @Named and @RequestScoped are used to declare the AppUser class as a CDI managed bean in the request scope. If we look into the AppUser class attributes, we will find the following JPA annotations:

- @Id annotation is used to mark the class attribute as a unique identifier.

- @Column annotation is used for explicitly setting the column name that the JPA class attribute maps to.

In the next section, we will see how to configure the JPA persistence unit and create the User Manager EJB.

Application Back End (EJB 3.2 + JPA 2.1)

Now we come to the part about the application back end, which is using EJB 3.2 and JPA 2.1, which are part of the Java EE 7 platform. In the previous section, we already saw the application's single JPA entity (AppUser) class, but we did not have any information about how to use the entity bean in performing the different database operations. In order to perform the database operation, we need to define the persistence.xml file which is shown in Listing 10-17.

Listing 10-17. persistence.xml File

```xml
<?xml version="1.0" encoding="UTF-8"?>
<persistence version="2.1" xmlns="http://xmlns.jcp.org/xml/ns/persistence"
xmlns:xsi="http://www.w3.org/2001/XMLSchema-instance"
xsi:schemaLocation="http://xmlns.jcp.org/xml/ns/persistence
http://xmlns.jcp.org/xml/ns/persistence/persistence_2_1.xsd">

    <persistence-unit name="weatherUnit" transaction-type="JTA">
        <provider>org.eclipse.persistence.jpa.PersistenceProvider</provider>
        <jta-data-source>jdbc/weatherDB</jta-data-source>
    </persistence-unit>
</persistence>
```

In the persistence.xml file (under /resources/META-INF), the persistence unit name "weatherUnit" is defined and transaction type is set to be "JTA" (Java Transaction API). Inside the persistence unit, we define both the JPA provider class (org.eclipse.persistence.jpa.PersistenceProvider) and the <jta-data-source> to be (jdbc/weatherDB). The <jta-data-source> element represents the JNDI name of the JDBC data source. Listing 10-18 shows the UserManager Local EJB interface.

Listing 10-18. UserManager Local EJB Interface

```java
package com.jsfprohtml5.weather.model;

import javax.ejb.Local;

@Local
public interface UserManagerLocal {
    public AppUser getUser(String userID, String password);
    public void registerUser(AppUser user) throws UserExistsException;
}
```

UserManager EJB implements UserManagerLocal interface as shown by Listing 10-19.

Listing 10-19. UserManager EJB

```java
package com.jsfprohtml5.weather.model;

import java.util.List;
import javax.ejb.Stateless;
import javax.persistence.EntityManager;
import javax.persistence.PersistenceContext;
import javax.persistence.Query;

@Stateless
public class UserManager implements UserManagerLocal {

    @PersistenceContext(unitName = "weatherUnit")
    EntityManager em;

    @Override
    public AppUser getUser(String userID, String password) {
        Query query = em.createQuery("select appUser from AppUser appUser where "
                    + "appUser.id = :id and appUser.password = :password");

        query.setParameter("id", userID);
        query.setParameter("password", password);

        List<AppUser> result = query.getResultList();

        if (result != null && result.size() > 0) {
            return result.get(0);
        }

        return null;
    }

    @Override
    public void registerUser(AppUser appUser) throws UserExistsException {
        Query query = em.createQuery("select appUser from AppUser appUser where "
                    + "appUser.id = :id");

        query.setParameter("id", appUser.getId());

        List<AppUser> result = query.getResultList();

        if (result != null && result.size() > 0) {
            throw new UserExistsException();
        }

        em.persist(appUser);
    }
}
```

@Stateless annotation defines the UserManager class as a stateless session EJB. @PersistenceContext annotation is used for injecting a container managed entity manager instance. Using the injected entity manager instance, we will be able to perform the database operations. In the UserManager EJB, there are two main methods:

1. getUser() method, which retrieves the user using the user name and password from the database. It returns null if the user does not exist.

2. registerUser() method, which does the following:

    • If the user ID already exists, it throws UserExistsException.

    • If the user ID does not exist, then the user is saved in the database.

Listing 10-20 shows UserExistsException class.

Listing 10-20. UserExistsException Class

```
package com.jsfprohtml5.weather.model;

public class UserExistsException extends Exception {
}
```

UserExistsException is a simple custom exception which extends Exception class.

The weather application is developed under GlassFish version 4.0. Listing 10-21 shows glassfish-resources.xml which defines the application data source.

Listing 10-21. Weather Application glassfish-resources.xml File

```
<?xml version="1.0" encoding="UTF-8"?>
<!DOCTYPE resources PUBLIC "-//GlassFish.org//DTD GlassFish Application Server 3.1 Resource
Definitions//EN" "http://glassfish.org/dtds/glassfish-resources_1_5.dtd">
<resources>
    <jdbc-connection-pool ...>
        <property name="serverName" value="localhost"/>
        <property name="portNumber" value="1527"/>
        <property name="databaseName" value="weatherDB"/>
        <property name="User" value="weather"/>
        <property name="Password" value="password"/>
        <property name="URL" value="jdbc:derby://localhost:1527/weatherDB"/>
        <property name="driverClass" value="org.apache.derby.jdbc.ClientDriver"/>
    </jdbc-connection-pool>
    <jdbc-resource enabled="true" jndi-name="jdbc/weatherDB" object-type="user"
pool-name="derby_net_weatherDB_weatherPool"/>
</resources>
```

In order to add the defined resources of glassfish-resources.xml in your GlassFish 4, you need to start your GlassFish server by running the following command from the bin directory of the server.

```
> asadmin start-domain
```

After the server starts, you can use asadmin add-resources command as follows in order to add the defined resources in your server.

```
> asadmin add-resources <<full path>>/glassfish-resources.xml
```

265

After running the previous command, the resources will be added to your GlassFish server. Finally Listing 10-22 shows the single APP_USER table we have in weatherDB.

Listing 10-22. APP_USER TABLE DDL Script

```
CREATE TABLE APP_USER (
    ID VARCHAR(64) PRIMARY KEY,
    FIRST_NAME VARCHAR(32),
    LAST_NAME VARCHAR(32),
    PASSWORD VARCHAR(32),
    PROFESSION VARCHAR(32),
    EMAIL VARCHAR(64),
    ZIP_CODE VARCHAR(32)
);
```

The weatherDB is a JavaDB Derby database; it is included with the application source code under (src/main/database) directory for your reference. In order to install the database in your GlassFish server, stop your GlassFish server if it is running as follows:

```
> asadmin stop-domain domain1
```

We are here assuming that your GlassFish domain name is (domain1). After stopping the server, also stop GlassFish Java DB as follows:

```
> asadmin stop-database
```

After stopping the server and Java DB, copy weatherDB directory located under (src/main/database) directory to your ([GlassFish server]/glassfish/databases) directory, and then start the server and Java DB. Java DB can start using the following command:

```
> asadmin start-database
```

After starting the server and Java DB, you can deploy the weather application in your GlassFish server and start using it.

■ **Note**　The weather application is a Maven web project, so in order to build it, you can use mvn clean install command and then deploy the output war file (weather-1.0-SNAPSHOT.war) in your GlassFish 4 server. Note that the output war file will be located under the target directory. In order to run the Maven command correctly, make sure that JAVA_HOME points to the Java 7 directory installed in your operating system.

Summary

In this chapter, you learned in detail how to create a Basic JSF 2.2 application in Java EE 7 environment. You understood how to structure the JSF 2.2 application. You learned how to utilize the JSF 2.2 Faces Flow in order to handle the flow between common pages. Finally, you learned how to utilize different Java EE 7 technologies (CDI, JPA 2.1, and EJB 3.2) in order to facilitate bean management, transaction management, and persistence in your JSF application.

■ ■ ■

JSF2 Advanced Topics

This chapter is a collection of advanced topics that JSF application writers must take into consideration when writing real-life JSF applications. We will also look at how to use the `<f:ajax>` tag to Ajaxify and improve the user experience. The Ajax section is followed up with examples of using JavaScript to tap into the JSF JavaScript API. Finally you cannot build a real-world application without thorough testing. We will examine the Arquillian testing framework sponsored by Red Hat through the JBoss Community.

Design Considerations for JSF Applications

This section highlights design considerations that you should take into account when building JSF applications. We will touch upon the importance of minimizing usage of session data, how to approach security, where to save state views, and finally managed bean scopes vs. CDI scopes.

Minimizing Use of Session-Scope

When developing JSF applications you should be particularly careful about using session-scoped beans. It may be tempting to store objects in the user session, as it is conveniently available throughout the application. The problem with this convenience is an increasing memory footprint per user. You may end up with large session objects that are not collected until the user ends the session. This will put limits on the number of concurrent users because the more users accessing the system the more physical memory is required for the application server, thereby making the application non-scalable. Session-scoped objects should be used only for storing data that should live from the beginning of a user session to the end. Common data that lives throughout a user session could be username, person names, login time, and preferences. You should avoid using session-scoped objects for storing data about selected objects in a master-detail or binary objects that may potentially be very big, such as a user profile picture. As a rule of thumb, you should have only one session-scoped managed bean in your JSF application. Seriously consider the architecture of your application if you feel the need for multiple session-scoped beans.

■ **Tip**   It is common for developers not to address application performance until the end of the software development lifecycle. However, when you use session objects in JSF you must pay attention to performance testing and profiling of the application early in the development process and throughout the whole process. It is particularly important to profile the memory footprint while simulating multiple user sessions. There are many Java profiles available. We recommend that you use a profiler that integrates well with your development environment to make it as easy as possible to profile your application during development. If the profiler is slow and cumbersome to use, you will likely avoid using it and you will not discover scalability issues early enough. Some IDEs have a built-in profiler that makes it easy to profile both memory and CPU consumption, as shown in Figure 11-1. To simulate multiple user sessions you can use an open-source tool like Apache jMeter (http://jmeter.apache.org), where you can build a test plan that simulates multiple users by spawning multiple threads over a period of time.

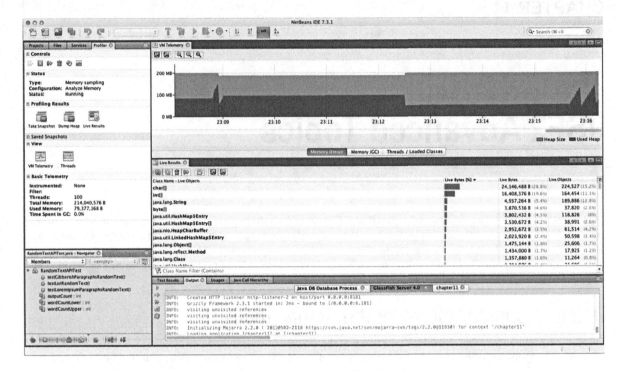

Figure 11-1. *Example of an IDE (NetBeans) that has a built-in profiler*

Using session-scoped beans also adds to complexity of session replication when operating in a clustered environment. In clustered environments the traffic would typically be balanced between the available nodes in the cluster. Even though the cluster tries to ensure that a single user session is served from the node where it was started, you still have situations where a node fail and the traffic must be redirected to another node. To avoid the user session being lost during node failure, sessions must be set up to replicate between the nodes. Luckily, this is taken care of by the application server, but it is an additional issue that must be addressed when using session-scoped beans.

Container-Managed Security

Many applications require securing some or all features with a username and password or through client certificates. The creators of the Java EE specification have defined a container-managed security framework that makes it easier for application developers to secure their application. Alternatively, the application developers will implement a custom security model, also known as application-managed security. Implementing application-managed security requires significant effort and skill, and in the end it may not provide any features or protection that is not already achievable through container-managed security.

Container-managed security is based on a model where resources (URLs) are protected by defined user roles. Upon logging in, users are assigned to user roles and the rest is taken care of by the application server. The only thing the application developer has to be concerned about is defining which resources are protected by which user roles. When the container detects that the user is not authorized to access a requested resource, it will automatically direct the user to a login mechanism. The login mechanism could be basic authentication, form authentication, or client certificate authentication. Basic authentication will prompt the user for a username and password through the native username and password dialog in the browser. Form authentication allows the application developer to provide her own login form, which as a minimum must include an input field for username and password. Lastly, client certificate authentication uses X.509 certificates to perform public key authentication. The rest of the security infrastructure is completely hidden from the application developer. The application developer communicates to the application server by specifying a security realm. The security realm is configured outside the application, in the application server. The security realm could specify that the users are located in an SQL database, an LDAP directory, or even a plain text file. It is the responsibility of the application server to provide security realms. Application servers typically expose interfaces for developers to implement their own security realms in case you have special requirements for how the user should log in. You could for example implement a security realm that authenticates against an online service such as Google or Yahoo. The implementation is custom to the application server but abstracts away how authentication is handled. This makes the container-based security very flexible and takes away complexity from the application developer. The application developer configures container-based security in /WEB-INFO/web.xml. Listing 11-1 shows an example of container-based security using basic authentication and different resources protected by different user groups. All JEE-complaint web application servers support the concept of container-managed security and thereby are portable.

Listing 11-1. Container-Based Security Configured for a Simple Application with a Couple of Protected Resources

```xml
<?xml version="1.0" encoding="UTF-8"?>
<web-app version="3.1" xmlns="http://xmlns.jcp.org/xml/ns/javaee"
xmlns:xsi="http://www.w3.org/2001/XMLSchema-instance"
xsi:schemaLocation="http://xmlns.jcp.org/xml/ns/javaee http://xmlns.jcp.org/xml/ns/javaee/web-app_3_1.xsd">
<servlet>
        <servlet-name>Faces Servlet</servlet-name>
        <servlet-class>javax.faces.webapp.FacesServlet</servlet-class>
        <load-on-startup>1</load-on-startup>
    </servlet>
    <servlet-mapping>
        <servlet-name>Faces Servlet</servlet-name>
        <url-pattern>/faces/*</url-pattern>
    </servlet-mapping>
    <welcome-file-list>
        <welcome-file>faces/index.xhtml</welcome-file>
    </welcome-file-list>

    <!--
        Security Contraints (protection) for the CUSTOMER role.
    -->
    <security-constraint>
        <display-name>Customer Constraints</display-name>
        <web-resource-collection>
            <web-resource-name>MyAccount</web-resource-name>
            <description>Account Pages</description>
            <url-pattern>/myaccount/*</url-pattern>
        </web-resource-collection>
        <auth-constraint>
            <description/>
            <role-name>CUSTOMER</role-name>
        </auth-constraint>

        <!--
            This section switches the transport from HTTP to HTTPS, thereby
            encrypting the traffic between the browser and server.
        -->
```

```
            <user-data-constraint>
                <description>Must switch to HTTPS as the page may contain confidential
information.</description>
                <transport-guarantee>CONFIDENTIAL</transport-guarantee>
            </user-data-constraint>
        </security-constraint>

        <!--
            Security Contraints (protection) for the ADMINISTRATOR role.
        -->
        <security-constraint>
            <display-name>Administrator Constrains</display-name>
            <web-resource-collection>
                <web-resource-name>AdministratorSection</web-resource-name>
                <description>Administrator pages</description>
                <url-pattern>/admin/*</url-pattern>
            </web-resource-collection>
            <auth-constraint>
                <description/>
                <role-name>ADMINISTRATOR</role-name>
            </auth-constraint>
        </security-constraint>
        <!--
            Specify which Login Mechanism and Security Realm to use. The details of
            the Realm itself is configured on the application server (outside the
            application).
        -->
        <login-config>
            <auth-method>BASIC</auth-method>
            <realm-name>CRMRealm</realm-name>
        </login-config>
        <!--
            Definition of the Security Roles used in the application
        -->
        <security-role>
            <description>A customer accessing the application</description>
            <role-name>CUSTOMER</role-name>
        </security-role>
        <security-role>
            <description>An administrator of the application</description>
            <role-name>ADMINISTRATOR</role-name>
        </security-role>
    </web-app>
```

State Saving

As we touched upon in Chapter 5, JSF 2.2 introduced the concept of stateless views. You can make a view stateless by specifying that a view should be transient as shown in Listing 5-23. This improves the performance of the application, as it will not have to store the view state between requests. This will obviously not work for all views, as we must retain the state for some views, but you should carefully consider if state retention is required for each of your views.

In situations where you do need state saving you should enable state saving on the server side rather than the client side. When view states are being saved on the client side, it is serialized into a string and stored in a hidden input field with the name javax.faces.ViewState. There are two performance penalties in doing this. First, there is an overhead in serializing and deserializing the view state every time the view is being processed. Second, you will use more bandwidth sending the state back and forth between the browser and server. The benefit of using client-side saving of the state is that you minimize the memory footprint of the application. You should carefully consider what is most critical for your application. Listing 11-2 shows the context parameter used to configure state saving in /WEB-INF/web.xml.

Listing 11-2. Example of Enabling Server-Side View State Saving

```
<?xml version="1.0" encoding="UTF-8"?>
<web-app version="3.1" xmlns="http://xmlns.jcp.org/xml/ns/javaee"
xmlns:xsi="http://www.w3.org/2001/XMLSchema-instance"
xsi:schemaLocation="http://xmlns.jcp.org/xml/ns/javaee http://xmlns.jcp.org/xml/ns/javaee/web-app_3_1.xsd">
    ...
    <context-param>
        <param-name>javax.faces.STATE_SAVING_METHOD</param-name>
        <!-- Replace server with client below to enable client-side state saving -->
        <param-value>server</param-value>
    </context-param>
    ...
</web-app>
```

Contexts and Dependency Injection (CDI)

When you develop JSF 2.x applications, you can choose between using the built-in managed bean scopes (@RequestScoped, @SessionScoped, and @ViewScoped) or use the Contexts and Dependency Injection (CDI) services defined in JSR 299. CDI provides an architecture where all Java EE components (Servlets, Enterprise JavaBeans, managed beans) follow the same programming model and lifecycle with well-defined scopes. It allows for Java EE components to be loosely coupled and injected where needed. CDI has proven to be such a success that the built-in managed scopes will be deprecated in future versions of JSF. If you start working on a new application you should use the CDI services from the beginning. If you are working on an existing application that you must continue to maintain, you should start planning a migration from the built-in managed bean scopes to CDI scopes.

Enabling CDI in JSF is simple. Create /WEB-INF/beans.xml specifying how CDI beans should be discovered as illustrated in Listing 11-3. Once the file is created, you can start using CDI Scopes in your application.

Listing 11-3. /WEB-INF/beans.xml Enabling CDI in Your JSF Application

```
<?xml version="1.0" encoding="UTF-8"?>
<beans xmlns="http://xmlns.jcp.org/xml/ns/javaee"
       xmlns:xsi="http://www.w3.org/2001/XMLSchema-instance"
       xsi:schemaLocation="http://xmlns.jcp.org/xml/ns/javaee
http://xmlns.jcp.org/xml/ns/javaee/beans_1_1.xsd"
       bean-discovery-mode="annotated">
</beans>
```

■ **Caution**   Do not attempt to mix and match CDI scopes and the built-in JSF managed bean scopes. It will end up causing confusion when your JSF beans start misbehaving because they are active in different scopes.

Ajaxifying JSF Applications

Prior to JSF 2.0 you had to implement your own support for Ajax or use third-party libraries such as RichFaces. Since JSF 2.0, Ajax has been supported out of the box using the <f:ajax> tag or the JavaScript API.

Using the <f:ajax> tag

<f:ajax> is a tag that registers Ajax behavior on UIComponents. Either the tag can be nested as a child inside a UIComponent, or it can embrace multiple UIComponents if the same Ajax behavior should be applied to all the UIComponents.

The tag offers a small but powerful selection of attributes for configuring the Ajax behavior. Table 11-1 outlines the available attributes.

Table 11-1. *Attributes for the <f:ajax/> Tag*

Attribute	Description
disabled	Determine if the Ajax behavior should not be rendered. Default is false.
delay	Number of milliseconds to delay the Ajax request. If multiple requests get in during the delay only the last request will be executed.
event	String specifying the DOM event that the Ajax behavior should respond to. It is important to note that it is just the event name (e.g., "click" and not "onclick"). The event must be emitted from the UIComponent using the tag; otherwise the Ajax behavior will never be triggered.
execute	Space-delimited list of components that should be executed when the Ajax behavior is triggered.
immediate	Determine if the Ajax behavior is triggered in the Apply Request Value phase (true) or the Invoke Application phase (false). Default is false.
listener	Reference to a listener that should process the AjaxBehaviorEvent triggered by the Ajax behavior.
onevent	Name of JavaScript function that should handle events emitted from executing the Ajax request.
onerror	Name of JavaScript function that should handle errors emitted from executing the Ajax request.
render	Space-delimited list of components that should be (re)rendered upon success of the Ajax request.

Listing 11-4 shows an example of using the <f:ajax> tag to update an output panel based on what is entered in an input text component. The Ajax behavior is hooked up to the keyup DOM event (typing a single key). When the event is received, the input text component will be executed and the value entered is stored in the outputMessage property of the ajaxDemo managed bean. When the request returns successful, the output-message panel is re-rendered and the message entered in the input text is displayed in the panel. The example also demonstrates the usefulness of the onevent attribute by passing all Ajax events to a JavaScript function called processInput, which toggles the visibility of an Ajax spinner when the requests begin and when it completes successfully.

Listing 11-4. Example of Using the <f:ajax/> Tag to Register Ajax Behavior When Updating a Text Field

```
<h:form id="my-message">
    <h:outputLabel value="Your message" for="input-message" />

    <h:inputText id="input-message" value="#{ajaxDemo.outputMessage}">
        <f:ajax event="keyup"
```

```
            onevent="function(data) { processInput(data, 'my-message:busy'); }"
            render="output-message" execute="@this" />
    </h:inputText>

    <h:graphicImage id="busy" library="images" name="spinner.gif" style="display: none; float: left;" />

    <h:panelGroup id="output-message">#{ajaxDemo.outputMessage}</h:panelGroup>

</h:form>

<script type="text/javascript">
// Handle for onevent
function processInput(data, id) {
    if (data.status === 'begin') {
        toggle_visibility(id);
    } else if (data.status === 'success') {
        toggle_visibility(id);
    }
}

// Utility function for toggling the visibility of an element
function toggle_visibility(id) {
    var e = document.getElementById(id);
    if (e.style.display == 'block')
        e.style.display = 'none';
    else
        e.style.display = 'block';
}
</script>
```

You will notice that we have used a special value in execute attribute. Both the execute and render attributes support a couple of special values. The special values are for convenience so that you do not have to enter specific component identifiers for components that are normally affected by the Ajax behavior. These values are outlined in Table 11-2.

Table 11-2. *Execute/Render Special Values*

Keyword	Description
@all	Execute or render all components
@none	Do not execute or render any components
@this	Execute or render the component that triggered the Ajax behavior
@form	Execute or render all the components in the form of the component that triggered the Ajax behavior

Using the JavaScript API

JSF comes with a JavaScript API that can be used together or instead of the <f:ajax> tag. The JavaScript API is available on all pages under the namespace jsf. Like <f:ajax>, the JavaScript API can be used to initiate Ajax requests. The JavaScript API can also be used for monitoring Ajax requests and handling errors.

The method signature for initiating an Ajax request using the JavaScript API is shown in Listing 11-5, and Table 11-3 explains the input parameters of the method.

Listing 11-5. Method Signature for Initiating an Ajax Request Using JavaScript

```
jsf.ajax.request(source, event, {options});
```

Table 11-3. *Input Parameters to jsf.ajax.request*

Parameter	Type	Necessity	Description
source	DOM Element object or String	Mandatory	The DOM Element that triggered the Ajax request. The unique identifier of the DOM Element is also sufficient.
event	DOM Event object	Mandatory	The DOM Event that invoked the Ajax request.
options	Associative array	Optional	Associative array of name/pair options specifying which components should be executed and rendered as well as callback functions for the Ajax event lifecycle. Valid options include execute and render, used for specifying a delimited list of client identifiers that should be executed and/or rendered upon the request. Two callback functions can be specified: onevent and onerror, used to handle the event lifecycle and errors, respectively. Lastly, it is possible to specify additional parameters using the params option.

Listing 11-6 shows an example of a button that executes a script that updates a panel grid using the JavaScript API.

Listing 11-6. Updating a Panel Grid Using the JavaScript API

```
<h:panelGroup id="clicks" layout="block">
    <h:outputLink id="refresh" onclick="refreshClicks(this, event); return false;">
        Refresh:
    </h:outputLink>
    <h:outputText value="#{javaScriptApiDemo.clicks}" />
</h:panelGroup>

<script type="text/javascript">
    function refreshClicks(source, event) {
        jsf.ajax.request(source, event, {render: 'clicks'});
    }
</script>
```

In Listing 11-6 we see that the JavaScript refreshClicks function is being called in the onclick event of the refresh output link. It is passing itself as the source and the event that was generated by onclick to the refresh function. It ends by returning false so that clicking the link does not invoke a full HTTP request. All the magic happens in the refreshClicks function. Here an Ajax request is triggered using the source and event passed to the function. The Ajax request has a single option that states that upon returning from the Ajax request the element with the ID clicks should be rendered. The element with ID clicks is a panel group containing the link and a value retrieved from a managed bean with the name javaScriptApiDemo. If the value of clicks has increased in the managed bean the refreshClicks function will update the display and show the current number of clicks.

■ **Tip** While tinkering with Ajax requests in JSF application you will eventually get an httpError stating "The Http Transport returned a 0 status code. This is usually the result of mixing ajax and full requests. This is usually undesired, for both performance and data integrity reasons" (see Figure 11-2). This warning message may seem cryptic but all it is saying is that you try trying to execute an Ajax request while you also perform a full HTTP request. This could occur if you forget to include return false in the end of onclick events that invoke Ajax requests, e.g.

WRONG: `<h:outputLink onclick="do-some-ajax();" />`

RIGHT: `<h:outputLink onclick="do-some-ajax(); return false;" />`

You can also execute the request lifecycle on selected components by using the execute option as shown in Listing 11-7.

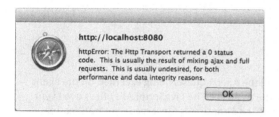

http://localhost:8080

httpError: The Http Transport returned a 0 status code. This is usually the result of mixing ajax and full requests. This is usually undesired, for both performance and data integrity reasons.

OK

Figure 11-2. *Error shown when executing Ajax and full HTTP requests at the same time*

Listing 11-7. Using the Execute Option to Execute the JSF Request Lifecycle on Selected Components

```
<h:form id="my-name-form">
    <h:outputLink onclick="saveName(this, event); return false;">Save name</h:outputLink>
    <h:inputText id="my-name" value="#{javaScriptApiDemo.myName}" />
    <h:panelGroup id="my-name-display">Your name is: #{javaScriptApiDemo.myName}</h:panelGroup>
</h:form>

<script type="text/javascript">
    function saveName(source, event) {
        jsf.ajax.request(source, event, {
            execute: '@form',
            render: 'my-name-form:my-name-display'
        });
    }
</script>
```

The example in Listing 11-7 shows an input field where the user can enter her name. The name is mapped to a property called myName on the javaScriptApiDemo managed bean. The name currently stored in the myName property is displayed below the input field inside a panel group. When the "Save name" link is clicked the saveName function is invoked. The Ajax request in the saveName function has the option execute set to @form, indicating that the form from which the request originates should execute the JSF request lifecycle. Upon returning from the request the my-name-display panel is updated inside the my-name-form form. It is worthwhile noting that Listing 11-7 is completely equivalent to Listing 11-8. The choice between using the `<f:ajax>` tag and the JavaScript API is up to the specific task you are trying to solve. It may make more sense to use the JavaScript API if other aspects of the page are controlled at the same time, collecting all the functionality in logically grouped JavaScript functions. If the page does not have any other JavaScripts being executed it may be overkill to use the JavaScript API and instead stick to the <f:ajax> tag.

Listing 11-8. Same Example as Listing 11-x but Using the <f:ajax> Tag Instead of the JavaScript API

```
<h:form id="my-name-form-pure-jsf">
    <h:outputLink>
        <f:ajax render="my-name-display-pure-jsf" execute="my-name-pure-jsf" />
        Save name
    </h:outputLink>
    <h:inputText id="my-name-pure-jsf" value="#{javaScriptApiDemo.myName}" />
    <h:panelGroup id="my-name-display-pure-jsf">
        Your name is: #{javaScriptApiDemo.myName}
    </h:panelGroup>
</h:form>
```

Monitoring Ajax Events

One thing that is not possible using the <f:ajax> tag is to monitor all the Ajax requests being executed on the client as well as general error handling of possible issues occurring from the requests. The JavaScript API offers two event listeners. One is an event listener for Ajax request events (addOnEvent) and another is for server error notification (addOnError). The Ajax request event listener emits three kinds of events outlined in Table 11-4. The server error event listener emits four kinds of events outlined in Table 11-5.

Table 11-4. Events Emitted from the Ajax Request Event Listener

Event	Description
begin	Emitted whenever an Ajax request begins
complete	Emitted whenever an Ajax request completes
success	Emitted whenever an Ajax request finishes successfully

Table 11-5. Events Emitted from the Server Error Event Listener

Event	Description
httpError	Emitted if the HTTP status is not in the 2xx Success range
serverError	Emitted when an error or exception occurred on the server side
malformedXML	Emitted when incorrect XML response is returned from the server
emptyResponse	Emitted when no response is returned from the server

Listing 11-9 is an example of a JavaScript that hooks into the two event handlers. The JavaScript can be used by any Facelets page by using the <h:outputScript/> tag as demonstrated in Listing 11-10.

Listing 11-9. JavaScript Hooking into the Event Listeners Exposed by the JSF JavaScript API

```
function outputAjaxEvent(data) {
    console.log(data);
}

function outputError(errorData) {
    console.log(errorData.type + " (" + errorData.status + "): " + errorName + ". " +
errorDescription);
    // Register error on a remote error logging server
}

function showProgress(data) {
    if (data.status === 'begin') {
        toggle_visibility('in-progress');
    } else if (data.status === 'success') {
        toggle_visibility('in-progress');
    }
}

// Utility function for toggling the visibility of an element
function toggle_visibility(id) {
    var e = document.getElementById(id);
        if (e.style.display == 'block')
            e.style.display = 'none';
        else
            e.style.display = 'block';
}
```

jsf.ajax.addOnEvent(outputAjaxEvent);
jsf.ajax.addOnEvent(showProgress);
jsf.ajax.addOnError(outputError);

Listing 11-10. Facelets Page Using the JavaScript File

```
<?xml version='1.0' encoding='UTF-8' ?>
<!DOCTYPE html PUBLIC "-//W3C//DTD XHTML 1.0 Transitional//EN"
"http://www.w3.org/TR/xhtml1/DTD/xhtml1-transitional.dtd">
<html xmlns="http://www.w3.org/1999/xhtml"
      xmlns:h="http://xmlns.jcp.org/jsf/html"
      xmlns:ui="http://xmlns.jcp.org/jsf/facelets"
      xmlns:f="http://xmlns.jcp.org/jsf/core">

    <ui:composition template="/base.xhtml">

        <ui:define name="title">
            Chapter 11 - JavaScript API Demo
        </ui:define>
```

```
<ui:define name="top">
    Chapter 11 - JavaScript API Demo
</ui:define>

<ui:define name="content">

    <h:outputScript name="events.js" library="js" />

    <h:form id="my-name-form-pure-jsf">
        <h:outputLink>
            <f:ajax render="my-name-display-pure-jsf" execute="my-name-pure-jsf"  />
            Save name
        </h:outputLink>
        <h:inputText id="my-name-pure-jsf" value="#{javaScriptApiDemo.myName}" />
        <h:panelGroup id="my-name-display-pure-jsf">
            Your name is: #{javaScriptApiDemo.myName}
        </h:panelGroup>
    </h:form>

    <!-
        Hidden by default. This is only shown when an Ajax
        request begins and hidden when a request completes successfully
    -->
    <h:panelGroup id="in-progress" layout="block" style="display: none;">
        <h:panelGroup style="font-weight: bold;">
            PLEASE WAIT - THE PAGE IS LOADING
        </h:panelGroup>
    </h:panelGroup>

</ui:define>
</ui:composition>

</html>
```

Testing JSF Applications

Any real-world application must have some level of testing. When you develop web applications it is typically not sufficient to write unit tests that verify the individual classes behind the functionality. You can test the logic behind your components and beans by using JUnit but that is typically not enough when you have a JSF application. There are many more aspects to testing a JSF application than just ensuring that the back-end logic is correct. In JSF applications you have the added complexity of HTTP (client-server interaction), Ajax requests, and web browser differences. The true test therefore requires a framework that can test a deployed version of the application and initiate a request (Ajax as well as full HTTP) and test the state of the application after the request. There are many popular functional testing frameworks available such as Selenium, FitNesse, and Cucumber. These testing frameworks could help us blackbox testing by verifying that the application behaves as expected on the user side. Ideally, we would like an integration-testing framework that will allow us to verify the behavior of our application and its components, as they would behave when they are deployed on the application server. This would allow for more accurate testing.

What Is Arquillian?

Arquillian is a complete platform for in-container testing of Java EE applications. Arquillian integrates with testing frameworks such as JUnit and TestNG making it easy to adopt for anyone comfortable writing unit tests. Arquillian uses an embedded application server of your choice to deploy the classes and resources subject to testing. Once the JSF application has been deployed in the embedded application server, you can test the behavior of the system by calling the classes and resources and inspecting their response. Out-of-the-box Arquillian is capable of testing JEE components such as EJBs and CDI beans. Several extensions have been built for Arquillian to support functional testing. Table 11-6 outlines popular extensions to Arquillian.

Table 11-6. *Popular Extensions for Arquillian*

Extension	Purpose	Maturity
Drone	Wrapper for the WebDriver API also used by Selenium. This extension makes it possible create simple functional tests. **Link:** http://arquillian.org/modules/drone-extension/	Stable
Warp	Simulating interactions on the client-side while examining the change of state on the server side at the different phases of the JSF request lifecycle. **Link:** http://arquillian.org/modules/warp-extension/	Alpha
Graphene	Enhances the Drone extension by gracefully supporting Ajax through guarding and interception of requests. **Link:** http://arquillian.org/modules/graphene-extension/	Stable
Persistence	Verify the persistence layer of the application. Allows for seeding the database using common data formats such as XML, XLS, YAML, JSON, and SQL. **Link:** http://arquillian.org/modules/persistence-extension/	Alpha
Performance	Verify that tests execute within a given time range. Will catch performance issues during regression testing. **Link:** http://arquillian.org/modules/performance-extension/	Beta
Seam 2	Allows testing of Seam libraries and injection points. **Link:** http://arquillian.org/modules/seam2-extension/	Beta

In this section we will explore how to use Arquillian and the Drone extension to do blackbox testing of JSF applications. First we will look at how to set up Arquillian and Drone for a Maven project followed by looking at how to write sensible JUnit tests using the Drone extension.

■ **Note** The Arquillian Warp Extension is the official replacement for the JSFUnit project, which is no longer being maintained. At the time of writing, the Warp extension is still in Alpha state and no production examples are available.

Setting Up Arquillian and Drone

In this section we will look at how to set up Arquillian and Drone in a Maven project. If you do not use Maven you can find guides on including the necessary dependencies in your project on the Arquillian website (http://www.arquillian.org).

Listing 11-11 shows the Maven project object model (POM) for including Arquillian and Drone in your project.

Listing 11-11. pom.xml Containing the Necessary Dependencies to Use Arquillian and Drone

```xml
<?xml version="1.0" encoding="UTF-8"?>
<project xmlns="http://maven.apache.org/POM/4.0.0" xmlns:xsi="http://www.w3.org/2001/XMLSchema-instance"
xsi:schemaLocation="http://maven.apache.org/POM/4.0.0
http://maven.apache.org/xsd/maven-4.0.0.xsd">
    <modelVersion>4.0.0</modelVersion>

    <groupId>com.apress.projsf2html5</groupId>
    <artifactId>chapter11</artifactId>
    <version>1.0-SNAPSHOT</version>
    <packaging>war</packaging>

    <name>chapter11</name>

    ...

    <dependencyManagement>
        <dependencies>
            <dependency>
                <groupId>org.jboss.arquillian</groupId>
                <artifactId>arquillian-bom</artifactId>
                <version>1.1.1.Final</version>
                <scope>import</scope>
                <type>pom</type>
            </dependency>
            <dependency>
                <groupId>org.jboss.arquillian.extension</groupId>
                <artifactId>arquillian-drone-bom</artifactId>
                <version>1.2.0.CR1</version>
                <type>pom</type>
                <scope>import</scope>
            </dependency>
        </dependencies>
    </dependencyManagement>

    <dependencies>
        <dependency>
            <groupId>org.glassfish.main.extras</groupId>
            <artifactId>glassfish-embedded-all</artifactId>
            <version>4.0</version>
            <scope>test</scope>
        </dependency>
        <dependency>
            <groupId>junit</groupId>
            <artifactId>junit</artifactId>
            <version>4.11</version>
            <scope>test</scope>
        </dependency>
```

```xml
<dependency>
    <groupId>org.jboss.arquillian.junit</groupId>
    <artifactId>arquillian-junit-container</artifactId>
    <scope>test</scope>
</dependency>
<dependency>
    <groupId>org.jboss.arquillian.container</groupId>
    <artifactId>arquillian-glassfish-embedded-3.1</artifactId>
    <version>1.0.0.CR4</version>
    <scope>test</scope>
</dependency>
<dependency>
    <groupId>org.jboss.arquillian.extension</groupId>
    <artifactId>arquillian-drone-impl</artifactId>
    <scope>test</scope>
</dependency>
<dependency>
    <groupId>org.jboss.shrinkwrap.descriptors</groupId>
    <artifactId>shrinkwrap-descriptors-api-javaee</artifactId>
    <scope>test</scope>
</dependency>
<dependency>
    <groupId>org.jboss.shrinkwrap.descriptors</groupId>
    <artifactId>shrinkwrap-descriptors-impl-javaee</artifactId>
    <scope>test</scope>
</dependency>
<dependency>
    <groupId>org.jboss.shrinkwrap</groupId>
    <artifactId>shrinkwrap-api</artifactId>
    <scope>test</scope>
</dependency>
<dependency>
    <groupId>org.jboss.arquillian.extension</groupId>
    <artifactId>arquillian-drone-webdriver-depchain</artifactId>
    <type>pom</type>
    <scope>test</scope>
</dependency>
<dependency>
    <groupId>org.jboss.arquillian.extension</groupId>
    <artifactId>arquillian-drone-selenium</artifactId>
    <scope>test</scope>
</dependency>
<dependency>
    <groupId>org.jboss.arquillian.extension</groupId>
    <artifactId>arquillian-drone-selenium-server</artifactId>
    <scope>test</scope>
</dependency>
<dependency>
    <groupId>org.seleniumhq.selenium</groupId>
    <artifactId>selenium-java</artifactId>
    <scope>test</scope>
</dependency>
```

```xml
        <dependency>
            <groupId>org.seleniumhq.selenium</groupId>
            <artifactId>selenium-server</artifactId>
            <scope>test</scope>
            <exclusions>
                <exclusion>
                    <groupId>org.mortbay.jetty</groupId>
                    <artifactId>servlet-api-2.5</artifactId>
                </exclusion>
            </exclusions>
        </dependency>
        <dependency>
            <groupId>org.slf4j</groupId>
            <artifactId>slf4j-simple</artifactId>
            <version>1.6.4</version>
            <scope>test</scope>
        </dependency>

        <dependency>
            <groupId>javax</groupId>
            <artifactId>javaee-web-api</artifactId>
            <version>7.0</version>
            <scope>provided</scope>
        </dependency>

    </dependencies>

    ...

</project>
```

Writing Tests Using Arquillian and Drone

We will use Arquillian to simulate the deployment of the web application to a web container. Once the web application is deployed in the embedded container, we will start running functional tests using the Drone extension by executing a request against the deployed application and verifying that it responds with the expected output. As an example we will test a simple application that asks the user for his name followed by greeting the user. A mock-up of the user interface is shown in Figure 11-3. Based on the mock-up, we need a Facelets file that shows the UI to the user and a CDI bean for storing the name as illustrated in Figure 11-4.

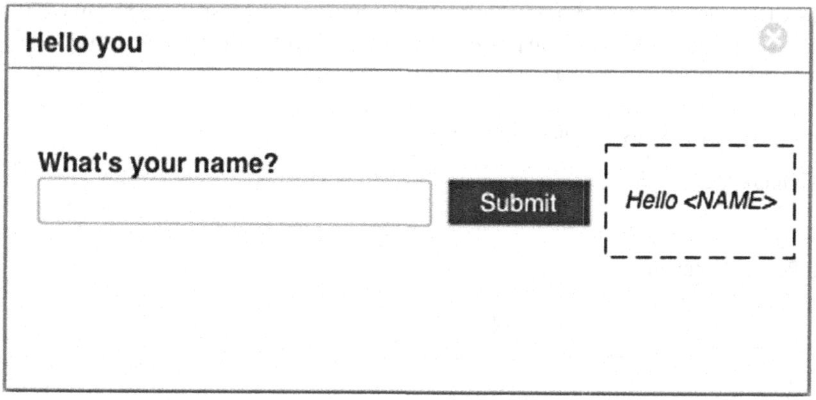

Hello you ⊗

What's your name?

[   ] [Submit] ┆ Hello <NAME> ┆

Figure 11-3. *Mock-up of the UI for the test application*

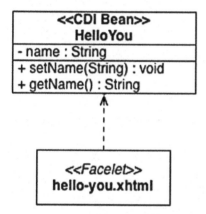

Figure 11-4. *Class diagram containing the CDI Bean and Facelets page used for the test application*

Based on the mock-up and class diagram we can write a couple of pseudo-tests using the Gherkin format that we will later implement using Drone.

Scenario: Entering my name

Given that I enter my name 'Clutch Powers' on the page

When I press the Submit Button

Then I will be greeted 'Hello Clutch Powers' by the application

---

Scenario: I enter the page

Given that I enter page

When I do nothing

Then there will be no greeting displayed

The actual implementation of the CDI bean can be seen in Listing 11-12. It is a simple request scoped bean with a single property called name. Listing 11-13 shows the Facelets file presenting the input field to the user including a submit button. Notice that we have a panel group that is displayed only if the CDI bean's name property is not empty.

Listing 11-12. Simple Request Scoped CDI Bean Exposing a name Property

```java
package com.apress.projsf2html5.chapter11.jsf;

import java.io.Serializable;
import javax.enterprise.context.RequestScoped;
import javax.inject.Named;

@Named(value = "helloYou")
@RequestScoped
public class HelloYou implements Serializable {

    private String name;

    public String getName() {
        return name;
    }

    public void setName(String name) {
        this.name = name;
    }
}
```

Listing 11-13. Facelets File Displaying the Input Box and Submit Button to the User

```xml
<?xml version='1.0' encoding='UTF-8' ?>
<!DOCTYPE html PUBLIC "-//W3C//DTD XHTML 1.0 Transitional//EN"
"http://www.w3.org/TR/xhtml1/DTD/xhtml1-transitional.dtd">
<html xmlns="http://www.w3.org/1999/xhtml"
      xmlns:h="http://xmlns.jcp.org/jsf/html"
      xmlns:ui="http://xmlns.jcp.org/jsf/facelets">

    <ui:composition template="/base.xhtml">

        <ui:define name="title">
            Chapter 11 - Testing - Hello You
        </ui:define>

        <ui:define name="top">
            Chapter 11 - Testing - Hello You
        </ui:define>

        <ui:define name="content">

            <h:form id="hello-form">
                <h:outputLabel value="What's your name?" for="input-name" />
                <h:inputText id="input-name" value="#{helloYou.name}" />
                <h:commandButton id="submit" value="Submit" />
```

```
            <h:panelGroup id="output-message" rendered="#{not empty helloYou.name}">
                Hello #{helloYou.name}
            </h:panelGroup>

        </h:form>

    </ui:define>
  </ui:composition>
</html>
```

The result of the CDI bean and the Facelet page can be seen in Figure 11-5.

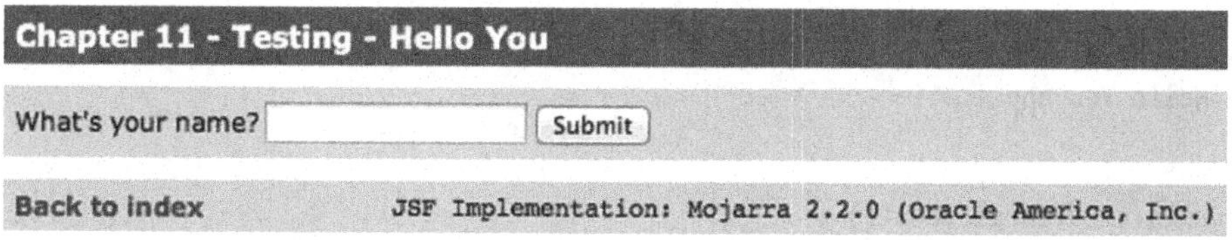

Chapter 11 - Testing - Hello You

What's your name? [   ] [Submit]

Back to index   JSF Implementation: Mojarra 2.2.0 (Oracle America, Inc.)

Figure 11-5. *The Hello You application*

We are now ready to test the application. Our test will be annotated with @RunWith to tell JUnit that we will use Arquillian as our test runner. We also use the @RunAsClient annotation to tell Arquillian that we will not be testing on the server side, but rather we will send a request as a web client. This is required for functional testing with the Drone extension. Next, we will specify the resources and classes that we want to test. This is done by creating a WebArchive object using the ShrinkWrap API. The WebArchive should contain all the resource and classes and only those. The purpose is to isolate the files being tested and to avoid adding unnecessary complexity. The method creating the WebArchive must be annotated @Deployment for Arquillian to detect what must be deployed before executing tests. Lastly we will write the actual tests. The complete test can be seen in Listing 11-14.

Listing 11-14. Arquillian Test Case for Testing the Hello You Application

```
package com.apress.projsf2html5.chapter11;

import com.apress.projsf2html5.chapter11.jsf.HelloYou;
import com.thoughtworks.selenium.DefaultSelenium;
import java.io.File;
import java.net.URL;
import org.jboss.arquillian.container.test.api.Deployment;
import org.jboss.arquillian.container.test.api.RunAsClient;
import org.jboss.arquillian.drone.api.annotation.Drone;
import org.jboss.arquillian.junit.Arquillian;
import org.jboss.arquillian.test.api.ArquillianResource;
import org.jboss.shrinkwrap.api.ShrinkWrap;
import org.jboss.shrinkwrap.api.asset.EmptyAsset;
import org.jboss.shrinkwrap.api.spec.WebArchive;
import org.junit.Test;
import org.junit.runner.RunWith;
import static org.junit.Assert.*;

@RunWith(Arquillian.class)
@RunAsClient
public class HelloYouTest {
```

```
/** This will give us the contextPath where the web application was installed. */
@ArquillianResource
URL contextPath;

/** This will give us access to a Drone that simulates a browser. */
@Drone
private DefaultSelenium browser;

/**
 * The method annotated with Deployment outputs the web archive representing
 * the application.The archive must contain all the resource and classes
 * being tested.
 *
 * @return {@link WebArchive} containing the resources and classes
 * representing the Hello You application
 */
@Deployment
public static WebArchive createDeployment() {
    return ShrinkWrap.create(WebArchive.class, "hello-you.war")
            .addClasses(HelloYou.class)
            .addAsWebResource(new File("src/main/webapp/hello-you.xhtml"))
            .addAsWebResource(new File("src/main/webapp/contracts/basic/base.xhtml"),
"contracts/basic/base.xhtml")
            .addAsWebResource(new File("src/main/webapp/contracts/basic/cssLayout.css"),
"contracts/basic/cssLayout.css")
            .addAsWebResource(new File("src/main/webapp/contracts/basic/default.css"),
"contracts/basic/default.css")
            .addAsWebInfResource(new File("src/main/webapp/WEB-INF/web.xml"))
            .addAsManifestResource(EmptyAsset.INSTANCE, "beans.xml");
}

/**
 * Scenario: Entering my name.
 * Given that I enter my name 'Clutch Powers' on the page
 * When I press the Submit Button
 * Then I will be greeted 'Hello Clutch Powers' by the application
 */
@Test
public void helloyou_EnterName_GreetingFound() {
    String startUrl = contextPath.toString() + "faces/hello-you.xhtml";

    // Open the hello-you page
    browser.open(startUrl);

    // Type name in the input field
    browser.type("id=hello-form:input-name", "Clutch Powers");

    // Click the submit button
    browser.click("id=hello-form:submit");

    // Wait for the page to load (max 5 seconds)
    browser.waitForPageToLoad("5000");

    // Check that the "Hello <name>" element is displayed on screen
    assertTrue(browser.isVisible("id=hello-form:output-message"));
```

```
        // Check that the name entered is the one expected
        assertEquals("Welcome message missing",
                browser.getText("id=hello-form:output-message"),
                "Hello Clutch Powers");
    }
    /**
     * Scenario: I enter the page.
     * Given that I enter page
     * When I do nothing
     * Then I there will be no greeting displayed
     */
    @Test
    public void helloyou_OpenPage_GreetingHidden() {
        String startUrl = contextPath.toString() + "faces/hello-you.xhtml";

        // Open the hello-you page
        browser.open(startUrl);

        // Check that the "Hello <name>" element is NOT displayed on the screen
        assertFalse(browser.isVisible("id=hello-form:output-message"));
    }
}
```

The DefaultSelenium Drone is capable of simulating many kinds of browser interactions. A sample of interesting methods are highlighted in Table 11-7.

Table 11-7. *Sample of DefaultSelenium Methods Used for Simulating User Interaction*

Method	Description
attachFile(fieldLocator, fileLocation)	Used for attaching files in a file input form field
Click(locator)	Clicks a given element with the specified locator
doubleClick(locator)	Double clicks a given element with the specified locator
dragAndDrop(locator, movements)	Simulates a drag and drop from a source to a location
getText(locator)	Gets the text in a given element
isVisible(locator)	Determines if a given element is visible on the screen
Open(url)	Opens a given page
typeKeys(location, value)	Types a value into a given input field
waitForPageToLoad(timeout)	Waits a given number of milliseconds for the page to load

Summary

In this chapter we explored design considerations for developing JSF applications such as security, performance, and memory consumption. We also looked at how to use the <f:ajax /> tag to Ajaxifying JSF applications. Using the <f:ajax /> tag it is possible to set up Ajax requests on individual as well as a group of JSF components. To supplement the <f:ajax /> tag we went behind the scenes to explore the JSF JavaScript API. Lastly we looked at testing JSF applications using the Aqullian testing framework coupled with the Drone extension that enables functional testing of the JSF applications.

CHAPTER 12

JSF2 Security and Performance

In this chapter, you will learn how to secure your JSF application using the security features provided by Java EE containers. You know how to apply container-managed authentication, authorization, and data protection in the weather application that was introduced in Chapter 10. In this chapter, you will also learn how to tune the performance of your JSF application in order to make your JSF pages more responsive.

JSF Application Security

Web application security can be divided into three main aspects which we will elaborate on in detail in this section:

- *Authentication* is the act of confirming to the system that the user identity is true.

- *Authorization* defines which parts of the system the user is allowed to access after performing authentication.

- *Data Protection* is about ensuring that the data between the user and the system cannot be modified or fabricated by unauthorized parties.

In Java EE, you can rely on the security features provided by Java EE containers in order to implement security requirements in your Java EE application (if your Java EE application depends on the security features provided by the Java EE container; this means that your Java EE application is using "container-managed security"). Instead of managing the security on the container level, you can also manage the security on the application level (this approach is called application managed security). Application managed security does not mean implementing all of the application security features from scratch; application managed security usually utilizes the security features provided by the Java EE container in order to implement custom security features in the application which are required by the customer.

Note If there is no reason for implementing custom security solution from the customer requirements, then container-managed security is highly recommended for Java EE application(s).

Java EE container-managed security provides container-managed authentication, authorization, and data protection. In the next subsections, we will illustrate these terms in detail.

Authentication

Java EE containers provide different types of authentication mechanisms:

- HTTP Basic

- Form-based

- Digest

HTTP Basic Authentication

In HTTP basic authentication, the server requests a user name and password from the web client and verifies that the user name and password are valid by comparing them against a database of authorized users in a specified or default realm. Basic authentication is the default when you do not specify an authentication mechanism in the web configuration file.

When basic authentication is used, the following steps occur:

- A client requests access to a protected resource.

- The web server returns a dialog box that requests the user name and password.

- The client submits the user name and password to the server.

- The server authenticates the user in the specified realm and, if successful, returns the requested resource.

■ **Note**   Realm is a store for the users and the groups of the system.

Form-Based Authentication

In form-based authentication, you can develop and customize login and error pages in your application. When form-based authentication is declared in the web configuration file, the following steps occur:

- A client requests access to a protected resource.

- If the client is unauthenticated, the server redirects the client to a login page.

- The client submits the login form to the server.

- The server attempts to authenticate the user.

- If authentication succeeds, the authenticated user's principal is checked to ensure that it is in a role that is authorized to access the resource (Authorization). If the user is authorized, the server redirects the client to the resource by using the stored URL path.

- If authentication fails, the client is forwarded or redirected to an error page.

For a complete example of form-based authentication, check the section "Applying Managed Security in the Weather Application."

■ **Note**   It is important to note that HTTP basic authentication sends user names and passwords as Base64-encoded text; while form-based authentication sends them as plain text, which means they are not secure, so they are recommended to be used with secure transport mechanism (such as SSL). In order to configure SSL you need to check the documentation of your application server because it is specific for every application server; for example in order to configure SSL in Tomcat 7, check the following link: `http://tomcat.apache.org/tomcat-7.0-doc/ssl-howto.html`.

Digest Authentication

Digest authentication authenticates a user based on a user name and a password (like basic HTTP authentication). However, unlike basic authentication, digest authentication does not send user passwords over the network. Instead, the client sends a one-way cryptographic hash of the password.

Configuring an Authentication Method

In order to configure the authentication method in your Java EE web application, you can use `<login-config>` element as shown here in the web configuration file (`web.xml`):

```
<login-config>
    <auth-method>FORM</auth-method>
    <realm-name>jdbcRealm</realm-name>
    <form-login-config>
        <form-login-page>/home.xhtml</form-login-page>
        <form-error-page>/error.xhtml</form-error-page>
    </form-login-config>
</login-config>
```

As you may notice, `<login-config>` element has the following sub-elements:

- `<auth-method>` element specifies the authentication mechanism for the web application. It can be DIGEST, BASIC or FORM or NONE.

- `<realm-name>` element specifies the realm name.

- `<form-login-config>` element specifies the login and error pages. It should be used when the form-based login is used.

Authorization

Authorization defines the role-based access control that determines what are the parts of the system which are allowed to be accessed by users. In Java EE, in order to achieve this, you can use `<security-constraint>` element in the `web.xml` as shown in Listing 12-1.

Listing 12-1. Sample <security-constraint> Example

```
<?xml version="1.0" encoding="UTF-8"?>
<web-app version="3.1" xmlns="http://xmlns.jcp.org/xml/ns/javaee"
xmlns:xsi="http://www.w3.org/2001/XMLSchema-instance"
```

```
xsi:schemaLocation="http://xmlns.jcp.org/xml/ns/javaee
http://xmlns.jcp.org/xml/ns/javaee/web-app_3_1.xsd">

    ...

    <security-constraint>
        <display-name>securityConstraint</display-name>
        <web-resource-collection>
            <web-resource-name>resources</web-resource-name>
            <url-pattern>/protected/*</url-pattern>
            <http-method>PUT</http-method>
            <http-method>DELETE</http-method>
            <http-method>GET</http-method>
            <http-method>POST</http-method>
        </web-resource-collection>
        <auth-constraint>
            <role-name>weatherUserRole</role-name>
        </auth-constraint>
        <user-data-constraint>
            <transport-guarantee>CONFIDENTIAL</transport-guarantee>
        </user-data-constraint>
    </security-constraint>
    <login-config>
        <auth-method>FORM</auth-method>
        <realm-name>WeatherRealm</realm-name>
        <form-login-config>
            <form-login-page>/home.xhtml</form-login-page>
            <form-error-page>/error.xhtml</form-error-page>
        </form-login-config>
    </login-config>
    ...

</web-app>
```

<security-constraint> element is used to define the access privileges to a collection of resources using their URL mapping. It can contain the following elements:

- Web resource collection (<web-resource-collection>): A list of URL patterns and HTTP operations that describe a set of resources to be protected.

- Authorization constraint (<auth-constraint>): Specifies whether authentication is to be used and names the roles authorized to perform the constrained requests.

- User data constraint (<user-data-constraint>): Specifies how data is protected when transported between a client and a server (will be illustrated in the "Data Protection" section).

A web resource collection (<web-resource-collection>) contains the following elements:

- <web-resource-name> (optional) is the name which you use for the web resource.

- <url-pattern> is the URL to be protected.

- <http-method> is used to specify which methods should be protected.

An authorization constraint (`<auth-constraint>`) contains the `<role-name>` element. You can use as many `<role-name>` elements as needed inside the `<auth-constraint>` element. The roles defined for the application must be mapped to users and groups defined on the application server (every application server has its own way for declaring this roles to users and groups mapping; check the section on "Applying Managed Security in the Weather Application" to understand how to do this on GlassFish application server version 4.0).

Data Protection

Data protection refers to securing data which is transferred between the client and the server. In Java EE, in order to do data protection, you can use `<user-data-constraint>` element of `<security-constraint>` in web.xml as shown in Listing 12-1 and highlighted in Listing 12-2.

Listing 12-2. <user-data-constraint> of <security-constraint> Element in web.xml

```
<security-constraint>
        <display-name>securityConstraint</display-name>
        <web-resource-collection>
                <web-resource-name>resources</web-resource-name>
                <url-pattern>/protected/*</url-pattern>
        </web-resource-collection>
        <auth-constraint>
                <role-name>weatherUserRole</role-name>
        </auth-constraint>
        <user-data-constraint>
                <transport-guarantee>CONFIDENTIAL</transport-guarantee>
        </user-data-constraint>
</security-constraint>
```

As shown in the bolded lines, the `<user-data-constraint>` element contains the `<transport-guarantee>` element. The `<transport-guarantee>` element specifies the communication between client and server, and it can have one of the following possible values: `NONE`, `INTEGRAL`, `CONFIDENTIAL`. `INTEGRAL` means that the application requires data (to be sent between the client and the server) to be sent in such a way that it cannot be changed from a third malicious party, while `CONFIDENTIAL` means that the application requires preventing other malicious third parties from observing the contents of the transmission. Both `INTEGRAL` and `CONFIDENTIAL` imply SSL.

Applying Managed Security in the Weather Application

In Chapter 10, we were introduced to the *Weather Application* as an example of a basic JSF 2.2 application. In the *Weather Application*, we handled the authentication (application login) and authorization (access to weather pages) from the application code. Handling security from application code is not recommended, especially when we are talking about typical authentication and authorization scenarios that do not have custom security requirements; therefore, let's apply container-managed security (form-based authentication and authorization) to the weather application.

First of all, let's modify home.xhtml to include the HTML form of the form-based authentication instead of handling the login requirement from the application code. Listing 12-3 shows the updates to home.xhtml.

Listing 12-3. Updates to home.xhtml Page

```
<?xml version='1.0' encoding='UTF-8' ?>
<!DOCTYPE html>
<html xmlns="http://www.w3.org/1999/xhtml"
        xmlns:ui="http://java.sun.com/jsf/facelets"
        xmlns:h="http://xmlns.jcp.org/jsf/html">

<ui:composition template="/WEB-INF/templates/main.xhtml">
    <ui:define name="title">
        #{bundle['application.loginpage.title']}
    </ui:define>
    <ui:define name="content">

        <!-- Form authentication -->
        <form action="j_security_check" method="POST">
           Username:<input type="text" name="j_username"></input><br/>
           Password:<input type="password" name="j_password"></input><br/>
           <input type="submit" value="#{bundle['application.login']}"></input>
        </form>
        <h:link value="#{bundle['application.loginpage.register']}" outcome="registration"/>

    </ui:define>
</ui:composition>

</html>
```

As shown in the bolded lines, in order to use form-based authentication and as per servlet specification, we have to use the HTML `<form>` tag (instead of the standard JSF `<h:form>`), setting the form action to `"j_security_check"` and the form method to `"POST"`, and setting the names of the username and password fields to `"j_username"` and `"j_password"`; finally, there is a submit button to submit the form. Listing 12-4 shows the form-based authentication configuration in `web.xml`.

Listing 12-4. Weather Application's Form-Based Authentication Configuration

```
<?xml version="1.0" encoding="UTF-8"?>
<web-app version="3.1" ...>
    ...
    <security-constraint>
        <display-name>securityConstraint</display-name>
        <web-resource-collection>
            <web-resource-name>resources</web-resource-name>
            <url-pattern>/protected/*</url-pattern>
        </web-resource-collection>
        <auth-constraint>
            <role-name>weatherUser</role-name>
        </auth-constraint>
        <user-data-constraint>
            <transport-guarantee>CONFIDENTIAL</transport-guarantee>
        </user-data-constraint>
    </security-constraint>
```

```
<login-config>
    <auth-method>FORM</auth-method>
    <realm-name>WeatherRealm</realm-name>
    <form-login-config>
        <form-login-page>/home.xhtml</form-login-page>
        <form-error-page>/error.xhtml</form-error-page>
    </form-login-config>
</login-config>
<welcome-file-list>
    <welcome-file>protected/weather.xhtml</welcome-file>
</welcome-file-list>
...
</web-app>
```

As shown in the bolded lines, in the security constraint part, only weatherUser role is able to access the resources under the protected folder (/protected/*). In the login configuration part, the authentication method is set to FORM (i.e., form-based Authentication), the realm name is set to WeatherRealm, and finally in the form login configuration, the login page is set to be home.xhtml (which is shown in Listing 12-3), while the error page (which will be shown when the user fails to log in) is set to error.xhtml. When the user login succeeds, the user will be forwarded to weather.xhtml page under protected folder.

weatherUser role defined for the application must be mapped to groups defined on the application server. For GlassFish, you can define the mapping between role and group in a configuration file (glassfish-web.xml) as shown in Listing 12-5.

Listing 12-5. glassfish-web.xml File

```
<?xml version="1.0" encoding="UTF-8"?>
<!DOCTYPE glassfish-web-app PUBLIC ...>
<glassfish-web-app error-url="">
  <context-root>/weather</context-root>
  <security-role-mapping>
    <role-name>weatherUser</role-name>
    <group-name>weather_user</group-name>
  </security-role-mapping>
  ...
</glassfish-web-app>
```

As shown in the configuration file, role name (weatherUser) is mapped to an actual group name (weather_user) which exists in the realm repository (WeatherRealm).

WeatherRealm is the store of the users and groups for the weather application; as you may remember, we had an APP_USER table which we used in order to store the application users. Thanks to JDBCRealm (which is supported in GlassFish and some of the other Java EE application servers), you can make your existing users/groups database a realm; however, we need to add another database table (APP_GROUP) in order to define the groups of the users as shown in Figure 12-1.

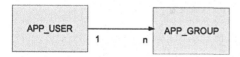

Figure 12-1. *Modifications in the weather application data model*

Listing 12-6 shows the SQL statements which contain the attributes of both APP_USER and APP_GROUP and the relation between them.

Listing 12-6. SQL Statements of the Weather Application Data Model

```
CREATE TABLE APP_USER (
    ID VARCHAR(64) PRIMARY KEY,
    FIRST_NAME VARCHAR(32),
    LAST_NAME VARCHAR(32),
    PASSWORD VARCHAR(32),
    PROFESSION VARCHAR(32),
    EMAIL VARCHAR(64),
    ZIP_CODE VARCHAR(32)
);

CREATE TABLE APP_GROUP(userid varchar(64) not null, groupid varchar(64) not null, primary
key(userid, groupid));

ALTER TABLE APP_GROUP add constraint FK_USERID foreign key(userid) references APP_USER(id);
```

Finally, in order to create our custom realm in GlassFish 4.0, click "Configurations -> server-config ->
Security -> Realms", enter the suitable realm information, and finally save the realm as shown in Figure 12-2.

Properties specific to this Class

JAAS Context: *	jdbcRealm
	Identifier for the login module to use for this realm
JNDI: *	jdbc/weatherDB
	JNDI name of the JDBC resource used by this realm
User Table: *	WEATHER.APP_USER
	Name of the database table that contains the list of authorized users for this realm
User Name Column: *	ID
	Name of the column in the user table that contains the list of user names
Password Column: *	PASSWORD
	Name of the column in the user table that contains the user passwords
Group Table: *	WEATHER.APP_GROUP
	Name of the database table that contains the list of groups for this realm
Group Table User Name Column:	USERID
	Name of the column in the user group table that contains the list of groups for this realm
Group Name Column: *	GROUPID
	Name of the column in the group table that contains the list of group names
Password Encryption Algorithm: *	none
	This denotes the algorithm for encrypting the passwords in the database. It is a security risk to leave this field empty.
Assign Groups:	
	Comma-separated list of group names
Database User:	weather
	Specify the database user name in the realm instead of the JDBC connection pool
Database Password:	password
	Specify the database password in the realm instead of the JDBC connection pool
Digest Algorithm:	none
	Digest algorithm (default is SHA-256); note that the default was MD5 in GlassFish versions prior to 3.1
Encoding:	
	Encoding (allowed values are Hex and Base64)
Charset:	
	Character set for the digest algorithm

Figure 12-2. Defining a new realm in GlassFish version 4.0

Table 12-1 shows WeatherRealm configuration properties.

Table 12-1. *Custom Realm Configuration Properties*

Property	Value
JAAS Context	jdbcRealm
JNDI	jdbc/weatherDB
User Table	WEATHER.APP_USER
User Name Column	ID
Password Column	PASSWORD
Group Table	WEATHER.APP_GROUP
Group Table User Name Column	USERID
Group Name Column	GROUPID
Password Encryption Algorithm	None
Assign Groups	[Leave this field blank]
Database User	Weather
Database Password	Password
Digest Algorithm	None
Encoding	[Leave this field blank]
Charset	[Leave this field blank]

Now, we configured container-managed security for the *Weather Application,* so we should remove AuthorizationListener class and its reference from faces-config.xml. WeatherBacking class has to be updated as well. Listing 12-7 shows the updated WeatherBacking managed bean.

Listing 12-7. Updated WeatherBacking Class

```
@Named
@RequestScoped
public class WeatherBacking extends BaseBacking {

    @EJB
    private UserManagerLocal userManager;

    @PostConstruct
    public void loadUser(ComponentSystemEvent event) {
        try {
            String userID = getRequest().getUserPrincipal().getName();
            AppUser sourceAppUser = userManager.getUser(userID);
            AppUser targetAppUser = (AppUser) evaluateEL("#{appUser}", AppUser.class);

            targetAppUser.setFirstName(sourceAppUser.getFirstName());
            targetAppUser.setLastName(sourceAppUser.getLastName());
            targetAppUser.setZipCode(sourceAppUser.getZipCode());
```

```
        } catch (Exception ex) {
            Logger.getLogger(WeatherBacking.class.getName()).log(Level.SEVERE, null, ex);
            getContext().addMessage(null, new FacesMessage(SYSTEM_ERROR));
        }
    }

    public String logout() {
        try {
            getRequest().logout();

            return "/home.xhtml?faces-redirect=true";
        } catch (ServletException ex) {
            Logger.getLogger(WeatherBacking.class.getName()).log(Level.SEVERE, null, ex);
        }

        return null;
    }
}
```

As shown in the code, loadUser() method retrieves the current user information using its ID (user ID can be retrieved from java.security.Principal, which can be gotten using getUserPrincipal() API of HTTPServletRequest). logout() calls the logout() method of HTTPServletRequest in order to log the user out from the current authenticated session. Listing 12-8 shows the updated weather.xhtml page.

Listing 12-8. Updated weather.xhtml Page

```
<?xml version='1.0' encoding='UTF-8' ?>
<!DOCTYPE html>
<html xmlns="http://www.w3.org/1999/xhtml"
      xmlns:ui="http://java.sun.com/jsf/facelets"
      xmlns:h="http://java.sun.com/jsf/html"
      xmlns:f="http://java.sun.com/jsf/core"
      xmlns:mashup="http://code.google.com/p/mashups4jsf/">

<ui:composition template="/WEB-INF/templates/main.xhtml">
    <ui:define name="title">
        #{bundle['application.weatherpage.title']}
    </ui:define>
    <ui:define name="content">
        <f:event listener="#{weatherBacking.loadUser}" type="preRenderView" />
        <h:form>
            #{bundle['application.welcome']}, #{appUser.firstName} #{appUser.lastName}! <br/><br/>

            #{bundle['application.weatherpage.currentInfo']} for #{appUser.zipCode}:
            <mashup:yahooWeather temperatureType="c" locationCode="#{appUser.zipCode}"/> <br/><br/>

            <h:commandLink value="#{bundle['application.weatherpage.logout']}"
                           action="#{weatherBacking.logout}"></h:commandLink> <br/><br/>
        </h:form>
    </ui:define>
</ui:composition>

</html>
```

As shown in the bolded line, in order to retrieve the current user information, loadUser() method of weatherBacking bean is called in the preRenderView event (which is called each time before the view is rendered). RegistrationBacking class has to be updated as well. Listing 12-9 shows the updated RegistrationBacking bean.

Listing 12-9. Updated RegistrationBacking Bean

```
@Named
@RequestScoped
public class RegistrationBacking extends BaseBacking {

    @EJB
    private UserManagerLocal userManager;

    public String register() {
        FacesContext context = FacesContext.getCurrentInstance();
        Map<Object, Object> flowScope = context.getApplication().getFlowHandler().getCurrentFlowScope();

        AppUser appUser = new AppUser();

        appUser.setId((String) flowScope.get("id"));
        appUser.setPassword((String) flowScope.get("password"));
        appUser.setEmail((String) flowScope.get("email"));

        appUser.setFirstName((String) flowScope.get("fname"));
        appUser.setLastName((String) flowScope.get("lname"));
        appUser.setProfession((String) flowScope.get("profession"));

        appUser.setZipCode((String) flowScope.get("zipCode"));

        //Assign a group to the user ...
        AppGroup appGroup = new AppGroup(appUser.getId(), "weather_user");
        List<AppGroup> appGroups = new ArrayList<>();

        appGroups.add(appGroup);
        appUser.setAppGroupList(appGroups);

        try {
            userManager.registerUser(appUser);
        } catch (UserExistsException ex) {
            Logger.getLogger(RegistrationBacking.class.getName()).log(Level.SEVERE, null, ex);
            context.addMessage(null, new FacesMessage(USERNAME_ALREADY_EXISTS));
            return null;
        } catch (Exception ex) {
            Logger.getLogger(RegistrationBacking.class.getName()).log(Level.SEVERE, null, ex);
            context.addMessage(null, new FacesMessage(SYSTEM_ERROR));
            return null;
        }

        return "flowReturn";
    }

    //...
}
```

As shown in the bolded lines, after appUser object is created and populated with the user information, it is assigned to "weather_user" group which is mentioned in the mapping file in Listing 12-5.

This is all what we need to do in order to apply container-managed security in the *Weather Application*. In order to get the full source code of *Weather Application*, download it from Chapter 12 source code that you can find in the book web site at www.apress.com/9781430250104.

JSF Application Performance

Tuning the performance of JSF applications is one of the most important aspects that every JSF developer needs to be aware of. In this part, we will talk about the most important aspects that can be tuned in order to enhance the performance of JSF 2.x applications.

Refresh Period

This interval specifies the amount of time that Facelets compiler has to wait until checking for changes in pages. In development, it is recommended to set the value of (javax.faces.FACELETS_REFRESH_PERIOD) parameter to a low value in order to help the JSF developers during development to be able to edit pages while the application is running. In production and in order to gain better performance, it is recommended to set the value of (javax.faces.FACELETS_REFRESH_PERIOD) parameter to -1 (which means that you don't want the compiler to check for changes once the page is compiled) as shown in the following.

```
<?xml version="1.0" encoding="UTF-8"?>
<web-app ...>
    ...
    <context-param>
        <param-name>javax.faces.FACELETS_REFRESH_PERIOD</param-name>
        <param-value>-1</param-value>
    </context-param>
    ...
</web-app>
```

Skip Comments

Setting (javax.faces.FACELETS_SKIP_COMMENTS) parameter to true can help reducing the amount of data sent across the network by removing comments from Facelets pages. These comments can be useful for understanding the code during development, but they are unnecessary during deployment, and in the same time, they can create a security risk by allowing the system users looking into the source code comments. Having an impact on both security and performance, it is important to set this parameter to true as shown in the following.

```
<?xml version="1.0" encoding="UTF-8"?>
<web-app ...>
    ...
    <context-param>
        <param-name>javax.faces.FACELETS_SKIP_COMMENTS</param-name>
        <param-value>true</param-value>
    </context-param>
    ...
</web-app>
```

Project Stage

Setting javax.faces.PROJECT_STAGE parameter to "Development" allows the JSF environment to print out debugging information in the pages. This can be helpful during development, but it has no useful purpose after deployment unless you are troubleshooting an error or problem in the testing environment. In production, always set this parameter value to "Production" in order to improve performance during production as shown in the following.

```xml
<?xml version="1.0" encoding="UTF-8"?>
<web-app ...>
    ...
    <context-param>
        <param-name>javax.faces.PROJECT_STAGE</param-name>
        <param-value>Production</param-value>
    </context-param>
    ...
</web-app>
```

State Saving Method

Setting javax.faces.STATE_SAVING_METHOD parameter to "server" (which is the default value) gives better performance than setting this parameter to "client". This is because server state saving does not require serialization of the state. The following is an example of setting state saving method to "server".

```xml
<?xml version="1.0" encoding="UTF-8"?>
<web-app ...>
    ...
    <context-param>
        <param-name>javax.faces.STATE_SAVING_METHOD</param-name>
        <param-value>server</param-value>
    </context-param>
    ...
</web-app>
```

However, it is important to know that if you do not have enough memory in the server, you can set the state saving method to "client".

Response Buffer

It is recommended to increase the response buffer size in order to reduce memory reallocations at rendering time, this can be achieved by setting javax.faces.FACELETS_BUFFER_SIZE parameter (and com.sun.faces.responseBufferSize parameter if you are using Mojarra) to proper values that are suitable to your application server memory capacity as shown in the following example.

```xml
<?xml version="1.0" encoding="UTF-8"?>
<web-app ...>
    ...
    <context-param>
        <param-name>javax.faces.FACELETS_BUFFER_SIZE</param-name>
        <param-value>500000</param-value>
    </context-param>
```

```
<context-param>
    <param-name>com.sun.faces.responseBufferSize</param-name>
    <param-value>500000</param-value>
</context-param>
...
</web-app>
```

As shown in the example, both javax.faces.FACELETS_BUFFER_SIZE and com.sun.faces.responseBufferSize parameters are set at 500000 bytes.

Number of Views in a Session

Number of views in session is represented by two different context parameters in Apache MyFaces and Oracle Mojarra:

- org.apache.myfaces.NUMBER_OF_VIEWS_IN_SESSION (in Apache MyFaces)
- com.sun.faces.numberOfViewsInSession (in Oracle Mojarra)

These parameters work only if the state saving method is set to "server". It defines the maximum number of serialized views stored in the session. By default it is set to 20 (in Apache MyFaces) or 15 (in Oracle Mojarra). For many applications, having this parameter to 15 or 20 may not be suitable, so if it is not a requirement in your JSF application to have such number of serialized views in the session, it is recommended to reduce it in order to save the server memory, as shown in the following.

```
<?xml version="1.0" encoding="UTF-8"?>
<web-app ...>
    ...
    <context-param>
        <param-name>org.apache.myfaces.NUMBER_OF_VIEWS_IN_SESSION</param-name>
        <param-value>3</param-value>
    </context-param>
    ...
</web-app>
```

In Mojarra, there is another related context parameter (which works also in server-side state saving) that you can tune, which is the (com.sun.faces.numberOfLogicalViews) parameter. This parameter represents the number of logical views of the application that are stored in the session. By default, it is set to 15. You can reduce this number when possible in order to save the server memory as shown in the following.

```
<?xml version="1.0" encoding="UTF-8"?>
<web-app ...>
    ...
    <context-param>
        <param-name>com.sun.faces.numberOfLogicalViews</param-name>
        <param-value>3</param-value>
    </context-param>
    ...
</web-app>
```

It is important to understand the semantics of both parameters:

- numberOfLogicalViews parameter refers to the number of logical views in the session which you can experiment by opening your JSF application in different browser tabs; every browser tab represents a logical view (**GET** view). For example, if the numberOfLogicalViews parameter is set to three and you open four different browser tabs in sequence, go to the first tab, and submit the form (assuming that the page contains form), then you will get ViewExpiredException because the first tab which represents the first logical view is removed from the LRU (Least Recently Used) map of the logical views. This also means that if you open three different browser tabs in sequence and you go to any of the tabs to submit the form, you will not face this exception because you did not exceed the maximum number of logical views, which is three.

- numberOfViewsInSession parameter refers to the number of **POST** views in the session, which you can experiment by submitting a form in a page many times. For example if numberOfViewsInSession parameter is set to three, and you submit a page form four times, press the browser back button four times, and then resubmit the first page form, you will get ViewExpiredException because the first page form which represents the first view is removed from the LRU map of the **POST** views. This also means that if you submit the form three times and you go back to resubmit the first page form, you will not face this exception because you did not exceed the maximum number of POST views, which is three.

Apache MyFaces Specific Tuning

If you have enough memory in the application server and because compression consumes CPU time, you can disable server state compression as follows.

```xml
<?xml version="1.0" encoding="UTF-8"?>
<web-app ...>
        ...
        <context-param>
                <param-name>
                        org.apache.myfaces.COMPRESS_STATE_IN_SESSION
                </param-name>
                <param-value>false</param-value>
        </context-param>
        ...
</web-app>
```

Note that the (org.apache.myfaces.COMPRESS_STATE_IN_SESSION) parameter works when the state saving method is set to "server". Another important parameter that you need to take care about when the state saving method is set to "server" is (org.apache.myfaces.SERIALIZE_STATE_IN_SESSION). Setting org.apache.myfaces.SERIALIZE_STATE_IN_SESSION parameter to false, you can disable serializing the state in session, which will give better performance as well, as follows.

```xml
<?xml version="1.0" encoding="UTF-8"?>
<web-app ...>
        ...
        <context-param>
                <param-name>
                        org.apache.myfaces.SERIALIZE_STATE_IN_SESSION
                </param-name>
```

```
            <param-value>false</param-value>
        </context-param>
        ...
</web-app>
```

Stateless JSF

One of the useful features of JSF 2.2 is the ability to create stateless views. Creating stateless views has two main advantages:

- Stateless view has a better performance than the default stateful view, because no time is spent for saving and restoring the state of the dynamic components inside <h:form>.

- Stateless view consumes less memory than the default stateful view (with <h:form>), because no memory is consumed for saving the state of the dynamic components inside <h:form>.

Although both the performance and memory gains can be relatively small for small and medium pages, this gain can be significant when you have large pages with many components in your application and also when your JSF application has a lot of concurrent users with limited hardware capabilities; this means that stateless views can serve for making JSF applications more scalable.

■ **Note**   Stateless views is one of the most powerful options if you are seeking to develop public web sites using JSF.

Because stateless views do not have state, it is important to realize that they will not work with both view and session scoped beans; this means that you should be aware that your managed beans are set in request scope.

■ **Note**   Stateless view may not be compatible with JSF component libraries such as PrimeFaces or RichFaces. So, generally, you have to verify whether the JSF component you are using is working well in stateless mode.

In order to apply stateless behavior to your JSF view, you need to set transient attribute of <f:view> to true as shown in the following.

```
<?xml version='1.0' encoding='UTF-8' ?>
<!DOCTYPE html>
<f:view xmlns="http://www.w3.org/1999/xhtml"
        xmlns:f="http://xmlns.jcp.org/jsf/core"
        xmlns:h="http://xmlns.jcp.org/jsf/html"
        transient="true">
    <html>
        <h:head>
            <title>Stateless Page</title>
        </h:head>
        <h:body>
                <!-- JSF HTML components -->
        </h:body>
    </html>
</f:view>
```

This is all what you need to do in order to make your JSF view stateless.

Best Practices

Adding to all of the previous recommendations, you need to take the following into consideration:

- Do not business logic which performs I/O operations in the getters of your managed beans because they may be called multiple times during the request processing life cycle, which can degrade the overall application performance. Business logic has to be moved to JSF action methods or event listeners.

- Avoid complicated EL expressions. In case you have a complicated expression, move its logic to Java managed beans.

- Always use pagination if you have to display data table with large number of records.

- Use Ajax (<f:ajax>) when possible for sending ONLY the parts of the page that you want the server to process and to render ONLY the parts of the page (NOT the whole page) that should be re-rendered.

- Minimize using session scoped managed beans in order to minimize the usage of the server memory and in order to increase application scalability.

Summary

In this chapter, you learned the differences between authentication, authorization, and data protection. You learned how to secure your JSF application using the security features provided by the Java EE container. You know how to apply container-managed authentication, authorization, and data protection in the weather application that was introduced in Chapter 10. You also learned how to tune the performance of your JSF application by modifying the default JSF context parameters and by applying a set of best practices.

CHAPTER 13

Applying It All: The Mega App

In this chapter, we will apply most of what we learned in the previous chapters in a sample application which we will call the Mega App. We will start from the application specification and wireframes and after understanding the application requirements, we will develop the application architecture including Data model, back-end services, front-end templates, application security including authentication, and authorization and error handling. And we will see how to implement this architecture using Java EE 7 technologies. The Mega App application utilizes many Java EE 7 technologies: it uses JSF 2.2 for handling the user interface interactions with the help of Twitter Bootstrap, EJB 3.2 for transaction handling, JPA 2.1 for persistence, CDI 1.1 for bean management, and Java Bean Validation for handling model validation. In this chapter, you will learn how to create a suitable application architecture and implementation for JSF 2.2 applications in the Java EE 7 space.

Mega App Specification

Mega App is an online library application that allows its users to search for books. After getting the available books from the search, the user can request a copy for one or more book(s) from the search results. In the back office, the application administrator(s) can approve or reject the requests for the books. If a book (or more) request(s) are approved, then the Mega App user will be able to download the approved book(s) from his/her approved book listing. Figure 13-1 shows the Mega application book request flow from the application user perspective.

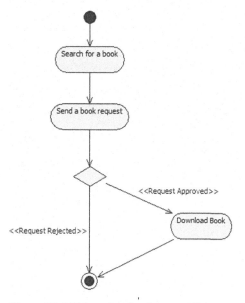

Figure 13-1. *Mega App book request flow*

The Mega App application has two roles:

- Application user
- Application administrator

Figure 13-2 shows the user case diagrams of both application user and application administrator.

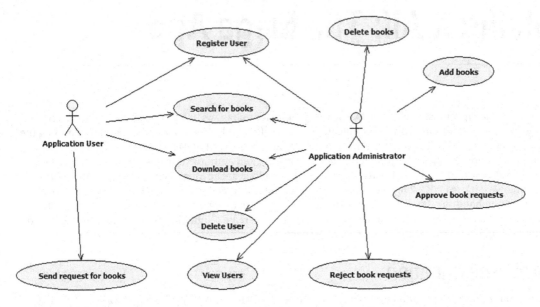

Figure 13-2. *Mega App use case diagram*

As shown by the use case diagram, the application user can perform the following operations:

- Register in the application.
- Search for books.
- Send requests for a books.
- Download approved books.

The application administrator can perform the following operations:

- Add book(s).
- Delete book(s).
- Approve book requests.
- Reject book requests.
- Search for books.
- Download books.
- Register users in the application.
- View all users.
- Delete user(s).

■ **Note** It is important to understand that a role (or an actor) can include one or more user(s) in the system. This means that in Mega App, we can have many application users and many application administrators as well.

Mega App Wireframes

Now, let's have a tour in the application wireframes in order to have a clear understanding of the application specification. We will illustrate the application page(s) which every actor in the application (application user and application administrator) can interact with. First of all, in order to access the application pages, the users need to register themselves using the registration page. Figure 13-3 shows the registration page.

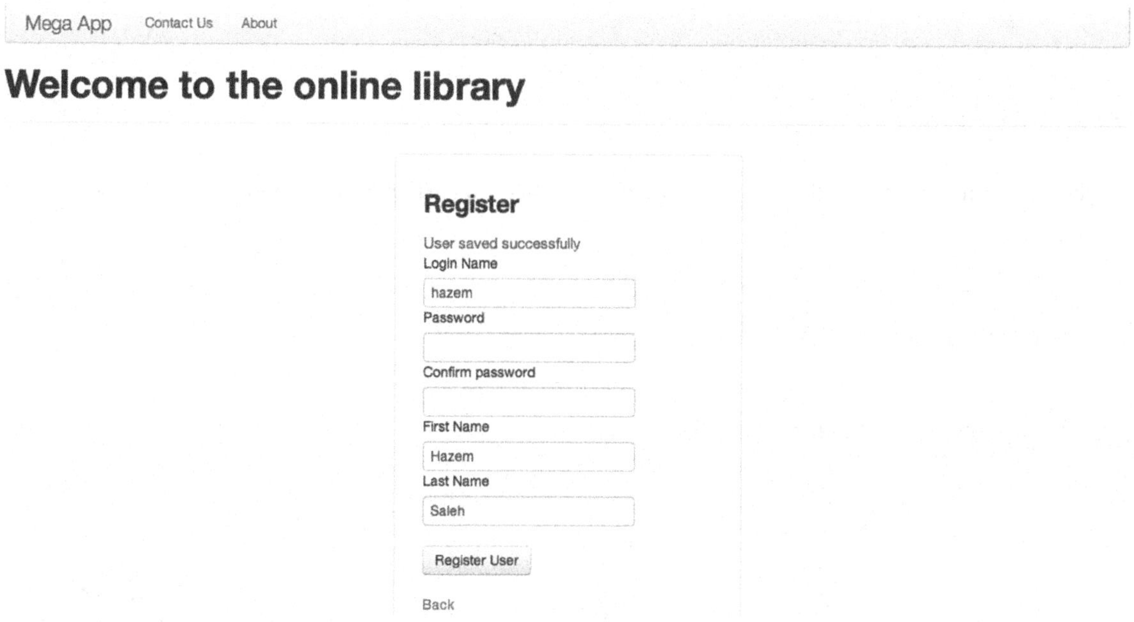

Figure 13-3. *Registration page*

In order to register, the user has to provide the following information:

- Login name, which has to be unique for every user in the application.
- Two identical passwords.
- The user first name.
- The user last name.

If the user enters correct information, the application will inform the user that his/her account is created successfully. After doing successful registration, the user should be able to login to the system. Figure 13-4 shows the Mega App login page.

Figure 13-4. *Login page*

After login to the application, the application user is introduced to the home page as shown in Figure 13-5.

Figure 13-5. *Application user home page*

As shown in the page, the user can perform the following operations using the side menu:

- Search for books.
- View Pending Requests.
- View approved requests.
- View rejected requests.
- Logout.

The user can search for books by title by entering the exact book title or by entering just part of the title. When the user enters book title and clicks the "Search for books" button, the search table will be populated with the results. For every book in the search result, the application user has the option to request a book copy. Once the user requests the book copy, the administrator user will be able to see the user request in his/her pending requests inbox as shown in Figure 13-6.

Figure 13-6. *Application administrator pending requests inbox*

As shown in the previous figure, the administrator user can perform the following operations on the pending requests of the application users:

- Approve user request.

- Reject user request.

- Download the book that the user wishes to have a copy of.

Adding to this, the administrator user has the following operations in the side menu:

- Search for books.

- View pending requests.

- View approved requests.

- View rejected requests.

- Add a book.

- View users.

- Log out.

The details of the administrator operations will be illustrated in the next few paragraphs.

Once the application administrator approves the book request, the application user will be able to see his/her request in his/her approved requests inbox as shown in Figure 13-7.

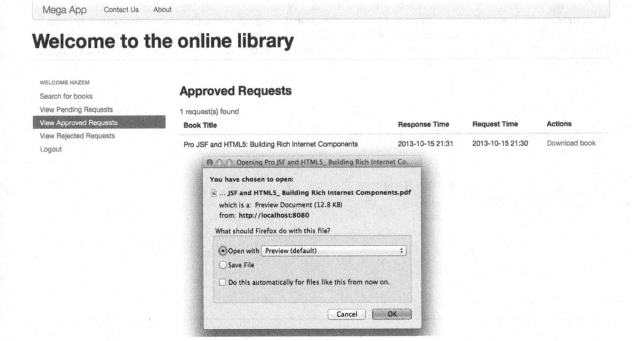

Figure 13-7. *Approved book requests for the application user*

In the approved requests inbox, the application user can download the book copy. If the application administrator rejects the user's book request then the user will see his/her rejected request in his/her "View Rejected Requests" inbox. The "View Pending Requests" inbox of the application user shows his/her current pending book requests which are not yet approved or rejected by the application administrator.

Now, let's move to the administrator user's pages: after the successful login of the administrator user, the administrator user can search for books by their titles (or part of their titles) as shown in Figure 13-8.

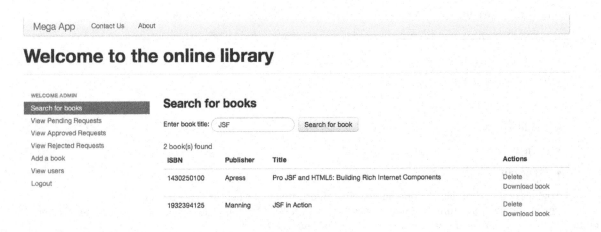

Figure 13-8. *Application administrator home page*

The administrator user can search for books in order to either download them or to delete them from the application. The administrator user's pending requests inbox is already illustrated in Figure 13-6. In this inbox, the administrator user can either approve or reject the book request or download the requested book.

Figure 13-9 shows the administrator user's approved requests inbox.

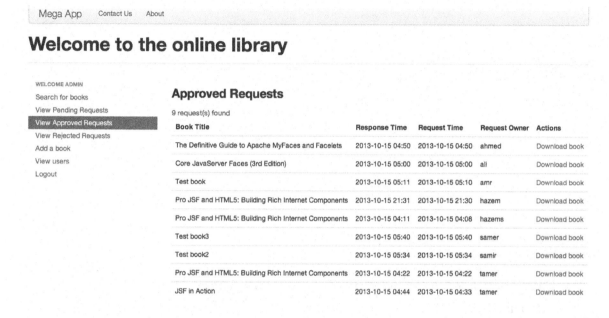

Figure 13-9. *Administrator user's approved requests inbox*

The administrator user's approved requests inbox includes the list of all the approved book requests. The administrator user also has a rejected requests inbox, which includes all of the rejected book requests. The approved or rejected book request information is as follows:

- Book title.
- Response time.
- Request time.
- Request owner.
- Available actions that can be done on the requests.

The administrator user can add books as shown by Figure 13-10.

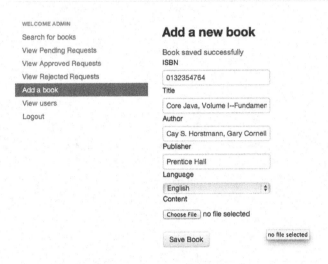

Figure 13-10. Administrator add book page

The administrator can add a book by entering the following book information:

- Book ISBN.

- Book title.

- Book author.

- Publisher name.

- Book language.

- Book content (which represents simply a PDF file).

Once the book is created, it will be available from the book search page. Finally, the administrator user can view all the users of the applications as shown in Figure 13-11.

Mega App   Contact Us   About

Welcome to the online library

WELCOME ADMIN

Search for books
View Pending Requests
View Approved Requests
View Rejected Requests
Add a book
View users
Logout

All Users

9 user(s) found

Login Name	First Name	Last Name	Actions
admin	admin	admin	Delete
hazems	Hazem	Saleh	Delete
tamer	Tamer	Tamer	Delete
hazem	Hazem	Saleh	Delete
ahmed	Ahmed	Ahmed	Delete
ali	Ali	Ali	Delete
amr	Amr	Amr	Delete
samir	samir	samir	Delete
samer	samer	samer	Delete

Figure 13-11. *Administrator user's user management page*

The administrator user can view all the users of the application and also delete any of them.

Mega App Architecture

Mega App application utilizes the following Java EE 7 technologies:

- JSF 2.2 for handling the user interface interactions.
- EJB 3.2 for transaction handling.
- JPA 2.1 for data persistence.
- CDI 1.1 for bean management.
- Bean Validation 1.1 for handling model validation.

In order to have nifty HTML5/CSS3 user interface, Mega App uses Twitter Bootstrap library: http://getbootstrap.com. Twitter Bootstrap is a lightweight HTML5/CSS3 library that contains nifty design templates for typography, forms, buttons, navigation, and other interface components, as well as optional JavaScript extensions.

For simplicity purposes, Mega App uses Oracle Java DB. Java DB is the Oracle's supported distribution of the Apache Derby open-source database. It supports standard ANSI/ISO SQL through the JDBC and Java EE APIs and is included in the JDK. Figure 13-12 shows the high-level components of the Mega App application.

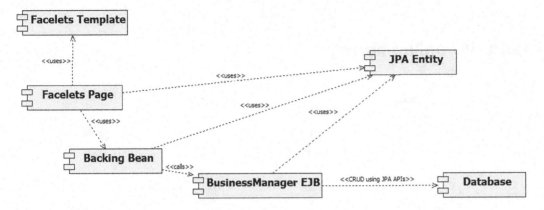

Figure 13-12. *Mega App high-level components*

As shown in the previous figure, the application has the following high-level components:

1. Facelets pages: They represent the Mega App pages. They use both the backing beans and JPA beans (which are managed using CDI) via the JSF expression language (EL). They also utilize the application Facelets templates.

2. Facelets Templates: They represent the templates that are used by the application pages. In Mega App, there are two templates (one for the public pages and the other for the protected pages).

3. Backing Beans: They are normal managed beans that are conceptually related to the UI pages and are not part of the application model. Backing beans are ideal for centralizing the handling of the page actions (sometimes backing beans are called controller classes). In Mega App, backing beans mainly use the JPA CDI managed beans to call the Business Manager (Service) EJBs in order to perform the required operation(s).

4. Business Manager EJBs: In order to perform the business operations, backing beans call Business Manager EJBs. Business Manager EJBs are stateless session EJBs which use the JPA entities and the JPA `EntityManager` in order to perform the required database operations. In Mega App, we have the following business manager EJBs:

    - Book Manager EJB to handle the book management operations such as (`registerBook`, `updateBook`, `deleteBook`, `getBookInformation`...etc).

    - Book Request Manager EJB to handle the book request flow operations (`sendBookRequest`, `approveBookRequest`, and `viewRequests`).

    - MegaUser Manager EJB to handle the Mega App user management operations (`getMegaUser`, `retrieveMegaUsers`, `registerMegaUser`, `removeMegaUser`).

5. JPA Entities (CDI managed beans): JPA entities represent the data classes that map to the database tables. In Mega App, the JPA entities are used as the application's CDI managed beans which are binded with the Facelets pages using EL.

Constructing Data Model

Let's start with creating the data model of Mega App. Figure 13-13 shows the Mega App logical data model.

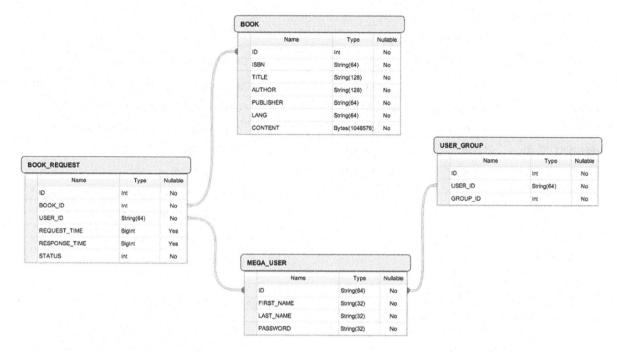

Figure 13-13. *Mega App logical data model*

As shown in the diagram, Mega App data model contains four entities:

1. BOOK Entity: BOOK entity is responsible for storing the book data. It has the attributes shown in Table 13-1.

Table 13-1. *Book Entity Attributes*

Attribute name	Logical Type	Nullable	Description
ID	Integer	Primary Key (NOT NULL)	Auto-generated ID that represents book ID
ISBN	String(64)	NOT NULL	Book ISBN
TITLE	String(128)	NOT NULL	Book title
AUTHOR	String(128)	NOT NULL	Book author
PUBLISHER	String(64)	NOT NULL	Book publisher
LANG	String(64)	NOT NULL	Book language
CONTENT	Bytes(1 MB)	NOT NULL	Book content

The relation type between BOOK Entity and BOOK_REQUEST is "one-to-many", which means that a book can have 0 or more book requests.

2. BOOK_REQUEST Entity: BOOK_REQUEST entity is responsible for storing the requests for the book that are performed by the application users. It has the attributes shown in Table 13-2.

Table 13-2. BOOK_REQUEST table

Attribute name	Logical Type	Nullable	Description
ID	Integer	Primary Key (NOT NULL)	Auto-generated ID that represents request ID
BOOK_ID	Integer	NOT NULL	Foreign key that represents the book ID
USER_ID	String(64)	NOT NULL	Foreign key that represents the user ID
REQUEST_TIME	Long	NULLABLE	Request time
RESPONSE_TIME	Long	NULLABLE	Response time
STATUS	Integer	NOT NULL	The request status. It has one of three values: 1, which represents pending status 2, which represents rejected status 3, which represents approved status

3. USER Entity: USER entity is responsible for storing the Mega App users. It has the following attributes as shown in Table 13-3.

Table 13-3. MEGA_USER Entity

Attribute name	Logical Type	Nullable	Description
ID	String(64)	Primary Key (NOT NULL)	The user login name
FIRST_NAME	String(32)	NOT NULL	The user first name
LAST_NAME	String(32)	NOT NULL	The user last name
PASSWORD	String(32)	NOT NULL	The user password

The relation type between USER Entity and BOOK_REQUEST is "one-to-many", which means that a user can perform 0 or more book requests.

The relation type between USER Entity and USER_GROUP is "one-to-many", which means that a user can be in 0 or more groups.

■ **Note** The Mega App code ensures that the user will be always a member in one group.

---

4. USER_GROUP Entity: USER_GROUP entity is responsible for storing the Mega App user groups. It has the attributes shown in Table 13-4.

Table 13-4. USER_GROUP Entity

Attribute name	Logical Type	Nullable	Description
ID	Integer	Primary Key (NOT NULL)	Auto-generated ID
USER_ID	String(32)	NOT NULL	Foreign key that represents the user ID
GROUP_ID	String(32)	NOT NULL	The group ID. It has one of two values:
			1, which represents "User" group
			2 which represents "Administrator" group

Listing 13-1 shows the equivalent SQL DDL (Data Definition Language) script of the indicated logical data model for Java DB.

Listing 13-1. Mega App SQL DDL Script

```
-- Create Table: USER_GROUP
--------------------------------------------------------------------------------
CREATE TABLE USER_GROUP
(       ID INTEGER NOT NULL PRIMARY KEY GENERATED ALWAYS AS IDENTITY (START WITH 1, INCREMENT BY 1)
        , USER_ID VARCHAR(64)
        , "GROUP_ID" INTEGER
);


-- Create Table: BOOK
--------------------------------------------------------------------------------
CREATE TABLE BOOK
(
        ID INTEGER NOT NULL PRIMARY KEY GENERATED ALWAYS AS IDENTITY (START WITH 1, INCREMENT BY 1)
        ,ISBN VARCHAR(64) NOT NULL
        ,TITLE VARCHAR(128) NOT NULL
        ,AUTHOR VARCHAR(128) NOT NULL
        ,PUBLISHER VARCHAR(64) NOT NULL
        ,LANG VARCHAR(64) NOT NULL
        ,CONTENT blob(1M) NOT NULL
);


-- Create Table: MEGA_USER
--------------------------------------------------------------------------------
CREATE TABLE MEGA_USER
(
        ID VARCHAR(64) NOT NULL PRIMARY KEY
        ,FIRST_NAME VARCHAR(32) NOT NULL
        ,LAST_NAME VARCHAR(32) NOT NULL
        ,PASSWORD VARCHAR(32) NOT NULL
);
```

```
-- Create Table: BOOK_REQUEST
-----------------------------------------------------------------------------
CREATE TABLE BOOK_REQUEST
(
        ID INTEGER NOT NULL PRIMARY KEY GENERATED ALWAYS AS IDENTITY (START WITH 1, INCREMENT BY 1)
        ,BOOK_ID INTEGER NOT NULL
        ,USER_ID VARCHAR(64) NOT NULL
        ,REQUEST_TIME BIGINT
        ,RESPONSE_TIME BIGINT
        ,STATUS INTEGER NOT NULL
);

-- Create Foreign Key: BOOK_REQUEST.USER_ID -> MEGA_USER.ID
ALTER TABLE BOOK_REQUEST ADD CONSTRAINT FK_BOOK_REQUEST_USER_ID_MEGA_USER_ID FOREIGN KEY (USER_ID)
REFERENCES MEGA_USER(ID);


-- Create Foreign Key: BOOK_REQUEST.BOOK_ID -> BOOK.ID
ALTER TABLE BOOK_REQUEST ADD CONSTRAINT FK_BOOK_REQUEST_BOOK_ID_BOOK_ID FOREIGN KEY (BOOK_ID)
REFERENCES BOOK(ID);

-- Create Foreign Key: USER_GROUP.USER_ID -> MEGA_USER.ID
ALTER TABLE USER_GROUP ADD CONSTRAINT FK_USER_GROUP_USER_ID FOREIGN KEY (USER_ID) REFERENCES MEGA_
USER(ID);
```

Constructing Service Layer (EJBs)

After creating the data model, we need to define the application APIs (services) which will be used from the JSF backing beans. Mega App utilizes EJB technology in order to expose the application services for the client (JSF Backing beans). In Mega App, we have the following three business manager EJBs:

- Book Manager EJB.
- Book Request Manager EJB.
- Mega User Manager EJB.

Book Manager EJB is responsible for handling the book management operations, which are

- Registering new books.
- Updating a book information.
- Removing a book.
- Getting the book information.
- Getting a book content.
- Getting all books.

Book Request Manager EJB is responsible for handling the book request flow operations, which are

- Sending a book request by an application user.
- Approving a book request by an application administrator.

- Rejecting a book request by an application administrator.

- Removing a book by an application administrator.

User Manager EJB is responsible for handling the user management operations, which are

- Registering a Mega App user.

- Getting a Mega App user information.

- Removing a Mega App user.

- Retrieving Mega App users.

Listing 13-2 shows the persistence.xml file (located under /resources/META-INF). persistence.xml file uses JPA version 2.1 and it defines the "megaAppUnit" persistence unit that uses "JTA" transaction type. Using "JTA" transaction type means that the container will handle the EntityManager creation and tracking for you, and you can obtain its instance using @PersistenceContext annotation. JTA data source is set to jdbc/mega data source, using which we will be able to access the Mega App database.

Listing 13-2. persistence.xml File

```xml
<?xml version="1.0" encoding="UTF-8"?>
<persistence version="2.1" xmlns="http://xmlns.jcp.org/xml/ns/persistence"
             xmlns:xsi="http://www.w3.org/2001/XMLSchema-instance"
             xsi:schemaLocation="http://xmlns.jcp.org/xml/ns/persistence
http://xmlns.jcp.org/xml/ns/persistence/persistence_2_1.xsd">

  <persistence-unit name="megaAppUnit" transaction-type="JTA">
    <jta-data-source>jdbc/mega</jta-data-source>
    <exclude-unlisted-classes>false</exclude-unlisted-classes>
    <properties/>
  </persistence-unit>
</persistence>
```

■ **Note**   It is good to note that in Java EE 7, most of the deployment descriptor namespaces are changed from the prefix to http://java.sun.com to http://xmlns.jcp.org.

Listing 13-3 shows the EJB interface of BookManager EJB, which is defined as an EJB Local interface using @Local annotation.

Listing 13-3. EJB Local Interface of BookManager EJB

```java
package com.jsfprohtml5.megaapp.service;

import com.jsfprohtml5.megaapp.model.Book;
import com.jsfprohtml5.megaapp.service.exception.BookAlreadyExists;
import com.jsfprohtml5.megaapp.service.exception.BookNotFound;
import java.util.List;
import javax.ejb.Local;
```

```
@Local
public interface BookManagerLocal {
    public Book getBookInformation(Integer bookID) throws BookNotFound;
    public Book registerBook(Book book) throws BookAlreadyExists;
    public Book updateBook(Book book) throws BookNotFound;
    public void removeBook(Integer bookID) throws BookNotFound;
    public byte[] getBookContent(Integer bookID) throws BookNotFound;
    public List<Book> getAllBooks(Book book);
}
```

■ **Tip** Using @Local annotation is suitable when the EJB client is running in the same JVM of the EJB itself. @Local annotation is more efficient than @Remote annotation as it does not require argument marshalling, transportation, and un-marshalling.

Listing 13-4 shows the BookManager EJB class's registerBook and updateBook methods.

Listing 13-4. BookManager EJB's Register and Update Book Methods

```
package com.jsfprohtml5.megaapp.service;

import com.jsfprohtml5.megaapp.model.Book;
import com.jsfprohtml5.megaapp.service.exception.BookAlreadyExists;
import com.jsfprohtml5.megaapp.service.exception.BookNotFound;
import java.util.ArrayList;
import java.util.List;
import java.util.logging.Level;
import java.util.logging.Logger;
import javax.ejb.Stateless;
import javax.persistence.EntityManager;
import javax.persistence.NoResultException;
import javax.persistence.PersistenceContext;
import javax.persistence.Query;

@Stateless
public class BookManager implements BookManagerLocal {

    @PersistenceContext(unitName = "megaAppUnit")
    EntityManager em;

    //Other interface methods ...

    @Override
    public Book registerBook(Book book) throws BookAlreadyExists {
        Query query = em.createQuery("select book from Book book where "
                    + "book.isbn = :isbn");

        query.setParameter("isbn", book.getIsbn());
```

```
    try {
        query.getSingleResult();
        throw new BookAlreadyExists();
    } catch (NoResultException exception) {
        Logger.getLogger(BookManager.class.getName()).log(Level.FINER, "No similar books found");
    }

    em.persist(book);
    em.flush();

    return book;
}

@Override
public Book updateBook(Book book) throws BookNotFound {
    Book updatableBook = em.find(Book.class, book.getId());

    if (updatableBook == null) {
        throw new BookNotFound();
    }

    mergeBookAttrs(book, updatableBook);

    em.merge(updatableBook);
    em.flush();

    return book;
}

private void mergeBookAttrs(Book book, Book updatableBook) {
    if (book.getAuthor() != null) {
        updatableBook.setAuthor(book.getAuthor());
    }

    if (book.getContent() != null) {
        updatableBook.setContent(book.getContent());
    }

    if (book.getIsbn() != null) {
        updatableBook.setIsbn(book.getIsbn());
    }

    if (book.getLang() != null) {
        updatableBook.setLang(book.getLang());
    }

    if (book.getPublisher() != null) {
        updatableBook.setPublisher(book.getPublisher());
    }
```

```
        if (book.getTitle() != null) {
            updatableBook.setTitle(book.getTitle());
        }
    }
}
```

@Stateless annotation defines BookManager class as a stateless session EJB. @PersistenceContext annotation is used for injecting a container-managed entity manager instance, using which we will be able to perform the database operations. The registerBook method checks if an already existing book ISBN matches the new book ISBN, and if it finds a case, it throws BookAlreadyExists exception, or else it persists the new book data in the database. The updateBook method throws BookNotFound exception if the book to be updated does not exist in the database; if the target book exists, it merges the new data updates with the existing book data using the mergeBookAttrs method. Listing 13-5 shows the remaining methods of BookManager EJB.

Listing 13-5. BookManager EJB's Remaining Methods

```
@Stateless
public class BookManager implements BookManagerLocal {

    @PersistenceContext(unitName = "megaAppUnit")
    EntityManager em;

    @Override
    public Book getBookInformation(Integer bookID) throws BookNotFound {
        Query query = em.createQuery("select book.id, book.isbn, book.title, "
                    + "book.author, book.publisher, book.lang from Book book where "
                    + "book.id = :id");

        query.setParameter("id", bookID);

        Object[] bookInfo = null;

        try {
            bookInfo = (Object[]) query.getSingleResult();
        } catch (NoResultException exception) {
            throw new BookNotFound(exception.getMessage());
        }

        Book book = new Book(
                    (Integer) bookInfo[0],
                    (String) bookInfo[1],
                    (String) bookInfo[2],
                    (String) bookInfo[3],
                    (String) bookInfo[4],
                    (String) bookInfo[5],
                    null);

        return book;
    }
```

```java
@Override
public void removeBook(Integer bookID) throws BookNotFound {
    Book book = em.find(Book.class, bookID);

    if (book == null) {
        throw new BookNotFound();
    }

    em.remove(book);
    em.flush();
}

@Override
public byte[] getBookContent(Integer bookID) throws BookNotFound {
    byte[] content = null;

    try {
        content = (byte[]) em.createQuery("Select book.content from Book book where book.id=:id")
                            .setParameter("id", bookID)
                            .getSingleResult();
    } catch (NoResultException exception) {
        throw new BookNotFound(exception.getMessage());
    }

    return content;
}

@Override
public List<Book> getAllBooks(Book searchableBook) {
    List<Book> books = new ArrayList<Book>();
    String searchableTitle = searchableBook.getTitle();

    Query query = em.createQuery("select book.id, book.isbn, book.title, "
                + "book.author, book.publisher, book.lang from Book book where "
                + "book.title like :title");

    query.setParameter("title", "%" + searchableTitle + "%");

    List<Object[]> bookList = (List<Object[]>) query.getResultList();

    if (bookList == null) {
        return books;
    }

    for (Object[] bookInfo : bookList) {
        Book book = new Book(
                (Integer) bookInfo[0],
                (String) bookInfo[1],
                (String) bookInfo[2],
                (String) bookInfo[3],
                (String) bookInfo[4],
```

```
                    (String) bookInfo[5],
                    null);

            books.add(book);
        }

        return books;
    }

    //...
}
```

The other methods of BookManager EJB are as follows:

- getBookInformation: Gets the metadata of the book (the book data without the book contents). It throws BookNotFound exception if the target book is not found.

- getBookContent: Gets only the book content as a byte array. It throws BookNotFound exception if the target book is not found.

- removeBook: Removes the book from the database. It throws BookNotFound exception if the target book is not found.

- getAllBooks: Takes a book object as a parameter for allowing the API to search with any of the book attributes. However, for now, the getAllBooks() implementation searches using only the title attribute of the book, using the SQL like operator. If there are no results, the API returns an empty list.

Now, let's check the details of Book JPA entity which holds the book attributes and the validation constraints which use Java Bean Validation APIs. Listing 13-6 shows Book JPA entity code.

Listing 13-6. Book JPA Entity

```
package com.jsfprohtml5.megaapp.model;

import java.io.Serializable;
import java.util.List;
import javax.persistence.Basic;
import javax.persistence.CascadeType;
import javax.persistence.Column;
import javax.persistence.Entity;
import javax.persistence.FetchType;
import javax.persistence.GeneratedValue;
import javax.persistence.GenerationType;
import javax.persistence.Id;
import javax.persistence.Lob;
import javax.persistence.OneToMany;
import javax.persistence.Table;
import javax.validation.constraints.NotNull;
import javax.validation.constraints.Size;
```

```java
@Entity
@Table(name = "BOOK")
public class Book implements Serializable {
    private static final long serialVersionUID = 197654646546456456L;

    @Id
    @GeneratedValue(strategy = GenerationType.IDENTITY)
    @Basic(optional = false)
    @Column(name = "ID")
    private Integer id;

    @Basic(optional = false)
    @NotNull
    @Size(min = 10, max = 20, message = "ISBN must be between 10 and 20 characters")
    @Column(name = "ISBN")
    private String isbn;

    @Basic(optional = false)
    @NotNull
    @Size(min = 5, max = 128, message = "Book title must be between 5 and 128 characters")
    @Column(name = "TITLE")
    private String title;

    @Basic(optional = false)
    @NotNull
    @Size(min = 3, max = 128, message = "Book author must be between 3 and 128 characters")
    @Column(name = "AUTHOR")
    private String author;

    @Basic(optional = false)
    @NotNull
    @Size(min = 3, max = 64, message = "Book publisher must be between 3 and 64 characters")
    @Column(name = "PUBLISHER")
    private String publisher;

    @Basic(optional = false)
    @NotNull
    @Size(min = 3, max = 64, message = "Book language must be between 3 and 64 characters")
    @Column(name = "LANG")
    private String lang;

    @Basic(optional = false)
    @Lob
    @Column(name = "CONTENT")
    private Serializable content;

    @OneToMany(cascade = CascadeType.ALL, mappedBy = "bookId")
    private List<BookRequest> bookRequestList;

    public Book() {
    }
```

```java
    public Book(Integer id) {
        this.id = id;
    }

    public Book(Integer id, String isbn, String title, String author, String publisher, String lang,
Serializable content) {
        this.id = id;
        this.isbn = isbn;
        this.title = title;
        this.author = author;
        this.publisher = publisher;
        this.lang = lang;
        this.content = content;
    }

    public Integer getId() {
        return id;
    }

    public void setId(Integer id) {
        this.id = id;
    }

    public String getIsbn() {
        return isbn;
    }

    public void setIsbn(String isbn) {
        this.isbn = isbn;
    }

    public String getTitle() {
        return title;
    }

    public void setTitle(String title) {
        this.title = title;
    }

    public String getAuthor() {
        return author;
    }

    public void setAuthor(String author) {
        this.author = author;
    }

    public String getPublisher() {
        return publisher;
    }

    public void setPublisher(String publisher) {
        this.publisher = publisher;
    }
```

```java
    public String getLang() {
        return lang;
    }

    public void setLang(String lang) {
        this.lang = lang;
    }

    public Serializable getContent() {
        return content;
    }

    public void setContent(Serializable content) {
        this.content = content;
    }

    public List<BookRequest> getBookRequestList() {
        return bookRequestList;
    }

    public void setBookRequestList(List<BookRequest> bookRequestList) {
        this.bookRequestList = bookRequestList;
    }

    @Override
    public int hashCode() {
        int hash = 0;
        hash += (id != null ? id.hashCode() : 0);
        return hash;
    }

    @Override
    public boolean equals(Object object) {
        if (!(object instanceof Book)) {
            return false;
        }
        Book other = (Book) object;
        if ((this.id == null && other.id != null) || (this.id != null &&
!this.id.equals(other.id))) {
            return false;
        }
        return true;
    }

    @Override
    public String toString() {
        return "com.jsfprohtml5.megaapp.model.Book[ id=" + id + " ]";
    }

}
```

Book JPA entity class has the following attributes:

- id: Marked as a primary key for the entity using @Id annotation. It is an auto-generated attribute.

- ISBN: Validated to be not null. ISBN is validated to be between 10 and 20 characters.

- title: Validated to be not null. Book title is validated be between 5 and 128 characters.

- author: Validated to be not null. Book author is validated to be between 3 and 128 characters.

- publisher: Validated to be not null. Book publisher is validated to be between 3 and 64 characters.

- lang: Represents the book language and it is validated to be not null. Book language is validated to be between 3 and 64 characters.

- content: Represents the book content and it is marked as a Lob (Large Object).

- bookRequestList: Represents the associated requests of the book; its cascade type is set to "All", which means that all of the operations (merge, persist, remove, refresh) will be cascaded.

■ **Note**   It is important to note that all of the following JPA entities will be used as CDI beans in the application Facelets pages: for more information, check the "Composing Page Templates" section.

Now, let's move to the second EJB Manager (MegaUserManager) EJB. Listing 13-7 shows the EJB Local interface of MegaUserManager EJB.

Listing 13-7. MegaUserManager EJB Local Interface

```
package com.jsfprohtml5.megaapp.service;

import com.jsfprohtml5.megaapp.model.MegaUser;
import com.jsfprohtml5.megaapp.service.exception.UserAlreadyExists;
import com.jsfprohtml5.megaapp.service.exception.UserNotFound;
import java.util.List;
import javax.ejb.Local;

@Local
public interface MegaUserManagerLocal {
    public MegaUser getMegaUser(String userID) throws UserNotFound;
    public List<MegaUser> retrieveMegaUsers();
    public MegaUser registerMegaUser(MegaUser user) throws UserAlreadyExists;
    public void removeMegaUser(String userID) throws UserNotFound;
}
```

Listing 13-8 shows the MegaUserManager EJB class implementation.

Listing 13-8. MegaUserManager EJB Class

```java
package com.jsfprohtml5.megaapp.service;

import com.jsfprohtml5.megaapp.model.Constants;
import com.jsfprohtml5.megaapp.model.MegaUser;
import com.jsfprohtml5.megaapp.model.UserGroup;
import com.jsfprohtml5.megaapp.service.exception.UserAlreadyExists;
import com.jsfprohtml5.megaapp.service.exception.UserNotFound;
import java.util.ArrayList;
import java.util.List;
import java.util.logging.Level;
import java.util.logging.Logger;
import javax.ejb.Stateless;
import javax.persistence.EntityManager;
import javax.persistence.NoResultException;
import javax.persistence.PersistenceContext;
import javax.persistence.Query;

@Stateless
public class MegaUserManager implements MegaUserManagerLocal {

    @PersistenceContext(unitName = "megaAppUnit")
    EntityManager em;

    @Override
    public MegaUser getMegaUser(String userID) throws UserNotFound {
        Query query = em.createQuery("select megaUser.id, megaUser.firstName"
                            + ", megaUser.lastName from MegaUser megaUser where "
                            + "megaUser.id = :id");

        query.setParameter("id", userID);

        Object[] megaUserInfo;

        try {
            megaUserInfo = (Object[]) query.getSingleResult();
        } catch (NoResultException exception) {
            throw new UserNotFound(exception.getMessage());
        }

        MegaUser megaUser = new MegaUser(
                (String) megaUserInfo[0],
                (String) megaUserInfo[1],
                (String) megaUserInfo[2],
                null);

        return megaUser;
    }

    @Override
    public MegaUser registerMegaUser(MegaUser user) throws UserAlreadyExists {
```

```java
        Query query = em.createQuery("select megaUser from MegaUser megaUser where "
                    + "megaUser.id = :userID");

        query.setParameter("userID", user.getId());

        try {
            query.getSingleResult();
            throw new UserAlreadyExists();
        } catch (NoResultException exception) {
            Logger.getLogger(BookManager.class.getName()).log(Level.FINER, "No user found");
        }

        List<UserGroup> userGroups = new ArrayList<UserGroup>();

        UserGroup userGroup = new UserGroup();
        userGroup.setUserId(user);
        userGroup.setGroupId(Constants.USER_GROUP);

        userGroups.add(userGroup);

        user.setUserGroupList(userGroups);

        em.persist(user);
        em.flush();

        return user;
    }

    @Override
    public void removeMegaUser(String userID) throws UserNotFound {
        MegaUser megaUser = em.find(MegaUser.class, userID);

        if (megaUser == null) {
            throw new UserNotFound();
        }

        em.remove(megaUser);
        em.flush();
    }

    @Override
    public List<MegaUser> retrieveMegaUsers() {
        Query query = em.createQuery("select megaUser from MegaUser megaUser", MegaUser.class);

        List<MegaUser> result = query.getResultList();

        if (result == null) {
            return new ArrayList<MegaUser>();
        }

        return result;
    }
}
```

The methods of UserManager EJB are as follows:

- getMegaUser: Retrieves the user information. It throws UserNotFound exception if the target user is not found.

- registerMegaUser: Registers the Mega App user in the Mega App database as an application user (i.e., it makes the user a member in the "User" group). It throws UserAlreadyExists exception if the user ID already exists in the database.

- removeMegaUser: Removes the Mega App user from the database. It throws UserNotFound exception if the target user is not found.

- retrieveMegaUsers: Retrieves all the users of the Mega App (whether they are normal users or administrator users).

Let's check the details of MegaUser JPA entity, which holds the User attributes and its associated validation constraints. Listing 13-9 shows MegaUser JPA entity class.

Listing 13-9. MegaUser JPA Entity Class

```
package com.jsfprohtml5.megaapp.model;

import java.io.Serializable;
import java.util.List;
import javax.persistence.Basic;
import javax.persistence.CascadeType;
import javax.persistence.Column;
import javax.persistence.Entity;
import javax.persistence.Id;
import javax.persistence.OneToMany;
import javax.persistence.Table;
import javax.persistence.Transient;
import javax.validation.constraints.NotNull;
import javax.validation.constraints.Size;

@Entity
@Table(name = "MEGA_USER")
public class MegaUser implements Serializable {
    private static final long serialVersionUID = 109890766546456L;

    @Id
    @Basic(optional = false)
    @Size(min = 3, max = 64, message = "ID must be between 3 and 64 characters")
    @Column(name = "ID")
    private String id;

    @Basic(optional = false)
    @NotNull
    @Size(min = 3, max = 32, message = "First name must be between 3 and 32 characters")
    @Column(name = "FIRST_NAME")
    private String firstName;
```

```java
@Basic(optional = false)
@NotNull
@Size(min = 3, max = 32, message = "Last name must be between 3 and 32 characters")
@Column(name = "LAST_NAME")
private String lastName;

@Basic(optional = false)
@NotNull
@Size(min = 6, max = 32, message = "Password must be between 6 and 32 characters")
@Column(name = "PASSWORD")
private String password;

@Transient
private String password2;

@OneToMany(cascade = CascadeType.ALL, mappedBy = "userId")
private List<UserGroup> userGroupList;

@OneToMany(cascade = CascadeType.ALL, mappedBy = "userId")
private List<BookRequest> bookRequestList;

public MegaUser() {
}

public MegaUser(String id) {
    this.id = id;
}

public MegaUser(String id, String firstName, String lastName, String password) {
    this.id = id;
    this.firstName = firstName;
    this.lastName = lastName;
    this.password = password;
}

public String getId() {
    return id;
}

public void setId(String id) {
    this.id = id;
}

public String getFirstName() {
    return firstName;
}

public void setFirstName(String firstName) {
    this.firstName = firstName;
}
```

```java
    public String getLastName() {
        return lastName;
    }

    public void setLastName(String lastName) {
        this.lastName = lastName;
    }

    public String getPassword() {
        return password;
    }

    public void setPassword(String password) {
        this.password = password;
    }

    public String getPassword2() {
        return password2;
    }

    public void setPassword2(String password2) {
        this.password2 = password2;
    }

    public List<UserGroup> getUserGroupList() {
        return userGroupList;
    }

    public void setUserGroupList(List<UserGroup> userGroupList) {
        this.userGroupList = userGroupList;
    }

    public List<BookRequest> getBookRequestList() {
        return bookRequestList;
    }

    public void setBookRequestList(List<BookRequest> bookRequestList) {
        this.bookRequestList = bookRequestList;
    }

    @Override
    public int hashCode() {
        int hash = 0;
        hash += (id != null ? id.hashCode() : 0);
        return hash;
    }

    @Override
    public boolean equals(Object object) {
        if (!(object instanceof MegaUser)) {
            return false;
        }
```

```
        MegaUser other = (MegaUser) object;
        if ((this.id == null && other.id != null) || (this.id != null &&
!this.id.equals(other.id))) {
            return false;
        }
        return true;
    }

    @Override
    public String toString() {
        return "com.jsfprohtml5.megaapp.model.MegaUser[ id=" + id + " ]";
    }

}
```

MegaUser JPA entity class has the following attributes:

- id: Marked as a primary key for the entity using @Id annotation. It is validated to be between 3 and 64 characters.

- firstName: Validated to be not null. It is validated to be between 3 and 32 characters.

- lastName: Validated to be not null. It is validated to be between 3 and 32 characters.

- password: Validated to be not null. It is validated to be between 6 and 32 characters

- userGroupList: Represents the associated groups of the user and its cascade type is set to "All", which means that all of the operations (merge, persist, remove, refresh) will be cascaded (as shown in Listing 13-8, the user belongs to one group).

- bookRequestList: Represents the associated book requests of the user and its cascade type is set to "All", which means that all of the operations (merge, persist, remove, refresh) will be cascaded.

■ **Note** password2 attribute in MegaUser entity class is used in order to confirm password entrance in the registration page. As shown, the attribute is annotated with @Transient annotation to indicate that this field not persistent.

UserGroup JPA entity class maps to the USER_GROUP table, which maps the application users to the application groups as shown in Listing 13-10.

Listing 13-10. UserGroup JPA Entity Class

```
package com.jsfprohtml5.megaapp.model;

import java.io.Serializable;
import javax.persistence.Basic;
import javax.persistence.Column;
import javax.persistence.Entity;
import javax.persistence.GeneratedValue;
import javax.persistence.GenerationType;
import javax.persistence.Id;
import javax.persistence.JoinColumn;
```

```java
import javax.persistence.ManyToOne;
import javax.persistence.Table;

@Entity
@Table(name = "USER_GROUP")
public class UserGroup implements Serializable {
    private static final long serialVersionUID = 1982138123123319321L;

    @Id
    @GeneratedValue(strategy = GenerationType.IDENTITY)
    @Basic(optional = false)
    @Column(name = "ID")
    private Integer id;

    @Column(name = "GROUP_ID")
    private Integer groupId;

    @JoinColumn(name = "USER_ID", referencedColumnName = "ID")
    @ManyToOne
    private MegaUser userId;

    public UserGroup() {
    }

    public UserGroup(Integer id) {
        this.id = id;
    }

    public Integer getId() {
        return id;
    }

    public void setId(Integer id) {
        this.id = id;
    }

    public Integer getGroupId() {
        return groupId;
    }

    public void setGroupId(Integer groupId) {
        this.groupId = groupId;
    }

    public MegaUser getUserId() {
        return userId;
    }

    public void setUserId(MegaUser userId) {
        this.userId = userId;
    }
```

```
    @Override
    public int hashCode() {
        int hash = 0;
        hash += (id != null ? id.hashCode() : 0);
        return hash;
    }

    @Override
    public boolean equals(Object object) {
        if (!(object instanceof UserGroup)) {
            return false;
        }
        UserGroup other = (UserGroup) object;
        if ((this.id == null && other.id != null) || (this.id != null &&
!this.id.equals(other.id))) {
            return false;
        }
        return true;
    }

    @Override
    public String toString() {
        return "com.jsfprohtml5.megaapp.model.UserGroup[ id=" + id + " ]";
    }

}
```

UserGroup JPA entity class has the following attributes:

- id: Marked as a primary key for the entity using @Id annotation. It is an auto-generated attribute.

- groupId: Represents the group ID (can be 1 for user group or 2 for administrator group).

- userId: Represents the associated user object.

The third and last EJB Manager is BookRequestManager EJB. Listing 13-11 shows the EJB Local interface of BookRequestManager EJB.

Listing 13-11. BookRequestManager Local EJB Interface

```
package com.jsfprohtml5.megaapp.service;

import com.jsfprohtml5.megaapp.model.BookRequest;
import com.jsfprohtml5.megaapp.service.exception.BookRequestAlreadyExists;
import com.jsfprohtml5.megaapp.service.exception.BookRequestNotFound;
import java.util.List;
import javax.ejb.Local;

@Local
public interface BookRequestManagerLocal {
    public BookRequest sendBookRequest(BookRequest bookRequest) throws BookRequestAlreadyExists;
    public void approveBookRequest(Integer bookRequestNumber) throws BookRequestNotFound;
    public void rejectBookRequest(Integer bookRequestNumber) throws BookRequestNotFound;

    public List<BookRequest> viewRequests(String userName, int status);
}
```

Listing 13-12 shows the first part of BookRequestManager EJB class.

Listing 13-12. First Part of BookRequestManager EJB Class

```java
package com.jsfprohtml5.megaapp.service;

import com.jsfprohtml5.megaapp.model.Book;
import com.jsfprohtml5.megaapp.model.BookRequest;
import com.jsfprohtml5.megaapp.model.Constants;
import com.jsfprohtml5.megaapp.model.MegaUser;
import com.jsfprohtml5.megaapp.model.UserGroup;
import com.jsfprohtml5.megaapp.service.exception.BookRequestAlreadyExists;
import com.jsfprohtml5.megaapp.service.exception.BookRequestNotFound;
import java.util.ArrayList;
import java.util.List;
import java.util.logging.Level;
import java.util.logging.Logger;
import javax.ejb.Stateless;
import javax.persistence.EntityManager;
import javax.persistence.NoResultException;
import javax.persistence.PersistenceContext;
import javax.persistence.Query;

@Stateless
public class BookRequestManager implements BookRequestManagerLocal {

    @PersistenceContext(unitName = "megaAppUnit")
    EntityManager em;

    @Override
    public BookRequest sendBookRequest(BookRequest bookRequest) throws BookRequestAlreadyExists {
        Query query = em.createQuery("select bookRequest from BookRequest bookRequest where "
                    + "bookRequest.bookId.id = :bookId and bookRequest.userId.id = :userId");

        query.setParameter("bookId", bookRequest.getBookId().getId());
        query.setParameter("userId", bookRequest.getUserId().getId());

        try {
            query.getSingleResult();
            throw new BookRequestAlreadyExists();
        } catch (NoResultException exception) {
            Logger.getLogger(BookManager.class.getName()).log(Level.FINER, "No book request found");
        }

        bookRequest.setRequestTime(System.currentTimeMillis());
        bookRequest.setStatus(Constants.PENDING_REQUEST); //pending status...

        em.persist(bookRequest);
        em.flush();

        return bookRequest;
    }
```

```java
    @Override
    public void approveBookRequest(Integer bookRequestNumber) throws BookRequestNotFound {
        BookRequest updatableBookRequest = em.find(BookRequest.class, bookRequestNumber);

        if (updatableBookRequest == null) {
            throw new BookRequestNotFound();
        }

        updatableBookRequest.setStatus(Constants.APPROVED_REQUEST); //approved status
        updatableBookRequest.setResponseTime(System.currentTimeMillis());

        em.merge(updatableBookRequest);
        em.flush();
    }

    @Override
    public void rejectBookRequest(Integer bookRequestNumber) throws BookRequestNotFound {
        BookRequest updatableBookRequest = em.find(BookRequest.class, bookRequestNumber);

        if (updatableBookRequest == null) {
            throw new BookRequestNotFound();
        }

        updatableBookRequest.setStatus(Constants.REJECTED_REQUEST); //rejected status
        updatableBookRequest.setResponseTime(System.currentTimeMillis());

        em.merge(updatableBookRequest);
        em.flush();
    }

    //...
}
```

The first methods of BookRequestManager EJB are as follows:

- sendBookRequest: Creates a book request in the BOOK_REQUEST table setting its status to 1 (which refers to pending) and the request time to the current system time. It throws BookRequestAlreadyExists exception if the user has already sent a request for the target book.

- approveBookRequest: Sets the book request status to 3 (which refers to approved) and the response time to the current system time. It throws BookRequestNotFound exception if the target book request is not found.

- rejectBookRequest: Sets the book request status to 2 (which refers to rejected) and the response time to the current system time. It throws BookRequestNotFound exception if the target book request is not found.

Listing 13-13 shows the second part of BookRequestManager EJB class.

Listing 13-13. The Second Part of BookRequestManager EJB Class

```java
@Stateless
public class BookRequestManager implements BookRequestManagerLocal {

    @PersistenceContext(unitName = "megaAppUnit")
    EntityManager em;

    // ...

    @Override
    public List<BookRequest> viewRequests(String userID, int status) {
        String requestQuery = "select bookRequest.id, book.id, book.title, bookRequest.requestTime, bookRequest.responseTime, bookRequest.userId.id "
                            + "from BookRequest bookRequest JOIN bookRequest.bookId book JOIN bookRequest.userId user "
                            + "where bookRequest.status = :statusID";

        Query query = null;

        UserGroup group = getUserGroup(userID);

        if (group.getGroupId() == Constants.USER_GROUP) {
            requestQuery += " and bookRequest.userId.id = :userId";

            query = em.createQuery(requestQuery);

            query.setParameter("statusID", status);
            query.setParameter("userId", userID);
        } else {
            query = em.createQuery(requestQuery);

            query.setParameter("statusID", status);
        }

        List<BookRequest> bookRequests = new ArrayList<BookRequest>();

        List<Object []> results = (List<Object []>) query.getResultList();

        if (results == null) {
            return bookRequests;
        }

        for (Object[] result : results) {
            BookRequest bookRequest = new BookRequest((Integer) result[0]);
            Book book = new Book();

            book.setId((Integer) result[1]);
            book.setTitle((String) result[2]);
```

```
            bookRequest.setBookId(book);
            bookRequest.setRequestTime((Long) result[3]);
            bookRequest.setResponseTime((Long) result[4]);

            bookRequest.setUserId(new MegaUser((String) result[5]));

            bookRequests.add(bookRequest);
        }

        return bookRequests;
    }

    private UserGroup getUserGroup(String userID) {
        Query query = em.createQuery("Select userGroup from UserGroup userGroup where userGroup.
userId.id=:userID", UserGroup.class);

        query.setParameter("userID", userID);

        UserGroup group;

        try {
            group = (UserGroup) query.getSingleResult();
        } catch (NoResultException exception) {
            throw new IllegalStateException(userID + " state is invalid as user does not belong to
any group!!!");
        }

        return group;
    }
}
```

viewRequest method is used in order to view the book requests for both the normal and administrator users. It takes two parameters:

- user ID: Represents the user ID that requests to view the book requests.

- status: Represents the status of the book requests that will be retrieved. It can be one of three values (1 for pending, 2 for rejected, and 3 for approved; these values are coded in the Constants interface that is shown in Listing 13-14).

Listing 13-14. Constants Interface

```
package com.jsfprohtml5.megaapp.model;

public interface Constants {
    public static int USER_GROUP = 1;
    public static int ADMIN_GROUP = 2;

    public static int PENDING_REQUEST = 1;
    public static int REJECTED_REQUEST = 2;
    public static int APPROVED_REQUEST = 3;

    public static String APP_PDF_TYPE = "application/pdf";
}
```

viewRequest method gets the user role using its provided user ID by calling getUserGroup private method. If the user role is ADMIN_GROUP, then the user will retrieve all of the requests under the provided status (pending, rejected, or approved). If the user role is USER_GROUP, then the user will retrieve only the requests which are sent by the provided user ID under the provided status (pending or rejected or approved).

viewRequest method will be called from backing beans in order to view pending, rejected, and approved book requests for the current logged in user.

Let's check the details of BookRequest JPA entity, which holds the book request attributes. Listing 13-15 shows BookRequest JPA entity class.

Listing 13-15. BookRequest JPA Entity Class

```java
package com.jsfprohtml5.megaapp.model;

import java.io.Serializable;
import javax.persistence.Basic;
import javax.persistence.Column;
import javax.persistence.Entity;
import javax.persistence.GeneratedValue;
import javax.persistence.GenerationType;
import javax.persistence.Id;
import javax.persistence.JoinColumn;
import javax.persistence.ManyToOne;
import javax.persistence.Table;
import javax.validation.constraints.NotNull;

@Entity
@Table(name = "BOOK_REQUEST")
public class BookRequest implements Serializable {
    private static final long serialVersionUID = 132123123120090L;

    @Id
    @GeneratedValue(strategy = GenerationType.IDENTITY)
    @Basic(optional = false)
    @Column(name = "ID")
    private Integer id;

    @Basic(optional = false)
    @Column(name = "REQUEST_TIME")
    private long requestTime;

    @Basic(optional = false)
    @Column(name = "RESPONSE_TIME")
    private long responseTime;

    @Basic(optional = false)
    @NotNull
    @Column(name = "STATUS")
    private int status;
```

```
    @JoinColumn(name = "USER_ID", referencedColumnName = "ID")
    @ManyToOne(optional = false)
    private MegaUser userId;

    @JoinColumn(name = "BOOK_ID", referencedColumnName = "ID")
    @ManyToOne(optional = false)
    private Book bookId;

    public BookRequest() {
    }

    public BookRequest(Integer id) {
        this.id = id;
    }

    public BookRequest(Integer id, long requestTime, long responseTime, int status) {
        this.id = id;
        this.requestTime = requestTime;
        this.responseTime = responseTime;
        this.status = status;
    }

    public Integer getId() {
        return id;
    }

    public void setId(Integer id) {
        this.id = id;
    }

    public long getRequestTime() {
        return requestTime;
    }

    public void setRequestTime(long requestTime) {
        this.requestTime = requestTime;
    }

    public long getResponseTime() {
        return responseTime;
    }

    public void setResponseTime(long responseTime) {
        this.responseTime = responseTime;
    }

    public int getStatus() {
        return status;
    }
```

```java
    public void setStatus(int status) {
        this.status = status;
    }

    public MegaUser getUserId() {
        return userId;
    }

    public void setUserId(MegaUser userId) {
        this.userId = userId;
    }

    public Book getBookId() {
        return bookId;
    }

    public void setBookId(Book bookId) {
        this.bookId = bookId;
    }

    @Override
    public int hashCode() {
        int hash = 0;
        hash += (id != null ? id.hashCode() : 0);
        return hash;
    }

    @Override
    public boolean equals(Object object) {
        if (!(object instanceof BookRequest)) {
            return false;
        }
        BookRequest other = (BookRequest) object;
        if ((this.id == null && other.id != null) || (this.id != null &&
!this.id.equals(other.id))) {
            return false;
        }
        return true;
    }

    @Override
    public String toString() {
        return "com.jsfprohtml5.megaapp.model.BookRequest[ id=" + id + " ]";
    }
}
```

BookRequest JPA entity class has the following attributes:

- id: Marked as a primary key for the entity using @Id annotation. It is an auto-generated attribute.

- requestTime: A long type field to represent the request time.

- responseTime: A long type field to represent the response time.

- status: An integer field to represent the request status. It can have one of three values (1 for pending, 2 for rejected, and 3 for approved).

- userId: Represents the request associated user object.

- bookId: Represents the request associated book object.

These are the available three service EJBs; as can be noticed in the previous code snippets, many methods of the manager EJBs throw instances of the following custom exceptions:

- BookAlreadyExists

- BookNotFound

- BookRequestAlreadyExists

- BookRequestNotFound

- UserAlreadyExists

- UserNotFound

All of these custom exceptions inherit from java.lang.Exception. Listing 13-16 shows BookAlreadyExists exception as an example.

Listing 13-16. BookAlreadyExists Exception

```
package com.jsfprohtml5.megaapp.service.exception;

import javax.ejb.ApplicationException;

@ApplicationException(rollback=true)
public class BookAlreadyExists extends Exception {
    public BookAlreadyExists () {
        this.message = "Book already exists";
    }

    public BookAlreadyExists(String message) {
        this.message = message;
    }

    @Override
    public String getMessage() {
        return this.message;
    }

    private String message;
}
```

■ **Note** It is recommended to annotate custom application exception with @ApplicationException in order to avoid having them wrapped in container exceptions. Doing this will allow the EJB client to catch the thrown exceptions directly without having to unwrap container exceptions.

Composing Page Templates

Mega App relies on two templates under WEB-INF/templates folder:

1. simple.xhtml template, which is used as a template for the public pages in the application such as the login and registration pages.

2. main.xhtml template, which is used as a template for all the protected pages in the application such as book requests and book search pages.

simple.xhtml template is a basic template which consists of a header, a content, and a footer. Listing 13-17 shows simple.xhtml template.

Listing 13-17. simple.xhtml Template

```
<?xml version='1.0' encoding='UTF-8' ?>
<!DOCTYPE html>
<html xmlns="http://www.w3.org/1999/xhtml"
      xmlns:ui="http://xmlns.jcp.org/jsf/facelets"
      xmlns:h="http://xmlns.jcp.org/jsf/html">

<h:head>
    <title><ui:insert name="title">Welcome to the Mega App</ui:insert></title>
    <meta name="viewport" content="width=device-width, initial-scale=1.0"></meta>

    <ui:include src="common/bootstrapCSS.xhtml"/>
</h:head>

<h:body>
    <div class="container">
        <ui:insert name="header">
            <ui:include src="common/header.xhtml"/>
        </ui:insert>

        <ui:insert name="content"></ui:insert>

        <ui:insert name="footer"></ui:insert>
    </div>
    <ui:include src="common/bootstrapJS.xhtml"/>
</h:body>
</html>
```

As shown in the template, there are three named content elements:

*   "header" element, which is currently initialized by header.xhtml file under /WEB-INF/templates/common folder.

*   "content" element, which can be defined by the page content.

*   "footer" element, which can be defined by the page footer.

header.xhtml contains the navigation bar, which includes links to the home page, contact us page, and About page. The header pages also contains the header text as shown in Listing 13-18.

Listing 13-18. header.xhtml Page

```
<html xmlns="http://www.w3.org/1999/xhtml"
      xmlns:ui="http://xmlns.jcp.org/jsf/facelets">
   <ui:composition>
       <div class="navbar">
           <div class="navbar-inner">
           <a class="brand" href="#{request.contextPath}/protected/pages/bookSearch.xhtml">Mega App</a>
           <ul class="nav">
               <li><a href="#{request.contextPath}/public/pages/contactUs.xhtml">Contact Us</a></li>
               <li><a href="#{request.contextPath}/public/pages/about.xhtml">About</a></li>
           </ul>
           </div>
       </div>
       <div class="page-header">
           <h1><ui:insert name="headerText">Welcome to the online library</ui:insert></h1>
       </div>
   </ui:composition>
</html>
```

■ **Note**   The navigation bar HTML fragment is simplified and converted to a JSF composite component, check "Composing JSF Components" section.

---

bootstrapCSS.xhtml file contains the bootstrap CSS files include which is shown in Listing 13-19.

Listing 13-19. bootstrapCSS.xhtml File

```
<html xmlns="http://www.w3.org/1999/xhtml"
      xmlns:ui="http://xmlns.jcp.org/jsf/facelets">
   <ui:composition>
        <!-- Bootstrap CSS -->
        <link href="#{request.contextPath}/css/bootstrap.min.css" rel="stylesheet" media="screen"></link>
        <link href="#{request.contextPath}/css/bootstrap-responsive.css" rel="stylesheet"></link>
        <link href="#{request.contextPath}/css/megaapp.css" rel="stylesheet"></link>
   </ui:composition>
</html>
```

bootstrapJS.xhtml file contains the bootstrap JavaScript files include which is shown in Listing 13-20.

Listing 13-20. bootstrapJS.xhtml File

```
<html xmlns="http://www.w3.org/1999/xhtml"
      xmlns:ui="http://xmlns.jcp.org/jsf/facelets">
   <ui:composition>

        <!-- Bootstrap JS -->
        <script src="#{request.contextPath}/js/jquery.js"></script>
        <script src="#{request.contextPath}/js/bootstrap.js"></script>
   </ui:composition>
</html>
```

main.xhtml template consists mainly of a metadata section, a header, a side menu, a content, and a footer. Listing 13-21 shows main.xhtml template.

Listing 13-21. main.xhtml Template

```
<?xml version='1.0' encoding='UTF-8' ?>
<!DOCTYPE html>
<html xmlns="http://www.w3.org/1999/xhtml"
      xmlns:ui="http://xmlns.jcp.org/jsf/facelets"
      xmlns:h="http://xmlns.jcp.org/jsf/html"
      xmlns:f="http://xmlns.jcp.org/jsf/core">

<f:view contentType="text/html">
    <ui:insert name="metadata"/>
    <h:head>
        <title><ui:insert name="title">Welcome to the Mega App</ui:insert></title>
        <meta name="viewport" content="width=device-width, initial-scale=1.0"></meta>

        <ui:include src="common/bootstrapCSS.xhtml"/>
    </h:head>

    <h:body>
        <div class="container">
            <ui:insert name="header">
                <ui:include src="common/header.xhtml"/>
            </ui:insert>

            <div class="row-fluid">
                <div class="span3">
                    <ui:insert name="menu"/>
                </div>

                <div class="span9">
                    <ui:insert name="content"/>
                </div>
             </div>

            <ui:insert name="footer"></ui:insert>
        </div>

        <ui:include src="common/bootstrapJS.xhtml"/>
    </h:body>
</f:view>
</html>
```

As shown in the template, there are mainly five named content elements:

- "metadata" element, which can be defined by the page in order to declare <f:metadata> with its children elements if needed.

- "header" element, which is currently initialized by the header.xhtml file.

- "menu" element, which can be defined by the page's side menu.

- "content" element, which can be defined by the page content.

- "footer" element, which can be defined by the page footer.

There is currently a unified side menu for all of Mega App users, Listing 13-22 shows menu.xhtml page.

Listing 13-22. menu.xhtml Page

```xml
<?xml version='1.0' encoding='UTF-8' ?>
<!DOCTYPE html>
<html xmlns="http://www.w3.org/1999/xhtml"
      xmlns:c="http://xmlns.jcp.org/jsp/jstl/core"
      xmlns:h="http://xmlns.jcp.org/jsf/html"
      xmlns:ui="http://xmlns.jcp.org/jsf/facelets">

    <h:form id="navForm">

        <ui:param name="currentPage" value="#{facesContext.viewRoot.viewId}#{(empty request.
queryString)?'':'?'.concat(request.queryString)}"/>

        <ul class="nav nav-list">
            <li class="nav-header">Welcome #{request.userPrincipal.name}</li>
            <li class="#{currentPage == '/protected/pages/bookSearch.xhtml'?'active':''}">
                <a href="#{request.contextPath}/protected/pages/bookSearch.xhtml">Search for books</a>
            </li>

            <li class="#{currentPage == '/protected/pages/bookRequests.xhtml?status=1'?'active':''}">
                <a href="#{request.contextPath}/protected/pages/bookRequests.xhtml?status=1">View
Pending Requests</a>
            </li>

            <li class="#{currentPage == '/protected/pages/bookRequests.xhtml?status=3'?'active':''}">
                <a href="#{request.contextPath}/protected/pages/bookRequests.xhtml?status=3">View
Approved Requests</a>
            </li>

            <li class="#{currentPage == '/protected/pages/bookRequests.xhtml?status=2'?'active':''}">
                <a href="#{request.contextPath}/protected/pages/bookRequests.xhtml?status=2">View
Rejected Requests</a>
            </li>

            <c:if test="#{request.isUserInRole('megaAppAdmin')}">
                <li class="#{currentPage == '/protected/pages/admin/bookAdd.xhtml'?'active':''}">
                    <a href="#{request.contextPath}/protected/pages/admin/bookAdd.xhtml">Add a book</a>
                </li>

                <li class="#{currentPage == '/protected/pages/admin/userList.xhtml'?'active':''}">
                    <a href="#{request.contextPath}/protected/pages/admin/userList.xhtml">View users</a>
                </li>
            </c:if>

            <li><h:commandLink action="#{logoutBacking.logout}">Logout</h:commandLink></li>
        </ul>
    </h:form>

</html>
```

There are two main things that needs to be highlighted in the menu:

1. currentPage parameter is constructed with the current JSF view ID and query parameter in order to highlight the current selected menu item.

2. There are two protected menu items that appear only for the application administrator which are "Add a book" and "View users" items.

Composing JSF Pages and Backing Beans

Figure 13-14 shows the structure of the application pages and resources.

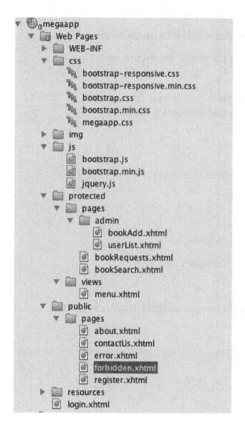

Figure 13-14. *Mega App pages and resources structure*

Under Web Pages folder there are

1. css folder: Contains the application CSS files (bootstrap CSS files "bootstrap*.css") and megaapp.css, which includes the custom application CSS customizations.

2. img folder: Contains bootstrap images.

3. js folder: Includes bootstrap JavaScript files and jquery.js which bootstrap depends on.

4. protected folder: Contains all of the protected pages. Only authenticated user are able to access pages inside this folder. Under the protected folder, there are two main folders:

    a. pages folder: Contains the protected pages that are accessible by all of the authenticated users, which are

        -   bookSearch.xhtml page, which allows the user to search for books.

        -   bookRequests.xhtml page, which allows the user to see his/her pending, approved, and rejected book requests.

        -   admin folder: Contains the admin protected pages, which are accessible only by administrator users. It has the following pages:

            bookAdd.xhtml page, which allows the administrator user to add new books.

            userList.xhtml page, which allows the administrator user to list and manage users.

    b. views folder: Contains the view fragments that are used by the pages. It contains only one file (menu.xhtml) which renders the side menu.

5. public folder: Contains all of the public pages that can be accessed by everyone (including unauthenticated users). Under public folder, there is one main folder (pages folder) which contains the application public pages:

    a. about.xhtml page, which represents the about page.

    b. contactUs.xhtml page, which represents the contact us page.

    c. error.xhtml page, which represents the general error page.

    d. forbidden.xhtml page, which the forbidden access page.

    e. register.xhtml page, which allows the application user to register.

6. resources folder: Contains all of the application composite JSF components.

7. login.xhtml is the application login page.

Now, let's go through the application pages. Mega App uses container-managed security in order to handle authentication and authorization. Listing 13-23 shows login.xhtml page.

Listing 13-23. login.xhtml Page

```
<?xml version='1.0' encoding='UTF-8' ?>
<!DOCTYPE html>
<html xmlns="http://www.w3.org/1999/xhtml"
      xmlns:ui="http://xmlns.jcp.org/jsf/facelets"
      xmlns:h="http://xmlns.jcp.org/jsf/html">

<ui:composition template="/WEB-INF/templates/simple.xhtml">

    <ui:define name="content">

        <form action="j_security_check" method="POST" class="form-center">
            Username:<input type="text"
                            name="j_username"
                            placeholder="login name"
                            class="input-block-level"></input>
```

```
               Password:<input type="password"
                               name="j_password"
                               placeholder="Password"
                               class="input-block-level"></input>

               <button type="submit"
                       class="btn btn-large btn-primary">Sign In</button>

               <br/><br/>

               <h:link value="Not registered? Register now"
                       styleClass="input-block-level"
                       outcome="/public/pages/register"/>
           </form>

       </ui:define>
</ui:composition>

</html>
```

As you know from Chapter 12, in order to use form-based authentication, we have to use the HTML <form> tag; setting the form action to "j_security_check" and the form method "POST", setting the names of the username and password fields to "j_username" and "j_password", and finally adding a submit button to submit the form.

When the user clicks the register link at the end of the login page, the user is directed to the registration page. Listing 13-24 shows the register.xhtml page.

Listing 13-24. register.xhtml Page

```
<?xml version='1.0' encoding='UTF-8' ?>
<!DOCTYPE html>
<html xmlns="http://www.w3.org/1999/xhtml"
      xmlns:ui="http://xmlns.jcp.org/jsf/facelets"
      xmlns:h="http://xmlns.jcp.org/jsf/html"
      xmlns:f="http://xmlns.jcp.org/jsf/core">

<ui:composition template="/WEB-INF/templates/simple.xhtml">

    <ui:define name="content">

        <h:form id="registerUserForm" styleClass="form-horizontal form-center">
            <h3>Register</h3>

            <h:outputText id="informationMessage"
                          value="#{userAddBacking.infoMessage}"
                          rendered="#{userAddBacking.infoMessage ne null}"
                          class="informationMessage">
            </h:outputText>

            <div class="form-group">
                <h:outputLabel value="Login Name" for="loginName"/>
```

```
                   <h:inputText id="loginName" value="#{newUser.id}"
                            class="form-control" required="true">
                       <f:passThroughAttribute name="placeHolder" value="Login Name"/>
                   </h:inputText>
               </div>

               <div class="form-group">
                   <h:outputLabel value="Password" for="password"/>
                   <h:inputSecret id="password" value="#{newUser.password}"
                            class="form-control" required="true">
                   </h:inputSecret>
               </div>

               <div class="form-group">
                   <h:outputLabel value="Confirm password" for="password2"/>
                   <h:inputSecret id="password2" value="#{newUser.password2}"
                            class="form-control" required="true">
                   </h:inputSecret>
               </div>

               <div class="form-group">
                   <h:outputLabel value="First Name" for="fname"/>

                   <h:inputText id="fname" value="#{newUser.firstName}"
                            class="form-control" required="true">
                       <f:passThroughAttribute name="placeHolder" value="First Name"/>
                   </h:inputText>
               </div>

               <div class="form-group">
                   <h:outputLabel value="Last Name" for="lname"/>
                   <h:inputText id="lname" value="#{newUser.lastName}"
                            class="form-control" required="true">
                       <f:passThroughAttribute name="placeHolder" value="Last Name"/>
                   </h:inputText>
               </div>

               <br/>
               <h:commandButton value="Register User" class="btn" action="#{userAddBacking.registerUser}">
                   <f:ajax execute="@form" render="@form"/>
               </h:commandButton>

               <br/><br/>
               <h:link outcome="/login.xhtml" value="Back"/>

               <br/><br/>
               <h:messages id="messages" class="errorMessage"/>
           </h:form>
       </ui:define>
   </ui:composition>
   </html>
```

The registration form includes the corresponding input fields to the Mega App user attributes, which were described in Listing 13-9. When the user clicks the "Register User" command button, and using the <f:ajax> tag, the registration form attributes are sent to the server, #{userAddBacking.registerUser} action method is executed, and finally either a success message or a failure message(s) is rendered to the client. Listing 13-25 shows UserAddBacking CDI managed bean.

Listing 13-25. UserAddBacking CDI Managed Bean

```
package com.jsfprohtml5.megaapp.backing;

import com.jsfprohtml5.megaapp.model.MegaUser;
import com.jsfprohtml5.megaapp.service.MegaUserManagerLocal;
import com.jsfprohtml5.megaapp.service.exception.UserAlreadyExists;
import java.io.Serializable;
import java.util.logging.Level;
import java.util.logging.Logger;
import javax.ejb.EJB;
import javax.enterprise.context.RequestScoped;
import javax.enterprise.inject.Produces;
import javax.faces.application.FacesMessage;
import javax.inject.Named;
import javax.faces.view.ViewScoped;

@Named
@ViewScoped
public class UserAddBacking extends BaseBacking implements Serializable {
    @EJB
    private MegaUserManagerLocal userManager;

    @Named
    @Produces
    @RequestScoped
    private MegaUser newUser = new MegaUser();

    private String infoMessage;

    public String getInfoMessage() {
        return infoMessage;
    }

    public void setInfoMessage(String infoMessage) {
        this.infoMessage = infoMessage;
    }

    public String registerUser() {
        if (! newUser.getPassword().equals(newUser.getPassword2())) {
            getContext().addMessage(null, new FacesMessage("Passwords must be identical"));

            return null;
        }
```

```
        try {
            userManager.registerMegaUser(newUser);
            infoMessage = "User saved successfully";

            newUser = new MegaUser();
        } catch (UserAlreadyExists ex) {
            Logger.getLogger(UserAddBacking.class.getName()).log(Level.SEVERE, null, ex);
            infoMessage = "Login name already exists";
        } catch (Exception ex) {
            Logger.getLogger(UserAddBacking.class.getName()).log(Level.SEVERE, null, ex);
            getContext().addMessage(null, new FacesMessage("An error occurs while registering user"));
        }

        return null;
    }
}
```

Before going into the registration details, there are two points that need to be highlighted:

1. `@javax.faces.view.ViewScoped` annotation: It is important to know that CDI does not have view scope but since CDI is an extensible framework, JSF 2.2 provided an implementation for CDI View scope and provided the `@javax.faces.view.ViewScoped` annotation.

2. `@Produces` annotation: A CDI annotation that is used to identify a method or a field as a producer method or field. A producer method or field is called whenever another bean in the application needs an injected object. If `@Produces` annotation is combined with `@Named` annotation with `@xxxScoped`, this will allow this producer field to be available in the JSF expression language for the specified xxx scope. In our case, a prototype `MegaUser` is being exposed using the named producer to the JSF expression language in the JSF Facelets page in the request scope, which means it can be accessed using `#{newUser.xxx}` expression.

■ **Caution** It is very important not to be confused by `@javax.faces.view.ViewScoped` and `@javax.faces.bean.ViewScoped` annotations; the first one is the JSF 2.2 CDI implementation for the view scope, while the second one is the JSF managed bean view scope, NOT the CDI one.

`registerUser` method validates that the entered user password is equal to the confirmed user password and then calls `registerMegaUser` method of `MegaUserManager` EJB to register the user.

After the user logs in to the system, the user is redirected "by default" to `bookSearch.xhtml` page. Listing 13-26 shows `bookSearch.xhtml` page code.

Listing 13-26. bookSearch.xhtml Page Code

```
<?xml version='1.0' encoding='UTF-8' ?>
<!DOCTYPE html>
<html xmlns="http://www.w3.org/1999/xhtml"
      xmlns:ui="http://xmlns.jcp.org/jsf/facelets"
      xmlns:h="http://xmlns.jcp.org/jsf/html"
      xmlns:f="http://xmlns.jcp.org/jsf/core"
      xmlns:c="http://xmlns.jcp.org/jsp/jstl/core">
```

```
<ui:composition template="/WEB-INF/templates/main.xhtml">
    <ui:define name="menu">
        <ui:include src="/protected/views/menu.xhtml"/>
    </ui:define>

    <ui:define name="content">
        <h3>Search for books</h3>
        <h:form id="searchForm" class="form-search">

            <h:outputText value="Enter book title: "/>
            <h:inputText id="searchTitle" class="search-query input-medium"
                        value="#{bookSearchBacking.searchTitle}"
                        required="true"/> 

            <h:commandButton value="Search for book" class="btn" action="#{bookSearchBacking.
retrieveBookList}">
                <f:ajax execute="searchTitle" render="results messages"/>
            </h:commandButton>

            <br/><br/>

            <h:panelGroup id="results" class="table-responsive">

                <h:outputText id="informationMessage"
                            value="#{bookSearchBacking.infoMessage}"
                            rendered="#{bookSearchBacking.infoMessage ne null}"
                            class="informationMessage"/>

                <h:dataTable value="#{bookSearchBacking.bookList}"
                            var="currentBook" class="table"
                            rendered="#{not empty bookSearchBacking.bookList}">

                    <h:column>
                        <f:facet name="header">
                            ISBN
                        </f:facet>
                        #{currentBook.isbn}
                    </h:column>
                    <h:column>
                        <f:facet name="header">
                            Publisher
                        </f:facet>
                        #{currentBook.publisher}
                    </h:column>
                    <h:column>
                        <f:facet name="header">
                            Title
                        </f:facet>
                        #{currentBook.title}
                    </h:column>
```

```
            <h:column>
                <f:facet name="header">
                    Actions
                </f:facet>

                <c:if test="#{request.isUserInRole('megaAppUser')}">
                    <h:commandLink value="Request Copy"
action="#{bookSearchBacking.requestBookCopy}">
                        <f:setPropertyActionListener
target="#{bookSearchBacking.selectedBook}" value="#{currentBook}" />
                        <f:ajax render=":searchForm:results :searchForm:messages" />
                    </h:commandLink>
                </c:if>

                <c:if test="#{request.isUserInRole('megaAppAdmin')}">
                    <h:commandLink value="Delete" action="#{bookSearchBacking.deleteBook}">
                        <f:setPropertyActionListener
target="#{bookSearchBacking.selectedBook}" value="#{currentBook}" />
                        <f:ajax render=":searchForm:results :searchForm:messages" />
                    </h:commandLink> <br/>
                    <h:commandLink value="Download book"
action="#{bookSearchBacking.downloadBook}">
                        <f:setPropertyActionListener
target="#{bookSearchBacking.selectedBook}" value="#{currentBook}" />
                    </h:commandLink>
                </c:if>

            </h:column>

        </h:dataTable>

    </h:panelGroup>

    <h:messages id="messages" class="errorMessage"/>
        </h:form>
    </ui:define>
</ui:composition>

</html>
```

When the user enters a book title in the "searchTitle" input text and then clicks the "Search for books" command button, and using the <f:ajax> tag, the "searchTitle" input value is sent to the server, the #{bookSearchBacking.retrieveBookList} action method is executed, and finally the "results" panel is rendered with the retrieved books list and the number of displayed books. The <h:dataTable> component inside the "results" panel is populated with the book list; every row in the data table renders a book with the following information:

- ISBN
- Publisher
- Title

As shown in the bolded lines, the Action column shows the available action based on the user role using #{request.isUserInRole}:

- If the user is a member in megaAppUser group (i.e., Mega App user), then the only available action is "Request Copy".

- If the user is a member in megaAppAdmin group (i.e., Mega App administrator), then the available actions are ("Delete Book" and "Download Book").

In all of the operations inside data table ("Request Copy", "Delete Book", and "Download Book"), a property action listener is executed in order to bind the currently selected book (#{currentBook}) with the (#{bookSearchBacking.selectedBook}) property before performing the actual action. Listing 13-27 shows BookSearchBacking CDI bean.

Listing 13-27. BookSearchBacking CDI Bean

```
package com.jsfprohtml5.megaapp.backing;
import com.jsfprohtml5.megaapp.model.Book;
import com.jsfprohtml5.megaapp.model.BookRequest;
import com.jsfprohtml5.megaapp.model.Constants;
import com.jsfprohtml5.megaapp.model.MegaUser;
import com.jsfprohtml5.megaapp.service.BookManagerLocal;
import com.jsfprohtml5.megaapp.service.BookRequestManagerLocal;
import com.jsfprohtml5.megaapp.service.exception.BookNotFound;
import com.jsfprohtml5.megaapp.service.exception.BookRequestAlreadyExists;
import java.io.IOException;
import java.io.OutputStream;
import java.io.Serializable;
import java.util.List;
import java.util.logging.Level;
import java.util.logging.Logger;
import javax.ejb.EJB;
import javax.faces.application.FacesMessage;
import javax.faces.context.ExternalContext;
import javax.inject.Named;
import javax.faces.view.ViewScoped;

@Named
@ViewScoped
public class BookSearchBacking extends BaseBacking implements Serializable {
    @EJB
    private BookManagerLocal bookManager;

    @EJB
    private BookRequestManagerLocal bookRequestManager;

    private List<Book> bookList;
    private String searchTitle;
    private String infoMessage;
    private Book selectedBook;
```

```java
    public String getSearchTitle() {
        return searchTitle;
    }

    public void setSearchTitle(String searchTitle) {
        this.searchTitle = searchTitle;
    }

    public List<Book> getBookList() {
        return bookList;
    }

    public void setBookList(List<Book> bookList) {
        this.bookList = bookList;
    }

    public String getInfoMessage() {
        return infoMessage;
    }

    public void setInfoMessage(String infoMessage) {
        this.infoMessage = infoMessage;
    }

    public Book getSelectedBook() {
        return selectedBook;
    }

    public void setSelectedBook(Book selectedBook) {
        this.selectedBook = selectedBook;
    }

    public String retrieveBookList() {
        Book searchableBook = new Book();

        searchableBook.setTitle(searchTitle);

        bookList = bookManager.getAllBooks(searchableBook);

        if (bookList.isEmpty()) {
            infoMessage = "No Book results found";
        } else {
            infoMessage = bookList.size() + " book(s) found";
        }

        return null;
    }

    public String requestBookCopy() {
        BookRequest bookRequest = new BookRequest();
        MegaUser megaUser = new MegaUser();
```

```
            megaUser.setId(getRequest().getUserPrincipal().getName());

            bookRequest.setUserId(megaUser);
            bookRequest.setBookId(getSelectedBook());

            try {
                bookRequestManager.sendBookRequest(bookRequest);
                infoMessage = "Book request sent";
            } catch (BookRequestAlreadyExists ex) {
                Logger.getLogger(BookSearchBacking.class.getName()).log(Level.SEVERE, null, ex);
                infoMessage = "You already sent a request for this book";
            } catch (Exception ex) {
                Logger.getLogger(BookSearchBacking.class.getName()).log(Level.SEVERE, null, ex);
                getContext().addMessage(null, new FacesMessage("An error occurs while sending book request"));
            }

            return null;
        }

    public String deleteBook() {
        try {
            Book currentSelectedBook = getSelectedBook();

            bookManager.removeBook(currentSelectedBook.getId());
            bookList.remove(currentSelectedBook);

            infoMessage = "Book deleted successfully";
        } catch (BookNotFound ex) {
            Logger.getLogger(BookSearchBacking.class.getName()).log(Level.SEVERE, null, ex);
            getContext().addMessage(null, new FacesMessage("An error occurs while deleting the book"));
        }

        return null;
    }

    public String downloadBook() {
        Book currentSelectedBook = getSelectedBook();
        Book book;
        byte[] content;

        try {
            book = bookManager.getBookInformation(currentSelectedBook.getId());
            content = bookManager.getBookContent(currentSelectedBook.getId());
        } catch (BookNotFound ex) {
            Logger.getLogger(BookSearchBacking.class.getName()).log(Level.SEVERE,
"No books found !!!", ex);
            return null;
        }

        ExternalContext externalContext = getContext().getExternalContext();
```

```
        externalContext.responseReset();
        externalContext.setResponseContentType(Constants.APP_PDF_TYPE);
        externalContext.setResponseContentLength(content.length);
        externalContext.setResponseHeader("Content-Disposition", "attachment; filename=\""
+ book.getTitle() + ".pdf\"");
        OutputStream output = null;

        try {
            output = externalContext.getResponseOutputStream();

            output.write(content);

            output.flush();
            output.close();
        } catch (IOException ex) {
            Logger.getLogger(BookSearchBacking.class.getName()).log(Level.SEVERE, null, ex);
        } finally {
            getContext().responseComplete();
        }

        return null;
    }
}
```

The main methods of BookSearchBacking CDI bean are as follows:

- retrieveBookList: Calls getAllBooks method of BookManager EJB passing searchableBook
  object, which contains the searchable title as a parameter. If there are no results returned, a
  "No Book results found" message is displayed to the user. If results are returned, a message
  with the number of returned books is displayed to the user including the books list.

- requestBookCopy: Calls sendBookRequest method of BookManager EJB passing bookRequest
  object (which contains the request owner user and the target book) as a parameter. If the request
  is sent successfully, a "Book request sent" information message is displayed to the user.

- deleteBook: Calls removeBook method of BookManager EJB passing the currently selected book
  ID as a parameter. If the operation is done successfully, a "Book deleted successfully"
  information message is displayed to the user.

- downloadBook: Calls getBookContent method of BookManager EJB passing the currently
  selected book ID as a parameter; in order to give the downloadable content a meaningful
  name, the book title is retrieved using getBookInformation method of BookManager EJB.

In order to follow up on the requests, the Mega App (administrator or user) can use the bookRequests.xhtml
page. Listing 13-28 shows the bookRequests.xhtml page.

Listing 13-28. bookRequests.xhtml Page

```
<?xml version='1.0' encoding='UTF-8' ?>
<!DOCTYPE html>
<html xmlns="http://www.w3.org/1999/xhtml"
      xmlns:ui="http://xmlns.jcp.org/jsf/facelets"
      xmlns:h="http://xmlns.jcp.org/jsf/html"
      xmlns:c="http://xmlns.jcp.org/jsp/jstl/core"
      xmlns:f="http://java.sun.com/jsf/core">
```

```xml
<ui:composition template="/WEB-INF/templates/main.xhtml">
    <ui:define name="metadata">
        <f:metadata>
            <f:viewParam name="status" value="#{bookRequestsBacking.status}">
                <f:validateLongRange minimum="1" maximum="3"/>
            </f:viewParam>

            <f:event listener="#{bookRequestsBacking.retrieveBookRequests}" type="preRenderView"/>
        </f:metadata>
    </ui:define>

    <ui:define name="menu">
        <ui:include src="/protected/views/menu.xhtml"/>
    </ui:define>

    <ui:define name="content">
        <h3>
            <c:if test="#{bookRequestsBacking.status eq 1}">
                Pending Requests
            </c:if>
            <c:if test="#{bookRequestsBacking.status eq 2}">
                Rejected Requests
            </c:if>
            <c:if test="#{bookRequestsBacking.status eq 3}">
                Approved Requests
            </c:if>
        </h3>
        <h:form id="bookRequestForm">
            <h:panelGroup id="results" class="table-responsive">
                <h:outputText id="informationMessage"
                              value="#{bookRequestsBacking.infoMessage}"
                              rendered="#{bookRequestsBacking.infoMessage ne null}"
                              class="informationMessage"/>

                <h:dataTable value="#{bookRequestsBacking.bookRequestList}"
                             var="bookRequest" class="table"
                             rendered="#{not empty bookRequestsBacking.bookRequestList}">

                    <h:column>
                        <f:facet name="header">
                            Book Title
                        </f:facet>
                        #{bookRequest.bookId.title}
                    </h:column>
                    <c:if test="#{bookRequestsBacking.status ne 1}">
                        <h:column>
                            <f:facet name="header">
                                Response Time
                            </f:facet>
```

```
                        <h:outputText value="#{bookRequest.responseTime}">
                            <f:converter converterId="com.jsfprohtml5.megaapp.TimeConverter"/>
                        </h:outputText>
                    </h:column>
                </c:if>
                <h:column>
                    <f:facet name="header">
                        Request Time
                    </f:facet>
                    <h:outputText value="#{bookRequest.requestTime}">
                        <f:converter converterId="com.jsfprohtml5.megaapp.TimeConverter"/>
                    </h:outputText>
                </h:column>

                <c:if test="#{request.isUserInRole('megaAppAdmin')}">
                    <h:column>
                        <f:facet name="header">
                            Request Owner
                        </f:facet>
                        #{bookRequest.userId.id}
                    </h:column>
                </c:if>

                <h:column>
                    <f:facet name="header">
                        Actions
                    </f:facet>

                    <c:if test="#{request.isUserInRole('megaAppUser')}">
                        <c:if test="#{bookRequestsBacking.status eq 1 or
bookRequestsBacking.status eq 2}">
                            NA
                        </c:if>
                        <c:if test="#{bookRequestsBacking.status eq 3}">
                            <h:commandLink value="Download book"
action="#{bookRequestsBacking.downloadBook}">
                                <f:setPropertyActionListener
target="#{bookRequestsBacking.selectedBookRequest}" value="#{bookRequest}" />
                            </h:commandLink>
                        </c:if>
                    </c:if>

                    <c:if test="#{request.isUserInRole('megaAppAdmin')}">
                        <h:commandLink value="Download book"
action="#{bookRequestsBacking.downloadBook}">
                            <f:setPropertyActionListener
target="#{bookRequestsBacking.selectedBookRequest}" value="#{bookRequest}" />
                        </h:commandLink>
                        <c:if test="#{bookRequestsBacking.status eq 1}">
                            <br/>
                            <h:commandLink value="Approve request"
action="#{bookRequestsBacking.approveRequest}">
```

```
                                    <f:setPropertyActionListener
target="#{bookRequestsBacking.selectedBookRequest}" value="#{bookRequest}" />
                                    <f:ajax render=":bookRequestForm:results
:bookRequestForm:messages" />
                                </h:commandLink>
                                <br/>
                                <h:commandLink value="Reject request"
action="#{bookRequestsBacking.rejectRequest}">
                                    <f:setPropertyActionListener
target="#{bookRequestsBacking.selectedBookRequest}" value="#{bookRequest}" />
                                    <f:ajax render=":bookRequestForm:results
:bookRequestForm:messages" />
                                </h:commandLink>
                            </c:if>
                        </c:if>

                    </h:column>

                </h:dataTable>

            </h:panelGroup>

            <h:messages id="messages" class="errorMessage"/>
        </h:form>
    </ui:define>
</ui:composition>

</html>
```

A view parameter is created to map the status parameter to the status attribute of bookRequestsBacking CDI bean via #{bookRequestsBacking.status}, and in the preRenderView event, the requests list under the indicated status (pending or rejected or approved) is retrieved using #{bookRequestsBacking.retrieveBookRequests} expression.

When the requests list is retrieved, the <h:dataTable> component is populated with the requests list; every row in the data table renders a book request with the following information per user role, as shown in Table 13-5.

Table 13-5. *Book Request Attribute Visibility*

Book request attribute	View condition
#{bookRequest.bookId.title}	All users (application administrators + application users)
#{bookRequest.responseTime}	All users (application administrators + application users) for only pending requests
#{bookRequest.requestTime}	All users (application administrators + application users)
#{bookRequest.userId.id}	Appears only for application administrator to show the book request owner

As shown in the bolded lines, the Action column shows the available action based on the user role using #{request.isUserInRole}:

- If the user is a member in megaAppUser group (i.e., Mega App user) and #{bookRequestsBacking.status} is equal to 3 (approved), then the only available action is "Download Book".

- If the user is a member in megaAppAdmin group (i.e., Mega App administrator), then the available actions are "Download Book" for all the book request statuses, "Approve Request", and "Reject Request" if #{bookRequestsBacking.status} equals to 1 (pending).

In all of the operations inside data table ("Approve Request", "Reject Request", and "Download Book"), a property action listener is executed in order to bind the currently selected book request (#{bookRequest}) with the (#{bookRequestsBacking.selectedBookRequest}) property before performing the actual action. Listing 13-29 shows BookRequestsBacking CDI bean.

Listing 13-29. BookRequestsBacking CDI Bean

```
package com.jsfprohtml5.megaapp.backing;
import com.jsfprohtml5.megaapp.model.Book;
import com.jsfprohtml5.megaapp.model.BookRequest;
import com.jsfprohtml5.megaapp.model.Constants;
import com.jsfprohtml5.megaapp.service.BookManagerLocal;
import com.jsfprohtml5.megaapp.service.BookRequestManagerLocal;
import com.jsfprohtml5.megaapp.service.exception.BookNotFound;
import com.jsfprohtml5.megaapp.service.exception.BookRequestNotFound;
import java.io.IOException;
import java.io.OutputStream;
import java.io.Serializable;
import java.util.List;
import java.util.logging.Level;
import java.util.logging.Logger;
import javax.ejb.EJB;
import javax.faces.application.FacesMessage;
import javax.faces.context.ExternalContext;
import javax.faces.event.ComponentSystemEvent;
import javax.inject.Named;
import javax.faces.view.ViewScoped;

@Named
@ViewScoped
public class BookRequestsBacking extends BaseBacking implements Serializable {
    @EJB
    private BookManagerLocal bookManager;

    @EJB
    private BookRequestManagerLocal bookRequestManager;

    private List<BookRequest> bookRequestList;
    private BookRequest selectedBookRequest;

    private int status = 1;
    private String infoMessage;
```

```
public List<BookRequest> getBookRequestList() {
    return bookRequestList;
}

public void setBookRequestList(List<BookRequest> bookRequestList) {
    this.bookRequestList = bookRequestList;
}

public BookRequest getSelectedBookRequest() {
    return selectedBookRequest;
}

public void setSelectedBookRequest(BookRequest selectedBookRequest) {
    this.selectedBookRequest = selectedBookRequest;
}

public int getStatus() {
    return status;
}

public String getInfoMessage() {
    return infoMessage;
}

public void setInfoMessage(String infoMessage) {
    this.infoMessage = infoMessage;
}

public void setStatus(int status) {
    this.status = status;
}

public void retrieveBookRequests(ComponentSystemEvent event) {
    bookRequestList = bookRequestManager.viewRequests(getRequest().getUserPrincipal().getName(),
                                                      status);

    if (bookRequestList.isEmpty()) {
        infoMessage = "No Requests found";
    } else {
        infoMessage = bookRequestList.size() + " request(s) found";
    }

}

public String downloadBook() {
    Book currentSelectedBook = getSelectedBookRequest().getBookId();

    Book book;
    byte[] content;
```

367

```
        try {
            book = bookManager.getBookInformation(currentSelectedBook.getId());
            content = bookManager.getBookContent(currentSelectedBook.getId());

        } catch (BookNotFound ex) {
            Logger.getLogger(BookRequestsBacking.class.getName()).log(Level.SEVERE,
"No books found !!!", ex);
            return null;
        }

        ExternalContext externalContext = getContext().getExternalContext();

        externalContext.responseReset();
        externalContext.setResponseContentType(Constants.APP_PDF_TYPE);
        externalContext.setResponseContentLength(content.length);
        externalContext.setResponseHeader("Content-Disposition", "attachment; filename=\""
+ book.getTitle() + ".pdf\"");
        OutputStream output = null;

        try {
            output = externalContext.getResponseOutputStream();

            output.write(content);

            output.flush();
            output.close();
        } catch (IOException ex) {
            Logger.getLogger(BookRequestsBacking.class.getName()).log(Level.SEVERE, null, ex);
            getContext().addMessage(null, new FacesMessage("An error occurs while downloading book"));
        } finally {
            getContext().responseComplete();
        }

        return null;
    }

    public String approveRequest() {
        BookRequest currentBookRequest = getSelectedBookRequest();

        try {
            bookRequestManager.approveBookRequest(currentBookRequest.getId());
            infoMessage = "Book Request Approved";
        } catch (BookRequestNotFound ex) {
            Logger.getLogger(BookRequestsBacking.class.getName()).log(Level.SEVERE, null, ex);
            getContext().addMessage(null, new FacesMessage("An error occurs while approving book
request"));
        }

        return null;
    }
```

```java
    public String rejectRequest() {
        BookRequest currentBookRequest = getSelectedBookRequest();

        try {
            bookRequestManager.rejectBookRequest(currentBookRequest.getId());
            infoMessage = "Book Request Rejected";
        } catch (BookRequestNotFound ex) {
            Logger.getLogger(BookRequestsBacking.class.getName()).log(Level.SEVERE, null, ex);
            getContext().addMessage(null, new FacesMessage("An error occurs while rejecting book
request"));
        }

        return null;
    }
}
```

The main methods of BookRequestsBacking CDI bean are as follows:

- retrieveBookRequests: Calls viewRequests method of BookRequestManager EJB passing the logged in user ID and requests list type (0 for pending, 1 for rejected, and 2 for approved) as parameters. If there is no results returned, a "No Requests found" message is displayed to the user. If results are returned, a message with the number of returned requests is displayed, including the requests list.

- downloadBook: Calls getBookContent method of BookManager EJB passing the currently selected book ID (using getSelectedBookRequest().getBookId()) as a parameter; and in order to give the downloadable content a meaningful name, the book title is retrieved using getBookInformation method of BookManager EJB.

- approveRequest: Calls approveBookRequest method of BookRequestManager EJB passing the book request ID as a parameter. If the operation succeeds, then the following "Book Request Approved" message will be displayed to the user.

- rejectRequest: Calls rejectBookRequest method of BookRequestManager EJB passing the book request ID as a parameter. If the operation succeeds, then the following "Book Request Rejected" message will be displayed to the user.

■ **Caution**   Currently in early builds of Mojarra 2.2, <f:viewParam> does not work if you use the new JSF 2.2 namespace, "http://xmlns.jcp.org/jsf/core". In order to fix this issue, just use the old JSF core namespace, "http://java.sun.com/jsf/core".

Now, it is the time to move to the administrator pages. Listing 13-30 shows bookAdd.xhtml, which is used for adding new books by the administrator.

Listing 13-30. bookAdd.xhtml Page

```xml
<?xml version='1.0' encoding='UTF-8' ?>
<!DOCTYPE html>
<html xmlns="http://www.w3.org/1999/xhtml"
      xmlns:ui="http://xmlns.jcp.org/jsf/facelets"
      xmlns:h="http://xmlns.jcp.org/jsf/html"
      xmlns:f="http://xmlns.jcp.org/jsf/core">
```

```
<ui:composition template="/WEB-INF/templates/main.xhtml">
    <ui:define name="menu">
        <ui:include src="/protected/views/menu.xhtml"/>
    </ui:define>

    <ui:define name="content">
        <h3>Add a new book</h3>
        <h:form id="bookAddForm" enctype="multipart/form-data" styleClass="form-horizontal">
            <h:outputText id="informationMessage"
                          value="#{bookAddBacking.infoMessage}"
                          rendered="#{bookAddBacking.infoMessage ne null}"
                          class="informationMessage"/>

            <div class="form-group">
                <h:outputLabel value="ISBN" for="isbn"/>

                <h:inputText id="isbn" value="#{newBook.isbn}"
                             class="form-control" required="true">
                    <f:passThroughAttribute name="placeHolder" value="Enter ISBN"/>
                </h:inputText>

            </div>
            <div class="form-group">
                <h:outputLabel value="Title" for="title"/>
                <h:inputText id="title" value="#{newBook.title}"
                             class="form-control" required="true">
                    <f:passThroughAttribute name="placeHolder" value="Enter Title"/>
                </h:inputText>
            </div>
            <div class="form-group">
                <h:outputLabel value="Author" for="author"/>
                <h:inputText id="author" value="#{newBook.author}"
                             class="form-control" required="true">
                    <f:passThroughAttribute name="placeHolder" value="Enter Author"/>
                </h:inputText>
            </div>

            <div class="form-group">
                <h:outputLabel value="Publisher" for="publisher"/>
                <h:inputText id="publisher" value="#{newBook.publisher}"
                             class="form-control" required="true">
                    <f:passThroughAttribute name="placeHolder" value="Enter Publisher"/>
                </h:inputText>
            </div>

            <div class="form-group">
                <h:outputLabel value="Language" for="language"/>
                <h:selectOneMenu id="language" value="#{newBook.lang}"
                                 class="form-control" required="true">
```

```
                    <f:selectItem itemValue="English" itemLabel="English"/>
                    <f:selectItem itemValue="Others" itemLabel="Others"/>
                </h:selectOneMenu>
            </div>

            <div class="form-group">
                <h:outputLabel value="Content" for="content"/>
                <h:inputFile id="content" value="#{bookAddBacking.filePart}"
                            class="form-control" required="true"
                            validator="#{bookAddBacking.validateFile}">
                </h:inputFile>
            </div>

            <br/>
            <h:commandButton value="Save Book" class="btn btn-default"
action="#{bookAddBacking.saveBook}">
                    <f:ajax execute="@form" render="@all"/>
            </h:commandButton>

            <h:messages id="messages" class="errorMessage"/>
        </h:form>
    </ui:define>
</ui:composition>

</html>
```

The book add form includes the corresponding input fields to the Book JPA entity attributes, which were described in Listing 13-6. When the user clicks the "Save Book" command button, and using the <f:ajax> tag, the book add form attributes are sent to the server, the #{bookAddBacking.saveBook} action method is executed, and finally either a success message or a failure message(s) is rendered to the client.

As you notice, the book add form uses the JSF 2.2 <h:inputFile> component in combination with <f:ajax> in order to upload the book content in an Ajaxified way. In order to have this functionality working, you have to make sure that the form enctype is set to "multipart/form-data".

■ **Caution** There is a bug in Mojarra JSF 2.2 <h:inputFile> component when used with <f:ajax>; this bug results in rendering an extra iframe when the response is returned from the server: https://java.net/jira/browse/ JAVASERVERFACES-2851. In order to solve this issue, you have to use @all in the render attribute of <f:ajax> tag.

Using #{bookAddBacking.validateFile} in the validator attribute of <h:inputFile>, the file size is validated for not exceeding 1 megabyte and the file type is validated to be of type PDF. BookAddBacking CDI bean which includes validateFile is shown in Listing 13-31.

Listing 13-31. BookAddBacking CDI Bean

```
package com.jsfprohtml5.megaapp.backing;
import com.jsfprohtml5.megaapp.model.Book;
import com.jsfprohtml5.megaapp.service.BookManagerLocal;
import com.jsfprohtml5.megaapp.service.exception.BookAlreadyExists;
import java.io.Serializable;
import java.util.ArrayList;
```

```java
import java.util.List;
import java.util.logging.Level;
import java.util.logging.Logger;
import javax.ejb.EJB;
import javax.enterprise.context.RequestScoped;
import javax.enterprise.inject.Produces;
import javax.faces.application.FacesMessage;
import javax.faces.component.UIComponent;
import javax.faces.context.FacesContext;
import javax.faces.validator.ValidatorException;
import javax.inject.Named;
import javax.faces.view.ViewScoped;
import javax.servlet.http.Part;
import org.apache.commons.io.IOUtils;

@Named
@ViewScoped
public class BookAddBacking extends BaseBacking implements Serializable {
    @EJB
    private BookManagerLocal bookManager;

    @Named
    @Produces
    @RequestScoped
    private Book newBook = new Book();

    private String infoMessage;
    private Part filePart;

    public String getInfoMessage() {
        return infoMessage;
    }

    public void setInfoMessage(String infoMessage) {
        this.infoMessage = infoMessage;
    }

    public Part getFilePart() {
        return filePart;
    }

    public void setFilePart(Part filePart) {
        this.filePart = filePart;
    }

    public String saveBook() {
        try {
            byte[] bytes = IOUtils.toByteArray(filePart.getInputStream());

            newBook.setContent(bytes);
```

```
            bookManager.registerBook(newBook);
            infoMessage = "Book saved successfully";

            newBook = new Book();
        } catch (BookAlreadyExists ex) {
            Logger.getLogger(BookAddBacking.class.getName()).log(Level.SEVERE, null, ex);
            infoMessage = "A book with the same ISBN already exists";
        } catch (Exception ex) {
            Logger.getLogger(BookAddBacking.class.getName()).log(Level.SEVERE, null, ex);
            getContext().addMessage(null, new FacesMessage("An error occurs while saving book"));
        }

        return null;
    }

    public void validateFile(FacesContext ctx, UIComponent comp, Object value) {
        List<FacesMessage> msgs = new ArrayList<FacesMessage>();

        Part file = (Part) value;

        if (file.getSize() > 1048576) {
            msgs.add(new FacesMessage("file size must not exceed 1 MB"));
        }

        if (! "application/pdf".equals(file.getContentType())) {
            msgs.add(new FacesMessage("Book format must be PDF"));
        }

        if (! msgs.isEmpty()) {
            throw new ValidatorException(msgs);
        }
    }
}
```

In saveBook and in order to save the book information, a call to registerBook method of BookManager is done passing the book information as a parameter. IOUtils.toByteArray is a utility function in Apache Commons IO that can be used to convert the file input stream to byte array in order to save the book content as a byte array.

Listing 13-32 shows userList.xhtml which is used for listing all the Mega App users to the administrator user(s).

Listing 13-32. userList.xhtml Page

```
<?xml version='1.0' encoding='UTF-8' ?>
<!DOCTYPE html>
<html xmlns="http://www.w3.org/1999/xhtml"
      xmlns:ui="http://xmlns.jcp.org/jsf/facelets"
      xmlns:f="http://xmlns.jcp.org/jsf/core"
      xmlns:h="http://xmlns.jcp.org/jsf/html">
```

```
<ui:composition template="/WEB-INF/templates/main.xhtml">
    <ui:define name="metadata">
        <f:metadata>
            <f:event listener="#{userSearchBacking.retrieveUserList}" type="preRenderView"/>
        </f:metadata>
    </ui:define>

    <ui:define name="menu">
        <ui:include src="/protected/views/menu.xhtml"/>
    </ui:define>

    <ui:define name="content">
        <h3>All Users</h3>
        <h:form id="userSearchForm">
            <h:panelGroup id="results" class="table-responsive">
                <h:outputText id="informationMessage"
                             value="#{userSearchBacking.infoMessage}"
                             rendered="#{userSearchBacking.infoMessage ne null}"
                             class="informationMessage"/>

                <h:dataTable value="#{userSearchBacking.userList}"
                             var="megaUser" class="table"
                             rendered="#{not empty userSearchBacking.userList}">

                    <h:column>
                        <f:facet name="header">
                            Login Name
                        </f:facet>
                        #{megaUser.id}
                    </h:column>
                    <h:column>
                        <f:facet name="header">
                            First Name
                        </f:facet>
                        #{megaUser.firstName}
                    </h:column>
                    <h:column>
                        <f:facet name="header">
                            Last Name
                        </f:facet>
                        #{megaUser.lastName}
                    </h:column>

                    <h:column>
                        <f:facet name="header">
                            Actions
                        </f:facet>

                        <h:commandLink value="Delete" action="#{userSearchBacking.deleteUser}">
                            <f:setPropertyActionListener target="#{userSearchBacking.selectedUser}"
value="#{megaUser}" />
```

```
                <f:ajax render="@form" />
            </h:commandLink>
        </h:column>

    </h:dataTable>

</h:panelGroup>

    <h:messages id="messages" class="errorMessage"/>
    </h:form>
    </ui:define>
</ui:composition>

</html>
```

In the preRenderView event, the users list is retrieved using #{userSearchBacking.retrieveUserList} expression.

When the users list is retrieved, the <h:dataTable> component is populated with the users list; every row in the data table renders a user information with the ability to remove any user using the "Delete" command link. The "Delete" command link sets the #{userSearchBacking.selectedUser} property with the current selected user (#{megaUser}) using a property action listener and then calls the #{userSearchBacking.deleteUser} action method in order to perform the delete user operation.

Listing 13-33 shows UserSearchBacking CDI bean.

Listing 13-33. UserSearchBacking CDI Bean

```
package com.jsfprohtml5.megaapp.backing;
import com.jsfprohtml5.megaapp.model.MegaUser;
import com.jsfprohtml5.megaapp.service.MegaUserManagerLocal;
import com.jsfprohtml5.megaapp.service.exception.UserNotFound;
import java.io.Serializable;
import java.util.List;
import java.util.logging.Level;
import java.util.logging.Logger;
import javax.ejb.EJB;
import javax.faces.application.FacesMessage;
import javax.inject.Named;
import javax.faces.view.ViewScoped;

@Named
@ViewScoped
public class UserSearchBacking extends BaseBacking implements Serializable {

    @EJB
    private MegaUserManagerLocal userManager;

    private List<MegaUser> userList;
    private String infoMessage;
    private MegaUser selectedUser;
```

```java
    public List<MegaUser> getUserList() {
        return userList;
    }

    public void setUserList(List<MegaUser> userList) {
        this.userList = userList;
    }

    public String getInfoMessage() {
        return infoMessage;
    }

    public void setInfoMessage(String infoMessage) {
        this.infoMessage = infoMessage;
    }

    public MegaUser getSelectedUser() {
        return selectedUser;
    }

    public void setSelectedUser(MegaUser selectedUser) {
        this.selectedUser = selectedUser;
    }

    public String retrieveUserList() {
        userList = userManager.retrieveMegaUsers();

        if (userList.isEmpty()) {
            infoMessage = "No Users found!";
        } else {
            infoMessage = userList.size() + " user(s) found";
        }

        return null;
    }

    public String deleteUser() {
        MegaUser currentSelectedUser = getSelectedUser();
        try {
            userManager.removeMegaUser(currentSelectedUser.getId());
            userList.remove(currentSelectedUser);
            infoMessage = "User deleted successfully";
        } catch (UserNotFound ex) {
            Logger.getLogger(UserSearchBacking.class.getName()).log(Level.SEVERE, null, ex);
            getContext().addMessage(null, new FacesMessage("An error occurs while deleting user"));
        }

        return null;
    }
}
```

The main methods of UserSearchBacking CDI bean are as follows:

- retrieveUserList: Calls retrieveMegaUsers method of UserManager EJB. If results returned successfully, a message with the number of returned users is displayed to the user including the users list (administrator and users).

- deleteUser: Calls removeMegaUser method of UserManager EJB passing the currently selected user ID (using currentSelectedUser.getId()) as a parameter. If the user is deleted successfully, the following "User deleted successfully" will be displayed to the user.

Mega App uses CDI version 1.1, and Listing 13-34 shows the application's bean.xml file under WEB-INF folder.

Listing 13-34. Mega App beans.xml File

```
<?xml version="1.0" encoding="UTF-8"?>
<beans xmlns="http://xmlns.jcp.org/xml/ns/javaee"
       xmlns:xsi="http://www.w3.org/2001/XMLSchema-instance"
       xsi:schemaLocation="http://xmlns.jcp.org/xml/ns/javaee
http://xmlns.jcp.org/xml/ns/javaee/beans_1_1.xsd"
       version="1.1" bean-discovery-mode="annotated">

</beans>
```

Applying Security

In Mega App, we have implemented container-managed security for application authentication, and page authorization. Listing 13-35 shows the Mega App security constraints which are defined in the application web.xml file.

Listing 13-35. Mega App Security Constraints

```
<?xml version="1.0" encoding="UTF-8"?>
<web-app xmlns="http://xmlns.jcp.org/xml/ns/javaee"
         xmlns:xsi="http://www.w3.org/2001/XMLSchema-instance"
         xsi:schemaLocation="http://xmlns.jcp.org/xml/ns/javaee
http://xmlns.jcp.org/xml/ns/javaee/web-app_3_1.xsd"
         version="3.1">

    ...

    <security-constraint>
        <display-name>securityConstraint1</display-name>
        <web-resource-collection>
            <web-resource-name>resources</web-resource-name>
            <description/>
            <url-pattern>/protected/*</url-pattern>
        </web-resource-collection>
        <auth-constraint>
            <role-name>megaAppUser</role-name>
            <role-name>megaAppAdmin</role-name>
        </auth-constraint>
    </security-constraint>
```

```
    <security-constraint>
        <display-name>securityConstraint2</display-name>
        <web-resource-collection>
            <web-resource-name>resources</web-resource-name>
            <description/>
            <url-pattern>/protected/pages/admin/*</url-pattern>
        </web-resource-collection>
        <auth-constraint>
            <role-name>megaAppAdmin</role-name>
        </auth-constraint>
    </security-constraint>
    <login-config>
        <auth-method>FORM</auth-method>
        <realm-name>MegaRealm</realm-name>
        <form-login-config>
            <form-login-page>/login.xhtml</form-login-page>
            <form-error-page>/public/pages/forbidden.xhtml</form-error-page>
        </form-login-config>
    </login-config>

    <security-role>
        <role-name>megaAppUser</role-name>
    </security-role>
    <security-role>
        <role-name>megaAppAdmin</role-name>
    </security-role>

    <welcome-file-list>
        <welcome-file>protected/pages/bookSearch.xhtml</welcome-file>
    </welcome-file-list>
</web-app>
```

The security constraints defined in Mega App defines the following rules:

1. Both MegaAppUser and MegaAppAdmin can access all the resources under /protected/ directory.

2. Only MegaAppAdmin can access all the resources under /protected/pages/admin/ directory.

3. login.xhtml is the form login page.

4. If a user is not authorized, the user will be directed to forbidden.xhtml page.

The default welcome page for the logged-in user is the book search page (bookSearch.xhtml) page.

As you know from Chapter 10, roles defined in the application's web.xml must be mapped to groups defined on the application server. For GlassFish, we can define the mapping between role and group in a configuration file (glassfish-web.xml) as shown in Listing 13-36.

Listing 13-36. glassfish-web.xml File

```
<?xml version="1.0" encoding="UTF-8"?>
<!DOCTYPE glassfish-web-app PUBLIC "-//GlassFish.org//DTD GlassFish Application Server 3.1
Servlet 3.0//EN" "http://glassfish.org/dtds/glassfish-web-app_3_0-1.dtd">
<glassfish-web-app error-url="">
```

```
  <security-role-mapping>
    <role-name>megaAppUser</role-name>
    <group-name>1</group-name>
  </security-role-mapping>

  <security-role-mapping>
    <role-name>megaAppAdmin</role-name>
    <group-name>2</group-name>
  </security-role-mapping>

<class-loader delegate="true"/>
  <jsp-config>
    <property name="keepgenerated" value="true">
      <description>Keep a copy of the generated servlet class' java code.</description>
    </property>
  </jsp-config>
</glassfish-web-app>
```

As shown in the configuration file, role names megaAppAdmin and megaAppUser are mapped to actual group names, which are "2" (Administrator group ID in MegaApp Database) and "1" (User group ID in MegaApp Database). MegaRealm is the store of the users and groups for the Mega App application; let's see the mapping between MEGA_USER and USER_GROUP tables and MegaRealm. Table 13-6 shows the configuration of MegaRealm.

Table 13-6. *MegaRealm Configuration*

Property	Value
Name	MegaRealm
Class Name	com.sun.enterprise.security.ee.auth.realm.jdbc.JDBCRealm
JAAS Context	jdbcRealm
JNDI	jdbc/mega
User Table	MEGA.MEGA_USER
User Name Column	ID
Password Column	PASSWORD
Group Table	MEGA.USER_GROUP
Group Table User Name Column	USER_ID
Group Name Column	GROUP_ID
Password Encryption Algorithm	None
Assign Groups	
Database User	Mega
Database Password	Password
Digest Algorithm	None
Encoding	
Charset	

Error Handling

In order to display proper error pages when an error occurs, the following error codes are mapped to the indicated pages in web.xml as shown in Listing 13-37.

Listing 13-37. Error Codes Mapping in web.xml File

```
<?xml version="1.0" encoding="UTF-8"?>
<web-app xmlns="http://xmlns.jcp.org/xml/ns/javaee"
        xmlns:xsi="http://www.w3.org/2001/XMLSchema-instance"
        xsi:schemaLocation="http://xmlns.jcp.org/xml/ns/javaee
http://xmlns.jcp.org/xml/ns/javaee/web-app_3_1.xsd"
        version="3.1">

    ...

    <error-page>
        <error-code>404</error-code>
        <location>/login.xhtml</location>
    </error-page>
    <error-page>
        <error-code>500</error-code>
        <location>/public/pages/error.xhtml</location>
    </error-page>
    <error-page>
        <error-code>403</error-code>
        <location>/public/pages/forbidden.xhtml</location>
    </error-page>

    ...
</web-app>
```

When error 404 (Resource not found) occurs, the user is redirected the login.xhtml page; when error 500 (Internal server error) occurs, the user is redirected to error.xhtml page; and finally when error 403 (Forbidden access) occurs, the user is redirected to forbidden.xhtml.

Composing JSF Components

In Mega App Facelets pages, there are some cases in which we can create JSF composite components in order to simplify creating page elements and have the ability to reuse these components in further cases. One of these cases is the navigation bar which is mentioned in Listing 13-18. In this section, we will create a navigation bar composite component in order to simply the code of the header page.

<projsfhtml5:navbar> composite component is a wrapper for bootstrap navigation bar that can be used as shown in Listing 13-38.

Listing 13-38. projsfhtml5:navbar Component

```
<html xmlns="http://www.w3.org/1999/xhtml"
        xmlns:ui="http://xmlns.jcp.org/jsf/facelets"
        xmlns:projsfhtml5="http://xmlns.jcp.org/jsf/composite/projsfhtml5">
```

```
    <ui:composition>
        <projsfhtml5:navbar label="Mega App"
                            value="#{request.contextPath}/protected/pages/bookSearch.xhtml">

            <projsfhtml5:navitem label="Contact Us"
                            value="#{request.contextPath}/public/pages/contactUs.xhtml"/>
            <projsfhtml5:navitem label="About"
                            value="#{request.contextPath}/public/pages/about.xhtml"/>
        </projsfhtml5:navbar>

        <div class="page-header">
            <h1><ui:insert name="headerText">Welcome to the online library</ui:insert></h1>
        </div>
    </ui:composition>
</html>
```

`<projsfhtml5:navbar>` is the navigation bar element; it has two main attributes that represent the label and the value of the navigation bar, while `<projsfhtml5:navitem>` represents the navigation item element and has two similar attributes for defining the navigation item value and label.

Listing 13-39 shows navbar.xhtml, which is located under resources/projsfhtml5 folder.

Listing 13-39. navbar.xhtml under resources/projsfhtml5 Folder

```
<html xmlns="http://www.w3.org/1999/xhtml"
    xmlns:cc="http://java.sun.com/jsf/composite">

    <cc:interface>
        <cc:attribute name="label" type="java.lang.String" default="Mega App" />
        <cc:attribute name="value" type="java.lang.String" default="#" />
    </cc:interface>

    <cc:implementation>
        <div id="#{cc.clientId}" class="navbar">
            <div class="navbar-inner">
                <a class="brand" href="#{cc.attrs.value}">#{cc.attrs.label}</a>
                <ul class="nav">
                    <cc:insertChildren />
                </ul>
            </div>
        </div>
    </cc:implementation>
</html>
```

Listing 13-40 shows navitem.xhtml, which is located under resources/projsfhtml5 folder.

Listing 13-40. navitem.xhtml under resources/projsfhtml5 Folder

```
<html xmlns="http://www.w3.org/1999/xhtml"
    xmlns:cc="http://java.sun.com/jsf/composite">
```

```
<cc:interface>
    <cc:attribute name="label" type="java.lang.String" required="true"/>
    <cc:attribute name="value" type="java.lang.String" required="true" />
</cc:interface>

<cc:implementation>
    <li><a href="#{cc.attrs.value}">#{cc.attrs.label}</a></li>
</cc:implementation>
</html>
```

■ **Note**   Another case that can be converted to a JSF composite component is the menu fragment which is located in Listing 13-22. We will leave this one for you as an exercise.

Packaging and Deploying the Mega App

First of all, in order to deploy Mega App in your local environment, you need to build the application using Maven 3 from the application pom.xml directory as follows:

```
> mvn clean install
```

After running this command, the application war file will be generated in the target directory of the application with the following name (megaapp-1.0-SNAPSHOT.war).

MegaApp is developed under Glassfish version 4. Listing 13-41 shows the application's glassfish-resources.xml, which defines the application data source.

Listing 13-41. MegaApp's glassfish-resources.xml

```
<?xml version="1.0" encoding="UTF-8"?>
<!DOCTYPE resources PUBLIC "-//GlassFish.org//DTD GlassFish Application Server 3.1 Resource
Definitions//EN" "http://glassfish.org/dtds/glassfish-resources_1_5.dtd">
<resources>
    <jdbc-connection-pool ...>
        <property name="serverName" value="localhost"/>
        <property name="portNumber" value="1527"/>
        <property name="databaseName" value="megaApp"/>
        <property name="User" value="mega"/>
        <property name="Password" value="password"/>
        <property name="URL" value="jdbc:derby://localhost:1527/megaApp"/>
        <property name="driverClass" value="org.apache.derby.jdbc.ClientDriver"/>
    </jdbc-connection-pool>
    <jdbc-resource enabled="true" jndi-name="jdbc/mega" object-type="user"
pool-name="derby_net_megaApp_megaPool"/>
</resources>
```

In order to add the defined application resources of glassfish-resources.xml in your GlassFish 4, you need to start your GlassFish server by running the following command from the bin directory of the server.

```
> asadmin start-domain
```

After the server starts, you can use asadmin add-resources command as follows in order to add the defined resources to your server.

```
> asadmin add-resources <<full path>>/glassfish-resources.xml
```

After running the previous command, the resources will be added to your GlassFish server and you will see the following message.

```
JDBC connection pool derby_net_megaApp_megaPool created successfully.
JDBC resource jdbc/mega created successfully.
Command add-resources executed successfully.
```

Mega App database is a JavaDB Derby database; it is included with the application source code under (src/main/database) directory for your reference. In order to install the database in your GlassFish 4 server, stop your GlassFish 4 server if it is running as follows:

```
> asadmin stop-domain domain1
```

We are here assuming that your GlassFish domain name is (domain1).
After stopping the server, also stop GlassFish Java DB by running the following command:

```
> asadmin stop-database
```

After stopping GlassFish server and its Java DB, copy megaApp directory located under (src/main/database) directory to your ([GlassFish server]/glassfish/databases) directory, and then start the server and Java DB. Java DB can start using the following command:

```
> asadmin start-database
```

After starting the server and Java DB, you can deploy the Mega App application in your GlassFish server using the GlassFish administration console, which can be accessed usually from the following URL:

```
http://localhost:4848/common/index.jsf
```

■ **Note** Application Deployment in GlassFish is a very straightforward process: after login to the administration console, click the "Applications" menu item in the administration console side menu and then upload the application war. You may need to change the default context root to a friendly name (for example: "megaapp") in order to access the application directly using a simple context root.

Finally, you need to configure the application realm in order to properly login to the application. You can do this by creating a new realm from configurations -> server-config -> security -> Realms and then entering the realm information typical for the ones mentioned in Table 13-6.
After doing the realm step, now you can access the application from

```
http://localhost:8080/megaapp
```

You can log in using the administrator account:

```
user name: admin
password: password
```

Also you can log in using the following application user account:

```
user name: hazems
password: password
```

After login, you can search for books with the title "JSF" in order to find some sample results.

You can create whatever number of users you need from the registration page and whatever number of books from the books addition page for the administration user.

■ **Note**   We are assuming the default ports will work (8080 and 4848); in your local environment, you may have different working ports.

Summary

This chapter takes you on a beginning-to-end journey for building a "complete" JSF 2.2 application in the Java EE 7 environment starting from the application specification and wireframes until developing and deploying the application. This chapter shows you how to architect and develop a nontrivial JSF 2.2 application, including modeling the application data, building the application services (APIs), constructing domain model, and finally creating nifty user interface using the latest Java EE 7 stack (JSF 2.2, EJB 3.2, JPA 2.1, CDI 1.1, and Java Bean Validation).

Index

A, B

Ajaxifying JSF applications, 272
    JavaScript API (*see* JavaScript API)
    <f:ajax> tag, 272–273
2.1 application, JSF, 6
    build and deploy
        command line, 19
        GlassFish 3.1.2, 20
        Tomcat 7, 20
    firstApplication development
        complete layout, 8
        configuration files, 9
        dependencies, 17
        facelets pages, 11
        login page, 7
        managed beans, 16
        Maven structure, 8
        welcome page, 8
    Maven project structure, 6
    software, 6
Arquillian and Drone
    definition, 279
    set up, 279
    writing test
        CDI bean, 284
        class diagram, 282–283
        DefaultSelenium methods, 287
        input box and submit button, 284–285
        mock-up, 282
        results, 285
        test case, 285–287

C, D

Color custom component
    Ajax requests, 172
    attributes, 168
    composite component creation, 169

fallback version, 175
input element, 168
supporting lists, 171
use of composite component, 169
CommandButton, 256
Container-managed security
    framework, 268
Contexts and Dependency Injection (CDI)
    services, 271
Conversion
    converter interface, 64
        ConverterException, 65
        getAsObject, 65
        getAsString, 65
        <f\:\convertNumber/> converter, 65
        multiple valueHolder components, 65
    converters, 66
        explicit converters, 68
        Implicit converters, 66
    custom converter, 70
        conversion error, 74
        @FacesConverter annotation, 72
        getAsObject method, 71–72
        getAsString method, 71–72
        location class, 70
        LocationConverter behavior, 74
        LocationConverter class, 71
        TestBean managed bean, 73
        XHTML test page, 73
Conversion and validation, 63
    Apply Request Values phase, 64
    error messages, 88
    Process Validations Phase, 64
    Render Response phase, 64

E

Error handling, 380
evaluateEL() method, 247

Event models
    application-related event listeners, 94
    definition, 96
    faces events
        action and value change events, 96, 98, 103
        execution scenarios, 97
    life cycle phases, 95
    listener, 93
    main interface, 93
    object hierarchy, 95
    phase events
        AuthorizationListener phase
            listener code, 108
        execution time, 107
        faces configuration file, 109
        methods, 108
        PhaseListener interface, 107
        updated user managed bean, 108
    PhaseListener interface, 95
    system events
        application level (extends SystemEvent), 110
        application screen, 111
        checkName method code, 114
        component level, 110–111
        custom SystemEvent listener, 111
        ErrorDisplayListener, 116
        ErrorDisplayListener class, 115
        <f, 113–114
        faces-config.xml, 113
        invalidInput style class, 115
        listeners, 94
        one/more validation errors, 116–117
        postValidate event, 114
        styles, 115
    types, 94
    view parameters
        browser address bar, 121
        car managed bean, 118
        car.xhtml page, 118
        facelets pages, 117–118
        input form, 120–121
        modification, 119
        UICommand, 121
        utilize validation, 119–120
Exception handling
    application error page, 60
    CustomExceptionHandler class, 59–60
    CustomExceptionHandlerFactory class, 60
    error handling page, 61
    JSF configuration file, 61
    steps, 58
Expression language (EL)
    different sets, 37
    flash scope

confirm.xhtml page, 48–49
    input.xhtml page, 46
    survey application, 46
    survey managed bean, 50
method expression
    beverage managed bean, 44
    beverages page, 43
    calculateAverage method, 45
    login page, 42
    output, 45
    public non-static methods, 42
    relational operators, 44
    valueChangeListener attribute, 45
navigation
    conditional navigation, 57
    flow chart, 56
    implicit navigation, 51
    input.xhtml page, 56–57
    NavigationHandler class, 58
    pages, 55
    rule-based navigation, 52
unified
    declaration, 39
    features, 38
    highlighted underlined list item, 39
    JSTL tags, 38
value expression, 40

■ **F**

Facelets pages
    declaration, 12
    internal layout, 14–15
    introductory page, 13
    message.properties file, 12
    method-binding expression, 15
    simple.css file, 12
    simple.xhtml Template File, 11
    sub-elements, 12
    welcome.xhtml page code, 15
Faces events
    action and value change events, 96, 98, 103
    execution scenarios, 97
Faces Flow
    backing bean class, 258–259
    definition, 254
    faces-config.xml, 255
    rules, 254
    xhtml page registration, 255

■ **G**

getUser() method, 247
GlassFish 3.1.2, 20

H

Handling errors. *See* Error handling
HTML5 components, 191
    color custom
        Ajax requests, 172
        attributes, 168
        composite component creation, 169
        fallback version, 175
        input element, 168
        supporting lists, 171
        use of composite component, 169
    data picker custom
        attributes, 176
        backing bean (composite component), 178
        composite compoent creation, 177
        HTML5 date input (example), 176
        unsupported browsers, 182
        use of (composite component), 180
    input types, 167
    media component, 191
        JSF Creation, 195
        media elements, 191
    progress bar component, 208
        attributes, 209
        composite component, 209, 211
        indicators, 209
        progress.js JavaScript, 210
        screenshot, 213
    slider custom component
        attributes, 184
        composite component creation, 185
        use of cmposite component, 186
    spinner custom component
        attributes, 187
        composite component, 188
        use of composite control, 189

I

Implicit navigation, 51

J, K

JavaScript API
    <f:ajax> tag, 276
    HTTP requests, 274–275
    input parameters, 273–274
    monitoring Ajax events, 276
    panel grid updates, 274
    request lifecycle selected components, 275
JavaServer Faces (JSF), 1. *See also* 2.1 application, JSF
    architecture
        MVC2 architecture, 5
        pattern, 5–6
    component libraries, 3, 215
        PrimeFaces (*see* PrimeFaces)
        RichFaces (*see* RichFaces)
    evolution 1.0-2.2
        advantages, 3
        enhancements, 4
        features, 4
        2.2 specification and implementation, 4
    framework, 1
    implementations, 1
    life cycle
        apply request values phase, 23
        favorites page, 22
        immediate attribute, 26
        invoke application, 25
        phases, 21
        process validations phase, 24
        render response, 26
        request processing phases, 21
        restore view, 21
        UI components tree population, 23
        update model values, 24
    pages and backing beans
        bookSearch.xhtml page code, 356–358
        login.xhtml page, 352–353
        register.xhtml page, 353–354
        registration details, 356
        structure, 351
        UserAddBacking CDI managed bean, 355–356
        Web Pages folder, 351–352
    performance, 300
        apache myfaces and oracle mojarra, 302–303
        FACELETS_BUFFER_SIZE parameter, 301
        numberOfLogicalViews parameter, 303
        numberOfViewsInSession parameter, 303
        practices, 305
        PROJECT_STAGE parameter, 301
        refresh period, 300
        skip comments, 300
        stateless views, 304
        STATE_SAVING_METHOD, 301
    requirements, 1
    roles, 2
    security (*see* Web application security)
JPA entity beans, 244, 260
JSF 2.2, 123, 241
    backwards compatibility, 143
    big ticket features, 123
    EJB 3.2 and JPA 2.1, Back End, 263
        DDL Script, 266
        getUser() method, 265
        glassfish-resources.xml, 265
        GlassFish server, 266
        persistence.xml file, 263
        UserExistsException class, 265

JSF 2.2 (*cont.*)
    UserManager class, 265
    UserManagerLocal interface, 263–264
  Faces Flow
    backing bean class, 258–259
    definition, 254
    faces-config.xml, 255
    flow definition, 133
    flow scope, 259
    overview, 132
    packaging, 135
    rules, 254
    starting and ending flows, 134
    storing flow data, 134
    xhtml page registration, 255
  HTML5-friendly markup
    attributes, 124
    passing through attributes, 125
    passing through elements, 127
    prefixed attributes, 126
  JPA entity beans, 260
  resource library contracts
    contracts, 131
    mapping contract, 130
    overview, 127
    session-scoped managed bean, 131
  significant changes
    Ajax request delay, 142
    <f, 138
    file upload, 140
    UIData, 137
    WAI-ARIA, 137
    XML namespaces, 142
  stateless views, 136
  weather application, 241
    backing bean class, 248, 250
    backing beans, 244, 246
    JPA entity beans, 244
    login page, 243
    main.xhtml template page, 251
    Mashups4JSF yahooWeather component, 249–250
    messages.properties file, 251
    structure, 244
    user manager EJB, 244, 247
    user registration, 241–242
    XHTML pages, 244–245
JSF applications, 267. *See also* Ajaxifying JSF applications
  design considerations
    CDI services, 271
    container-managed security framework, 268
    session-scoped beans, 267
    state saving, 271
  testing (*see also* Arquillian and Drone)
    Arquillian, 279
    set up Arquillian and Drone, 279

■ L

logout() method, 251

■ M, N, O

Managed beans. *See also* Expression language (EL)
declaration
  annotations, 30
  scope, 30
  usage, 29
dependencies
  profession attribute, 34–35
  user instance, 35
initialization
  EE annotations, 31
  faces configuration file, 31, 33
  favoriteSports and spokenLanguages map, 32
  initialize method, 32
  @ManagedProperty annotation, 31
  map property, 33–34
  @PostConstruct and @ PostDestroy
    annotations, 32
  @PreDestroy method, 32
  sub-elements, 31
  XHTML page, 33
Java code, 36
@Named and @inject annotations, 36–37
POJO model, 29
Maven project object model (POM), 280
Media component
  JSF creation
    attribute value, 196
    Boolean attribute, 196
    component interface, 196
    composite component root, 198
    <f\:\passThroughAttribute/>, 196–197
    sources and track elements, 201
    using video component, 207
  media elements
    attributes, 192
    audio and vedio elements, 191, 193
    Flash SWF, 195
    HTMLMediaElement interface, 191
    multiple audio and vedio elements, 194
    subtitles in Multiple Languages, 194
Mega application, 307. *See also* Service layer
    construction (EJBs)
architecture
  high-level components, 316
  technologies, 315
composing page templates
  bootstrapCSS.xhtml file, 348
  bootstrapJS.xhtml file, 348
  header.xhtml page, 347–348

main.xhtml template, 349
menu option, 351
menu.xhtml page, 350
simple.xhtml template, 347
WEB-INF/templates folder, 347
composite components, 380
bootstrap navigation bar, 380
navbar.xhtml, 381
navitem.xhtml, 381–382
data model construction
entities, 317
logical data model, 317
one-to-many, 318
SQL DDL script, 319–320
USER entity, 318
USER_GROUP entity, 318
error handling, 380
JSF pages and backing beans (*see* JSF pages and
backing beans)
packaging and deploying, 382
security constraints
glassfish-web.xml file, 378–379
MegaRealm configuration, 379
rules, 378
web.xml file, 377–378
specification
application administrator, 308
book request flow, 307
case diagrams, 308
wireframes
administrator add book page, 314
application users, 311
approved book requests, 312
approved/rejected book request
information, 313
approved requests inbox, 313
book information, 314
home page, 310, 312
login page, 310
order of, 309
pending requests inbox, 311
registration page, 309
side menu, 310
user management page, 315
Monitoring Ajax events, 276

■ P, Q

Phase events
AuthorizationListener phase listener code, 108
execution time, 107
faces configuration file, 109
methods, 108
PhaseListener interface, 107
updated user managed bean, 108

PrimeFaces
configuration file, 215, 225–226
county navigator application, 221
bean code, 222–223
page code, 224–225
panel part, 222
ring component, 221
UI components, 221
defaultcommand, 217
dialog panel, 217
features, 215
fieldset, 217
IdleMonitor, 217
skinning framework, 215
UI components, 216
accordionpanel, 216
autocomplete, 216
breadcrumb, 216
Captcha component, 216
carousel, 216
colorpicker, 216
commandbutton, 216
ContextMenu, 216
DataGrid, 217
Drag&Drop, 217
features, 216
FeedReader, 217
galleria, 217
graphic image component, 217
growl, 217
HotKey, 217
imagecropper, 218
inplace, 218
inputmask, 218
layout component, 218
legacy, 217
lightbox, 218
MegaMenu, 218
menubar, 218
mindmap, 218
notificationbar, 218
overlaypanel, 219
PanelGrid, 219
photocam, 219
poll, 219
progressbar, 219
remotecommand, 219
resizable component, 219
selectbooleanbutton, 219
SelectManyCheckbox, 219
slidemenu, 220
socket, 220
spinner, 220
stack, 220
TagCloud, 220

PrimeFaces (*cont.*)
    tooltip, 220
    tree, 220
    wizard, 220
Progress bar component, 208
  attributes, 209
  composite component, 209
  Facescomponent, 211
  indicators, 209
  progress.js JavaScript, 210
  screenshot, 212

■ R

Resource library contracts
  contracts, 131
  mapping contract, 130
  overview, 127
  session-scoped managed bean, 131
RichFaces
  JBoss public repository, 228
  main tag libraries, 226
  myfaces-impl.jar, 227
  push CDI integration, 227
  push JMS integration, 227
  rightcountry application, 233
    bean code, 237
    drop source panel code, 233
    drop target panel, 234
    Egypt drop target, 235–237
    processDrop method, 235
  structure, 229
  UI components, 230
    collapsiblepanel, 230
    DataGrid component, 230
    DragIndicator, 230
    droptarget, 230
    hash map, 231
    HotKey, 231
    jQuery, 231
    notifystack, 232
    togglepanel, 232
    tooltip, 232
Rule-based navigation, 52

■ S

Service layer construction, (EJBs)
  book JPA entity code, 326
  book management operations, 320
  BookManager, 321
  book request flow operations, 320
  business manager, 320
  getAllBooks, 326
  getBookContent, 326

  getBookInformation method, 326
  persistence.xml file, 321
  registerBook and updateBook methods, 322–323
  remaining methods, 324–326
  removeBook, 326
  user management operations, 321
Server-side view state saving, 271
Session-scoped beans, 267
Slider custom component
  attributes, 184
  composite component creation, 185
  use of composite component, 186
Spinner custom component
  attributes, 187
  composite component, 188
  use of composite control, 189
Stateless views, 136
System events
  application level (extends SystemEvent), 110
  application screen, 111
  checkName method code, 114
  component level, 110–111
  custom SystemEvent listener, 111
  ErrorDisplayListener, 116
  ErrorDisplayListener class, 115
  <f:event> tag, 113–114
  faces-config.xml, 113
  invalidInput style class, 115
  one/more validation errors, 116–117
  postValidate event, 114
  styles, 115

■ T, U

Tomcat 7, 20

■ V

Validation. *See also* Conversion and validation
  custom validators, 77
  error messages, 85
  JSR Bean validation, 80
    Default validation group, 86
    @EmailAddress annotation, 82
    EmailValidator Validation Class, 83
    group attribute, 83
    message attribute, 83
    payload attribute, 83
    person managed bean, 81, 86
    subscriber application, 81, 84
    updated index, 87
  validator interface, 75
    EditableValueHolder components, 75
    <f:\:validateLongRange>, 76
    <f:\:validateRequired>, 76

Process Validations phase, 75
ValidatorException, 75
validators, 76
Value expression, 40

■ W, X, Y, Z

Web application security
authentication, 289–290
digest authentication, 291
form-based, 290
HTTP Basic authentication, 290
methods, 291
authorization, 289
constraint, 293
definition, 291

URL mapping, 292
web resource collection, 292
web.xml, 291
data protection, 289, 293
weather application
custom realm properties, 297
data model modification, 295
Form-Based configuration, 294
glassfish-web.xml File, 295
home.xhtml Page, 294
loadUser() method, 298
RegistrationBacking class, 299–300
SQL statements, 296
Update weatherbacking class, 297
Update xhtml page, 298
Web resource collection, 292

Get the eBook for only $10!

> Now you can take the weightless companion with you anywhere, anytime. Your purchase of this book entitles you to 3 electronic versions for only $10.

This Apress title will prove so indispensible that you'll want to carry it with you everywhere, which is why we are offering the eBook in 3 formats for only $10 if you have already purchased the print book.

Convenient and fully searchable, the PDF version enables you to easily find and copy code—or perform examples by quickly toggling between instructions and applications. The MOBI format is ideal for your Kindle, while the ePUB can be utilized on a variety of mobile devices.

Go to www.apress.com/promo/tendollars to purchase your companion eBook.